Organizational Dimensions *of* Global Change

David L. Cooperrider

Jane E. Dutton

Editors

Organizational Dimensions *of* Global Change

No Limits to Cooperation

HUMAN DIMENSIONS
OF GLOBAL CHANGE

SAGE Publications
International Educational and Professional Publisher
Thousand Oaks London New Delhi

For information:

SAGE Publications, Inc.
2455 Teller Road
Thousand Oaks, California 91320
E-mail: order@sagepub.com

SAGE Publications Ltd.
6 Bonhill Street
London EC2A 4PU
United Kingdom

SAGE Publications India Pvt. Ltd.
M-32 Market
Greater Kailash I
New Delhi 110 048 India

Printed in the United States of America

Library of Congress Cataloging-in-Publication Data

Main entry under title:

Organizational dimensions of global change: No limits to
cooperation / edited by David L. Cooperrider and Jane E. Dutton.
    p. cm.
  Includes bibliographical references and index.
  ISBN 0-7619-1528-1 (cloth: alk. paper)
  ISBN 0-7619-1529-X (pbk.: alk. paper)
  1. Social change—Congresses. 2. Organizational
change—Congresses. 3. International cooperation—Congresses.
I. Cooperrider, David L. II. Dutton, Jane E.
  HM101.072   1998
  303.4—ddc21   98-40069

99 00 01 02 03 94 95 10 7 6 5 4 3 2 1

Acquiring Editor:	Marquita Flemming
Editorial Assistant:	MaryAnn Vail
Production Editor:	Diana E. Axelsen
Editorial Assistant:	Denise Santoyo
Typesetter/Designer:	Janelle Lemaster
Indexer:	Mary Mortonsen
Cover Designer:	Candice Harman

CONTENTS

Part I: SENSEMAKING AND GLOBAL CHANGE

To our children:

Daniel, Matt, and *Hannah Cooperrider*
Cara and *Emily Sandelands*

PREFACE

Today's global forces for change are moving us into a remarkable new set of circumstances, one in which human social organizations inherited from the modern era may be unequal to the challenges posed by overpopulation, environmental damage, technology-driven revolutions, gross imbalances between rich and poor, and the onslaught of treatment-resistant diseases. Although very different in form, these various trends, from ozone depletion to 24-hours-per-day trading, are transnational by nature, crossing borders all over the globe, simultaneously affecting local-global realities, and reminding us that the earth, for all its historically reproduced divisions, is a single unit (for a powerful analysis of this point, see Kennedy, 1993). A world of thoroughgoing interdependence is upon us, and along with it is a historic opportunity to anticipate and imagine, to discover and design a new vision of the world's cooperative potential.

THE LAUNCHING OF A NEW SERIES

This pioneering volume is the first in a new series at Sage Publications that is devoted to advancing our knowledge of the Human Dimensions of Global Change. The series is designed to support a broader, worldwide movement—a call to all of the social sciences—to create an interdisciplinary domain seeking better understanding of the earth as a total system and to define ways in which human activities are both a source and a potentially positive response to alterations in earth and human systems that are not and cannot be localized; in short, the rapidly growing global agenda for change. The series is created out of concern for the future of humanity and the earth and recognizes that how humanity responds today to the consequences of ecological and economic global change will reverberate well into the future and across generations. What sets this series apart is its special attempt to augment the largely deficit-focused science of global change with special emphasis on constructive human response to the global agenda. In particular, it will attempt to search for new forms of human cooperation and global action. Thus, the call is to: (a) help build a foundation within the human dimensions of global change community for a scholarship of transformation that seeks to interpret basic new trends in humanity's global cooperative capacity; (b) anticipate new possibilities in organizational forms and processes; and (c) study the new relational practices that can contribute to a deeper understanding of the life-giving interrelation of humanity and world ecosystems, cooperative forms, and global society.

BACKGROUND AND BRIEF OVERVIEW

This volume grows from a special national Academy of Management conference hosted at Case Western Reserve University in the spring of 1995 that was intended to "begin building a solid Foundation under the Organization Dimensions of Global Change as a coherent intellectual enterprise . . . to explore how global change research needs organizational theory and change scholarship, and vice versa." The logic is simple: There is not one item on the global agenda for change that can be understood (much less responded to) without a better understanding of organizations. More than anywhere else, the world's direction and future are being created in the context of human organizations and institutions. Today, as the walls to global cooperation have tumbled, new spaces have opened for transboundary corporations, networks, nongovernmental organizations (NGOs), regimes, associations, grassroots groups, and many others to proliferate. The significance, in many respects, of the relatively small number of decisions made by our nation-state leaders pales in comparison to the billions of decisions made every day by members and leaders of such organizations. It is within this context that the editors of this volume offer an orientation and normative focus for organizational dimensions of global change (ODGC) inquiry as follows:

> ODGC research is an enterprise dedicated to the study and development of worldwide organizations and leaders that is capable of addressing the complex and pressing global issues of our time. In the transformative mode, ODGC research is deliberately capacity or "opportunity focused" and is "radically appreciative"—where inquiry itself is constructed as an intervention for the better and where the very framing of questions is recognized as a crucial choice-point for the kind of world that the "scientific construction of social reality" helps bring to focus, and perhaps fruition. Methodologically, it proceeds from the premise that there are "no limits to cooperation" and that virtually every item on the global agenda can be addressed, given the creation organizations and other cross-boundary cooperative systems that have as their primary task a world future of (a) human and ecological well-being; (b) sustainable economic development; and (c) an articulation of a set of values (emerging global ethics) capable of inspiring human action in the service of the widest possible good.

The book is divided into three parts. The chapters in Part I by Karl Weick, Kathryn Kaczmarski and David Cooperrider, Frances Westley, and Ram Tenkasi and Sue Mohrman explore and broaden our understanding of organizational sensemaking and knowledge exchange—it is called Sensemaking and Global Change. Part II is about the structuring of global cooperation and argues that organizations working on the global agenda are almost everything but unitary organizational forms. Part II, therefore, is titled Collaboration and Partnership Arrangements: The Structures of Global Change. Included are chapters by L. David Brown and Darcy Ashman, Mayer Zald, Barbara Gray, Julie Fisher, and John Aram. Part III is titled Social Constructionism and Global Change and invites greater attention to ethical discourse and inquiry into ever-evolving visions of the good. It invites greater disciplinary self-critique and reflexivity. It seeks expansion of voices participating in the world of global change science and action. And it invites anticipatory theorizing, constructing future images, propositions, and languages of positive possibility. Again, the authors are leading thinkers in their fields: Kenneth Gergen; Raza A. Mir, Marta B. Calás, and Linda Smircich; Rene Bouwen and Chris Steyaert; Nancy J. Adler; and Stuart Hart.

Although the contributors to this volume come from the arena of organization studies, this book should be of greater interest to human dimensions of global change scholars and practitioners all over the world and from an array of disciplines, including interdisciplinary fields of organization and management science, policy studies, international relations and development studies, and earth systems science, as well as the disciplines of sociology, economics, anthropology, political science, and psychology.

ACKNOWLEDGMENTS

In addition to the featured authors who contributed the chapters to this volume, our friends and colleagues from Case Western Reserve University and the University of Michigan have offered continuous goodwill, inspirational input, and support.

At Case Western Reserve University, we owe a large debt to faculty and students at the Weatherhead School of Management and its SIGMA Program on Human Cooperation and Global Action. Together, they hosted the conference with great hospitality and enthusiasm. In particular, we want to thank those faculty who made an important contribution in their willingness to give of their time and energy to lead a variety of sessions: Lisa Berlinger, Diana Bilimoria, Richard Boland, Richard Boyatzis, Ron Fry, Michael Ginzberg, David Kolb, Eric Neilsen, William Pasmore, and Don Wolfe. One of our richest sources of inspiration, as always, was Suresh Srivastva. He was the person who insisted that the conference needed a clearer direction; his suggestion to add "No Limits to Cooperation" as a subtitle for the event assisted in giving it a more affirmative and normative focus. Likewise, tremendous energy and a sense of purpose were infused throughout the conference by doctoral students from the Department of Organizational Behavior. Its success owes much to Kathryn Kaczmarski, Gurudev Khalsa, and Punya Upadhyaya, who were key organizers as well as visionaries about the importance of this domain for the future of the field. They, in turn, were assisted by a number of other doctoral student colleagues serving in a variety of ways: Don Austin, Ilma Barros, Rama Bhalla, Chet Bowling, Carla Carten, Tom Conklin, Mary Finney, James Ludema, Angela Murphy, Alice Yoko Oku, Charleyse Pratt, Cheryl Scott, Param Srikantia, Jane Wheeler, and Rob Wright. We are also grateful to Retta Holdorf and Bonnie Copes for their responsible, never-ending assistance in managing the conference and making sure that all of those who attended felt at home. In addition, two of our greatest advocates throughout have been Claudia Liebler and Ada Jo Mann, mainstays of our Global Excellence in Management Program. Their consistent sustenance for our efforts is gratefully received. In addition to the above, our very deep appreciation is given to the Dean of the Weatherhead School, Scott Cowen. Scott has always been an exceptional leader to all of us; and without his inspiration, encouragement, and ability to facilitate action, this conference (and, indeed, SIGMA) might not have happened. We are particularly grateful to him for his conviction that schools of management have a special, noble responsibility to society vis-a-vis the global agenda for change. He has been unfailing in his support for us personally and professionally and for the SIGMA Program.

Likewise, there were many from the University of Michigan who helped us with the conference. We appreciated the input and enthusiasm of several doctoral students: Gelaye Debebe, Bill Dethlefs, Stephanie Mackie-Lewis, Gina McLaughlin, and David Obstfeld. Dean Joseph B. White of the University of Michigan Business School lent his presence, ideas, and support for the conference. In his own leadership style, Joe has opened endless possibilities for inspiration and collaboration. Finally, Cheryl Vereen has helped with all of the details, assembling and caring for the production of this book. Without her help, the book would not have happened. This is her first book production, and, based on her enthusiasm, our guess is that it will not be her last.

In addition, we wish to thank a number of institutions and individuals who made this whole experience possible. The invitation and the seed grant funding came from a special initiative of the Academy of Management. Overall leadership and further funding came from two groups of the Academy: the Division of Organization and Management Theory and the Division of Organization Development and Change. Individual contributions were offered by a number of people; most notably, a generous gift from Jane Seiling was provided in support of SIGMA. Likewise, outside the Academy, inspiration and encouragement for the idea came from conversations with Tom Baerwhald at the National Science Foundation's Global Change Research Program and with John P. Grant and Elise Stork from the Office for Private Voluntary Cooperation (PVC) at the U.S. Agency for International Development. PVC's direct support in the field of Case Western Reserve University's Global Excellence in Management initiative provided a much-needed grounded context for the more academic theorizing about the organizational dimensions of global change.

As mentioned earlier, this volume is the first in a new Sage series. Marquita Flemming, our editor, has been a wonderful colleague, friend, and guide throughout this entire process. Instinctively, she knows that management today is a matter of world affairs and that the entire field is being called to aim higher. Her courage and commitment to work with us to connect organizational thinking to the research domain of global change cannot be overstated. We both want to thank Marquita and each of her colleagues at Sage for their professional assistance, encouragement, and willingness to open new pathways for the study of human cooperation and global action in the new century.

—David L. Cooperrider
Case Western Reserve University

—Jane E. Dutton
University of Michigan

1

NO LIMITS TO COOPERATION

An Introduction to the
Organizational Dimensions
of Global Change

DAVID L. COOPERRIDER
JANE E. DUTTON

S ometimes, a short anecdote can express more than many words, especially
when the anecdote is true. Ours is actually very simple. It is about a letter
we received several years ago, the content of which became the focus of our
very first conversation and the starting point of our first collaboration, culmi-
nating in contributions to *Advances in Strategic Management*, Volume 9,
1993.

At the outset, it must be said that the letter's query was surprising,
formidable, disconcerting—and totally compelling. It signaled the lack of
input from organizational scholars into the policy-relevant conversation about
global change. It was written by members of the UN's International Facilitating Committee (IFC) for the "Earth Summit" (recall that the conference was
the largest meeting on environment and development in history). In essence,
the call said:

We are about to step into an unprecedented experiment in global cooperation. And frankly, there is cause for concern. The issues to be discussed and acted upon are tremendously complex, scientifically uncertain, interrelated, dynamic, and monumental. Consider just a sampling of the issues requiring deliberation:

- World population, in the lifetime of those born after World War II, will soar from 2 billion to 10 billion—although it took 10,000 lifetimes for the population to first reach 2 billion.
- The world's forests are being destroyed at a rate of one football field-sized area every second, and every day, a species becomes extinct; and since mid-century, it is estimated that the world has lost nearly one fifth of the topsoil from its cropland.
- A continent-sized hole is opening up in the earth's protective ozone shield as the world's emissions of chlorofluorocarbons doubles every decade, having already increased 40 times over since World War II.
- Fossil fuel use has, in the same time period, increased 10 times over, flooding the atmosphere with unprecedented levels of carbon dioxide.
- The economy, which grew five times in size, is pushing human demands on the ecosystem beyond what the planet (our soils, water supplies, fisheries, etc.) has the ability to regenerate; and with around a billion new mouths being born each decade, the pressures on the entire ecosystem will multiply.
- Every day, 37,000 children under age 5 die of starvation or preventable diseases; nearly a billion are suffering in desperate poverty (and the conflicts and wars associated with it) while a precarious global debt burden grows by $7.5 billion every month.
- Questions: Can the world survive as one fourth rich and three fourths poor, half democratic and half authoritarian, with oases of human development surrounded by deserts of human deprivation?

We are, in so many ways, infants when it comes to our cooperative capacity for building a global society congenial to the life of the planet and responsive to the human spirit. So, as you know, more than 30,000 people with diverse disciplinary backgrounds from all over the world—from the earth sciences, from economics and business, from governmental and nongovernmental organizations, from religious and cultural institutions, and from the grassroots to the ivory tower, not to mention the myriad of cultures from hundreds of nations—will be assembling in Rio de Janeiro for what we call a summit, and what your field would call strategic planning. So we have a puzzle for you.

Your answer is important. Indeed, what happens at this meeting in response to ecological and economic global change will reverberate well into the future and across generations. Critics argue, and many of us actually agree, that the world could be worse off as a result of this ambitious meeting (it could result in greater loss of hope, increases in cynicism in international institutions, identification of irreconcilable conflicts, waste of resources, much talk with no action, empty platitudes and promises, and others). So we are asking for answers—from organization and management theory.

To help us organize and ensure a successful meeting, what knowledge can your field offer? Can you point us to the specific pieces of research, the theories, the principles and practices that could truly make the difference?

There are at least three ways to make meaning of this call. The first is to raise questions about the appropriateness of the recipients of the letter. Would not the IFC do better writing for help from schools of international relations, political science, geostrategic studies, or others? Second, maybe the anecdote's importance resides in its metaphorical contribution, that is, that organizing, in all domains of endeavor, is beginning more and more to resemble a global meeting (i.e., saturated in temporary relationships, information overload, metaproblem complexity, nonroutine tasks, structural dispersion, backlash from the crises mentality, diversities of every kind, and others). Or third, perhaps the anecdote is best understood at face value—simply as an urgent invitation to an increasingly important field of scholarship and knowledge whereby organization and management studies are now viewed on a much broader scale than ever before, indeed, as a matter of world affairs.

This volume is offered in anticipation of a new and expanding role for the students, scholars, and educators in organization and management studies. It takes as its challenge to address how organizational scholarship and thinking can inform understanding issues of global change. Its mandate is broad, its theoretical boundaries are open-ended, and it is inspired by a conviction that organizational studies has a pivotal role to play in both defining an agenda of relevant research on global change and providing theoretical lenses for understanding these research questions. Although it is risky business to herald an advance or bold new agenda without much evidence that it is already happening, we hope to at least begin making the case in this introductory chapter, considering developments like these:

■ Something quite extraordinary has been occurring on the world scene over the past 7 short years across the physical and social science disciplines. Around the world, an unprecedented interdisciplinary program of research has been envisioned, mobilized financially and programmatically, and organized almost like a global social movement organization. Its purpose, its vision, and its name have combined to galvanize levels of cooperation like few other initiatives in the history of social science—it is called "the human dimensions of global change research program."

■ The more productive the global change research domain has become (the 1996 Encyclopedia of World Problems now, sadly, catalogues some 15,000 transboundary problems), the more people are recognizing, or rediscovering, the role of organizations: Growing throughout the domain of global change science is the recognition and conviction that there is not one single item on the global agenda for change that can be understood outside of the role and functioning of organizations. Any effort to understand, much less come to terms with, global change that does not include a sustained commitment to improving our knowledge of the organizational dimensions cannot succeed.

■ More positively, the logic of rediscovering institutions can be taken one important step further. Although there may be limits to growth as far as the world's ecosystems are understood, there are no necessary limits to cooperation as human beings seek to constructively organize and respond. To an extent unimaginable a decade ago, the ideals of building a healthy, prosperous, and sustainable world future are taking on form and substance. Obstacles to cooperation and human enterprise that long seemed immovable have collapsed in humanity's path. In their classic volume *Our Common Future,* the World Commission on Environment and Development (1987) in fact suggested that virtually every item on the global agenda for change can be addressed (at least technically and economically)—"providing that *institutional arrangements* [italics added] permit the constructive interrelations of many intellectual resources and insights involving people from many countries with a myriad of cultures, traditions, languages, aspirations, and so on" (p. 8).

The book explores the potential of cooperation as a practice, an organizing accomplishment, and as a value for understanding issues of global change. It opens up conversations, research paths, and opportunities for dialogue around global change research. It addresses basic questions such as, What do we mean by global change research? What can organizational scholarship contribute to understanding the human dimensions of global change? If we were to offer a priority agenda for research and inquiry, what questions would we be asking, and what kinds of research would have a high probability of making a large contribution to knowledge as well as timely relevance for action? Is the global change domain likely to grow in future importance? And what would such inquiry do for organization scholarship? Will an expanded focus to include the organization dimensions of global change open our field to broad vistas of learning and compel changes in our current theories of human organization, management, and processes of change? Where are the exemplars?

In the rest of this chapter, we will begin exploring this new call, the opportunities raised, and the implications for both organization theory and society.

The chapter unfolds in three sections. The first provides a brief account of what has been internationally formulated as the domain of global change research, and it seeks to do so in ways that make these developments come alive for our own discipline. The second section, more importantly, previews the original pieces of work written for this volume. They are offered in the three parts of the book: Sensemaking and Global Change, Collaboration and Partnership Arrangements: The Structures of Global Change, and Social Constructionism and Global Change. We then conclude with a hope that we have for the future. It begins in a speculative way to envision broad reconsideration of the field's priorities focused on research, education, and innovation that is deliberately "opportunity focused" (Dutton, 1993) and "appreciative" (Cooperrider, 1990)—where inquiry itself is constructed as an intervention for the better and where the very framing of questions is recognized as a crucial choice-point for the kind of world that the scientific construction of social reality helps bring to focus, and perhaps fruition.

GLOBAL CHANGE RESEARCH DOMAIN:
A BRIEF REVIEW

The dominant changes that affect the environment and the course of life on Earth are natural ones, induced by such inexorable forces as natural selection, the shifting of winds and rivers, changing inputs from the Sun, the turbulent dynamics of the atmosphere and oceans, the drifting of the continental plates, the building of mountains, and the expansion and contraction of ice masses. But imposed on these is now another set of changes, more recent and immediate in consequence, that is the clear result of human activities. Our uses of energy and practices of intensive farming and technology have altered the albedo of the Earth, the composition of soil and waters, the chemistry for the air, the areas of forests, the diversity of plant and animal species, and the balance of global ecosystem.

International Council of Scientific Unions (1986, p. 1)

Do you think you can take over the universe and improve it?

—Lao-tzu

As used throughout this volume, the term *global change* is meant broadly to refer to alterations (positive or negative) in human or environmental systems whose effects are not and cannot be localized and for which appropriate human response is likely to require transboundary thought, organizing, and action (e.g., depletion of ozone; the transboundary movement of HIV/AIDS; species loss; emergence of global civil society; the global eradication of smallpox). As a research domain, global change science, especially that which is focused on the human dimensions, is young, dynamic, and emerging so rapidly that there is some risk of trying to say anything definitive about it. But there can be no mistake. Something quite extraordinary is occurring, and it has escaped the view of all but a relative handful of close observers, or those who are in the midst of creating the new directions. Place this in conjunction with the domain of actual practice—where social inventions across the local-global nexus are far outpacing our theories—and the potential of something like the organization dimensions of global change begins to expand in many exciting directions. Let us start with a brief review of the domain, the call to research in the area of global change.

The United States and International
Global Change Research Program (GCRP)

The USGCRP was created as a Presidential Initiative in 1989 and was formalized by the Global Change Research Act of 1990. At about the same time, the phrase "human dimensions" was added to the vocabulary of global change and in programmatic terms gave birth to the International Human Dimensions on Global Change Research Program (IHDGC), again in 1990. The major piece of writing giving direction internationally is generally taken as Turner, Clark, Kates, Richards, and Mathews's (1991) edited volume on *The Earth as Transformed by Human Action*; in the United States, there was, most notably, the framework-creating volume by Paul Stern, Oran Young, and Daniel Druckman (1992) *Global Environmental Change: Understanding the Human Dimensions*. Both had their roots in an invitation, a call, perhaps even a plea that can only be described as something of a scientific social movement, led by people such as Harold Jacobson at the University of Michigan's Institute for Social Research, as well as many others, such as Ian Burton (Director of the International Federation of Institutes for Advanced Study), Roland Fuchs (United Nations University), and Luis Ramallo (International Social Science Council). What brought these people to work tirelessly around the world over a period of several years was the conviction that the physical sciences (which had been defining the global change research agenda since the 1950s in the form of the international Geosphere-Biosphere Program) could go only so far without understanding the anthropogenic (a) sources of global change; (b) consequences of global change, both through other components of the geosphere-biosphere as well as directly to the human use systems; and (c) management of global change, that is, the prevention of harm, adaptation to change, and the rehabilitation and restoration of systems where changes of a deleterious nature are occurring. Speaking with conviction and passion to the entire social science community—disciplines such as economics, sociology, psychology, anthropology, and organization studies—the challenge was articulated rhetorically with two simple questions:

> Why does leadership come from the natural sciences, when the problems of global change are so much a function of human action? Should not the human sciences be expected to provide the lead, to set the agenda, and determine the priorities? (Burton & Timmerman, 1989, p. 304)

Momentum to address the question was generated. It was especially visible at the Sixteenth General Assembly of the International Social Sciences Council in December of 1986, and then it was used skillfully to build a consensus at the next major gathering in Tokyo 2 years later. The world's most ambitious social science cooperative endeavor was about to be inaugurated. For the catalysts, the obstacles, of course, were immense, including the challenges to science's claims to value neutrality, detached objectivity, tendencies toward ethnocentric knowledge, and limited methodological tools for dealing with truly global data sets. Even the design of the Tokyo event itself called for an extraordinary level of technical communication and mutual cooperation by the main sponsors, the International Foundation of Institutes of Advanced Study, the United Nations University, the International Social Sciences Council, and others. The myriad of geographically dispersed parties needed to overcome disciplinary, political, cultural, and language difficulties across all time zones. The Tokyo meeting, in particular, was a roller-coaster session, but people stayed in dialogue with the clear intuition that the outcomes of the deliberations might well be historic. Although no scientific or social consensus existed (or yet exists) about the scope and significance of issues such as climate warming, ozone depletion, acid precipitation, and the linkages between economy and ecology (e.g., the consequences of extreme poverty and/or overconsuming societies), something even more basic, according to the catalysts, was at stake: "Perhaps more importantly, there is no truly *global context* within which to *think* about these problems, let alone to begin to manage the problems themselves. This is the driving force behind HDGCP" (Burton & Timmerman, 1989, p. 298). In Kuhnian terms, fortunate observers at the meeting were witnesses to a paradigmatic revolution in the making. Lest one has any doubts, just type the words "global change" into a web search. The expedition will go on for hours (more on this later).

The Tokyo meeting resulted in an "extraordinary" and "urgent consensus" (Burton & Timmerman, 1989, p. 297). There were moments when differences of theoretical backgrounds and culture seemed unbridgeable. What emerged, however, was a unanimous conviction:

> Response to global change by one nation acting alone, or even by a few of the more powerful acting in concert will not suffice. The global community must become involved. The common welfare and moral solidarity of human-kind being at stake . . . a new relationship has to be forged between human society and environment, which will be morally, economically, and ecologi-cally sustainable. (Burton & Timmerman, 1989, pp. 299-300)

Visions of the new domain were given voice, one after the other. However, just as quickly as convictions and commitments were made, there were voices of caution, even fear, about setting sail on a course that the human science community was scarcely prepared to undertake:

> Given the magnitude of the task proposal—to create an international program that can contribute effectively to the understanding and management of global change—it has been asked whether the international community of scholars and human scientists is fully prepared to undertake it. Our own judgment is unequivocal: we are not fully prepared, and that is part of the problem. Were we more ready in intellectual and organizational terms, the world might not face quite a daunting prospect. . . . A great opportunity lies before us, and a great responsibility. (Burton & Timmerman, 1989, p. 303)

These words were written at precisely the same time that the Berlin Wall was falling, and events in Moscow signaled the end of the cold war. Signal events such as these marked an opportunity to approach the human sciences in a more integrated and whole-system way.

It is probably safe to say also that participants had precious little idea that within a few short years, there would be a mass mobilization of human dimensions conferences on every continent, dozens of new and related journals, the birth of literally hundreds of centers worldwide devoted to the human dimensions of global change, and, not incidentally, dedicated funding. As just one example, the piece of the U.S. Global Change Research Program budget devoted to the human dimensions (which also includes separate research budgets on climate and hydraulic systems, human interactions, biochemical dynamics, ecological systems, earth systems history, solid earth processes, and solar influences) has surged from $20.1 million in 1990 to more than $200 million in 1997 (see Office of Science and Technology Policy, 1997). This development in the United States has parallels across all continents and is all the more striking in view of the decline that was simultaneously under way in many other, more traditional areas of support in the humanities and social science research in general. In a recent article, Daniels (1996) asks, "How will future historians of science account for this rapid progress in only five years?" (p. 18).

The upshot of this brief review, of course, is not the dollars. What is important is the fact that a stage has been set. The phrase "human dimensions of global change" has and will increasingly become a powerful integrative theme bringing people together internationally across disciplines. The invitation is the following:

- To improve understanding and increase awareness of the complex interactions of environmental systems, including the atmosphere, biosphere, geosphere, and hydrosphere, as well as human systems, including economic, political, cultural, and sociotechnical systems
- To strengthen efforts to study, explore, and anticipate social change—attitudes and beliefs, population growth, markets, sociocultural systems, organizations and institutions, and international structures of cooperation—affecting the global environment
- To identify broad strategies to prevent, or mitigate, undesirable impacts of global change, or to adapt to changes that are already unavoidable
- To expand strategic options for dealing with global change and promoting the goal of sustainable development

Few developments have conveyed the sense of globality—and the need for global, transboundary methods for understanding and acting—as strongly as the growing realization that all depend on the earth's ecological resources and are vulnerable in the face of their degradation. For years, people have been talking about how globalization will set in motion a revolution in the intellectual world and compel refiguration in disciplinary boundaries, identities, methods, commitments, and agendas. Now it is beyond talk. Many are doing it. The domain of global change research, we believe, will burgeon in the next several years as issues of global concern will increasingly be identified through advances in theory and method and through advances in the world's communication capacity. How will organization theories respond? What can the organization and management sciences contribute to understanding the human dimensions of global change?

We now consider how the empirical forms of organizational life create additional urgency and possibility for the development of understanding of the organizational dimensions of global change.

From the Abstract to the Concrete:
New Organizing Forms for Global Change

Until very recently in history, people have responded to global phenomena as if they were local; they have not effectively institutionalized their responses across sectors or societies, nor have they been able, in organizational terms, to respond by deliberately altering the course of global changes themselves. But things are different now from what they have been for millennia. One example (drawn from material in Cooperrider & Bilimoria, 1993, p. 118) can be used to quickly illustrate the point:

> Future historians of global change will surely rank May 8, 1980 among the big dates. For on May 8, when the World Health Assembly declared that small-pox had been eradicated from the planet, smallpox became the first, and as yet only, global problem in history to have been eradicated or solved by organized action on a local-global world scale. The achievement can scarcely be overstated. Involving nearly a quarter million staff from 69 countries, including a multidisciplinary, multicultural group of 700 leaders, this global change response successfully addressed, in 10 years, a dreaded world boundary-crossing disease that had deadly effects on the human population since the time of the Neolithic age. Citation of this effort has happened more than a thousand times in the medical literatures. This is scarcely surprising, given the life-saving import of such an achievement, as well as the implications for other global health concerns, such as HIV/AIDS, and many other childhood diseases. But to this day, there has yet to emerge one theoretical or empirical study of this organizational breakthrough—from the perspective of leadership, decision making, organization design, management, strategic alliances, human motivation, managing change, multicultural management, or others.

We bring attention to this illustration for several reasons. The first is to underscore the point that it really is no longer utopian or romantically idealistic to be using the language of global change. The development of global cooperative capacity, across boundaries of all kinds, is part of the evolution of human efforts to organize life in response to transboundary problems and opportunities. We believe that these processes will accelerate in coming years.

The second is to bring attention to what we feel is a vast opportunity for organization theory. Indeed, the observable fact is this: Since World War II, more than 30,000 transnational nongovernmental (NGO) and intergovernmental (IGO) organizations have emerged to manage concerns related to issues of ecology and development (Union of International Associations, 1997). Many of the organizations to which we are referring are now familiar names: World Wildlife, Nature Conservancy, The Body Shop, Merck, Save the Children, United Nations, World Business Academy, Stonybrooke Farms, Sarvodaya Shramadama, and so on.

And this may be the tip of the iceberg. A study by the Club of Rome has called it a global "barefoot revolution" (Schneider, 1988); sociologists describe the axial age we are in as "the building of the global civic culture" (Boulding, 1988; de Oliveira & Tandon, 1994); Worldwatch Institute simply refers to new worldwide "people power"—with grassroots groups fighting poverty and environmental decline now numbering in the millions (Durning, 1989). Likewise, in other related spheres, political scientists are describing the accelerating formation of "institutions for the earth" (Haas, Keohane, & Levy, 1993) and of "global regimes" (Young, 1989); and at the same time, business thinkers at The World Business Academy are now even talking about the leading-edge "corporations as agents of positive global change" (Harman & Hormann, 1990) or the new "ecocentric organization" (Shrivastava, 1996).

So what ties these organizations conceptually? In connection with the language of the human dimensions of global change research program, we would like to refer to the type simply as global change organizations. The bridge is a useful one, we believe, because the language of the human dimensions of global change will continue to enlarge the boundary-crossing dialogue across disciplines—included in this rapidly growing dialogue are fields such as earth systems science, as well as the disciplines of sociology, economics, political science, international relations, anthropology, psychology, and management studies. Likewise, it is increasingly clear that what is happening and what the world is calling for is the birth of new organizational arrangements that allow for the closing of what some have called the institutional gap—the dichotomy between organizations born of the modern bureaucratic eras of the past several centuries and the new demands of a postmodern, supranational, globally linked world system of change (see Cooperrider & Bilimoria, 1993). As the World Commission on Environment and Development (1985) put it in clear and practical terms, "The real world of interlocked economic and ecological systems will not change; but the policies and institutions concerned must" (p. 9). In this spirit, the term *global change organization* is useful also to avoid the tired and outworn distinctions of profit, not for profit, public and private, governmental and nongovernmental, and so on. Global change organizations, as proposed below, have several minimal but important characteristics that can be used to help support interdisciplinary inquiry:

- Global change organizations assert, as their primary task, a commitment to serve as an agent of change in the creation of environmentally and socially sustainable world futures—their transformational missions are articulated around the real needs of people and the earth.

- They have discovered and mobilized innovative social-organizational architectures that make possible human cooperation across previously polarizing or arbitrarily constraining boundaries.

- They hold values of empowerment, or people-centered forms of action, in the accomplishment of their global change mission, emphasizing the central role of people as both means and ends in any development process.

- They are globally-locally linked in structure, membership, or partnership and thereby exist, at least in identity and practice (maybe not yet legally), as entities beyond the nation-state.

- They are multiorganizational and often cross-sectoral. They can be business, governmental, or not-for-profit. Indeed, many of the most significant global change organizing innovations involve multiorganization partnerships bridging sectoral boundaries in new hybrid forms of business, intergovernmental, and private voluntary sectors.

From here, many interesting questions surge to the fore. How many global change organizations are there? Can we create a mapping of this largely nonterritorial invisible continent where people are organizing to bridge barriers between nations, races, religions, sectors, professions, cultures, and distances in the service of a global imperative? What are their linkages and interactions? How do the designs and dynamics of complex organizations mediate humanity's sensemaking ability—its capacity to understand and respond to global change? How is the world's cooperative capacity enlarged or diminished in and through the evolution of organization structures that are locally and globally linked, multisectoral, cross-cultural, and multi-institutional? What is the effect of chronic disaster on people's sense of hope that constructive response to global change is possible? On a more micro level, can we create typologies or modes of enacting global change? What about transitions from old to new organizational forms? How do companies, for example, make rapid transition from being harmful agents of global change to active and constructive agents of global conservation, restoration, or renewal? What about questions of global change leadership? Gender relations? Oppression? How can we frame human response to global change so that all voices from different and unequal positions can be heard in organizational settings with equivalent seats? Equally important, how can global change partnerships be formed and guided effectively in the absence of authority? Will the people of the world ever evolve a shared global ethic, and what role will global change organizations play in this arena? What is the relationship between international regimes and transnational social movement organizations? Do global change organizations provide a powerful counterpoint to the dominant cost-minimization, benefit-maximization paradigm in the management sciences—where, at best, organizations are seen as utilitarian inducement/contribution (contract) systems, where hierarchy and control are designed to minimize shirking and agency costs, and where self-interested opportunism is assumed to prevail? Will organization theory rise to the positive challenge of building concepts whereby the self-sacrificing quality of the people and organizations—a public goods orientation—is, in fact, noticed and thus becomes a central, as opposed to a peripheral or tangential, focus?

OVERVIEW OF THE CONTENTS

The remaining 14 chapters making up this book were originally written in response to a worldwide call from the Academy of Management to begin a new dialogue on questions exactly like these. The authors, leading thinkers in the fields of organization studies, were invited in the context of discovery

> to open new doors to understanding and action . . . to view this as opportunity to accept Toynbee's well-known challenge "to dare in scholarship" and to generate systematic propositions that will give vision and direction to an

enterprise that will count, and count affirmatively, as it relates to the complex and growing global change agenda of our time.

The chapters, selected from more than 90 submissions, are expansive, vibrant, and thought provoking. Conceptually, they are grouped into three theoretical configurations beginning with questions of sensemaking (How do complex human organization dynamics mediate humanity's ability to understand and respond to global change?). Second, there are priority questions of new collaborative and partnership structures (How is the world's cooperative capacity enlarged or diminished in and through the evolution of organization structures that are locally and globally linked, multisectoral, cross-cultural, and multi-institutional?). Finally, Part III deals with broad questions related to promising paradigmatic approaches that take into account the socially constructed nature of reality in a pluralistic global change arena of multiple voices, diverse value systems, reflexive knowledge systems, and a world of interdependence. We now turn to an overview of each of the contributions.

Part I: Sensemaking and Global Change

Research on the human dimensions of global change strives to understand the interactions among and between human systems and environmental systems, including the atmosphere, biosphere, geosphere, and hydrosphere, as well as human systems, including economic, political, cultural, and institutional arrangements that make choices, take action, and so forth (see Stern et al., 1992). The question that concerns the authors of Part I is related to the latter emphasis: How do the workings of complex organizations mediate humanity's sensemaking ability—its capacity to understand and constructively respond to global change?

A sensemaking lens on the organizational dimensions of global change is rooted in the recognition that the global change domain is made up of issues that have unclear cause-effect structures, unintended side effects, are linked as metaproblems that are multilayered (cutting across entire societies), are essentially contested phenomena, have consequences that are often irreversible, and simultaneously, because of the reverberations into the future, create an imperative to act regardless of the endless uncertainties. In short, to organize for global change is an act of sensemaking. Sensemaking, we contend, is the birthplace for human response to global change because sensemaking sets the frame for decision making, becomes the basis for envisioning possible futures, creates the communication context for linking with others, and is itself transformed in the designs and processes of organizing. The chapters that fit in this section all locate the possibilities for accomplishing global change in the processes by which knowledge is created, shared, and acted upon. They share with each other a belief that small actions are consequential in the generation of meaning, that organizing with consequences for global change is an ongoing accomplishment, and that making sense is a critical part of the process. All four chapters are rich with example, helping us see how a sensemaking lens identifies important new ways to both think about and organize for global change.

Karl Weick's chapter on "Sensemaking as an Organizational Dimension of Global Change" opens Part I and unpacks the core premise that different organizational forms shape how people make sense by affecting the sensemaking resources available. He elaborates seven properties of sensemaking that afford different capacities for individuals to act in different situations. As a prolific writer about the importance of sensemaking in all of organizational life, Weick is well suited to extend his analysis to implications for global social change. He does this in a surprising way, by using examples to bring alive the connection between form (design), sensemaking resources, and outcomes.

As a starting point, Weick asserts that individual sensemaking in different organizational designs has critical consequences. The consequences from inadequate and adequate sensemaking are conveyed dramatically through the contrasting stories of firefighters in the Mann Gulch and the sensemaking by members of the Worker's Defense Committee in Poland. In the former case, 13 men die in a tragic fire. In the latter case, a small group of members of an opposition movement create a nearly miraculous large-scale change toward achievement of democracy. Sensemaking fails in the first and triumphs in the second.

The stories that Weick contrasts are powerful in their own right. However, they are especially compelling as reminders of the challenge in global social organizing: that strangers come together with diverse experience, only having face-to-face contact for limited periods, with leaders unknown or by chance, in temporary systems, facing solutions that make no sense, with limited or nonexistent ways of communicating and sharing experience, in unfamiliar terrain, and with strong consequences implied. Yet despite this challenge, by thinking systematically about the sensemaking resources available in an organizational form, one acquires a way of seeing the possibilities for enhancing global organizing. The window that Weick opens helps us to see that answering several design (organizational form) questions in the affirmative enables global social change: Does the form encourage conversation and give people a distinct, stable sense of who they are and what they represent? Does the form preserve elapsed data and legitimate the use of those data? Does it enhance the visibility of cues, enable people to be resilient in the face of interruptions, encourage people to accumulate and exchange plausible accounts, and encourage action or hesitations? According to Weick, the more affirmative the answers are to these questions, the better suited the form is for global social change.

Chapter 3, by Kathryn Kaczmarski and David Cooperrider, provides a different window into the possibilities for global organizing that arise from a focus on leadership. Like Weick, these authors locate the possibility for global organizing in the social processes that different structures afford. Rather than call these social processes sensemaking resources, these authors call the organizing potential *constructionist leadership*. They breathe new life into the concept of leadership by example and by contrast.

The example is a powerful one. The chapter traces the emergence of leadership during the creation of the Mountain Forum, a global-level alliance that, over the course of 11 years, brought together mountain-centered organizations, NGOs, international agencies such as the World Bank, mountain researchers and land managers, various national governmental representatives, donors, policymakers, academics, and IGOs, all of whom had a shared interest in increasing global interest in the conservation of the world's mountains. The story of the alliance's evolution documents the enormous challenges of scale and diversity that make the alliance's creation so remarkable. It also illustrates the pushes and pulls, planned and unplanned events, and large- and small-scale meetings that jointly enabled the emergence of this alliance. Although formalized by name in 1995 as the Mountain Forum, the alliance organized itself using a form that resisted bureaucracy, hierarchy, and formalization. As the authors put it,

> A pioneering image of the Mountain Forum emerged. Visualized by the participants was a coalition of organizations strung together by geographic region but with no identifiable center and no formal secretariat. . . . Within this coalition, boundaries would fade and no hierarchy of organizations or positions would exist, consistent with the consensus that a relational network of mountain NGOs and agencies was necessary to function successfully at

the global level . . . reflective of the basic values of the Mountain Forum:
open, democratic, decentralized, accessible, transparent, accountable, and
flexible. (Chapter 3, p. 72)

Kaczmarski and Cooperrider help us to see the power of constructionist
leadership in helping this forum come to life. They distinguish the leadership
task as one of organizing by bridging across diverse cultures of inquiry.
Constructionist leadership enables "productive connections at the deepest
levels . . . of belief and method" (Chapter 3, p. 76). Such a leader "works at a
nonmaterial, epistemic level of promoting appreciation of the 'intelligibility
nuclei' across often-conflicting communities" (Chapter 3, p. 76), and in
"building knowledge systems, open and indeterminate, capable of generating
intellectual breakthrough and action time and again" (Chapter 3, p. 76).

These authors distinguish this leadership form by three qualities: "(a) an
appreciative approach to knowledge, (b) a generative approach to language
that is rich in metaphor and narrative form, and (c) the formation of 'out of
control' organizations through the web of inclusion" (Chapter 3, p. 77). The
appreciative approach to knowledge means actively trying to use processes
that "[seek] to discover, learn about, and bring to prominence the 'life-giving'
best of every culture of inquiry" (Chapter 3, p. 78). The importance of
narrative and metaphor are described in terms of their bridging power, their
capacity to embrace complexity and ambiguity, and their ability to create and
sustain hope in the face of such diversity. It is all about a kind of leadership
that enables the kind of sensemaking so well articulated by Karl Weick in the
previous chapter. The authors bring to life these sensemaking constructions
by describing a series of meetings of Mountain Forum participants held in
circular Mongolian-styled yurts. Here, the place for gatherings was rich in
metaphoric possibility, and the social process used to encourage dialogue in
the sessions relied explicitly on metaphors and images as means for opening
up conversation and encouraging multiple interpretations. The use of appreciative approaches and metaphor and narration invites confusion, ambiguity,
and a sense of potential chaos. Kaczmarski and Cooperrider celebrate the
delicate balancing that a constructionist leader must create to open up the
dialogue through these methods and ways of relating without surpassing the
collective's capacity to extend and elaborate its potential.

The final element in constructionist leadership is captured by the idea of
web of inclusion, which describes a leader's commitment to inclusive structures and inclusive processes that ensure an "ever-expansive domain of relat-

edness" (Chapter 3, p. 86). In the evolution of the Mountain Forum, this feature was ensured through the creation and use of an open electronic network; through the commitment of values that support inclusion (open, democratic, decentralized, etc.); open membership; and a reliance on temporary leadership groups.

By chapter's end, one has a strong sense of the value of constructionist leadership for global organizing in its capacity to generate and bridge cultures of inquiry—in short, for making collective sense of a global agenda for change. One gains an intellectual and emotional appreciation for the possibilities derived from this form of leadership, as well as an understanding of some of its defining features. Interestingly, these ideas are brought to life in the Mountain Forum case, where no one leader or leadership group is ever named or identified.

In Chapter 4, Frances Westley addresses one of the greatest threats to humanity's sensemaking capacity—the impact of chronic disaster. Building on Kai Erikson's recent book *A New Species of Trouble* (1994), this chapter begins by looking at a uniquely contemporary experience of disaster that gathers force slowly and insidiously, creeping around people's defenses rather than smashing through them. People become unable to mobilize against the threat, sometimes because they feel there is nothing that can be done to avoid it, sometimes because they have been misinformed, but mostly because they have elected consciously or unconsciously to ignore it, to avoid anxiety by constricting awareness. In short, there is a dangerous constriction in sensemaking capacity, and it happens at every level of human system, from individuals to groups to organizations to the whole of society.

The disasters today, explains Westley, are different from many that human beings have dealt with throughout history because they (a) are chronic and insidious rather than acute and dramatic; (b) are humanly generated, or human-made; and (c) often involve toxins that seem to permeate the very ground of being, rendering the environment that surrounds us and of which we are a part "defiled and unreliable." The dread, slowly and progressively, appears to grow with time. It has the capacity to make people feel demoralized, helpless, and traumatized in a "peculiarly inaccessible way." It often incapacitates the very fabric of community, organization, and joint action—it raises questions about human beings' contemporary capacity to comprehend the global agenda, much less respond in viable and vigorous ways. The case in point: One of the most critical issues confronting the globe today is the rapid extinction of species. Estimates are that some 24 species are becoming extinct every day. Westley believes that although we may clean up our rivers and the atmosphere, learn new technologies for curing disease and for destroying toxic wastes, invent substitutes for environmentally destructive energy sources, and return to chemical-free forms of agriculture, we as a species have not learned to re-create the miracle of life.

A new species of solution, what we earlier talked about as the global change organization, may, in fact, be one antidote to the hopelessness and constricted sensemaking associated with the experience of chronic disaster. It is here where Westley makes her inspiring contribution. Her research, which traces the story of a worldwide network called the Conservation Breeding Specialist Group, takes a look at their effectiveness as a organization, but more importantly, she documents the human impact that such organizing has on its members. Through in-depth interviews, surveys (87% response rate), and participant observation, Westley provides insights into ways that organizing can transform the debilitating experiences of chronic disaster into informed and sustainable action.

Do organizations restrict our human capacity to make sense of our world, or are they centers that have broad potential for helping human beings reclaim and enlarge their sensemaking capacity? The question, theoretically, is important because it may help differentiate the sensemaking perspective on organizations from classic theories of decision making that stress constricted awareness and the satisficing effects of organization. Westley's scholarship, we believe, invites consideration of the latter.

In Chapter 5, Ramkrishnan Tenkasi and Susan Mohrman craft a series of arguments for why global change requires the creation of contexts in which collaborative knowledge can be created and used. These authors locate the possibility for global change in the social process by which knowledge is created and shared between interacting units or organizations. Their chapter directly critiques traditional ideas that knowledge can be realized objectively, applied universally, and considered complete. They substitute these traditional claims with ideas: (a) knowledge is subjectively constructed and subjectively consumed; (b) knowledge requires contextual adaptation; and (c) knowledge is incomplete. Throughout their chapter, they use examples in which knowledge transfer failed or succeeded depending on the consistency of actions with the collaborative knowledge creation perspective.

For these authors, successful global change requires the intentional and careful creation of what they call interpretive spaces, where joint meaning between parties can take place and where joint learning is enabled. They mention several techniques and perspectives used in contexts of global collaboration that enable these interpretive spaces: the dialogic method, search conferencing, appreciative inquiry, and interpretive interactionism.

Part II: Collaboration and Partnership Arrangements: The Structures of Global Change

In our view, we are already witnessing a significant transformation in the central preoccupation of organizational scholarship away from the individual or unitary organization and toward some more globally conceptualized entity. On one level, the shift signals a change in organizational forms. At another level, many are now arguing that cooperation is a higher-order adaptive strategy than, for example, competition (see The Club of Lisbon's report "Limits to Competition," 1994). One is reminded of Astley and Fombrun's (1983) notion of "collective strategy" (p. 181), which, as they ardently reason, specifically refutes the conception of organizations as autonomous, self-sufficient units and stresses the fact that all organizations are inevitably participants in a multitude of interorganizational associations that overlie and interpenetrate one another, thus constituting an intricate, functionally integrated network of vital relationships. To understand organizations as unitary and competitive (the vast majority of organization theorizing and research are indeed still founded on such assumptions) may no longer be relevant to understanding what is happening in the world of global change. In effect, by giving priority to the unitary form, organizational theory might well be underestimating the cooperative resources in the world. But more debilitating to the generative potential of the field is the problem of paradigm blindness; the field simply may not see the higher-order adaptive strategies. Only in this way does it make sense that still, almost 20 years after the classic global eradication of smallpox, not one single piece of organizational research can be found based on this unprecedented cooperative achievement. Have we painted a picture of the world's cooperative potential with a whole series of colors as missing?

As the authors in Part II demonstrate, the organizations responding to the agenda for global change are almost everything but unitary organizations—they are all hybrids. Whether termed strategic bridging institutions, social movement organizations, public-private partnerships, regimes, networks, referent organizations, or locally-globally linked NGOs, virtually all involve organizational arrangements that use resources and/or governance structures from more than one existing organization. Such "hybrid organizational arrangements" are no longer the exception but the norm and invite more relationally informed theorizing (e.g., concepts such as social capital, the strength of weak ties, cooperative advantage, and others). They also, as any leader in the arena of global change will attest, pose a myriad of new challenges for managerial practice. Imagine the hybrid organizational dynamics involved in the dramatic response to the depletion of the earth's layer of ozone. Literally thousands of organizations—corporations such as DuPont, social movement organizations, academies of science, intergovernmental agencies, trade associations, grassroots NGOs—combined their capacities to address the global environmental problem. Some observers say that it was the most successful form of human cooperation and global action ever recorded, at least as it involved worldwide mitigation response to destructive activities affecting the world's ecosystems (Haas et al., 1993). What do we know about this kind of organizing?

In Chapter 6, L. David Brown and Darcy Ashman argue that items on the global agenda for change are systems of self-reinforcing difficulties, or "messes" (using Russell Ackoff's colorful language), and are intractable to problem-solving activities by single organizations focused on limited aspects of the problem system. Planned global change—such as dealing with chronic poverty, maldevelopment, and hunger in large parts of the world, including debt-ridden economies whose instabilities are intensified by growing gaps between rich and poor—will inevitably demand changes at several levels of analysis. Global problems are often approached through macrolevel changes that can alter the policy environment. They also begin as microlevel reforms vis-à-vis locally focused projects that alter local behavior and institutions. But long-term global change, where vast increases in interdependence and uncertainty abound, requires both the macro and micro in the form of mesolevel programs and institutional relations. The mesolevel, as described by the authors, is neither top down nor bottom up and offers an alternative to free-market or central planning approaches to societal regulation. It involves global change partnerships that are both lateral and vertical; lateral partnerships join diverse professional skills and capacities across organizations and sectors, whereas vertical partnerships join parties across the divides of power, from the policy levels to the grassroots. This kind of hybrid arrangement has the earmark of a seminal idea and, as the authors demonstrate, can have high leverage effects on large systems with seemingly intractable problems.

The strength of the chapter is its research base in combination with a theoretical elaboration of Robert Putman's concept of social capital in the global change domain. Thirteen cases of hybrid partnerships from 12 countries in Africa and Asia are examined seeking to "identify ingredients associated with successful cooperation across differences in sector and power" (Chapter 6, p. 140). Three factors are used to explain successful cooperative efforts: (a) preexisting social capital in the form of previously experienced networks, norms, and trust; (b) settings of dialogue that maximized mutual influence among organizations in spite of sector and power differences; and (c) face-to-face group learning processes that used conflict (moderate to high levels of conflict were more productive than low levels of reported conflict) to enable new choices and new behaviors by interorganizational systems. The Bangladesh Immunization Health Program, for example, involved more than 1,000 partner organizations, transforming the vertical and lateral dimensions into a hybrid for change that has had a positive impact on the health of millions of Bangladeshi children. The cases, one after the other, are compelling. But equally important are the innovations in research practice leading to the case writing. The case studies and the initial comparative analyses were conducted by an international team of researchers. The medium, in this chapter, is also the message.

Mayer Zald turns his attention to a different kind of organization, one of the great catalytic forms that often sparks efforts at regime formation—transnational social movement organizations (SMOs). Zald's starting question is fundamental: How do people around the globe sometimes come to act in concert? His analysis is conceptually rich. It is guided by modern social movement theory, especially the writings that focus on resource mobilization, political opportunity, and cultural framing. But there is a paradox, says Zald: Cooperation across national boundaries to alleviate hunger, contain and eliminate the spread of AIDS, combat environmental deterioration, and so on also creates the conditions for large-scale conflicts. Groups and cultures that were once fairly isolated from each other are now brought into contact, and, almost by definition, SMOs generate conflict precisely because they are born with social transformation and change as their reason for existence. So, although the idea of cooperation across national boundaries to achieve desirable social goals has intuitive appeal, there are always groups and organizations with opposing priorities, goals, and values. The more effective the SMO is in generating cooperative transboundary action, the more conflict there will likely be in the world. A case in point is the role that SMOs played in helping to virtually eliminate slave trade globally across national boundaries. So, like the chapter by Brown and Ashman, cooperation and conflict go hand in hand; they are not opposites along a continuum.

Admittedly, Zald's writing is in an assertive mode, as if we knew a lot about the operation of transnational social movements. On a descriptive level, histories of particular social movements have been written. Yet on a comparative and theoretical level, much remains to be done. Concludes Zald, "The trends in globalization will inevitably lead to more transnational social movements and a more complex interweaving of conflict and cooperation" (Chapter 7, p. 183).

Most observers of the human response to global environmental change believe that the key to solving problems of collective action is in the creation of international regimes—and this is Barbara Gray's focus in Chapter 8. Regimes are interlocking sets of framework conventions and obligations that govern interactions among international actors. Although most of the study on international regimes concerns economic regimes, interest has mounted rapidly in the study of environmental regimes. To manage the myriad of environmental changes that are forecast (e.g., sea level increases from global warming) requires organizing at both the local and global levels. But such organizing presents a supreme challenge—it is about governing without government, it is about organizing a world of uncorrelated stakeholders in the absence of authority. It is about underorganized systems where interdependence is high but where most actors are approaching global-level phenomena through local, uncoordinated action and where no party has sufficient power to force unilateral decisions.

For Gray, the search for solutions to life-threatening issues at the global level involves four classifications of environmental problems: commons; shared natural resources; transboundary externalities; and linked issues, such as environmental and economic development linkages. In the absence of authority, the only real option, argues Gray, is collaboration: "'Collaboration involves a process of joint decision making among key stakeholders of a problem domain about the future of that domain'" (Chapter 8, p. 191). Like Brown and Ashman earlier, the author identifies a number of factors, such as social capital, that are critical to the successful development of regimes. Theoretically, Gray looks at how leadership, culture, structure, and technology become the mechanisms for negotiating the development of a domain and then quickly turns her attention to practical requirements or "how tos." What is most needed, she contends, is the formation of active trust. Her chapter identifies three major challenges to the successful creation of international regimes: how to effectively frame problems, how to deal with power differences, and how to select a convener. Her chapter identifies a range of solutions to these practical and structural organizing challenges. Her discussions of solutions suggest that organizing for global change is not simply about cold structures and mechanistic power relations. Much needed in the area of global change is a scholarship of human process. Although the structures of collaboration must likewise be better understood, Gray's call is for a better understanding of the difficult human processes of negotiation, interaction, and trust development that lie at the foundation of the collaborative forms.

Julie Fisher's chapter puts some numbers to such trends. For example, she maps out the breathtaking growth of indigenous NGOs committed to addressing issues of poverty and environmental decline in the Third World. The chapter explores characteristics of regionally and globally linked grassroots organizations (GROs), horizontal networks between GROs, grassroots support organizations (GRSOs), and horizontal and vertical GRSO networks that are connecting across cyberspace in a virtual global community. Organizations such as EarthCare Africa, The Latin American Network for Child Welfare, ANGOC (Asian NGO Coalition for Agrarian Reform and Rural Development), and dozens of others are described in ways that give the reader a feel—the barefoot revolution is on and the organizations being born have been hybridized with traditional ways of practicing cooperation in villages and cultures throughout the developing world. In Africa, for example, thousands of GROs were organized in response to the droughts of 1973 and 1985. In Kenya, there were 1,600 women's GROs by 1987. All of them must be understood through the lens of their cultural roots and traditional relational forms.

In reading Fisher's chapter, one is reminded of Pradeep Khandwalla's (1988) pioneering work intended to make the organization and behavioral sciences more directly relevant to sustainable development, especially socioeconomic growth in developing cultures. Fortunately, as Fisher's chapter so aptly shows, the opportunities and materials for studying the organizational dimensions of global change from the perspective of the developing world context are tremendous. These organizations, as the reader will see from the descriptions, offer exceptionally rich sites for natural experiment and participatory types of research where "before," "during," and "after" data on structure, leadership, boundary spanning, human relations approaches, organization revitalization, and change methodologies can be learned from in vivo. An organizational study for social development is an exciting and overdue paradigm; it is an area where practice is truly outpacing theory.

In the final chapter of Part II, John Aram argues that the sheer numbers, the size and magnitude of the recent explosion of global change organizations, suggests the need for a wholesale rethinking and revision of management assumptions and concepts. Conceptually and practically, global change organizations provide a powerful counterpoint to the dominant cost-minimization, benefit-maximization paradigm in the management sciences—where, at best, organizations are seen as utilitarian inducement/contribution (contract) systems, hierarchy and control are designed to minimize shirking and agency costs, and self-interested opportunism is assumed to prevail. The global change organizations are public or collective goods organizations. The matters of concern—human rights, environmental protection, biodiversity, women's rights, and community development—are meant by members to be commonized, not privatized. In terms of the influential theory of collective action (Olson, 1965), these behaviors should not be evident where large numbers prevail and group membership is heterogeneous. However, the enormous magnitude of the global change movement demonstrates the widespread prevalence of a different set of principles. From the standpoint of theory development, Aram proposes, the challenge is to build concepts in which the self-sacrificing quality of "people and organizations that create public goods is the central, as opposed to the peripheral or tangential, issue" (Chapter 10, p. 238). The organizational significance, the real story of the global change movement, lies in the incontrovertible and widespread evidence of public-goods behavior.

So, where do we go for insights into the growth of global change organizations, their innovativeness, and their ability to take public goods producing collective action? Here again is the idea of hybrid forms, of global change as requiring anything but unitary organizations. And in place of rational choice theories, Aram draws on the theory of weak ties in sociological network studies to cast an important light on the phenomenon. This theory explains how a social system organized by a greater number of acquaintances (weak ties) rather than close friends (strong ties) will exhibit greater aggregate innovativeness, cohesiveness, and adaptability. The decentralized, diffuse nature of membership in most global change efforts, especially aided by modern electronic communications, builds issue-oriented, low-density organizational networks.

At the same time that Aram identifies the insights applicable to global change organizations from network theory, he offers an important critical perspective in the global change movement. He illustrates the diverse intellectual influences that compose this movement (e.g., communitarian, social reformist), making the contradictions between influences more transparent. The existence of these differences means that effective organizing is a challenge. In addition, Aram raises three global needs—expressions of ethnonationalism, global crime organizations, and differing views of justice and fairness—as developments that further challenge the design of effective collaborative forms. Coupled with Aram's convincing case against the universality of the widely accepted utilitarian models of management, this perspective opens the door for fresh ideas for organization research and theory building.

Part III: Social Constructionism and Global Change

In the interest of establishing priorities and achieving clarity of exposition, the Committee on the Human Dimensions of Global Change made a series of focused recommendations for the national program on global change research. One, for example, zeroes in on the relational aspects of a growing global change agenda—especially the enormous intensification of worldwide conflicts over values and choices:

> Proposals deserve priority to the extent they are likely to enhance understanding of processes of decision making and conflict management in response to global change. . . . How will global environmental change intensify existing social conflicts or engender new forms of conflict? What technologies of conflict resolution or conflict management are likely to prove effective in coming to terms with these conflicts? (Stern et al., 1992, pp. 243, 247).

Interestingly, the committee also raises significant ethical questions about global change science itself, realizing that traditional science conventions— such as value freedom, detached objectivity, the picture theory of language, and the like—might well suppress the potential of a human dimensions research program. "Novel theoretical constructs and research methods are needed" (Stern et al., 1992, p. 167). For example, the stakes may be quite high: "The reflexivity of human activity makes knowledge itself a driving force of the system that is the object of that knowledge" (Stern et al., 1992, p. 167). Even further, in light of the dramatic plurality inherent in global-level inquiry, it is no longer possible or desirable to sustain patterns of insularity from the views, values, and understandings of those not quite like us.

Recently, social constructionist approaches to knowledge have begun to surface (see Gergen, 1994) that offer many exciting and promising ways of enriching the enterprise of human science, especially in a domain where questions of human relatedness (dealing with difficult issues of values, cultures, conflicts, and beliefs) and reflexivity (where knowledge itself transforms the phenomenon) are increasingly of preeminent concern. Unlike earlier versions of social constructionism that appeared as inherently critical of virtually every aspect of conventional science, current expressions not only place great value on empirical methodologies and other traditional accomplishments, but they also forge ahead with new methods demonstrating the advantages of breaking disciplinary boundaries, entering interrelated dialogues, and approaching concerns of reflexivity not as contaminating limitation but as unique opportunity (e.g., the 1987 accounts of ozone depletion reflexively turned back on human beings and prompted unprecedented reality-shaping forms of human cooperation and global action, including major alterations in corporate behaviors, changes in the agendas of international regimes, the birth of whole new connections among grassroots environmental movements, and rapid transformations in popular vocabularies and awareness).

For purposes here, constructionism is an approach to human science and practice that replaces the individual (or any single entity) with the relationship as the locus of knowledge. Philosophically, it involves a decisive shift in Western intellectual tradition from *cogito ergo sum* to *communicamus ergo sum*. The common thread in most constructionist writing is a concern with the processes by which human beings, their values, and commonsense and scientific knowledge are both produced in, and reproduce, human communities. In practice, constructionism replaces absolutist claims or the final word with the never-ending collaborative quest to understand and construct options for better living (for the major statement in this area, see Gergen, 1994).

One of the prominent strengths of the constructionist perspective, from the vantage point of developing a truly global human dimensions research program, is that it is always seeking to open the door to a fuller interweaving of the disparate communities of meaning. Although descriptions of social constructionism vary widely and are subject to an enormous and rapidly expanding body of scholarship, there are at least four exciting ways that social constructionism can expand the scope and significance of research on the organization dimensions of global change: It invites greater attention to ethical discourse and inquiry into ever-evolving visions of the good; it invites greater disciplinary self-critique and reflexivity; it seeks expansion of voices participating in the world of science and action; and it invites anticipatory theorizing, constructing future images, propositions, and languages of positive possibility. All of these, it would appear, are important forms of scholarship to the emergent domain. And each of these invitations is illustrated, at least partially, in Part III of our volume.

For example, Ken Gergen's chapter on "Global Organization and the Potential for Ethical Inspiration" demonstrates how social constructionism does not avoid but engages with full priority the thorny questions of values, concerns of power, and how social constructionism has practical uses in the arena of "an enormous intensification of ethical conflict" (Chapter 11, p. 257). For Gergen, the sources of conflicts in the global change domain are not essentially problems of malignant intention ("we should not think in terms of the evil practices of the multinationals as against the purity of traditional culture [or vice versa]" [Chapter 11, p. 258]) or ruthless and colonizing groups seeking world domination ("[these terms] are the epithets of the outsider" [Chapter 11, p. 258]). Rather, the problem is that of multiple and competing constructions of the good.

After dismissing and showing the weaknesses inherent in many conventional approaches to conflict resolution—including the long-standing attempt to generate universal and binding ethical principles, and when those do not work, the additional strategy of reactive international sanctions—Gergen finds compelling potential in new organizational forms and postmodern organizational theory.

The pivotal metaphor for simultaneously achieving organizational viability and ethical well-being, for Gergen, is found in conceptualizing ethical construction as relational process. Proposed is a shift in the Western intellectual tradition from conceptions of ethical principles, from which proper behaviors are later derived, to forms of ethically generative practices that give rise to conjoint action and the synergistic valuing of realities. From the social constructionist stance, global values and ethics will always be interminable and unsettleable; they are also contingent and parochial, reflecting the ongoing constructions of reality of parties in concrete relationship. Postmodern organizing, therefore, is to be valued for its relational globalizing potential to the extent to which it continuously opens the opportunities for intelligibilities to commingle, to interpenetrate in cooperative practice, and where the pervasive pluralism of international life is met not with dismay but with a sense of reassurance. Concrete illustrations of the abstract argument are usefully offered, such as that from a multinational pharmaceutical company, where the voices of ecological activists in essence became part of the management of the firm (the outside and inside of the corporation was obviously blurred)— leading the company to champion an international policy of bioethics. In the postmodern organization, writes Gergen, boundaries are loose and permeable; there are no single individuals making autonomous decisions; there are multiple centers of intelligibility and rapidly obsolete rationality; there are many nonhierarchical and overlapping networks of group configurations, lattices, matrices, temporary systems—and there is healthy appreciation for incoherent policies. A formula for chaos? Just the opposite, says Gergen. In the relationally rich circular organization, intelligibility is not as likely to ossify. Images of the good and the right do not become frozen, where my reality is the reality. Conventions of negation, so often created when intelligibilities are walled off from one another, are softened. And a subtle shift is accomplished. Relational practice gives rise to livable ethics. Embedded in the hurly-burly of everyday vocabularies and constructed understandings, these ethics are fluidly reconstructed in the course of living, in the processes of practical dialogue. Much needed, argues Gergen, is transformation of our fundamental quest. The ethically generative question for the global change community of researchers and practitioners is not "What is the good?" but instead, given the heterogeneity of the world's peoples, must become "What are the relational means by which we can help bring about dialogue and mutually satisfactory conditions?"

In Chapter 12, Raza Mir, Marta Calás, and Linda Smircich demonstrate one of the truly unique commitments of the social constructionist perspective—reflexive deliberation. Too often in scientific and scholarly pursuits, attention is focused "out there" with little open reflection inside the discipline. Hidden from view, frequently, are perhaps oppressive tendencies, values, or even innocent but detrimental consequences of the work. For the constructionist, there is recognition that, whether a primitive society or a scientific subculture, we develop working languages, and with those words (concepts, theories, professional vocabularies), accounts are furnished on what is real, rational, and right. Without reflexive deliberation—exploration into the historically and culturally situated character and consequence of the accounts, including our own—there is always risk of settling in too quickly. Univocal agreement tends to occlude critique. Outsiders not sharing the premises are rendered suspect, often dismissed or denigrated. Many disciplines obviously operate this way. But it is not a good foundation for building a program of inquiry into the human dimensions of global change. The all-too-familiar process of disciplinary fragmentation is antithetical to truly global learning. From this perspective, it is essential to build into global change science some processes of reflexive deliberation. And by doing it in this chapter, Mir, Calás, and Smircich offer a message that is demonstrated in its medium. It is a great piece of writing; something we need more of in organization theory.

The chapter begins in complete and utter protest with the theme of the present book. That we should hold up the value of cooperation as a positive and universal good appears at first glance to be a seductive vision. But not so quick, say the authors. Could it be that the language of cooperation is mainstream smoke; that it is fraught with historical connections to traditions, views, economic requirements, social systems, and practices that are oppressive? The possibility exists, say the authors. So, as theorists striving for less constriction in the discourse, "we have no option but to be rebelliously uncooperative" (Chapter 12, p. 277).

The scholarship of dislodgment that follows challenges all of us to retrace the historical continuities involved in the language of cooperation, including Frederick Taylor's call for cooperation, Mayo's human relations approaches, and others, including recent machinelike methods to organization reengineering. The continuities are disturbing. The authors wonder if anything like authentic cooperation, or full voice, is ever possible in the global domain.

In the modern age, argue the authors, new forms of domination are increasingly embodied in the social relations of science and technology, which organize knowledge and production systems. The story becomes further disturbing as a spotlight is placed on GE's strategic business moves in India—and its implicatures in female infanticide. Hailed by mainstream organizational writers as a move of great entrepreneurial vision, the authors show how the voices of women were systematically excluded in the broadest societal discourses. (One can easily transpose the argument to many global change concerns, such as trying to understand loss of rain forests and the indigenous voices.) Trying to understand the situation is complicated. But the problem, in the end, is not one of lack of explanations but one of who can explain. Are we "bound to remain trapped in [an] inability to produce a participative epistemology"? (Chapter 12, p. 290) ask the authors, and "is the West (knowledgeable enough to be) even capable of listening?" (Chapter 12, p. 290).

René Bouwen and Chris Steyaert continue the constructionist perspective almost seamlessly with their chapter "From a Dominant Voice Toward Multivoiced Cooperation." To understand human response to issues of global change, from inconsolable poverty to interrelated environmental pressures, we must complement the institutional, legal, and political perspectives with new understandings about how interactions among the world's peoples are framed in and through organizations. The question they add to Gergen's earlier one is this: "How can we frame human response to global change so that all voices from different and unequal positions can be heard in organizational settings with equivalent seats?" No, this is not an invitation to a Tower of Babel negatively interpreted, argue the authors. It is an invitation to recognize an original polylinguism. The care of our world and strengthening of cooperative capacity can be approached through the care of languages: "'No language to waste'—that is the polyphonic cry that can ground every global development or cultural project" (Chapter 13, p. 303).

Organizing, to be sustainable and effective, is about expansion of voice. The ideal, proposes the authors, is the development of "a polyphony of fully valid voices." Writing from their home in Belgium, the authors explain polyphony as a metaphor they are using from the oldest of musical repertoires. In the 15th and 16th centuries, the Flemish Primitives created a furor throughout Europe with their paintings. At the same time, a musical composition form was developed that eventually became an artistic production throughout all Europe. The composition technique was called polyphony—literally, multivoicedness. Two or more independent but organically related voice parts sound against one another. The authors describe how, in polyphonic partiture, we find multiple melodic lines (not just melody and chorus), and every line could, in theory, be performed separately. But performing all of the lines simultaneously creates a rich and complex musical totality. Most important, next to the independent horizontal lines, vertical lines emerge that also form a totality. In this way, a network of horizontal and vertical lines is created, in which every voice is meaningful but, at the same time, gains meaning in relation to other voices. Characteristic of Flemish polyphony is equivalence of all. There is no soloist part, nor a chorus part. The different voices are created simultaneously in and through one another in relational practice. The authors propose that this is the central priority for building new knowledge regarding global changes organization dimensions. Quoting from Bakhtin (1981), they conclude,

> We must renounce our monologic habits so that we might come to feel at home in the new artistic sphere which Dostoevsky discovered, so that we might orient ourselves in that incomparably more complex *artistic model of the world* which he created. (chap. 13, p. 318)

Nancy Adler, in Chapter 14, seeks broad expansion of voices in her search for new leadership: "Where are we going to find the kind of leaders that we need for 21st-century society. . . . What do we know about the women who hold the most senior global leadership positions?" (Chapter 14, pp. 323, 324).

For Adler, the central task of the final years of this century is the creation of a new model of coexistence among the world's various cultures, peoples, races, and religious spheres within a single, interconnected civilization. In relationship to the rapidly growing agenda for global change, we face the task of recreating virtually all of our organizations. Government organizations are encapsulated in increasingly obsolete domestic structures. Companies increasingly have the transnational structures and outlook necessary to address worldwide global issues, but they lack the mandate and vision to do so. But are there exceptions? Are there corporations, for example, that have dedicated themselves to addressing global issues? What are their characteristics, especially with regard to leadership?

After creating a mapping of the world's women leaders in both the governmental and global corporate sectors, Adler sets out on a fascinating search for the themes and patterns of women leaders. She traces the leaders' unique paths to power, how they leveraged the fact that they are women, their rising numbers, their diverse styles and backgrounds, and their promising strengths. Adler notes that "some strikingly unexpected patterns in the women leaders' paths to power differentiate them from most of their male contemporaries, and these very differences appear to fit well with the needs of 21st century society" (Chapter 14, p. 333).

Picture, for instance, Anita Roddick, founder and CEO of The Body Shop, whose U.K.-based company operating worldwide has become renowned for its global change commitments, including environmental campaigns, job creation efforts, leadership in the area of environmental auditing, and human rights advocacy. Roddick describes an image of organizing that fits our earlier definition of a global change organization: "'Leaders in the business world should aspire to be true planetary citizens. They have global responsibilities since their decisions affect not just the world of business but world problems of poverty, national security and the environment'" (Chapter 14, p. 334). Indeed, the Body Shop's mission statement states their reason for being is to "dedicate our business to the pursuit of social and environmental change."

It is important to note that Anita Roddick's vision is not the same as the important, but more familiar, call for socially responsible enterprise. It is more about organizations as leaders of needed change. With economic globalization and changing local conditions, business leaders will increasingly be involved with a broader field of issues that affect not only their shareholders, employees, and customers, but also the quality of life in communities and cities, our ecosystems, and people in countries throughout the world. In many ways, Roddick's views on leadership are iconoclastic. The conjoining of profits and social ideals is a disquieting proposition for some people. There is business, and there are good works, and never the twain shall meet. Is it an accident that this kind of future is being envisioned by a woman?

This is not the place for detailed commentary on Adler's courageous—and perhaps for some, provocative—findings. But her chapter points to deep-level changes—whole system transformations in values, beliefs, basic assumptions, and commitments—taking place in society. Most of us grew up in organizations that were dominated by men and their theorists—Henry Ford, Frederick Taylor, and Max Weber—the fathers of the classic bureaucratic system. These are not the organizations that will likely deal effectively with the transboundary concerns involved in the human response to global change. So, from where will the new cooperative forms come? For Adler, the women in her exploration represent a dialogue with future history. And the new voices, in polyphonic fashion, are offering a prophecy: "approaches that appeared to work well in the 20th century but foretell disaster for the 21st century" (Chapter 14, p. 343).

In the final chapter in Part III, Stuart L. Hart responds to a fourth constructionist invitation—to participate in the construction of new worlds. Many business, nonprofit, and government leaders talk about global environmental sustainability, but few have been able to advance anticipatory theory that moves beyond good critique into an actionable agenda for organizations. As anticipatory theory, Hart's work suggests that the task of good organization theory is not only to hold a mirror to the world as it is, nor to merely provide critiques of debilitating assumptions and practices, but to study that which has not yet occurred, that is, create alternative conceptions of the future through theory. From a constructionist stance, theories and discourses of the profession are themselves constitutive of societal life. Some theories, as they enter the common discourse of the culture, prepare the way to the future by sustaining taken-for-granted assumptions, whereas others, in more critical terms, serve the task of dislodgment. Hart's work, which he calls "prospective" theory, points to yet another direction: It responds to a mandate for social transformation. Rather than telling it like it is, this chapter tells it as it may become.

Like it or not, argues Hart, the responsibility for ensuring a sustainable world falls largely on the shoulders of the world's enterprises. The environmental revolution has been almost three decades in the making, and it has changed forever how companies do business. However, suggests Hart, the distance traveled to date will seem small when, in 30 years, we look back to the 1990s. Beyond greening, beyond competitive strategy, lies an enormous challenge. Hart's interest is in how the changing relationship between the world's ecosystems and the economy will change the whole paradigm of management where competitive strategy should give way to cooperative action. More than that, Hart's chapter is a call for systematic inquiry into corporations as agents of global change—pathfinders who have accepted the enormous challenge of developing a sustainable global economy. Although the social and technological issues exceed the mandate and the capabilities of any corporation, at the same time, corporations are the only organizations with the resources, the global reach, and, ultimately, the market motivation to achieve sustainability.

For Hart, the future of enterprise lies not just in pollution prevention (minimizing or eliminating waste before it is created) or even product stewardship (minimizing pollution from manufacturing and also all environmental impacts involved with the full life cycle of a product) but in leading the way to sustainable development (vision-led companies that are finding ways to act on three goals—environmental and social sustainability, and economic development—at the same time). Sustainability implies moving beyond incremental change to complete revision. This process might involve a creative destruction process as originally advocated by Schumpeter (1942), where creative new industries are born from the ashes of the old. By implication: Corporations can and should lead the way in helping to shape public policy, driving change in consumers' behavior, shaping new relationships to suppliers and other companies, and becoming educators rather than mere marketers of products. Obviously, there are very few examples of firms operating at the third level.

Hart's chapter illustrates these possibilities with powerful examples, including Monsanto's move from petrochemical to biological products and Amory Lovins's concept of the hypercar. Hart's prospective propositions are meant to hasten discovery of corporate leaders in the global change domain. His conclusion is that those who think that sustainability is only a matter of pollution control are missing the bigger picture. We are poised at the threshold of a historic moment in which many of the world's industries may be transformed. As a field, we are being invited into a research arena where the stakes are real. We need, as theorists, to be willing to set sail from the shores of the familiar. Much needed, argues Hart, is research into the firms and industries that are first movers.

CONCLUDING COMMENTS

In this discussion, we have attempted to bring thematic focus to the chapters to follow and have pointed to the central contours of a contemporary research agenda of tremendous importance and exciting implication. There is little question that globalization and global-level concerns are calling for the transformation of all social sciences in terms of their research and learning priorities, agendas, metatheoretical commitments, and methodologies. As it relates to the organization dimensions, we have proposed that:

- there is not one single item on the global agenda for change that can be understood outside of the role and functioning of organizations. Any effort to understand, much less come to terms with, global change that does not include a sustained commitment to improving our knowledge of the organizational dimensions cannot succeed.
- an increasingly important field of scholarship and knowledge is being born whereby organization and management studies will be viewed on a much broader scale than ever before, indeed, as a matter of world affairs.

In many ways, our common future will depend on the extent to which today's executives, grassroots citizens, and political leaders develop their visions of a better world, the shared will to achieve it, and the organizations capable of embodying humanity's cooperative potential. And so, finally, with important caveats as expressed, for example, in the chapters by Mir et al. and Aram, we would like to end this chapter with an opportunity-focused, affirmative direction for future research, dialogue, and experimentation in the domain of the organizational dimensions of global change (ODGC). Our suggestion and vision:

> ODGC research is an enterprise whose focus and task is to interpret basic new trends in humanity's global cooperative capacity, anticipate new possibilities in organizational forms and processes, and study the new relational practices that can contribute to a deeper understanding of the "life-promoting" interrelation of humanity and world ecosystems, cooperative forms, and global society.

REFERENCES

Astley, W. G., & Fombrun, C. (1983). Collection strategy: Social ecology of organizational environments. *Academy of Management Review, 8,* 576-587.

Bakhtin, M. (1981). *The dialogic imagination.* Austin: University of Texas Press.

Burton, L., & Timmerman, P. (1989). Human dimensions of global change: A review of responsibilities and opportunities. *International Social Science Journal, 121,* 297-313.

Club of Lisbon Report. (1994). *Limits to competition.* Brussels: Vubpress.

Cooperrider, D. L. (1990). Positive imagery, positive action: The affirmative basis of organizing. In S. S. Srivastva & D. L. Cooperrider, *Appreciative management and leadership: The power of positive thought in organizing* (pp. 91-125). San Francisco: Jossey-Bass.

Daniels, E. (1996). A future history of research on the human dimensions of global change. *Environment, 34,* 1-21.

Durning, A. (1989). People power and development. *Foreign Policy, 2,* 66-82.

Haas, P., Keohane, R., & Levy, M. (Eds.). (1993). *Institutions for the earth.* Cambridge: MIT Press.

Kennedy, P. (1993). *Preparing for the twenty first century.* New York: Random House.

Khandwalla, P. (1988). Strategic organizations in social development. In P. Khandwalla (Ed.), *Social development: A new role for the organizational sciences* (pp. 13-21). New Delhi: Sage.

Office of Science and Technology Policy. (1997). *Our changing planet: The FY 1997 research plan.* Washington, DC: Author.

Schneider, B. (1988). *The barefoot revolution.* Paris: Report to the Club of Rome.

Shrivastava, P. (1996). *Greening business: Profiting the corporation and the environment.* Cincinnati, OH: Thomson.

Stern, P., Young, O., & Druckman, D. (1992). *Global environmental change: Understanding the human dimensions.* Washington, DC: National Academy Press.

Turner, B. L., Clark, W. C., Kates, R. W., Richards, J. F., & Mathews, J. T. (Eds.). (1991). *The earth as transformed by human action.* New York: Cambridge University Press.

Union of International Associations. (Ed.). (1997). *Encyclopedia of world problems and human potential.* New York: Springer-Verlag.

PART

I

SENSEMAKING AND GLOBAL CHANGE

2

SENSEMAKING AS AN ORGANIZATIONAL DIMENSION OF GLOBAL CHANGE

KARL E. WEICK

Global issues that involve organizing on a massive scale have been described as contested, nonlinear metaproblems with long lead times, unintended side effects, unclear cause-effect structures, and consequences that are often irreversible (Cooperrider & Bilimoria, 1993, p. 110). Issues demanding change on a global scale are like an onrushing wall of fire and are just as tricky to manage. Normally, managing complexity on a global scale, especially when it is framed in a strategic framework, as Cooperrider and Bilimoria have done, means that the primary organizational issue is one of strategies for decision making. Decision making is certainly involved in managing complexity in global change, and this is evident when people refer to transboundary relations, development of environmentally sound technologies, translation of complex global realities into decisive action, environmental governance, establishment of international norms, and the management of strategic global social change organizations (GSCOs).

But I want to argue that to organize for global change is also a problem in sensemaking, a problem that partly subsumes Cooperrider and Bilimoria's interest in the management of meaning, vision, and relationships (p. 126). Precisely because global change is so difficult to comprehend, organizations designed to deal with it must be organizations designed as much to develop a coherent story of what is going on as to decide what should be done given that unfolding story. Thus, a potentially crucial organizational dimension of global change is the effect of organizational form on the kind of sense that people are able to make of what they face. I want to argue that at least seven resources affect sensemaking, and that organizational designs used in global organizations can strengthen or weaken these resources. These effects of design on resources for sensemaking, in turn, make it easier or harder to build a common idea of what is happening and what decisions need to be made.

I will contrast a system whose design weakens the resources for sensemaking (the firefighting crew at Mann Gulch) with a system in which the design strengthens the resources for sensemaking (the Worker's Defense Committee in Poland). In the case of the weak sensemaking system, the outcome was tragedy. In the case of the strong sensemaking system, the outcome was success against overwhelming odds.

Before I discuss sensemaking and two examples of how it unfolds differently in response to different designs, I should say a word about the two systems I will describe, because they have little obvious resemblance to GSCOs such as World Vision. By this I mean that, compared with global organizations, my two examples involve fewer people who are more homogeneous, who span fewer boundaries, whose contacts are more transient, and who are less dominated by visionary missions, although this may be a matter of degree. The firefighters and the defense committee are not, however, irrelevant to organizing on a global scale. They resemble GSCOs in the sense that they have singular focus on a relatively clear issue (a fire that is consuming wildland, a totalitarian regime that is eroding liberty); they are complex in their own ways; they each contain subsets of players that frame issues differently; they are more cooperative than competitive; and collaboration is essential for their success.

Aside from debates about whether firefighters and opposition movements are organized in ways that resemble organizing for global social change, the more important point is that my purpose here is to present a perspective rather than a model organization to be imitated. Given the way that global change has been depicted, it appears that variations in the ease with which potential participants can make sense of their own participation, the participation of others, and the referent problem itself affect both their willingness to expend energy and their decision about how to deploy that energy. I want to introduce the image of organizational sensemaking as a language to describe part of what determines the enthusiasm, improvisation, and persistence on the part of people who organize for global change. I introduce the sensemaking perspective by contrasting two systems, chosen not for their involvement in global change but for their ability to make the notion of sensemaking vividly visible.

THE PHENOMENON OF SENSEMAKING

Imagine an EMS technician arriving at the scene of an accident; a representative of World Vision walking into a newly discovered "Home for the Deficient and Unsalvageable" in Romania; a firefighter crew chief sizing up a fire, part of which is burning downhill and part of which is burning uphill (see picture on page 38 of Thoele, 1995, for an illustration of this situation); a United Airlines pilot turning the control wheel after a sudden loud noise and finding that none of the control surfaces on the DC-10 aircraft respond (the experience of Captain Al Hcyns on UA flight 232); or finding a pocket of smallpox cases in a remote village in 1996 after the World Health Assembly has declared smallpox eradicated. What these circumstances all share, aside from their possible dramatic overkill, is that they all consist of a pile of cues in need of some frame to organize them. There is also an imperative to act. In each case, small, familiar cues can have a disproportionate influence in framing what one feels one is dealing with. Sensemaking is about sizing up a situation, about trying to discover what you have while you simultaneously act and have some effect on what you discover. Sensemaking, in other words, is seldom an occasion for passive diagnosis. Instead, it is usually an attempt to grasp a developing situation in which the observer affects the trajectory of that development. Object and subject are hard to separate in sensemaking, as when a physician starts several different treatments with a patient who is slow to respond and soon finds that he or she is treating the treatments rather than the presenting symptom.

Although size-ups may seem short-lived, their influence is enduring because once a hypothesis is formed, people tend to look for evidence that confirms it. This tendency is especially strong if people are under pressure to act quickly and if it is hard for them to find time to question their initial beliefs (Gilbert, 1991). Furthermore, initial actions are often publicly chosen and hard to revoke (Salancik, 1977), which means that people are bound to those actions and search for reasons that justify the actions as rational.

Thus, sensemaking involves the ongoing retrospective development of plausible images that rationalize what people are doing. When people engage in acts of sensemaking, it is more precise to think of them as accomplishing reality rather than discovering it. Discovery is a less appropriate description because in order for people to make sense of something, they often have to *ignore* much that others might notice. Reality is not so much discovered as buried in the interest of sensemaking. To make sense is to focus on a limited set of cues, and to elaborate those few cues into a plausible, pragmatic, momentarily useful guide for actions that themselves are partially defining the guide that they follow. Once a sense of the situation begins to develop, that sense can be terribly seductive and can resist updating and revision. The feeling of relief one gets the moment there is some idea of what might be happening makes it that much harder to remain attentive and willing to alter one's sense of what is happening and one's own position in that altered scenario.

These considerations seem relevant to global social change because there, too, people develop some sort of sense regarding what they are up against, what their own position is relative to what they sense, and what they need to do, including walking away from the scene. In discussions of organizational dimensions of global change, I feel it is important to separate sensemaking from decision making because sensemaking sets the frame within which decisions are made. In many cases, sensemaking may even do the bulk of the "deciding" that is present in any organized activity. So-called decision making may simply ratify what was made inevitable much earlier when an innocent-appearing set of judgments mapped an issue out of a much larger set of possibilities that has now been forgotten.

Sensemaking is such a sprawling topic that it seems arbitrary to choose some portion of it as being especially relevant to global social change. That danger notwithstanding, I want to discuss seven properties that have an important effect on sensemaking. These seven are (a) social context, (b) personal identity, (c) retrospect, (d) salient cues, (e) ongoing projects, (f) plausibility, and (g) enactment. These seven can be remembered by means of the acronym SIR COPE. They are important in any discussion of organizing for global social change for at least two reasons. First, these seven properties affect not only the initial sense one develops of a situation—this initial sense is often overdetermined by one's own personal history—but more importantly, the extent to which people will update and develop their sense of the situation.

In other words, these properties have an effect on the willingness of people to disengage from, discard, or "walk away" from their initial story and adopt a newer story that is more sensitive to the particulars of the present context. Second, these seven properties are affected by organizational designs, as will be clear in the examples I contrast. There appear to be organizational conditions that facilitate sensemaking and conditions that thwart sensemaking. Given the complexity of global change issues and of the structures needed to manage that change, any adjustments that increase the collective capability to grasp this complexity should be given serious consideration. Obviously, there is far more to organizing for global change than the process of sensemaking. All I want to argue is that, given a choice between organizational forms, all of which seem to manage other issues equally well, the choice should favor a form that allows for more conversations, clearer identities, more use of elapsed action as a guide, unobstructed access to a wider range of cues, more focused attention on interruptions whenever projects are disrupted, wider dissemination of stories, and deeper acceptance of the reality that people face in situations that are of their own making.

THE SEVEN PROPERTIES OF SENSEMAKING

When people talk about sensemaking in an organizational setting, they discuss at least seven properties of that setting that have an effect on their efforts to size up what they face. These seven are discussed in detail in Weick (1995, pp. 17-62), and the interested reader is referred to that source.

For the sake of the present discussion, the seven are summarized in a highly minimalist form that relies heavily on a commonsense understanding of the terms employed.

1. *Social context:* Sensemaking is influenced by the actual, implied, or imagined presence of others. Sensible meanings tend to be those for which there is social support, consensual validation, and shared relevance. To change meaning is to change the social context. When social anchors disappear and one feels isolated from a social reality of some sort, one's grasp of what is happening begins to loosen.

2. *Personal identity:* A person's sense of who he or she is in a setting; what threats to this sense of self the setting contains; and what is available to enhance, continue, and render efficacious that sense of who one is all provide a center from which judgments of relevance and sense fan out. When identity

is threatened or diffused, as when one loses a job without warning, one's grasp of what is happening begins to loosen.

3. *Retrospect:* The perceived world is actually a past world in the sense that things are visualized and seen *before* they are conceptualized. Even if the delay is measured in microseconds, people know what they have done only after they do it. Thus, sensemaking is influenced by what people notice in elapsed events, how far back they look, and how well they remember what they were doing. When people refuse to appreciate the past and instead use it casually, and when they put their faith in anticipation rather than resilience, then their acts of retrospect are shallow, misleading, and halfhearted, and their grasp of what is happening begins to loosen.

4. *Salient cues:* If sensemaking is about nothing else, it is about the resourcefulness with which people elaborate tiny indicators into full-blown stories, typically in ways that selectively shore up an initial hunch. The prototype here is a self-fulfilling prophecy or an application of the documentary method. Both elaborate an initial linkage between a particular and a category into a confident diagnosis through successive rounds of selective search for confirming evidence. Thus, both individual preferences for certain cues as well as environmental conditions that make certain cues figural and salient affect one's sense of what is up. When cues become equivocal, contradictory, or unstable, either because individual preferences are changing or because situations are dynamic, people begin to lose their grasp of what is happening.

5. *Ongoing projects:* Experience is a continuous flow, and it becomes an event only when efforts are made to put boundaries around some portion of the flow, or when some interruption occurs. Thus, sensemaking is constrained not only by past events, but also by the speed with which events flow into the past and interpretations become outdated. The experience of sensemaking is one in which people are thrown into the middle of things and forced to act without the benefit of a stable sense of what is happening. These handicaps are not attributable to personal shortcomings but rather to the stubborn, ongoing character of experience. When people lose their ability to bound ongoing events, to keep pace with them by means of continuous updating of actions and interpretations, or to focus on interrupting conditions, they begin to lose their grasp.

6. *Plausibility:* To make sense is to answer the question "What's the story here?" To answer this question, people usually ask a slightly different question: "What's a story here?" Sensemaking is about coherence, how events hang together, certainty that is sufficient for present purposes, and credibility. Plausibility should not be mistaken for fantasy, however, because a sense that survives has been influenced by the other six properties. Thus, plausible sense is constrained agreements with others, consistency with one's own stake in events, the recent past, visible cues, projects that are demonstrably under way, scenarios that are familiar, and actions that have tangible effects. When one or more of these sources of grounding disappears, stories may strain credibility, leave too many cues unaddressed, or be impossible to compose, in which case people begin to lose their grasp.

7. *Enactment:* Action is a means to gain some sense of what one is up against, as when one asks questions, tries a negotiating gambit, builds a prototype to evoke reactions, makes a declaration to see what response it pulls, or probes something to see how it reacts.

Having done any of these interventions in the interest of sensemaking, one will never know for sure what might have happened had no intervention been made. It is that sense in which it is part of what one sees in any moment of sensemaking that is a partial reflection of oneself. But to stay detached and passive is not to improve one's grasp, because much of what any situation means lies in the manner of its response. When probing actions are precluded, or avoided, or unduly narrow, it becomes more difficult to grasp what one might be facing.

These seven properties can be arrayed into a sensemaking process in at least two ways. First, sensemaking seems to follow roughly a sequence in which people concerned with identity in the social context of other actors engage ongoing events from which they extract cues and make plausible sense retrospectively while enacting more or less order into those ongoing events. This sequence breaks down as identity and the social context and cues become more ambiguous, retrospect becomes more difficult, ongoing events become more resistant to bounding, plausibility becomes more tenuous, and action becomes more constrained. A second way to animate these seven properties of sensemaking into a process is by means of the familiar recipe, "How can I know what I think or feel until I see what I say and do?" When people enact this recipe, they are affected by the social context (what I say and do is affected by the audience that I anticipate will audit the conclusions I reach); identity (the recipe is focused on the question of who I am, the answer to which lies partly in what my words and deeds reveal about what I think and feel); retrospect (to learn what I think and feel, I look back over what I said and did); cues (what I single out from what I say and do is only a small portion of all possible things I might notice); ongoing (my talk and action are spread across time, which means my interests early in the scanning may change by the time the scanning concludes); plausibility (I need to know only enough about what I think to keep my project going); and enactment (the whole recipe works only if I produce some object in the first place that can be scrutinized for possible thoughts and feelings).

ORGANIZING FOR SENSEMAKING

Given those seven properties of sensemaking and their potential sequencing, it remains to link them with issues of organizational design. The linkage is straightforward. The operative question is, What happens to these seven resources for sensemaking when people organize to accomplish tasks that cannot be done alone? If the design maintains or strengthens these seven resources, then people will be able to continue making sense of what they face. If the design undermines or weakens these resources, then people will tend to lose their grasp of what may be occurring. For each resource, there is a corresponding question about the organizational form that coordinates their activities. These questions are crude, more suited for practice than theory, and are currently being refined. Nevertheless, they are an initial means to raise issues related to sensemaking in the context of organizing for global social change. The initial questions are these:

1. Social context: Does the form encourage conversation?
2. Identity: Does the form give people a distinct, stable sense of who they are and what they represent?
3. Retrospect: Does the form preserve elapsed data and legitimate the use of those data?
4. Salient cues: Does the form enhance the visibility of cues?
5. Ongoing projects: Does the form enable people to be resilient in the face of interruptions?
6. Plausibility: Does the form encourage people to accumulate and exchange plausible accounts?
7. Enactment: Does the form encourage action or hesitation?

As I will now show, the organizational form associated with the crew that fought the Mann Gulch fire made it difficult for them to access many resources for sensemaking. As a result, they were unable to grasp what was happening to them, and most of these young men lost their lives as a result. The contrasting case of the KOR opposition movement in Poland is one in which access to sensemaking resources is not as difficult. As a result, people were able to make sense of their actions and could sustain them under oppressive conditions.

THE MANN GULCH DISASTER
AS PROBLEMATIC SENSEMAKING

The Mann Gulch disaster, made famous in Norman Maclean's (1992) book *Young Men and Fire,* unfolded in the following sequence, which is a composite of Maclean (1992), Weick (1993), and Rothermel (1993).

On August 5, 1949, at about 4 p.m., 15 smoke jumpers—trained firefighters but new to one another as a group—parachuted into Mann Gulch. The crew's leaders originally believed that the blaze was a basic "ten o'clock fire," meaning that the crew would have it under control by 10 a.m. the next morning. Instead, the fire exploded and forced the men into a race for their lives.

The fire at Mann Gulch probably began on August 4 when lightning set a small fire in a dead tree. The temperature reached 97°F the next day and produced a fire danger rating of 74 out of a possible 100, indicating the potential for the fire to spread uncontrollably. When the fire was spotted by a lookout on a mountain 30 miles away, 16 smoke jumpers were sent at 2:30 p.m. from Missoula, Montana in a C-47 transport plane. (One man became ill and did not make the jump.) A forest ranger posted in the next canyon, Jim Harrison, was already on the scene trying to fight the fire on his own.

Wind conditions that day were turbulent, so the smoke jumpers and their cargo were dropped from 2,000 feet rather than the usual 1,200. The parachute connected to their radio failed to open, and the radio was pulverized as it hit the ground. But the remaining crew and supplies landed safely in Mann Gulch by 4:10 p.m. The smoke jumpers then collected their supplies, which had scattered widely, and grabbed a quick bite to eat.

While the crew ate, foreman Wagner Dodge met up with ranger Harrison. They scouted the fire and came back concerned that the thick forest near which they had landed could become a "death trap." Dodge told the second-in-command, William Hellman, to take the crew across to the north side of the gulch, away from the fire, and march along its flank toward the river at the bottom of the gulch. While Hellman did this, Dodge and Harrison ate a quick meal. Dodge rejoined the crew at 5:40 p.m. and took his position at the head of the line moving toward the river.

He could see flames flapping back and forth on the south slope as he looked to his left. Then, Dodge saw that the fire had suddenly crossed the gulch about 200 yards ahead and was moving toward them. He yelled at the crew to run from the fire and began angling up the steep hill toward the bare ridge of rock.

The crew was soon moving through slippery grasses two-and-a-half feet high but was quickly losing ground to the flames—eventually towering at a height of 30 feet—rushing toward them at a rate that probably reached a speed of 660 feet per minute. Sensing that the crew was in serious danger, Dodge yelled at them to drop their tools. Two minutes later, to everyone's astonishment, he lit a fire in front of the men and motioned to them to lie down in the area it had burned. No one did. Instead, they ran for the ridge and what they hoped would be safety.

Two firefighters, Robert Sallee and Walter Rumsey, made it through a crevice in the ridge unburned. Dodge survived by lying down in the ashes of his escape fire. The other 13 perished. The fire caught up with them at 5:56 p.m.—the time at which the hands on Harrison's watch melted in place.

We see the collapse of sensemaking when firefighters persist in calling the exploding fire a ten o'clock fire even though their senses tell them it is something more than this. We also see the collapse of the relating that is so crucial for sensemaking when individuals are torn between leaders, forget about their buddies, disobey orders, fail to share information, and ignore the solution that would have saved them. Access to resources for sensemaking was made difficult by the way the firefighters were organized.

Firefighters in Mann Gulch lost their *social anchors* when they found it hard to communicate, when they were uncertain how much trust they could put in their leader, and when they remained strangers to one another. The form and the environment discouraged conversation.

Firefighters in Mann Gulch found their *identity* threatened when they were told to drop their tools, which was the reason they were in Mann Gulch in the first place. It became increasingly unclear whether they were smoke jumpers or victims, and whether they were fighting or fleeing the fire.

Firefighters in Mann Gulch found it hard to resort to *retrospective sensemaking* because they did not know what was going on, their actions were unclear, and there was no explanation of why their foreman was adding a new fire when they already had all the fire they could deal with.

Firefighters in Mann Gulch faced *cues* that were difficult to interpret. They did not know whether they were retreating from the fire or flanking it, whether it was big or small, whether their foreman was scared or not, whether the grass they were walking in burned the same way as the trees where the fire was not located, and whether this was a fire they should flee or face.

Firefighters in Mann Gulch faced an *ongoing* dynamic fire that was becoming more intense and moving faster, and which they could neither stop nor avoid.

Firefighters in Mann Gulch, having spent all their lives fighting small fires, did not find it *plausible* that the small fire they expected to find had grown monstrous. The question "What's the story here?" remained fatally unanswerable.

Firefighters in Mann Gulch were unclear where and when they would take a stand to suppress the fire, what their actions were accomplishing, and whether they might even be making things worse by *enacting* a new fire.

Firefighters in Mann Gulch may have experienced a crisis in sensemaking that was due in part to the way in which they were organized. Their organization cut off access to crucial resources for sensemaking, which meant they persisted too long with the definition they carried into Mann Gulch when they first sized it up. It is this fate that global change organizations should take seriously.

There are alternative ways of organizing, as we will now see in the case of the opposition movement in Poland.

THE WORKER'S DEFENSE COMMITTEE
AS SUCCESSFUL SENSEMAKING

The democratic opposition movement in Poland, which started with the Worker's Defense Committee (KOR) in September 1976, is a dramatic example of heedful interrelating on a local scale that results in large changes on a national scale. Jonathan Schell (1987) has described the unfolding of these relationships in sufficient detail that we are able to encode them into resources for sensemaking.

The KOR movement started in Adam Michnik's clear thinking about what could and could not be changed in Poland. The Polish people said that it was impossible to defeat the threat of nuclear weapons, the 200 divisions of the Russian army, and General Jaruzelski's totalitarian rule; therefore, resistance was hopeless and doomed to fail. "It was Michnik's genius to separate the two halves of the propositions and to accept the first (the impossibility of defeating the armies and police forces) and reject the second (the hopelessness of all resistance)" (Schell, 1987, p. xxiii). Michnik rejected the idea that resistance was hopeless and defined areas of permissible maneuver in the "minutiae of their local environment" (p. xxiii).

The reasoning went like this. What if 10 people gathered in an apartment and listened to an uncensored lecture on Polish history? "What if a group of workers began to publish a newsletter in which factory conditions were truthfully described?" (Schell, 1987, p. xxiv). What if people did social work and gave direct medical, financial, and legal aid to those who needed it? Would this not set up an alternative set of institutions that the government would eventually accept? The important theme was direct local activity done independent of government that would "restore social bonds outside official institutions" (p. xxix). Rather than seize power and then use that power to do the good things in which they believed, KOR did the opposite: They did the good things first and worried about the state later (p. xxx).

The beauty of their actions was that each one both exemplified a democratic value they thought was important and, at the same time, accomplished something. For example, when KOR wrote their declaration of purpose, people signed the document and listed their addresses and phone numbers, a small action that both exemplified the value of open public action and allowed networking. The group made autonomy (the capacity to act freely) a principle for their own actions and encouraged people to do anything that was not contrary to the principles of the movement (Schell, 1987, p. xxviii). People were encouraged to *act* freely within small local areas even though their right to act freely (liberty) was supposedly constrained. Notice that every act proved to be a test of just how much liberty they might have, and in these tests were valuable learnings. When people put autonomy into practice, they formed associations around whatever issues they thought were important (e.g., pollution, trade, working conditions), which created diversity, contagion, and enthusiasm in many different areas of the country.

Schell (1987) describes this combination of open, truthful, autonomous, trusting local action as "militant decency" (p. xxix). The strength of the movement came from peaceful activities in a normal civic life, which set a new tone for that life. The guiding principle was simple but radical:

> Start doing the things you think should be done, and . . . start being what you
> think society should become. Do you believe in freedom of speech? Then
> speak freely. Do you love the truth? Then tell it. Do you believe in a decent
> and humane society? Then behave decently and humanely. (p. xxx)

What is radical and revolutionary is that when all of this is put in motion,
it is not one more hollow promissory note from the government that says that
if you are loyal and comply today, we will guarantee you a better tomorrow.
Polish people had heard these lies for years and years. What KOR did was use
multiple, parallel, small wins to reverse the Polish political experience. Their
program created an immediate, visible, day-to-day community of free people.
KOR did not promise a better tomorrow. It delivered a better today. It did not
try to seize power from the government. Instead, it created new power by
building up society and enacting new order and organization.

KOR did not get carried away by its success nor lose sight of its aims,
nor did it finally come to resemble the bureaucratic nightmare it resisted. In
their final, and perhaps most dramatic, act exemplifying democracy and the
subordination of ego, pride, and vanity, KOR voted itself out of existence in
September 1981 when people decided that their role was being filled by
Solidarity (Schell, 1987, p. xxix). KOR had carved out a sphere of compromise within the totalitarian, violent Polish system without themselves resort-
ing to domination and violence. Having demonstrated that it was possible to
do this, KOR dissolved, symbolizing that the people themselves had learned
how to act locally and enact a just society.

The lessons are clear. Large consequences can be produced by small
actions when people change the only thing they can change: their own actions.
In the case of Poland, the actions were controllable opportunities that generated tangible accomplishments (e.g., signatures, discussions, documents,
medical aid, networks). The actions uncovered latitude within the totalitarian
system, attracted allies and deferred government intervention, and lowered
the necessity to confront the government head-on. The demands for strategizing, planning, calculation, and suspicion were made manageable when people
were encouraged to behave in whatever truthful, trusting, open, autonomous,
nonviolent way made sense in their local community. They improvised, and
they acquired details of how the system worked. Thousands of uncorrelated
variations sprang up all over Poland, some of which proved adaptive and were
retained and circulated. Evolution was discovered to be a powerful form of
revolution when it combined nonviolence, rehearsal of important values in

immediate action, a social order based on small acts of decency, and patience and persistence. KOR demonstrated that control and freedom are to be found in the micro-action of sensemaking even when macro structures appeared confining and coercive.

KOR did not plan all of this in advance. Instead, direct local acts of decency, undertaken wherever an opportunity presented itself, created tangible outcomes that attracted attention, uncovered new opportunities, built confidence, enlarged the number of people who tried to improve civic life, and built a bandwagon from small beginnings. Adam Michnik gave voice and substance to changes. He spotted the patterns and portrayed what was happening in stirring rhetoric. KOR changed the words, actions, sensitivities, and images with which the Polish people had to work. KOR changed what people saw when they looked back at the indeterminate flow of events that was the Poland of the 1970s. KOR did *not* change the realities of indeterminacy, flow, and thrownness. Instead, what KOR *did* change were actions and words that were added to that flow (e.g., this is a self-limiting revolution that will not attempt to overthrow the government). They changed the interpretations that were imposed retrospectively on those flows (e.g., we have enough faith in the people of Poland to dissolve KOR). And KOR encouraged people to enact reliable periods of determinacy in an otherwise indeterminate set of events (e.g., the government may renege on its promises of a better tomorrow, but here is a better today; our promises come later). KOR knew that just as indeterminacy, flow, and thrownness constrained them, they also constrained the government's response. KOR knew that there were seams in a totalitarian world, and so did Jaruzelski. Large retaliation against small acts of decency was as unthinkable for Jaruzelski as were small acts of violence to overthrow a vast army for Michnik. In the space between these two versions of the unthinkable, there is room to maneuver. The maneuvering room is small, but it is not trivial.

And the room to maneuver consists of nothing more or less than the power of local interaction to create a new sense of what is possible. What could be more local than yourself, and what could be more immediate than your own action? The Polish people demonstrated the power of this lesson in the context of much more oppressive organizational structures than many of those in global change.

This account of KOR's strategy and mode of organizing can be coded into the seven resources for sensemaking introduced earlier. When we do so, we find that KOR is as rich in these resources as Mann Gulch was bereft of them. Before we do this coding, we need to review key aspects of the organizational design evolved by KOR that affected sensemaking. The following seem relevant:

1. There are just a few guiding principles, and they provide wide latitude for autonomy and locate interpretation of the meaning of those principles. People are urged to follow their own enthusiasms and initiatives and to create new centers of autonomous activity. This configuration resembles tight coupling on a handful of core values and loose coupling on everything else (Peters & Waterman, 1982).

2. There is a clear adversary whose power could squash any direct effort at overthrow.

3. There are seams created by the fact that neither overthrow by the opposition movement nor military oppression by the group in power will be politically successful. These common interests create small but tangible spaces for compromise.

4. There is ongoing articulation by intellectuals such as Michnik of what is happening and what it means. These accounts are not filled with stirring, visionary rhetoric or simplistic accounts of good and evil. Instead, there is a calming tone of "angerless wisdom" (Schell, 1987, p. xi), reaffirmation of the importance of living one's beliefs, discussion of being ready to die but unwilling to kill, and renewed emphasis on scrutinizing the local scene for opportunities to build an alternative society.

5. There are highly diverse activities done simultaneously across the country that amount to independent experiments from which people learn that totalitarianism has variable resistance to change.

6. Acts of militant decency create an alternative society, which means that people become less dependent on the totalitarian society and effectively ignore it in more and more of their dealings.

7. There is an ongoing effort to act "as if" Poland were already a free country, which, in Schell's (1987) words, enables the "as if to melt away" (p. xxx), with substance replacing pretense.

Minimal as this organizational design may seem, it does foster sensemaking even if it also might well make decision making more difficult. Specific examples in KOR of access to sensemaking resources include the following:

1. *Social context:* There are gatherings, groups that publish newsletters, attempts to restore social bonds, networking by means of signed documents, trust in local action, the formation of associations, and an ongoing focus on

"independent public opinion" rather than on totalitarian power (Schell, 1987, p. xxvi). The form encourages conversation.

2. *Identity:* People see themselves as agents who do what they think needs to be done to exemplify democratic values. They see themselves as engaged in a new form of revolution, as a community of free people, as rehearsing values that matter, and as helping a self-limiting revolution. The form provides a distinct, stable, workable sense of who the participants are as individuals.

3. *Retrospect:* People act in order to discover how much liberty they actually have. There is ongoing discovery of what the revolution is about based on seeing what works and what does not. The form thrives on elapsed data and uses those data to form an emerging definition of what the opposition stands for.

4. *Salient cues:* Close attention is directed to local activities to find spaces of permissible maneuver. People are urged to pay attention to things they can improve using only the skills and sensitivities they now possess. The counsel is to "scrutinize the minutiae of their local environment" (Schell, 1987, p. xxiii), which means that the form enhances the visibility of cues from which sense can be made.

5. *Ongoing projects:* The "revolution" consists basically of peaceful activities in a normal, ongoing civic life that sets a new tone. There is a day-to-day community of people acting as if they are free and carving out small areas of compromise as they do so. Life does not stop for the revolution to start. Life and the revolution fold together. The revolution keeps pace with the relentless flow of experience and, in doing so, loses some of its conspicuousness, gains pragmatic relevance, is made more manageable and doable, and, because of its close affinity with ongoing, everyday action, is eminently sensible. The form accommodates to the flow of experience and, in doing so, enables people to keep up with dynamic events.

6. *Plausibility:* The accounts of what is happening tell a coherent, meaningful story, a story of militant decency, a better today that replaces empty promises, and the creation of a new society. These are stories of possibilities being realized, and they provide reasonable explanations for what is happening and what can happen. The form gains its energy from stories of tangible accomplishments within an alternative social order.

7. *Enactment:* What is perhaps most characteristic of KOR is the dominance of action that creates a different order. People are counseled to "do what you think needs to be done." There is action at every turn—action such as lectures, publishing, providing medical or financial aid, performing small acts of decency, consumer protection, social work, concrete assistance in legal trials—action that even includes dissolving KOR itself. The form encourages action. Perhaps more accurately, the form is action.

CONCLUSION

The Mann Gulch firefighting crew and the KOR opposition group exemplify variations in organizational design that have an effect on the capability for sensemaking. Variations in sensemaking, in turn, affect enthusiasm, the willingness to sustain complex collaboration, and resourcefulness in the face of setbacks. Although Mann Gulch and KOR may seem far removed from organizing for global change, there is a sense in which they incorporate many of its conditions.

To see this parallel, consider the following more general and more stark rendering of the story of Mann Gulch.

> Individuals who are strangers to one another
> are spread out,
> unable to communicate,
> unfamiliar with the terrain,
> in disagreement about who their leaders are, and
> they're told to do something they've never done before,
> or they will die.
> They don't do it.
> They die.

When people organize for global change, their organizational challenges look a lot like those in Mann Gulch. In organizing for global change, leaders also will face

1. Strangers with diverse experience
2. Face-to-face contact for intermittent, short periods
3. Unknown leaders
4. Temporary systems
5. Proposed solutions that make no sense
6. An inability to communicate and share experience
7. Terrain consisting of unfamiliar troubles (or opportunities)
8. Failures and possible fatalities

The context for efforts at global change may often bear an uncomfortable resemblance to the context at Mann Gulch. But if some of the organizational dysfunction at Mann Gulch can be understood as a failure to organize for sensemaking, then efforts at global change can be redesigned to strengthen this capability. That is what appears to have happened with the Worker's Defense Committee in Poland.

The promise of KOR is the suggestion that challenges such as those of Mann Gulch can be overcome. KOR is organized in such a way that

a community replaces strangers,
closeness replaces separation,
the familiar replaces the unfamiliar,
agreements replace disagreements,
acceptance replaces noncompliance, and
renewal replaces death.

3

CONSTRUCTIONIST LEADERSHIP IN THE GLOBAL RELATIONAL AGE

The Case of the Mountain Forum

KATHRYN M. KACZMARSKI
DAVID L. COOPERRIDER

THE EMERGENCE OF GLOBAL CIVIL SOCIETY

The global symbols of the Material Age—the Berlin Wall, the Iron Curtain, and the Super-power rivalry—are gone. They have been replaced by a peaceful united Germany, in a united Europe, in a rejuvenated United Nations committed to collective global security and free markets. These are the global symbols of the new Relationship Age. Earth has been in the Material Age since before human civilization. It is now entering the Relationship Age, the period when personal and planetary activities will be based on the assumption that *all is relationship, not matter.* (Mollner, in Combs, 1992, p. 204)

Welcome to the relational age! Whether on a local or global scale, within the private sector, between governments on an international level, or nongovernmental organizations in local communities, people are working together

An earlier version of this chapter was published in 1997 under the same title in *Organization and Environment, 10,* 235-258.

through partnership. We are seeing and experiencing an indication of the "burgeoning interest in collaboration in every sector of society" (Gray, 1989, p. 25). In the business world, words like *strategic alliance* and *partnership* proliferate in many annual reports and are celebrated as *best practices*. And in the public sector, the emergence of civil society on local, national, regional, and global levels indicates this trend. People are coming together to help each other solve problems, either in their own backyards or in other parts of the world (de Oliveira & Tandon, 1994; Wood, 1995).

One clear manifestation of the increase in global civil society is the increase in the appearance of global social change organizations (GSCOs):

> GSCOs appear to represent an emergent organizational form with some characteristics which distinguish them from other types of organizations. They may be known by a variety of labels (international non-government organizations, inter-sectoral partnerships, transnational development organizations to name just a few), but are distinct in at least four different ways (Cooperrider & Pasmore, 1991):
> 1. Many have as their primary task a commitment to serve as an agent of change in the creation of a healthier and sustainable world;
> 2. They have discovered and mobilized innovative social-organizational arrangements that make possible human cooperation across previously polarizing and constraining boundaries;
> 3. They hold values of empowerment, egalitarian and people-centered forms of social action in the accomplishment of mission;
> 4. They function or have membership across two or more countries without primary loyalty, identification, or reliance on national governments (i.e. they exist as entities beyond the nation state). (Johnson & Cooperrider, 1991, p. 225)

The number of these organizations has multiplied rapidly since the end of World War II. The *Encyclopedia of Human Problems* lists 10,233 global challenges that confront humanity (Johnson & Cooperrider, 1991). Increasingly, GSCOs are emerging to answer the call of these challenges. A few examples of such organizations include the International Physicians for Prevention of Nuclear War, The Nature Conservancy, The Hunger Project, and the Institute for Cultural Affairs.

Whereas these examples point to specific organizations formed to address global issues, Morgan, Power, and Weigel (1993) present other categories of "transition strategies" aimed at addressing the global change agenda. One such strategy is the creation of global issue regimes.

> The function of such regimes is to institutionalize a set of norms, principles, or procedures for guiding the conduct of states and international organizations with respect to a particular issue area (e.g., environmental degradation, ozone depletion, absolute poverty, the debt crisis, deep sea bed mining, resource exploitation in Antarctica). (p. 1915)

Formation of such a global issue regime "focuses on the creation and/or reconfiguration of international institutions that are issue-based, functioning as both think tanks and conduits for the enhancement, diffusion and institutionalization of new global norms" (p. 1916).

A second category of strategies presented by these authors and related to GSCOs is the creation of alternative institutions. These are largely nongovernmental institutions whose creation mostly "bypasses (and occasionally usurps) traditional governmental prerogatives and domains. Hence the process in institution building and reform is seen more as something that parallels, co-opts or redirects the governing structures of nation states" (Morgan et al., 1993, p. 1920).

Both of the strategies presented by these categories allude to the role of bridging organizations (Brown, 1991) or strategic bridging (Westley & Vredenburg, 1991) between organizations to address global issues. Bridging organizations enact horizontal and vertical linkages in order to promote grassroots influence at the policy level (Brown, 1991, p. 807). Although GSCOs have appeared over the past 50 years to address worldwide issues, increasingly, these organizations are now seeking ways to collaborate with other like-minded individuals and organizations to provide the infrastructure for the formation of a global regime.

Yet our knowledge is limited on how to create such global efforts, not to mention what kind of *leadership* is called for in such highly complex cooperative and collaborative systems. Research on the leadership processes that lead to successful regime formation at the global level is just beginning; analysis in this area is in its infancy and has been advanced most empirically in the classic work of Oran R. Young: "Efforts to elucidate the role of leadership in international society have engendered more confusion than illumination" (Young, 1991, p. 286). Therefore, the focus of this chapter is to explore this confusion and attempt to highlight aspects of leadership demanded by an emerging global civil society.

WHAT WE KNOW ABOUT THE LEADERSHIP
DIMENSIONS OF GLOBAL ORGANIZING

Leadership for Global Organizing

Young, one of the leading scholars in the international Human Dimensions of Global Environmental Change research program, has identified "three forms of leadership that regularly come into play in efforts to establish international institutions: structural leadership, entrepreneurial leadership, and intellectual leadership" (Young, 1991, p. 281). In this definition, structural leadership refers to an individual who represents a party (usually a state) and engages in institutional bargaining in the interest of that party. The aim of the structural leader is to leverage his or her party's structural power regarding specific issues of interest. According to Young, structural leaders are typified by individuals who possess the ability to assemble and nurture effective coalitions and take appropriate actions to hinder the development of blocking or counter coalitions. Structural leaders are often public servants who are well compensated to negotiate on behalf of states (Young, 1991, p. 293), regardless of the result of these negotiations, to produce timely and mutually acceptable outcomes. Structural leadership is able to break through barriers of regime formation largely through the structural power (material, size, etc.) of the nation-state structure. Although hegemony is always a concern, there is clear evidence that use of this kind of power can be quite important, if not essential, to regime formation.

The entrepreneurial leader, the second analytic type, is defined as "an individual who relies on negotiating skills to frame issues in ways that foster integrative bargaining and to put together deals that would otherwise elude participants endeavoring to form international regimes through institutional bargaining" (Young, 1991, p. 293). Those who function as entrepreneurial leaders have a number of roles from which to choose. First, they can act as *agenda setters* by crafting the framework for presenting issues at an international level. Second, they might assume the role of *popularizers* by drawing attention to specific issues over others. Third, they can enact an *inventor* role by devising alternative, creative policy options to overcome obstacles in the negotiation process. And fourth, they can pose as *brokers* by making deals and abetting support for favored options. Yet according to Young, entrepreneurial leaders are to be differentiated from mediators because their interests are not neutral. "They work to frame the issues at stake and intervene energetically in the substance of the negotiations, endeavoring to invent attractive options and to persuade the parties to back the options they espouse" (Young, 1991, p. 295).

One key differentiating aspect between this form of leadership and the other two is the emergence of multiple leaders when entrepreneurial activities are at hand. The activities engaged in under these conditions allow for simultaneous efforts by a number of individuals and, therefore, the presence of numerous entrepreneurial leaders. In particular, the presence of multiple leaders appears most strong when centered around the entrepreneurial acts of popularizing issues and brokering interests.

An intellectual leader is one who relies on the power of ideas to produce intellectual capital. "While the structural leader seeks to translate power resources into bargaining leverage, the intellectual leader relies on the power of ideas to shape the intellectual capital available to those engaged in institutional bargaining" (Young, 1991, p. 300). It is through this intellectual capital that differences are bridged and cooperative processes achieved. Hence, this serves to play an important role in the negotiation process, either constructing or deconstructing consensus around issues in international society. A classic example here was the power of the idea of sustainable development, and how environment and economy were so powerfully put back together. There is both a similarity and a distinction between entrepreneurial leadership and intellectual leadership:

> Both the entrepreneurial leader and the intellectual leader rely on their wits to make their efforts felt. Whereas the entrepreneurial leader is an agenda setter and popularizer who uses negotiating skill to devise attractive formulas and to broker interests, however, the intellectual leader is a thinker who seeks to articulate the systems of thought that provide the substratum underlying the proximate activities involved in institutional bargaining. Accordingly, entrepreneurial leaders often become consumers of ideas generated by intellectual leaders. (Young, 1991, pp. 300-301)

Young's definition of intellectual leadership runs parallel to what Peter M. Haas (1992) has defined as an "epistemic community." Most commonly used to refer to scientific communities or networks of knowledge-based experts, members of epistemic communities generally share a way of knowing, patterns of reasoning, and values (Haas, 1992). Epistemic communities have been shown to generate momentum for international cooperation leading to regime formation (Haas, 1990; Haas, 1989, 1992; Krasner, 1983; Young, 1989), particularly in the environmental sector. It is the intellectual capital generated by an epistemic community—usually a group of scientists or researchers sharing common academic interests and generating a common discourse around these interests—that becomes the backbone of thought for intellectual leadership.

Trist (1983) has identified and defined the functions of referent organizations, playing an integral leadership role in interorganizational domain formation. Such organizations come about to serve in a centering capacity; yet a tricky balance needs to be maintained in providing this function. "To be acceptable the referent organization must not usurp the functions of the constituent organizations, yet to be effective it must provide appropriate leadership" (Trist, 1983, p. 275). In providing such "appropriate leadership," referent organizations have three broad functions:

1. *Regulation* of present relationships and activities; establishing ground rules and maintaining base values;
2. *Appreciation* of emergent trends and issues; developing a shared image of a desirable future; and
3. *Infrastructure support*—resource, information sharing, special projects, etc. (Trist, 1983, p. 275)

Most importantly, through the enactment of these functions, it is the referent organization that ensures the continuity of the domain over time by integrating emerging trends and issues into its evolution. Hence, by their very nature, referent organizations are themselves *discontinuous*. While serving to bring together, or convene, representatives of the constituent organizations comprising the domain, referent organizations themselves are more virtual than actual in existence, and they change as required by the evolution of the domain and/or regime.

The emergence of a newly formed global alliance, the Mountain Forum, presents what we believe is a rare and relevant example of leadership enacted during a process of global regime formation and organization development, an initiative designed to respond to urgent issues of global environmental change in mountain regions throughout the world. Building on Young's three forms of leadership and Trist's conceptualization of referent organizations, we propose another analytic type to Young's (1991) tripartite typology of structural, entrepreneurial, and intellectual leadership. In what follows, we articulate our methodology, explore what we know about the leadership dimensions of global change organizing, and then build hypotheses about "constructionist leadership," a fourth type, emerging from our grounded research into the story of the global Mountain Forum.

METHODOLOGY

We followed the case study method in our efforts to make sense of the global organizational development of the Mountain Forum. More specifically, our approach could be classified as a hypothesis-generating case study. Thachankary, Tenkasi, and Cooperrider's (1996) study of the classic global eradication of smallpox is a good example of this kind of research. The objective is to generate theoretical propositions for further empirical investigation and learning based on the observations of the case.

Our inquiry into the regime formation of the Mountain Forum relied on a number of primary and secondary data sources. Our primary data source was a diverse team of intergovernmental, nongovernmental, and academic/scientific leaders involved with the effort with whom we held extensive interviews (see Kaczmarski, 1996, for a published account of an entire verbatim interview). We also were involved as participant observers, primarily in an organizational development role, in many hours of meetings over the past 2 years, as well as at key formative conferences that ultimately gave birth to the new worldwide organization. Data from field notes, transcribed meeting tapes, and interviews were analyzed for common themes. Specifically, we asked, What was the type of leadership associated with the birth of this regime and, ultimately, new global organization? What was the leadership type that made the essential difference (i.e., without it, the development of the new organization might not have happened)? Before addressing these questions, however, we need to outline the case study, or rather story, of this global organization.

THE STORY OF THE MOUNTAIN FORUM

Background

Covering one fifth of the world's surface and inhabited by 10% of its population, mountains are home to unique communities and cultures, maintaining lifestyles intimately interwoven with fragile ecosystems. These global ecosystems are sensitive living laboratories for monitoring climate change, cultivating a significant environment for biological diversity, and serving as a source of more than 80% of the world's fresh surface water. Most of all, mountains represent some of the world's most precious and sacred human and natural resources.

In recent decades, mountains have been threatened by global forces such as inappropriate economic development, human conflict, air-quality deterioration, and deforestation. Yet mountains have never been recognized as a distinct environmental sector worthy of ecological or political attention. Mountain peoples, who live in some of the most remote, rugged, and impoverished regions of the earth, historically have had little voice or influence over policies pertaining to, and the treatment of, their homelands. Even governments are themselves outliers as the official structures representing these areas: Consequently, all those concerned with mountain cultures and environments have historically been marginalized. Both local, grassroots, nongovernmental organizations (NGOs) and governments of mountainous regions, such as Nepal, typically encounter massive power imbalances when dealing with the political and economic institutions responsible for broad-based policy and economic development. This has allowed for continued oversight by regional and worldwide policymakers.

A Short History

Prior to the late 1980s and early 1990s, there was little collective action concerning mountains other than in scientific circles. Activities were scattered, and different governments and mountain organizations either were not in contact or regarded each other with suspicion. Historically, mountain NGOs and other mountain-centered organizations fostered their own agendas, resulting from having to scramble for limited resources and funding. Composed of roughly 300 groups worldwide, the mountain NGO sector is one of the smallest among all environmental groups. Because mountains had not been recognized as an environmental sector, NGOs found it nearly impossible to solicit funding from donors or to influence governments on the basis of a mountain-specific focus. Interdependent with the plight of NGOs, governments of these regions were themselves struggling to gain visibility for issues unique to mountainous areas and therefore had little support to offer.

Likewise, there was little interagency or intergovernmental cooperation on mountain development because this concept did not exist. International agencies, such as the World Bank and the United Nations's Food and Agriculture Organization (FAO) were working under the assumption of "upstream protection for downstream use." Many governments viewed upland people as the culprits responsible for destroying the land, or else they were victims and were targets for poverty alleviation or compensation for the adverse impact of development. Indigenous peoples were given little regard for their vision, strengths, uniqueness, and resourcefulness, and they were viewed as incapable of or lacking the capacity for self-reliance. This perception of mountain peoples and cultures resulted in a lack of motivation to join forces between the different parties involved.

In spite of this fragmentation and lack of cooperation, a small band of geographers and environmentalists had been working since the mid-1970s to raise awareness of the unique nature of mountains. Because some were members of the International Mountain Society (IMS), primarily an organization of mountain researchers and land managers with global reach, they served to promote integrated mountain ecosystem development and conservation through their interests and efforts as researchers and writers. *Mountain Research and Development*, a scientific journal of joint publication between the IMS and the United Nations University, contained articles covering every major and many lesser-known mountain regions of the world. Despite a limited audience, this publication planted seeds for a burgeoning global dialogue on environmental and cultural mountain development.

The workings of this collection of individuals began to spread. In December 1983, the International Centre for Integrated Mountain Development in Kathmandu, Nepal was inaugurated; it was an intergovernmental organization concerned with sustainable mountain development in the Hindu Kush-Himalayas. A few years later, in 1986, the first international mountain conference took place at the Mohonk Mountain House in upstate New York. In December 1990, a small group of geographers and environmentalists involved in these efforts met in Appenberg, Switzerland and formally adopted the name "Mountain Agenda." The aim of their project was to put mountains on the world's environmental map. With the upcoming United Nations Conference on Environment and Development (UNCED) in Rio de Janeiro scheduled for June 1992 (i.e., the Earth Summit), the Mountain Agenda recognized an extraordinary opportunity to create momentum.

Quickly obtaining funding from the Swiss government and involving a wider circle of colleagues, the Mountain Agenda championed the publication of *The State of the World's Mountains* (Stone, 1992) in May 1992, just before UNCED. This was a global report in book form with contributions by development and environment authorities. A second and most important activity taken on by the Mountain Agenda was to become involved in the preparation process for the Earth Summit.

The Earth Summit: June 1992

The process leading up to UNCED consisted of a series of four preparatory committees, or PrepComs, beginning late in the summer of 1990. Held in different parts of the world, these PrepComs were an intermediary step to allow extensive preparations to take place for the upcoming intergovernmental conference. More important, these sessions were the primary vehicle to involve NGOs—a first for a summit meeting.

The Mountain Agenda group, while compiling chapters for their soon-to-be-released book, searched for an opening by which to enter the summit preparation process. It was not until the third PrepCom that they found an ally: the Swiss government. By making an excited appeal for the inclusion of a separate chapter on mountains as part of Agenda 21, five members of the Mountain Agenda joined the Swiss delegation in Geneva, the site of the third session. The Swiss approached mountainous countries such as Nepal, Ethiopia, Canada, New Zealand, Austria, and others to canvass their support for a separate chapter. The strategy paid off: At the end of the third PrepCom, their collective efforts resulted in securing a distinct place for mountains in UNCED and Agenda 21. Between the third and fourth PrepComs, further inputs were provided by UNCED's Secretariat, the World Bank, and the Mountain Institute (a mountain NGO based in West Virginia), among others. The effort resulted in the delivery of Chapter 13, *Managing Fragile Ecosystems: Sustainable Mountain Development,* adopted at the fourth PrepCom and incorporated into Agenda 21 in time for UNCED in Rio.

The inclusion of this chapter on mountain ecosystems gave this sector international legitimacy for the first time; it was a definitive event. However, because the chapter was drafted late in the presummit process, it did not benefit from the full participation of NGOs and people working in the world's mountain regions, nor from the full influence and ownership of governments and UN agencies. Nevertheless, the chapter was endorsed along with the rest of Agenda 21 and delegated to the UN's Food and Agriculture Organization (FAO), the designated task manager to coordinate follow-up of implementation within the UN system.

Equally if not more important, those present at the summit realized the necessity of collective efforts in getting mountain-related issues foremost in the minds of international policymakers. Rio changed the course of history. Many realized that they could no longer afford to work alone. Strategic bridging would be essential in forming an active coalition and furthering the direction established at Rio, including the full participation of NGOs, governments, scientists, and indigenous mountain peoples. The real impact for development of mountain-specific policies and global-level advocacy required cooperation on all levels.

The FAO Intervention: March 1994

In spite of Chapter 13, neither governments nor donors rushed to support new major initiatives in sustainable mountain development, even with numerous ongoing activities by the Mountain Agenda group, IMS, and others. Although the need was becoming more widely recognized, no one had a clear understanding of how to forge a strategic mountain alliance or how to form partnerships across NGOs, UN agencies, and private-sector and government organizations. No clear mechanism or motivational force existed to direct the energy from Rio into the organization of a global alliance.

Not much changed until the FAO convened an interagency meeting as a follow-up to the Earth Summit. In addition, the FAO task manager decided to invite select NGOs and intergovernmental organizations (IGOs) to the meeting, including these organizations, which would normally not have access. In March 1994, the FAO hosted the session on Chapter 13 at its headquarters in Rome. This was the opportunity many had been anticipating: Both nongovernmental and governmental forces came together and collectively laid out a possible procedure for advancing a follow-up to Agenda 21. It was a highly productive event.

One recommendation that emerged, given the late stage of introduction of this chapter into the UNCED preparatory process, suggested convening a larger gathering of NGOs to undertake a detailed review of Chapter 13, the mountain agenda. This would allow the mountain NGO community to engage in a similar process from which other sectors benefited during the PrepCom process leading up to the summit. They agreed to create an interagency mechanism that was inclusive of NGOs and leading up to a possible intergovernmental World Conference on Mountain Sustainable Development in 1998. In the interim, five intergovernmental regional conferences were proposed: Latin America, Africa, Europe, North America, and Asia and the Pacific.

The UN Interagency Group now invited NGOs and their supporting governments into full partnership to develop a more inclusive, detailed, and agreed-upon mountain agenda. This highly symbolic show of support and the meeting itself allowed for organizing energies to be mobilized once again. Not only did this invitation pave the way for additional NGO participation, but it also anticipated the forging of stronger relationships among NGOs, governments, and other organizations working in this arena. A multisector, global mountain alliance began to take shape.

In July 1994, the NGO Workshop on the Mountain Agenda was held at The Mountain Institute's conference and education facility, Spruce Knob Mountain Center, located in the West Virginian Appalachians. In attendance from around the world were 30 mountain NGO leaders, donors, academics, environmentalists, and others concerned with worldwide mountain policy. The intent of this gathering was to deliberate on the agenda, process, and plan for the International NGO Consultation on the Mountain Agenda—the first-ever global meeting for the sustainable development and preservation of mountain environments and cultures. The meeting was a terrific success: The agenda, conference structure, design considerations, themes, participation criteria, facilitation process, and plans for follow-up for the NGO consultation flowed from and were agreed upon by the group.

The Lima Meeting: February 1995

With much-needed support from donor governments and organizations, and extensive cooperative effort between the organizations involved, the February international meeting in Lima, Peru marked a key and critical turning point in the evolution of the mountain story. In attendance were 110 NGO leaders, academics, donors, policymakers, environmentalists, and organizational representatives with a stake in raising awareness of the state of the world's mountains to a global level. The expected outcomes of this meeting were twofold. The first intent was to create an ongoing network for information sharing and mutual learning, leading to innovative partnerships to implement actions. The second motive was to develop consensus on a prioritized action plan to implement the mountain agenda and distribute it to all governments through the high-level meeting of the United Nations Commission on Sustainable Development (UNCSD) in April 1995—only 2 short months away.

As the first half of the event unfolded, the sheer complexity of the global issues and the diversity of backgrounds and perspectives severely tested collaboration. Complicating this was the fact that few participants had experience with large group processes and had never previously met. When papers were presented by some well-established scientists and researchers, some participants criticized the content and presenters, claiming a display of ignorance of the "real" issues. This fostered little substantive dialogue. The NGO representatives, each with his or her own cultural perspective, wants, and aspirations, found few forums that valued their contributions. Some wondered if the whole event was not simply a charade of the power-structures-that-be that would ultimately control the outputs.

For 3 days, the push-pull dynamics and defensive stances continued; influence, control, and voice were sought and negotiated among individuals and factions. At an ad hoc meeting of the premeeting planners, it was agreed that a new approach was needed that favored solid thematic working groups to be suggested by the participants. In addition, there were many other positive developments beginning to take shape: People intermingled and were getting to know each other, multiple coalitions formed, interest groups gathered with interest groups, new friendships began, and cards were exchanged. As the groups congealed and became more intimate, their involvement grew at the macro level, and through all of this commotion, participants were gaining ground.

On the next to last day, several representatives from NGOs, agencies, and academia shepherded the process forward. In their remaining time together, participants extended the original six thematic topic areas into ten and self-divided into groups around topics that responded more adequately to their local contexts. These topics were cultural diversity; sustainable development; production systems and alternative livelihoods; local energy demand and supply in mountains; tourism; sacred, spiritual, and symbolic significance of mountains; mountains as water towers; mountain biodiversity; climate change; and natural hazards. Some of the recommendations that emerged from these groups included the need for decisional autonomy for mountain peoples, the need for mountain languages to be protected as primary carriers of traditions and identity, the importance of recognizing intellectual property rights for indigenous knowledge systems, a call for recognizing the true value of mountain resources in terms of economic return, and the need to recognize and embrace the importance of mountains as "water towers to humanity."

In the final 2 days of the consultation, participants proposed and decided to create a world mountain forum based on the urgent need to continue the dialogue initiated in Lima. All interested parties would be invited to join together to promote conservation and sustainable development in the world's mountains. The charted purpose was "to provide a forum for mutual support and the exchange of ideas, experiences and peoples to raise mountain issues on local, national, regional, and international agendas and to promote policies and actions for equitable and ecologically sustainable mountain development."

With this recommendation, the congregation split into regional groups with the intent of electing regional representatives to serve on the Initial Organizing Committee (IOC) of the Mountain Forum. Clearly, the circle had widened from the original Mountain Agenda members to include and involve a larger, more diversified mountain community. The voices at the table had multiplied: indigenous groups, environmental scientists, NGO leaders, intergovernmental organization officials, donors, academics, and others. An IOC of 14 conference participants was formed with the intent to lead a global advisory committee that would work with regional networks in activities such as advocacy, information exchange, implementation of the mountain agenda, cooperative and joint efforts, and monitoring and evaluation. This group planned to meet at the end of September 1995 to take the next concrete step in the organizational development of a world "Mountain Forum."

The Initial Organizing Committee: September 1995

After Lima, a quick and intense effort produced the *Summary Report and Recommendations* document of the Lima NGO consultation in time for the April UNCSD session. The secretary-general of the UNCSD, along with representatives of governments and UN agencies, lauded the efforts of the consultation as one of the "salient achievements" in the follow-up and implementation of Agenda 21. The UNCSD displayed its endorsement by including a two-page statement of support for mountain ecosystems and cultures, incorporating many of the key points of the Lima document, as part of their final report. The much-sought-after support from the international policy community was now in place. In September 1995, the IOC for the Mountain Forum gathered at Spruce Knob to begin the organizing task.

The meeting began with a process of storytelling from all participants, providing a narrative account of regional successes and developments since the Lima gathering. However, this was the simplest activity in which the participants would engage for the next 4 days. Asked to articulate in metaphoric form their various images for the Mountain Forum, a wide variety of possibilities were given: a web, a movement, a cyber-community, a coffee shop, a solar system, a Roman forum, a big family, a federation, a bridge, a morphic field, a polyphony, and others. There was no clear and consistent image of how this group of mountain organizations and interests should come together and be organized, despite the clarity of purpose and intent of all present. However, one thing was strikingly clear because of its conspicuous absence. No one, at least in metaphoric form, articulated a vision of a conventional hierarchy: a secretariat with a secretary general, an organization with a large center and physical structure, and so on. By working with metaphoric language and not the literal language of organization, many varied and complex new images were allowed to enter the deliberations. But again, the complexities and diversities of an already diverse global effort were growing. Complicating this was the spectrum of participants: grassroots organizers to international policymakers. This was a microcosm of the Lima meeting.

Over the next few days, a number of different breakout group configurations emerged in the hope of converging on some common way to proceed with the organizational development of the Mountain Forum. Through this activity, the group continued to tack back and forth between organizational form and function, recognizing the tightly coupled relationship between the two. The sensitivity to structure became apparent. No one organization or individual readily rose to assume leadership. The experienced leaders in the room clearly understood that creating a center of authority or power would be the kiss of death. Furthermore, the institutionalization of one organization or individual as leader was antithetical to forming a global coalition, because this would center the Mountain Forum in one place. Having one organization formally in charge would negate the notion of a global alliance of equal partners.

The language used also pointed to the struggle to organize differently, attempting to honor a global alliance. Words that implied a formalized structure, such as having a "secretariat" to operate the Forum, or having the Forum "centered" somewhere geographically, were unacceptable—indeed, strongly resisted—by the participants. On an unarticulated level, what was collectively conceptualized required different language that was reflective of the differences people perceived between their organizational experiences and the opportunity presented with this new global configuration.

One consistent theme throughout the meeting and during prior gatherings was the expressed need for an electronic information network, a recommendation giving concrete form and action to the notion of a Mountain Forum. This idea was articulated repeatedly as a necessary component of the Forum because it had the potential to address numerous issues: the remoteness of mountains from more densely populated areas, the lack of information that reaches mountain communities, and the inconsistent advocacy of mountain issues across different ranges and continents.

On the final day of the meeting, a pioneering image of the Mountain Forum emerged. Visualized by the participants was a coalition of organizations strung together by geographic region but with no identifiable center and no formal secretariat. The emphasis on organizing based on regional or geographic "nodes" was seen as the best way to bridge the local and the global, serving the interests of both. Within this coalition, boundaries would fade and no hierarchy of organizations or positions would exist, consistent with the consensus that a relational network of mountain NGOs and agencies was necessary to function successfully at the global level. Membership would be broad and completely open to individuals and institutions—nongovernmental, governmental, and private-sector—and reflective of the basic operational values of the Mountain Forum: open, democratic, decentralized, accessible, transparent, accountable, and flexible.

The electronic information network would act to serve the entire mountain community, providing Internet access and allowing for mutual exchange of information, but would not encompass a position of power or authority. Any individual involved in creating the network and ensuring smooth operation would be considered a resource to the Forum, but not a manager. Each region would designate an organization to act as the regional node responsible for providing the bridge between mountain NGOs and interests and the server node of the Forum. The server node would perform a technical function only. A global node would cater to organizations not fitting into any one region. Yet any organization would be able to communicate directly with another through the network without traveling through any one node. These nodes would be primarily responsible for promoting membership and interregional linkages among interested organizations, along with disseminating timely and consistent information. The electronic information network would be a primary means of enacting mutual support across geographic and organizational boundaries, advancing the Mountain Agenda through information sharing and connecting all concerned parties. The proposed graphic to illustrate the organizing of the Forum is given in Figure 3.1.

At the conclusion of the meeting, participants agreed to establish an Interim Facilitating Committee for the next 2 years, consisting of representatives from each of the regional nodes and the server node, the task manager of the UN interagency committee on Chapter 13, and a representative

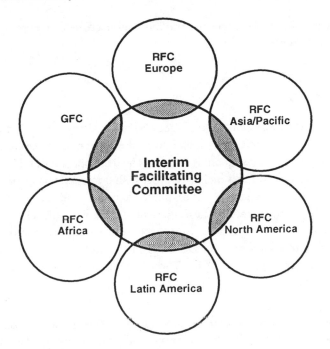

Figure 3.1 The Mountain Forum
SOURCE: Report of the Initial Organizing Committee of the Mountain Forum.
NOTE: Shaded areas indicate representatives to the Interim Fascilitating Committee.
RFC = Regional Facilitating Committee; GFC = Global Facilitating Committee.

from a primary donor organization, The Swiss Agency for Development and Cooperation (SDC). This interim committee, expected to experience a change in membership after the initial 2-year period, would be responsible for guiding operations of the Mountain Forum and monitoring and evaluating its performance, drafting proposals for the next evolution of governance, soliciting funding in support of the Mountain Forum, convening additional meetings as needed, and catalyzing direct contributions to the General Review of Agenda 21 Implementation by a Special Session of the UN General Assembly in 1997.

Although many details still needed discussion and attention, the session closed with participants expressing sentiments of great hope for the future of the Forum, with expectations fulfilled and exceeded. The meeting had produced the results desired at the outset: a delineation of the functions of a global alliance around mountains and the shape such an alliance would take, agreed upon by an international community of mountain NGOs and interagency and government organizations. All had been able to set aside their individual interests and, through an innovative collaboration, create and serve something larger than themselves.

Going Forward

The Mountain Forum Project Document, outlining a detailed plan for organization and operation, resulted from the September meeting and was developed during the last quarter of 1995. The development of this document continued the iterative and inclusive process that marked this effort from its inception: The report largely developed over e-mail and fax lines as those concerned continued crafting the document and giving feedback. Just weeks after the writing of the report, which set forth the agreed-upon vision of organization and purpose, the SDC stepped forward and provided the half-million dollars needed for start-up. The world's first global Mountain Forum was born. As one person concluded,

> None of us can begin to imagine the thousands of projects, the international network of relationships, the information sharing, the impact, the global learning, and other benefits that will emerge through just the electronic network alone. I feel more hopeful somehow. The world's mountains are sacred spaces. Helping give birth to this living entity was the most significant initiative of my career.

THE FOURTH FORM: CONSTRUCTIONIST LEADERSHIP[1]

The first step can be nothing less than a broad-based attempt by people from these cultures to understand one another, and to understand each other's right to existence. Only then can a kind of worldwide, pluralistic meta-culture . . . evolve. It is only in the context of such a meta-culture that a new sense of political responsibility—global responsibility—can come into being. . . . Yes, it is clearly necessary to invent organizational structures appropriate to the multicultural age.

—Vaclav Havel

To understand what we discovered in terms of a fourth type of leadership, it is useful first to say something about the context of global change organizing. In a word, the single most salient aspect of the global change domain is the enormous proliferation of *knowledge* and, concomitantly, mounting diversities in knowledge systems—in the proliferating interactions of varieties of cultures of inquiry.

Since World War II, humankind has entered a totally new era of history, perhaps even of evolution, as it relates to the changing role of knowledge and its far-reaching implications for newly emerging societal dynamics and organizational potentials. More scientific information has been generated in the past 30 years than during humanity's previous several million years. In the global change domain, humanity has extended its knowledge on an all-planetary scale to the far reaches of the universe, as well as to the infinitely small—the atom, the cell, the gene. The world has taken stock on a global scale of this total knowledge in a series of remarkable world conferences: the first ever held.

Today, we can literally open encyclopedias that catalogue more than 15,000 global problems, and we can reference some 6,000 new scientific articles published each day. This march of knowledge, coupled with the global communications revolution in satellites, computers, and emerging innovations, will go on. This story is certainly being told today in many places and through voluminous literature on the knowledge society and the emergence of the *intelligent organization.* Yet implications have scarcely been "unpacked" for understanding leadership in the global change domain.

One executive, who has spent more than 15 years in leadership at the UN, has written about, from a leadership perspective, the challenges of the myriad of cultures of inquiry:

> Many of them think that they hold the ultimate truth, that others are wrong and that the rest of the world should accept their truth, way of life and beliefs. The sociology of *this* cosmos has barely retained humanity's attention. . . . Thinkers believed that everything could be solved, explained and furthered by means of the intellect. We seem to have come to an end of that belief. How many times do we see in the United Nations that world problems are insoluble because of the excessive intelligence of the antagonists? . . . Humanity has done marvels in the last few hundred years in developing human senses and comprehension through stupendous scientific and technological inventions. . . . The miracles of knowledge must be repeated now in the fields of sentiment and relationship. (Muller, 1993, pp. 20-21)

The leadership that made the indelible difference in the development of the Mountain Forum was a kind that sees organizational development as the construction of an *organization-as-knowledge-system,* where organizing is a bridge among diverse cultures of inquiry. The fundamental task of an organization in this account is to provide a context for the bridging of diverse systems of intelligibility, and a medium for building a kind of worldwide metaculture of knowing, akin to that about which Vaclav Havel continues to speak.

Furthermore, the demonstration of leadership that led to the creation of the Mountain Forum displayed an overarching concern with "structuring the unknown" (Waterman, 1990, p. 41). Such is the work of sensemaking, which involves "placement of items into frameworks, comprehending, redressing surprise, constructing meaning, interacting in pursuit of mutual understanding, and patterning" (Weick, 1995, p. 6). Central concepts to sensemaking that are illustrated by the leadership of the Mountain Forum and discussed further in our analysis are concerns with the effects of language (because sense is generated by words), making sense of the past (retrospective), and attempting to make sense of the future (prospective).

The fundamental and historical task of what we will soon illustrate and talk about in this case as constructionist leadership is to enable productive connections, at the deepest levels of belief and method, among paradigms or cultures of inquiry. Unlike Young's structural leader; sophisticated primarily in the mobilizing capacity of material or economic power for overcoming the barriers to regime formation, the constructionist leader works at a nonmaterial, epistemic level of promoting appreciation of the "intelligibility nuclei" across often-conflicting communities. Likewise, because the constructionist leader is working at deeper levels of connecting knowledge communities, the skills and methods used look quite different from the brokering and negotiating of the entrepreneurial leader (more on this later). Finally, in contrast to intellectual leadership, conceived in Young's typology as the generator of whole new ideas that mobilize actions across groups and nations, the constructionist leader is involved fundamentally in building relational knowledge *systems,* open and indeterminate, capable of generating intellectual breakthrough and action time and again. The focus, then, is not with the truth power of a single idea; nor is the constructionist leader often engaged with an exclusive content or advocacy stance. Indeed, in the most radical sense, the constructionist leader operates as if words such as the "unassailable" truth, the "superior way of knowing," the "objective validity of the facts," and so on, are not useful—at least as they relate to the fragile and global formation of organizations as metacultures of inquiry. As we will illustrate, the constructionist leader often uses language in purposefully ambiguous ways. Metaphor and narrative form are opted over seemingly precise scientific precision and appear related to a number of positive relational consequences: being open to multiple and contradictory meanings; fostering complicated understanding; softening the boundaries between intelligibilities; pushing open the envelope of conventionally conceived limitations; creating a fertile space for more voices; and, through the forging of a new relationship, instilling hope.

Based on our analysis, we propose that constructionist leadership, as a complementary fourth and missing type in our understandings of global regime formation and organizational development, can be understood as a process involving three basic dimensions: (a) an appreciative approach to knowledge, (b) a generative approach to language that is rich in metaphor and narrative form, and (c) the formation of "out of control" organizations through the web of inclusion. In the remainder of this chapter, we provide illustration and elaboration on each of these dimensions and conclude with a call for future research.

Leadership Through Appreciation

One of the key individuals involved in the evolutionary process of the Mountain Forum reflected on the inception of the Mountain Agenda and praised the work of the handful of courageous scientists who brought to the world's attention the state of the world's fragile mountain ecosystems. But she also reflected on what might be called the global change paradox: that the very methods and vocabularies of understanding that are used to diagnose and place global problems on the world agenda are, when applied to human organization, likely to create a sense of threat, separation, and distance in fragile new forms of relatedness, thereby successfully undermining efforts to organize and take action globally. The all-too-frequent result: a retreat of the initial epistemic community and the formation of warring camps that speak only to themselves.

After evidence of this dynamic taking place at the Lima gathering, not one of the subsequent conferences or meetings included the presentation of formal papers on the degradation of the mountain ecologies and cultures. The professional vocabularies of deficit, whether consciously planned or not, were not given the same platform. There was a clear shift in agenda, process, and iquiry methodology introduced by leadership. Following Srivastva and Cooperrider (1990), Bunker (1990), and Barrett (1996), we can refer to the dramatically different form of leadership as *appreciative.* When asked about this shift, one of the leaders explained,

I mean, it wasn't that we sat together and plotted and had a conscious plan to make this happen. . . . I think that whether you call it a feminine style of leadership, or a horizontal or a networking or a facilitating style, it was markedly different from what had characterized the interactions of this group before. . . . The biggest learning I've had, not just in this experience in relationship to appreciative inquiry, is the very difficult work of holding people's attention to the vision (the opportunity) of what we are trying to do—is very hard.

In contrast to Young's entrepreneurial type, negotiating and brokering agreements, the appreciative approach functions as kind of a metaepistemological stance, working to build a metaculture of inquiry that actively seeks to discover, learn about, and bring to prominence the "life-giving" best of every culture of inquiry. Again building on Barrett's (1996) recent work, the term "appreciative" has several meanings. First, as Sir Geoffrey Vickers (1968) wrote in his classic work *Value Systems and Social Processes,* appreciative systems are a culture's system of values, beliefs, and expectations that guide perception and action. The appreciative system "resides in a particular *readiness* to see and value and respond to its situation in a certain way" (Vickers, 1968, p. 27). In Vickers's scheme, a culture's valuing processes are self-reinforcing systems that generate anticipation, expectation, and perception and therefore hasten the anticipated results.

A second meaning comes from the root of the word *appreciate*, meaning to grow in value, in this case to value what is best about a human system or culture. In this sense, "it refers to a system's capacity to deliberately notice, anticipate, and heighten positive potential" (Barrett, 1996, p. 37). As one of the key people said,

It matters how we framed this whole thing right from the beginning. To construct our challenge as a "threat" or response to a threat is not what I felt would move things. . . . For me, I kept being swept up in the excitement, the incredible miracle really happening, the boundary-crossing potential and possibility.

The art of constructionist leadership is the art of creating contexts of appreciative interchange where people from different traditions of knowing come together to create a new culture of valuing where differences are embraced rather than being a source of dominance and conformity pressures. It was not by accident, we discovered, that the next major conference, following the Peru event, began with systematic inquiry into all of the

successes, innovations, and strengths of each of the regions—everything that
was happening and had happened that could be drawn upon as resources for
building the global forum. In small groups, people explored, through uncon-
ditionally positive questions (Wilmot, 1996), the best in people's cultures and
traditions. For example, affirmative (not diagnostic) questions like these were
used to set the stage for discovery:

> As you reflect on our conference task, what are the regional or local devel-
> opments, events, or milestones that are most positive or promising—achieve-
> ments or trends since our Peru event that give you the most hope in the
> possibility of someday creating a vital and effective world Mountain Forum?
> Have you ever been part of the successful development of a global organiza-
> tion or collaborative alliance of diverse organizations? What were the critical
> challenges, and, more important, how were they dealt with?

Such gestures of data collection were contagious, creating a context for
generative dialogue. It was not long before inquiry was expanding beyond
local histories as positive possibility to joint envisioning of what might be—an
affirmation of the future as an opportunity versus a threat.

Interestingly, recent research in organization theory begins to help explain the power of the kind of radical appreciation that began to occur. The
assumptions behind the research include the following: (a) Interpretation
matters for patterns of organizational development; (b) organizational issues
are ambiguous and equivocal, and making language and labels are powerful
punctuating, expressing, and motivational devices; and (c) framing the organizational development task as a threat or a problem will have both social
psychological and organization-level repercussions quite different from framing organizational issues as an opportunity (Dutton, 1993; Isen, Nygen, &
Ashby, 1988; Weick, 1979). Especially in global situations, where there is
often a plurality of voices vying for the right to "reality," for their views to be
accepted as legitimate expressions of the true and the good, it appears that the
power of appreciation is considerable. In this case, we observed that where
appreciative learning is alive and diverse cultures of inquiry are connected to
another through an opportunity frame, relationships grow and metaculture
expands. Everyone, it would appear, brings to the table the desire to have an
essential voice and to be valued for the exceptional capacity that he or she has.
The constructionist leader creates an affirmational context and practice for
this to happen.

Construction Through Metaphor and Narrative Form

To be sure, the appreciative approaches—where people were actively engaged in gathering data into the strengths, potentials, achievements, and visions of the Other—did not create a rose-colored world or a wonderful utopia free from conflict. Indeed, although the vast majority of people did experience being valued, listened to, and included in substantive ways, there were other tempests in the making. One person put it like this, after a session of broad sharing of perspectives:

> There was so much, I just was overwhelmed. I had a sense of vertigo, like the bottom had fallen out. . . . I thought the whole thing would fall apart at any minute. I went into the session with my elegant and clear priorities and came out confused and restless.

This person, trained in economics and primarily concerned with issues of poverty alleviation and job creation (many mountain regions are home to the world's poorest people), had just come out of a group session with a diversity of knowledge systems represented: forestry specialists (cloud forests have been disappearing faster than lowland tropical rain forests); biodiversity researchers (mountain regions often function as sanctuaries and refuges for plants and animals that have long since disappeared from the lowlands); an indigenous spiritual adviser (prior to colonial control, most mountain societies existed for generations as earth-centered agrarian societies); and a recreational ecologist (the impacts of tourism, golf courses, and ski resorts often permanently fragment forest habitat and often lead to soil erosion from cleared areas). As one might expect, complexities among points of view and vocabularies of understanding were tremendous. Most began to experience the same sense of vertigo. Not only did each account differ, but it would appear that as people began to swim in the sea of competing intelligibilities, they began to acknowledge the validity of the Others' realities. They simultaneously became more conscious of their own limited assumptions, contextual biases, and perhaps how thin the veneer of objectivity and value neutrality really might be. For many, this reflexive turn, this sense of arbitrariness of priority and point of view, was like the ground underfoot beginning to give way unexpectedly.

It is at this stage at international meetings that there is a rush for Robert's Rules of Order, entrepreneurial brokering and negotiating, and the canonizing of the "consensus" text. Each of these—especially the rush to create the precisely termed and unambiguous text—can be read as an attempt to return to a world of certainties lost. It is here that structural leadership uses structural power to keep things moving forward. Entrepreneurial leadership, again, uses brokering and negotiating in search of compromise. And intellectual leadership returns to the persuasive clarification, reinforcement, and simplification of the substantive and compelling idea. The pattern that connects the three is the turning away from relativization and relationship, and supplying language, text, and order that quiets the chaos of plurality. Organization as metaculture is undermined. But the constructionist leader does just the opposite.

Consider these occurrences:

- The next set of meetings is not held at well-equipped hotel conference centers or UN offices but in poverty-stricken mountain regions and in Mongolian-style yurts—where every meeting and eating room is round and where the views of the mountainsides are seen everywhere in panoramic, 360-degree turns. The question is, Why?

- Breaks begin to occur at seemingly haphazard, nonscheduled times. The breaks turn into long walks on trails, or occasions for storytelling. Again, why this emergent social process?

- In the meeting, when the crucial and sensitive questions of form, structure, location, and leadership of the new organization are finally brought to deliberation, a ground rule is proposed: Subgroups should report back to the plenary only in the form of metaphors and images of organization. Each group is encouraged to return with at least five different, even contradictory, metaphors. The complexity is so high that the questions of organizational form and leadership are put to rest and are not addressed directly for 2 more days. Yet a sense of palpable hope is articulated by many. Courage is growing. And again, the question is why: Why the new ground rule, continuing the ambiguity?

- Each morning's session is preceded by some kind of outdoor game involving teamwork, connection, and cooperative discovery, planning, and action. Everyone participates.

Drawing from the examples listed above, the second vital and defining aspect of constructionist leadership can be discerned. The leader's tools are again in the form of language, in ways of talking and constructing:

The constructionist leader recognizes and knows how to use the bridging power of *metaphor and narrative form* as the single most important way of sustaining the dialogue between radically different knowledge systems. In nurturing a metaculture, the pattern of discourse is of greater significance than any particular feature of it (e.g., the overarching vision, the best analysis, the content of the text)—although each feature is valued because it contributes to the pattern of the whole. As the pattern shifts from deficit to appreciation, from negotiation to narrative, and from grand vision to multiple metaphor— hope grows and heterogeneity becomes not that which divides but that which relates.

Although the examples listed above may seem like inconsequential acts in response to the immense challenge of building systems of international cooperation, they are of great significance. The creation of an environment rich in metaphor—for example, the circular physical architecture of the Mongolian yurts coupled with the metaphoric deliberations, where all visions of organization could be expressed through metaphor—appeared to free plenary discourse from dependence on well-developed idiom and cognitive frameworks. Interestingly, differences could be expressed at levels of abstraction that augmented rather than destroyed the widening circle of dialogue; in fact, differences were often expressed not by challenging the conclusions of a discipline but by questioning the aesthetic design of the metaphor and by creating contrast and perspective through the use of countermetaphors. All of this invited participatory engagement: Multiple interpretation made the "exercises" more interesting, and because there was nothing to be decided, there was room for great improvisation on the spot. Interestingly, not one of the metaphors had any linkage to familiar international organization terms or images. Conspicuously absent were hierarchies, secretariats, centralized authority structures, and so on. A sense of unanimity was discovered—about that which the group did not want. Later, one of the participants spoke about the metaphoric impact of meeting in the Mongolian yurts:

> The place created a seating space of equality. You had no head of the room. . . . Wherever we went, while eating, while meeting, while taking breaks, we were always in circular relation to one another. Outsiders came in and reported that they could not tell who the leaders of the meeting were, or who were the funders or scientists, and the doers. . . . The Mountain Forum would not have been born if we were in the boxed-in architecture of a Hyatt-Regency.

It was no accident that the environment created multiple metaphors as opposed to single vision, and that just at the time that reflexive doubt and uncertainties soared, there was abandonment of negotiation as the relational form and a move toward narration—the opting for storytelling over debate.

For example, one morning, before beginning the meeting, group members are asked to share stories from their own local traditions and cultures about community rituals, prayers of thanksgiving, events, and sources of wisdom concerning the fall harvest. People are moved to laughter and tears, and not incidentally, every parable had a message related to the task at hand. All had to do with successful "barn-building" processes, of communities coming together in sharing and caring ways for the good of the whole. Although much has been written in recent years about the narrative structure of organizational life (Weick, 1995), very little attention has been paid to the deliberate use of "narrative inquiry" (Ludema, 1996) as a way of bridging diverse cultures of inquiry. In Ludema's (1996) pathbreaking work, narrative inquiries have exhibited eight characteristics that imbue them with the power to unleash hope, create new knowledge, and empower collaborative action: They impart intergenerational wisdom, affirm varieties of experience and encourage full voice, foster relational connections, convey holistic knowledge, establish perceptual and contextual frame, provide presumptions of logic, transmit a system of values, and extend hopeful visions of possibility. The task of narrative inquiry, concludes Ludema (1996),

> is to provide a space in which organizational members can come together in full voice to share their most inspiring stories, build strong relational bonds, create a compelling moral vision of a desired future, and then support each other in creating a world of vital human significance and hope. (p. 196)

In a speech at a scientific meeting on the mountain ecologies, one of the Mountain Forum leaders was telling of the vision of the newly forming entity. She ended the speech with an apt Romanian proverb: "Stories have wings, and they fly from mountain to mountain top."

For the constructionist leader, no constructive purpose is served by running away from the impact or dislodgment of certainty that is (in counter-intuitive ways) accelerated through appreciative processes of interchange in global groups. From the perspective of building a metaculture of inquiry, the moment of mounting chaos can be the wildest life-giving engagement of all. The delicate challenge is to find sanctuary from destructive chaos—where alternative modes are immediately dismissed, suppressed, or totally divorced from one another—and to move toward transformational dialogue, where ambiguity is embraced and the commingling of vocabularies continues as long as possible without having to press for token consensus. The winds of confusion are not eliminated by the constructionist leader: They are actually sought after, valued, built up, and concentrated through the use of metaphor and narrative inquiry—much like a sail is used to gather and hold the force of the gale. The longer the winds can be held in the space of the sail, the more dynamic and alive the sailboat ride becomes. The seemingly inevitable breaking point of global meetings does not, as a result, occasion return to the dungeon of the text, rules of order, or the glossing of differences through structural or compromise activities. Indeed, at the very time the circumscribed conclusions of the disciplines are rendered vulnerable, they are opened to extension, elaboration, and enrichment. Opened wide is an enormous world of long-term potential and alternatives. Embryonic is a relational system capable not just of transfer of knowledge but the co-generation of something emergent.

The Web of Inclusion

The Mountain Forum has emerged as an innovative face-to-face *and* electronic network of networks between diverse nongovernmental, governmental, intergovernmental, scientific, and private-sector organizations and individuals. Its purpose is to serve people all over the world who want to do advocacy work and take action on behalf of the Mountain Agenda.

As a global network, the Mountain Forum's design is the least structured organization form that can be said to have any structure at all. Like other networks, the Mountain Forum has been constructed through design that is marked by (a) the absence of centralized structure, (b) the autonomous nature of subunits, (c) high connectivity between subunits, and (d) the "webby" nonlinear causality of peers influencing peers. Like other networks, it is designed for supreme adaptability and change: It is boundless in terms of potential membership; it is highly resilient; and like the grand network known as the Internet, it is noncontrollable. It is a system where there is no authority in charge to supervise emergent communications or collaboratively conceived projects (perhaps in the millions over the years). The leadership does its work by nurturing a metaculture of inquiry and endlessly opening the boundaries of membership by working with the web of inclusion.[2] One person tried to put words to the process:

> I think this nurturing style is a very feminine style of leadership. And I think
> it would have been harder for many of the senior men to accept both the small
> group process and the group responsibility coming from a man. They are all

strong—many of them come out of command-and-control hierarchical systems and had been spending years butting their heads together like a bunch
of mountain rams! [Laughter] . . . But this is not well-suited for the work we
needed to do. So we invented a different way. . . . And it's really not managing
pieces—it is facilitating, empowering, activating—but the more you get into
the language, the hokier it sounds, frankly, . . . to use language that is soft and
connected—you know, how could you have the "nurturing node"?

In terms of a process, the web of inclusion was constructed in several
ways: (a) through the articulation of operational values: "the Mountain Forum
is open, democratic, decentralized, accessible, transparent, accountable, and
flexible"; (b) through temporary and facilitative leadership groups (e.g., 2-
year service on the "interim facilitating committee"—note the special care to
resist terms such as "central," "secretariat," or "chairperson"); (c) through a
state-of-the-art development of an out-of-control information network; and
(d) a completely open membership pulsating across sectoral lines, nation-state
lines, and system-level lines—that is, memberships of individuals, organizations, communities, regional associations, nation-states, international bodies
such as the UN, and others. Most important, however, is how the web of
inclusion can be framed in knowledge or epistemic terms—as the coevolu-
tionary meeting ground between global and local systems of knowledge. What
was needed, argued one of the leaders, is a global-local interdiscourse or
knowledge alliance:

There is a corresponding need for interdisciplinary approaches to sustainable
mountain development. . . . The cultural expressions of mountain peoples
should be recovered and fostered. In this context, protecting indigenous
peoples' interests, including their knowledge, should be an integral part of
efforts toward sustainable development . . . through research, database development, pilot projects, information exchanges, and in-country training of
scientists and technical experts and local natural resource managers.

At a more theoretical level, the Russian literary theorist Mikahail Bakhtin
(1981) has introduced the term *heteroglossia,* referring to the fact that the
languages of knowing of any culture of inquiry are a polyglot. Essentially,
there are no thoroughbred languages or cultures of inquiry. However, as
Gergen (1995) argues, Bakhtin's concept of heteroglossia may be properly
reconstituted as dimension. That is, we can view subcultures as varying in the
degree to which they incorporate and supplement the languages of surrounding disciplines and cultures of inquiry. Relevant to the leadership stance of

organizing *through* an ever-expanding web of inclusion, one can propose that organizational forms acting to increase internal heteroglossia, up to a point, are those most capable of surviving in a global, postmodern society. For the constructionist leader, the world of organization and global cooperation is a world not of knowledge per se but of interknowing—rationality, wisdom, and new knowledge are preeminently products not so much of method but of social collaboration. In this sense, organization might properly be conceived of as a method of knowing.

> The constructionist leader makes this wager: The wider the web of inclusion, the better the emerging organization will be able to generate the knowledge needed to address the global agenda. Because the web of inclusion is inherently open-ended, every moment of insight can give way to further exploration, expanding outward from the initial organizing group to the ever-expansive domain of relatedness.

CONCLUSION: A CALL FOR FUTURE RESEARCH

In summary, we propose adding a fourth type to Young's stated structural, entrepreneurial, and intellectual leadership. We believe this fourth type, which we have called *constructionist,* is particularly relevant in global regime formation, where multiple voices, perspectives, and truths are involved and the complexities of organizing are most unfathomable.

Many people perceive mountains as powerful symbols of pristine wilderness and natural strength. But these perceptions belie the vulnerabilities of mountain environments: All over the world, expanding economic pressures are degrading mountain ecosystems while confronting mountain peoples with increasing cultural assimilation, poverty, and political disempowerment. In this chapter, we have traced the human response to the growing global agenda for change in relation to the world's precious mountain environments, beginning with the global regime formation associated with Chapter 13 of Agenda 21 at the 1992 Earth Summit and resulting in the construction of a new worldwide organization, the Mountain Forum. In particular, the study built on the regime formation literature surrounding the three widely acknowledged leadership types—structural, entrepreneurial, and intellectual—and proposes constructionist leadership as a fourth complementary, but missing, leadership type. Through grounded theory analysis of this unique and successful global change organizing effort, themes have been developed about a kind of leadership that enables productive connections, at the deepest levels of belief and method, among paradigms or cultures of inquiry. Helping to expand our understanding of the organizational dimensions of global change, this chapter concludes that the most challenging task in global regime formation and organizational development is the bridging of diverse systems of intelligibility, allowing for the establishment of a worldwide metaculture of knowing.

NOTES

1. Use of the term *constructionist* or *constructing* is deliberate, as opposed to meaning-making leadership (Morgan, 1986) or sensemaking (Srivastva & Associates, 1983; Weick, 1995). As Dutton (1993) points out, the term emphasizes the effort that individuals exert to craft or portray an organizational inquiry in a certain way. Following Webster's dictionary as well, construction is defined as the process of building, devising, or forming. The idea that organizational issues are constructed rather than passively perceived by people emphasizes the active component involved in enacting the environments we then react to as "objective" (see Weick, 1979, for an analysis of the "enactment of limitations" phenomenon in organizations). Finally, the word *constructionist* usefully links this conceptualization to the important epistemological work of Gergen's (1994) social construction of reality.

2. The term *web of inclusion* was first proposed by Sally Helgesen (1990) in her book *The Female Advantage*. In her later book, Helgesen (1994) moves beyond gender and discovers that web leadership, female or male, involves five strategies: Webs operate by means of open communications across levels, blur distinctions between conception and execution, create lasting networks that redistribute power constantly, embrace the outside world, and serve as a vehicle for constant reorganization. In our study, the term is used to help understand the knowledge linking process we have discussed as building a metaculture of inquiry.

4

NOT ON OUR WATCH

The Biodiversity Crisis and Global Collaboration Response

FRANCES WESTLEY

This chapter concerns a particular kind of crisis and the human and organizational capacities best designed to address it. The focus is on a network of scientists and managers centrally preoccupied with the problem of conserving endangered species. This group, all members of the Conservation Breeding Specialist Group, a nongovernmental organization (NGO) based in Minnesota, forms an international network working separately and together to fight the ever-increasing speed of extinctions threatening biodiversity on this planet. As such, they represent an example of a new form of organization, the global social change organization (GSCO).

This chapter will explore a number of theoretical questions. The first is the nature of the crisis. What is the impact of ecological crisis and change on individuals? Is it the same or different from other forms of crisis from the point of view of human response?

Second, what motivates and enables individuals involved in confronting this crisis to work effectively and with commitment? What are the elements of the social organization that facilitate or block their efforts?

Finally, this chapter will tell a story of a particular kind of dedication and motivation. In doing so, it will raise the question of what kinds of satisfactions and rewards are offered by GSCOs and to what extent they differ from those found in more traditional organizations.

The Biodiversity Crisis

One of the most critical issues confronting the globe today is the rapid extinction of species. The loss of biodiversity has profound implications for our societies: economic, psychological, aesthetic, moral, and biological. To stem this tide, however, demands profound changes in the way in which we organize at a global level.

A NEW SPECIES OF TROUBLE

A chronic disaster is one that gathers force slowly and insidiously, creeping around one's defenses rather than smashing through them. People are unable to mobilize their normal defenses against the threat, sometimes because they have elected consciously or unconsciously to ignore it, sometimes because they have been misinformed about it, and sometimes because they cannot do anything to avoid it anyway (Erikson, 1994, p. 21).

In a recent book, titled *A New Species of Trouble,* Kai Erikson describes what he sees as an increasingly common occurrence of the modern world, disasters that, instead of stemming from acts of God, are the result of human choices and activities, the side effects of our technologies and our relentless quest to control the world and its resources to our own ends. Erikson suggests that these disasters are different from many that communities have dealt with through history because (a) they are chronic and insidious rather than acute and dramatic; (b) they are of our own making; and (c) they often include toxins that seem to permeate the very ground of being, rendering the environment that surrounds us, and of which we are a part, "defiled and unreliable" (Erikson, 1994, p. 155).

Such disasters are a new species of trouble because humans seem to be constitutionally poorly equipped to handle them. The dread that such disasters evoke seems out of proportion to the real danger. It appears to grow with time instead of resolving itself. It has the capacity to make people feel demoralized and helpless, traumatized in a peculiarly inaccessible way. It rends the very fabric of community in a way not easily repaired.

Erikson amasses data from a whole series of such disasters, from the nuclear leak at Three Mile Island to the mercury contamination of Grassy Narrows. He notes that these disasters, unlike classic tragedies, had no beginning, middle, and end. Because they are perceived to be caused by humans, those who are affected feel the need to attribute blame. Blame, however, is often diffuse and difficult to pin down, especially if there is no one company responsible for the problem. And the end of the story is even more difficult to formulate in an intelligible way, because we have, as yet, little understanding of the ultimate effects of such disasters, and those affected wait, seemingly endlessly, to see what the costs will be. This is what gives such disasters their chronic quality, as well as an aspect of the severe trauma that those affected experience.

In addition, Erikson seems to indicate that the dread that individuals experience in such situations is disproportionate to the real danger. He suggests that this dread may have a primal quality, as something "naturally loathsome, inherently insidious—a horror, like poison gas, that draws on something deeper in the human mind" (Erikson, 1994, p. 147). Erikson himself hesitates to push this further, arguing that it is "odd conceptual terrain for a sociologist to be wandering around in" (p. 147). He argues, however, that it has something to do with the sense that "poisons are now lodged in the tissues of the body, and that the surrounding countryside is contaminated as well, that the whole natural envelope in which people live out their lives has become defiled and unreliable . . . 'dead ground'" (p. 155). This is put in mythic terms by the elders of the Indian tribe of Grassy Narrows, who feel that a land that had once been good, a "land that would give people strength," has been taken over by bad spirits:

> We call it "pijibowin." This is the Ojibwa word for poison. You can't see it or smell it, you can't taste it or feel it, but you know it's there. You know it can hurt you, make your limbs go numb, make your spirit sick. But I don't understand how the land can turn against us. (p. 39)

Erikson's comment on the above quote was that he felt that the use of the term "poison" by the elder was symbolic as well as literal. It referred to the mercury that had literally poisoned their bodies, and it referred to "a pervasive fear that the world of nature and the world of human beings can no longer be relied on in the old way." This fear, and the numbness, apathy, and alienation that the elder described, Erikson argues, are characteristic of all chronic disasters, whether or not they include "real" poisoning.

Whereas Erikson may feel that such primal dreads are uncertain grounds for sociologists to tread, E. O. Wilson, biologist and father of sociobiology, has no such difficulty. In his recent work, Wilson (1984) has increasingly championed the idea of biophylia, which he defines as "the innate tendency of humans to focus on life and lifelike processes" (p. 122). Wilson argues that although many have noted the potential economic, social, aesthetic, and even moral costs of the destruction of biodiversity, little has been said about the biological costs for human beings. Since primitive times, Wilson notes, humans have built on their innate, genetically programmed responses to the natural world to construct a rich human symbolism of language and art. It is still the natural world, not the world of machines, that provokes the most primitive, irrational emotions, whether of dread or pleasure. For example, take the universal response of dread that snakes evoke and that has caused them to figure so centrally in human myths and images cross-culturally. This dread exceeds the dread of cars; in urbanites, it is therefore irrational but peculiarly hard to eradicate. Wilson argues not so much that it is instinctive (i.e., inbred), because it is a fear that grows with age in humans as well as in primates. But the tendency to be particularly stimulated, both to pleasure and to fear, by certain kinds of natural stimuli is innate:

> How could it be otherwise? The brain evolved into its present form over a period of about two million years. . . . Snakes mattered. The smell of water, the hum of a bee, the directional bend of a plant stalk mattered. . . . And a sweet sense of horror, the shivery fascination with monsters and creeping forms that so delights us today, even in the sterile hearts of the cities, could see you through to the next morning. Organisms are the natural stuff of metaphor and ritual. Although the evidence is far from in, the brain appears to have kept its old capacities, its channelled quickness. We stay alert and alive in the vanished forests of the world. (Wilson, 1984, p. 100)

Increasingly, Wilson argues, he has been convinced of the fact that much of what we perceive as aesthetic, as well as much of what motivates us to explore, innovate, and invent, is grounded in our biological relationship to other species. In fact, we have been programmed for diversity and for survival within that diversity. From the diversity itself comes our excitement with exploration, our restless pursuit of variety, our imaginative capacities. From our need to survive comes our preference for certain kinds of landscapes (high, with sweeping vistas, by water: the choice of dwelling for those free to exercise a choice); for certain colors and shapes (which stimulate reproductive urges); and our desire to control the natural world. Both the need for variety and the need for control and safety are programmed in our genes, argues Wilson. But the modern human lives in a world that has been too successfully controlled, and the subsequent reduction in variety threatens not only other species, but our own as well:

> The brain is prone to weave the mind from the evidences of life, not merely to minimal contact required to exist, but a luxuriance and excess spilling into virtually everything we do. People can grow up with the outward appearance of normality in an environment largely stripped of plants and animals, in the same way that passable looking monkeys can be raised in laboratory cages and cattle fattened in feeding bins. Asked if they were happy, these people would probably say yes. Yet something vitally important would be missing, not merely the knowledge and pleasure that can be imagined and might have been, but a wide array of experiences that the human brain is peculiarly equipped to receive. (Wilson, 1984, p. 118)

Taken together, Erikson's notion of a new species of trouble and Wilson's theory of biophylia suggest that a healthy environment, one with natural biodiversity, is more closely linked to psychological health than we had thought previously. It is not merely economic gains or aesthetic satisfactions that we lose when we contaminate or destroy that environment. We risk evoking lingering feelings of dread, trauma, alienation, and/or numbness when we tamper either deliberately or accidentally with the fundamental balance of nature. As human beings, we have the capacity to compensate, to overcome such feelings, but their primitive and enduring potential should not be underestimated.

RESPONSES TO THE CRISIS

> What event likely to happen during the next few years will our descendants most regret? Everyone agrees, defense ministers and environmentalists alike, that the worst thing possible is global nuclear war. If it occurs the entire human species is endangered; life as normal human species wish to live it would come to an end. With that terrible truism acknowledged, it must be added that if no country pulls the trigger the worst thing that will probably happen—in fact is already well underway—is not energy depletion, economic collapse, conventional war, or even the expansion of totalitarian governments. As tragic as these catastrophes would be for us, they can be repaired within a few generations. The one process going on that will take millions of years to correct is the loss of genetic and species diversity by the destruction of natural

habitats. This is the folly our descendants are least likely to forgive us.
(Wilson, 1984, p. 121)

The rapid disappearance of biological species, and the resulting reduction
in biodiversity, is an example of the kind of chronic disaster that Erikson
described. It is happening rapidly, and it is changing our environment forever.
Wilson argues that of all the crises facing the modern world, this is the worst:
"This is the folly our descendants are least likely to forgive us." Species are
disappearing at a truly alarming rate. Some say as many as 24 species are
disappearing every day, more than 10,000 species per year (Wilson, 1984,
p. 122).

For many urban dwellers, however, it is a crisis about which we only hear.
We still consider ourselves unaffected and may be only dimly aware of the
psychological trauma that Wilson described of living in an increasingly
uniform and "dead" environment. For those whose livelihood, profession, or
love is centered on animals, however, the experience of chronic disaster
associated with species extinction is real and oppressive. The North American
Indians were deeply affected by the disappearance of the buffalo; today, the
fishers of the eastern seaboard have watched their source of livelihood dry up
almost overnight, the seemingly inexhaustible bounty of the sea unaccount-
ably exhausted. And those whose career and passion is the study or care of
animals (zoologists, biologists, naturalists) mourn the passing of species with
the same sense of inestimable loss:

The tropical rain forest . . . is being clear-cut from the edge inward. It is being
lifted up from the ground entire like a carpet rolled off a bare floor, leaving
behind vast stretches of cattle range and cropland that need artificial fertilization to sustain even marginal productivity. . . . Tens and thousands of
species have been scraped away as by a giant hand and will not be seen in
that place for generations, if ever. The action can be defended (with difficulty)
on economic grounds, but it is like burning a Renaissance painting to cook
dinner. (Wilson, 1984, p. 25)

In addition, observers speak with some despair of the possibility of
stemming the tide of extinctions. The complexity of the problem, the numbers
of human actors (individuals and organizations) required to solve the problem,
and the deeply rooted nature of the desire and need to exploit nature for
economic gain all seem to argue against hope for the future.

However, a small but effective group of individuals has responded to this chronic disaster not with hopelessness but with action. The Conservation Breeding Specialist Group, based in Minneapolis, Minnesota, is not only an excellent example of a global organization for social change, but an interesting exception to Erikson's profile of community reaction to an insidious, chronic environmental disaster. Instead of responding with numbness and alienation, they have responded with unprecedented energy.

A New Species of Solution:
The Conservation Breeding Specialist Group

The Conservation Breeding Specialist Group (CBSG) is a subcommittee of the Swiss-based International Union for the Conservation of Nature (IUCN). The IUCN had established a series of taxon-based specialist groups to act as advisory groups regarding the status of particular taxons in the wild. CBSG was formed initially to act as a liaison between these groups and the captive breeding community (represented by zoos worldwide, but most particularly in England and North America). It remained largely inactive, however, until Ulysses Seal was appointed chairman in 1979.

Dr. Ulysses Seal came at the problem of endangered species and the conservation of biodiversity from a rather unusual angle. He was trained initially in psychology (BA and MA), then switched fields, and in 1957, he received his PhD in biochemistry. Seal had always had a personal interest in animals, and his research led him to seek out the zoos as sources of blood samples of exotic species with which to work. In exchange, he helped them develop more effective immobilization drugs to facilitate sampling. In the process, Seal championed a scientific "medical" approach to the management of zoo animals, an approach he found sorely lacking in the management of zoo collections.

> What I did in the course of time I spent with [zoo people] was to hear about problems. These guys would all tell me: "Here's a problem. Here's something we don't know, here's something we can't do." Wherever I thought I could bring to bear what I knew about human medicine, I did. At one time I had over thirty projects going with field people on a variety of species all over North America.

Seal carried this approach of applying knowledge across disciplines and of entrepreneurial action to solve the problems he identified in his role as chairman of CBSG. His work with captive animals made him aware of the need to genetically manage small populations if the endangered species were to survive. Seal recognized that to solve this problem, an intensification of the kind and quality of information available about individual animals was needed, as well as far greater collaboration between the individuals and organizations where the information was "stored."

Upon taking over the leadership of CBSG, Seal took on the challenge. In the early years, he worked largely alone. Until 1990, CBSG was a one-man operation, staffed by Seal himself on a part-time basis. In that year, an executive officer was hired, and then a secretary in 1991. By 1995, the staff had grown to three program officers and three office staff, with Seal, having retired from his research position at the Veterans Administration Hospital in Minneapolis, devoting himself full-time to CBSG activities.

Funding, like staffing, has always been low. The group is supported by donations from its members, which are largely zoos. Beginning with 15 members in 1984, CBSG now has a formal membership of 653 from 150 countries; 140 members are donor institutions and organizations. From this donor base, CBSG works with an operating budget of $300,000 per year.

In the 1993 *Futures Search Report,* drafted by a group of staff, board members, and interested stakeholders, the first highly valued characteristic of CBSG was summarized as follows:

> One of the primary qualities identified was the priority that CBSG places on the exchange and sharing of information, with free dissemination of products and data. CBSG's communication network was seen as critical—keeping members and constituents up-to-date on technology and new programs. Its facilitation of problem-identification and problem-solving, as well as being a forum for discussion of global conservation issues are highly valued. Its ability to facilitate mutual problem-solving by people with diverse interests is appreciated, and was identified as the foundation upon which most, if not all, the workshop successes are based. (CBSG, 1993, p. 34)

This quote summarizes well the interesting organizational aspects of CBSG. It is a far-flung network, held together by modern communication technology. In the 16 years that Seal has been chair, it has developed a set of processes and products upon which it relies to facilitate the identification, discussion, and resolution of extinction crises. CBSG has been described as "an endangered species fire brigade which careens from crisis to crisis with state-of-the-science advice on the emergency moves best calculated to avert calamity" (Alvarez, 1994, p. 356). The small staff of the Minneapolis office can act only as a catalyst and an adviser. The actual saving of the species is in the hands of the approximately 5,000 to 6,000 people who have participated in the initiatives.

This group of people (which CBSG refers to as the "network") may be further divided into peripheral and core members. Peripheral members are those who may have participated in a CBSG workshop (some 3,000 participated in Population and Habitat Viability Assessment [PHVA] workshops in 1994), who may be on the CBSG mailing list for the quarterly newsletter (circulation: 7,000 in 170 countries), or may be a member whose support is largely financial but who attends CBSG annual meetings (653 individual members). In addition, there is a "core" group of 100 to 200 people. These people have been identified by Seal as primary resources, and they donate their time, energy, and expertise repeatedly for CBSG workshops, consultations, or the design of new initiatives. These core representatives come from all levels of hierarchy and all parts of the world; they are recruited by Seal at workshops or meetings, brought there because of their reputation, or else they themselves seek out CBSG because of their own convictions. For the most part, these individuals have full-time jobs as researchers, zoo employees, or government officials. Yet they give extensive hours, indeed, weeks of free time, sometimes with the support of their home organizations, to make the products and processes of CBSG successful.

The network is "convened" only rarely and incompletely. CBSG has an annual meeting each year at which 200 to 300 members meet. Most important, however, the network members are called in on workshops on endangered species. These include Population and Viability Assessment (PHVA) Workshops, where members act as facilitators and experts in multistakeholder meetings to determine how to manage threatened species all over the world. The workshop process was designed to help maximize the good scientific analysis of the current status of endangered species.

It is a process in which conflict management and cross-cultural management are crucial skills. PHVAs seem designed to maximize conflict; an organizer or facilitator must be adept at handling such dynamics. Most members of the core group of CBSG have received no formal training in facilitation or management skills; they are scientists by training. The amount of effort, on both a professional and personal basis, required to participate in these exercises is phenomenal. To organize one of these exercises can take up to a year, and even to participate in one takes up to a week (including preparation and travel time). It is time fraught with setbacks and frustrations as well as gratifications. The work is intense, demanding, and emotionally draining.

And yet a large group of dedicated professionals has given its time, often on a voluntary basis, to make these exercises a success. And considering the complex and nearly hopeless proportions of the task, CBSG has had some astounding success. The volume has been enormous. In 1994 alone, the "node" conducted or participated in 63 workshops, prepared 96 workshop reports and similar documents, and responded directly to more than 3,200 queries from people in 120 countries. More important, to date, some 20 species have been temporarily "saved" by captive breeding programs in which the information from the International Species Inventory System and the collaborative processes of Species Survival Programs have played an important role (Tudge, 1991, p. 29). The PHVA and Conservation Assessment Management Plan processes can be credited with helping some 40 other species. The sheer (and ever-increasing) volume of these workshops qualifies as a measure of the initiative's ability to convene stakeholders. Anecdotal testimonials support this assumption. For example, one CBSG member working in India stated at the close of a recent workshop that "PHVAs had become one of the most important tools in assessing wildlife conservation in our country" and that "PHVAs are now considered an integral part of the management scenario." In addition, a U.S. commentator involved in the almost certainly doomed struggle to save the Florida panther summarized succinctly, if pessimistically, "Without the CBSG, there would be no movement at all." No stakeholder group has been credited with doing more to organize the domain in the interests of constructive action.

How, then, does CBSG work, on the level of process and in terms of the motivations of individuals who give of their time and energy, often voluntarily and also surprisingly tirelessly? These individuals are waging an almost hopeless battle, truly a chronic disaster, in Erikson's terms, with very limited means. Why do they persist? The work keeps them long days, weeks, sometimes months from home and family and friends. What keeps them going? Why do they not succumb to the apathy, numbness, and alienation described by Erikson?

In an effort to understand the motivations, we sent a query to 47 core members of the CBSG network, those who were identified by Seal as having participated in numerous CBSG processes over time and as being a group that could consistently be relied upon to give of their time and energy. Thirty-seven of these (83%) responded in writing, at length and in very moving terms. In addition, we interviewed the CBSG staff and several key individuals closely associated with the office. This combined database provides a surprisingly clear picture of both the degree to which CBSG core members view the current situation as a chronic disaster and the emotional, intellectual, and moral reasons they have for continuing the effort.

"Not on Our Watch": Motivations and Misgivings

Because most battles are being lost at the ecosystem, landscape, and species levels, this is discouraging and gloomy stuff. A steady diet of the gloom is depressing. Aldo Leopold said that one of the costs of being an ecologist was that everywhere you look, you see only wounds.

It must first be noted that while many in the CBSG network describe themselves as inherently optimistic, they are nevertheless acutely aware of the grave and hopeless nature of the problem with which they are struggling. This paradox is present in many of their statements.

Fundamental to all the efforts—so much so that it can probably be taken as a given—is an urgent and critical need to change the relationship that people have with the rest of the natural world—both for our sake and for the sake of the health of the rest of the biota. As one respondent said,

> I am discouraged about the likely status of the world—the standard of living for people and all other organisms (what's left anyway)—in future decades and centuries. In fact, this is one reason that I would not want to bring offspring into the world. . . . I'm not confident that we are leaving the world in very good shape for the future.

The above quote renders very personal the sense of desolation. In this respondent's view, the world is unlikely to be a fit place for offspring—as soon as a generation or so into the future. Although this view may strike the reader as doom and gloom, reflect that it is not the viewpoint of a defeatist, rather of one of the key members of the CBSG whose efforts for conservation can be (with no exaggeration) deemed tireless. One respondent described the discrepancy between effort and possible success as reflecting a "kind of craziness." Others referred to it as blind determination:

> We are in a crisis and we must succeed, but I am not optimistic that—in the broad sense—we will. In part, I think that my perspective is that we will almost certainly fail, but we cannot not try to change the course of things. It

is as if you are lost in a snowstorm, and sense that you are almost certainly going to die—you still try to get through it and survive.

On a more mundane level, it is not unusual to hear complaints from CBSG network members about the tremendous pace set by Seal and the difficulty in coping with the demands of a seemingly endless problem. The staff in the CBSG headquarters often struggles with exhaustion and potential burnout. As one network member said:

> At times, the staff simply can't keep up with the workload. I have seen them in tears, frazzled beyond words. When Ulie is away he sends them a fax a day, with 3000 new things to do and they are still working on last week's. They never get a break, it is unremitting. I know they feel extraordinarily proud and honoured to be part of something so important, but they sometimes just can't handle the frenetic pace, and the fact that it never ends.

For the volunteers who are part of the far-flung but active network of CBSG, the problem is somewhat different. They, too, confront the fact that the ambitions of CBSG seem to expand to exhaust all available time and energy. It is hard to draw lines around global challenges of this nature.

> It is not that I wish all this would go away, but working with CBSG is like opening the shallow top drawer of a bureau. You are invited to make a contribution, you make it and then you discover, that the real problem lies in the deep second drawer, and you get through that and discover yet a deeper drawer. This keeps exploding in more and more indepth reviews and pretty soon you are talking to people all over the world, and it is never finished. It is exciting, but never ending. You go into one project and if you've got your eyes open you know it isn't enough by the time you're done. It's frustrating. And it consumes the volunteers. After all, they have the rest of their lives, their jobs, their families. There are just not enough hours in the day. It would be nice if you could say it was done, but it never is.

In addition, network members sometimes find the work lonely. This may be an impediment that is poorly documented in networks in general. To the extent that motivation is, at least in part, a social construction, it is sometimes hard to keep motivation high in the long stretches between contact with other, like-minded individuals:

When you are sitting in rainy California and it is eight o'clock at night and you're trying to put together some data and you haven't talked to anyone in five months because Ulie hasn't been there and pretty soon you give up and turn on the TV or go to bed. It's a unique situation as people are spread all over the world. And when it comes to these bigger products, the global action plans, etc. really need his input. I was sorry to see Tom go, not because he was Tom, but because if you couldn't get hold of Ulie you could always get hold of Tom. And we need a few more warm bodies that you could contact.

Despite the loneliness, the ever-expanding expectations, the pressures and the exhaustion, members of the CBSG network gave a rich description of the motivations that informed their efforts. These motivations turned out to span the gamut from emotional and visceral, to intellectual and professional, to moral and spiritual. Analysis of their extensive and often moving statements revealed five distinct themes:

1. The emotional impact of working with animals
2. The satisfaction of working with others in the CBSG network
3. The sheer love of the work itself
4. An intense excitement with the CBSG approach
5. A profound sense of duty and responsibility

Because each of these contributes to the overall picture of motivation, they will be discussed in the text that follows.

The Emotional Impact of Working With Animals

In many of his books, Wilson describes how his love of insects, snakes, and the natural world informed his life for as long as he could remember. This would appear to be true for many of the biologists and zoologists who work for CBSG as well. As one respondent noted,

Most people such as botanists, entomologists, horticulturists and zoologists find a real joy in working with living things. They are not working just for a financial return. This is often manifest through a very deep affinity with living things of a particular taxon, or with a particular organism. The sense of responsibility is strong. We are trusted with that particular organism, it requires our attention. There is a deep fear of loss, therefore, not just a "management failure," but a personal loss.

An interesting element of this statement is the degree to which the attachment to the animal world begins with the particular and moves to the general. Members of CBSG (and probably all naturalists) joke about having a particular totem animal or plant. Although it is not universally true, many "specialize," focusing their particular sense of responsibility on a particular organism. As the speaker just quoted notes, the sense of affinity is deep, the sense of being entrusted is the equivalent of the sense of being entrusted that we express about the people we love; the threat is tangible and highly personal. It is also deeply visceral, in a sense that seems to support Wilson's notion of the innate biophyliac tendencies of humans:

> I love the animals and nature. The research is exciting. Personally, I think I do it for my own pleasure. Field work is very exciting for me, because I'm very close with the deer and when a deer looks me in the eyes, I surprise myself with the deep happiness I feel. I feel hopeless when I find a dead animal, angry and worried if I notice habitat alteration and I feel discouraged when I think that at this moment, I can do nothing to change the situation.

This claim to working for "my own pleasure" is a reflection of the strong emotional/visceral sense of connection to animals. As another respondent said,

> Perhaps it is also altruism, the survival of future generations on this planet that drives me. However, its [sic] probably more accurately selfishness. I love wildlife and wild places. I am moved emotionally when I see the vast herds of wildebeest on the Serengeti or a single butterfly landing in my garden to sip nectar or lay eggs.

This intense love of other species, which Wilson describes so well and which makes altruism feel selfish and hard, and hopeless work feel like self-indulgence ("for my own pleasure"), is noteworthy. In addition, it is at times supported by early childhood experiences of family or friends who simply "took the world seriously," as one interviewee noted. This was not necessarily only the world of nature; it was just a view that the world had value, both emotionally and intellectually, apart from an environment for the self. It deserved to be cared for, in its own right. One respondent whose father felt an affinity for the disappearing breeds of domestic livestock in England tells of the following "shaping" incident:

My father's passion was the conservation of old English breeds of domestic livestock. So my childhood was spent travelling around collecting individuals from the last herds/flocks in the U.K. Many of these were maintained by old farmers who were having to break up bloodlines maintained for generations. On one occasion I was taken out of school by my father to see the last pure bred Norfolk Horn ram before he died. I was collected from school that evening, the next morning the breed was extinct. The sense of loss was very tangible.

These respondents, therefore, do seem motivated to struggle against overwhelming odds because of what they see as an affinity to the animals that are disappearing, an affinity that is fundamental to their own identities at a visceral level. So, although Wilson's theory might seem to support Erikson's in that fundamental disturbances in the natural environment are a new species of trouble that undermines people's relationship to themselves and their environment, it would appear that, for some, that sense of connection is also the source of an (unreasoning) determination to work to rectify the situation, to *not* give in to the sense of hopelessness that Erikson describes. However, there are other motivations at work here as well.

The Satisfaction of Working With Others in the CBSG Network

One of the interesting things about the CBSG global network that may, in fact, be characteristic of all well-functioning networks but has not, I believe, been well documented in the literature to date is that the network acts as an important reference group for members.

Reference groups is a term used to connote informal groupings that are important identity-creating and -maintaining units for the focal individual. Generally more complex than friendship groups, in that they are not only important social but also professional reference points, they represent important resocializing forces for adults and can act as important emotional alternatives to families, as well as offer new ego ideals and identities to adherents.

Most of the discussion on reference groups, however, suggests that a certain amount of fairly intensive contact is a necessary condition. In the past, this meant that global reference groups were fairly rare. However, changes in communication technology (without which an organization such as CBSG could not exist at all) have expanded the affective as well as instrumental possibilities of global networks.

Although physical contact might be severely limited, telephone, fax, and especially e-mail allowed for an intimacy and a regularity of exchange. "While I may not see them often," one interviewee noted, "these are some of my best friends." This reference group aspect of CBSG represents an important motivation for adherents, energizing them to work seemingly endlessly and against the odds:

> I have enjoyed the interaction (and cultural learning) associated with all the terrific people that participate in CBSG activities. For whatever reason, there are some really nice and intensely dedicated people working in conservation. They certainly are not doing it for the money. Perhaps it is a mothering instinct within all of us, a drive to preserve what is close to us. In any case, the horrific decline in habitat makes all of us want to work together, and the commonality in interest/commitment spins us to an extended family-like relationship, friendships that likely will last for a lifetime. That in itself is a pretty good reason to work with CBSG.

In this quote, the elements of friendship, family, admiration, and common purpose are all clustered to suggest that the emotional affiliation with other humans is as important as the emotional affiliation with animals mentioned in the first theme. Somehow, the sense of community acts as a bulwark against the horror of the problem; the two are often mentioned in the same breath. Others in the network are referred to almost as comrades in arms:

> On the other hand, getting to know people from all over, with whom you share some fundamental value, is a great reward. Learning to work with them in some way, where cooperation is the theme, is equally rewarding. And, no matter how small, there is a sense of making a contribution, and engaging in a fight that is truly historical.

In particular, several of the leaders, notably Seal himself, are mentioned as sources of inspiration and even energy. As one respondent noted succinctly, "Ulie is a recharge point for many of the people in this network." Seal and the deputy chair of CBSG, David Wildt, were respected not only for their dedication, drive, and energy, but also as notable scientists who had advanced the field in general. They inspired confidence and emulation:

> Having "grown up" working with Ulie, Dave Wildt and his group and countless others gave me quite an advantage in knowledge and perspective.

These men are all pioneers in the field and watching them work hard and take chances is certainly inspirational.

From a theoretical view, it is interesting to note that Erikson identified the erosion of community as one of the truly pernicious attributes of the new species of trouble with which he was concerned. Along with the numbing, alienated effects of feeling that the environment could no longer be trusted was the sense that other human beings could no longer be trusted, either. Although Erikson noted that literature on crisis often identifies a new sense of community as being one of the positive side effects of crisis, in chronic disasters, with their insidious disturbance of the very ground of community, he found no examples of a heightened sense of community. Again, he attributes this to the subtly different nature of these crises—perhaps (although Erikson does not specify this) the boundaryless nature of the problem, which puts it outside the control of traditional communities. If this is so, the voices of members of CBSG suggest to us that global, boundaryless networks represent the appropriate community unit for responding to chronic disasters, and that when such global networks are both affective and instrumental, they represent real bulwarks against despair and apathy.

The Sheer Love of the Work Itself

A disproportionate number of CBSG network members are highly trained professionals, holding advanced degrees and often with admirable reputations in research and practice. They are professionals who understand their work and love to do it. As one respondent noted:

Your question certainly caused me to stop long enough to reflect on my life and why I do what I do. I find it most interesting that you ask this, because it is rare that someone that is self motivated and consistently produces is asked to explain why. Most people either find more work for them, or are just glad it's not them.

The intense pleasure that respondents found in working, however, had a double focus. For some, such as myself, it was the day-to-day tasks of the job that provided the critical motivation, that fueled the extracurricular activities. As one respondent said:

Then why do I go beyond the normal demands of my job to participate in CBSG activities? Of course, I am passionately engaged in the conservation of species. I do not need utilitarian arguments for saving species. I just want them to stay alive. Still, I do not think that is a complete explanation. What keeps me working for another hour, and another is probably not the cause, it is the work itself. I do feel discouraged about the state of our environment and exhausted at times, but it does not stop my work. It is a bit like the mouse in the wheel: he know he is not getting anywhere, still he keeps running, just for the fun of it!

For others, however, the relationship was reversed. CBSG depends on professionals who, once established, find that the day-to-day demands of their job are not entirely satisfying. They miss a sense of making a contribution, of "doing something real" that CBSG can provide. Many of them went into zoo work because of a "fascination with animals" and a desire to "keep them around." They then discovered, to their chagrin, that "the routine day-to-day work in a zoo has almost nothing to do with such goals." For such individuals, participation in CBSG processes provides a sense of meaning and contribution that gives a purpose and a shape to their daily activities. And for everyone, participating in CBSG provides a historical opportunity: There is also the sense of real involvement with a Big Issue of Our Time. For anyone with biological interests, the current biodiversity crisis is the biggest issue since the Cretaceous period (i.e., in 60 million years!). Besides, public radio here points out that environmental interest is emerging as a dominant theme of world culture, right up there with rock music and its descendants, and Coca-Cola.

Finally, it is hard to deny that CBSG core group participants are characterized by an exceptional amount of energy. They like to work, and they do so longer and harder than the average person. At most CBSG workshops, participants work 16- to 18-hour days. Although this is partly motivated by the cause, it is also clearly part of the basic disposition of members. There is an elective affinity between those who simply like to work hard and the kind of never-ending challenge that the problem of saving endangered species presents:

Being a workaholic certainly helps and work is probably the only thing that I've ever been consistently good at. I guess I feel that if you are not part of the solution, that you are part of the problem, and ignorance is no excuse for lack of activity.

In sum, CBSG core group members work for the sheer love of the job, as well as for the love of the animals they are trying to save. Because much of what they do is above and beyond their normal job requirements, they are self-selected for their high energy and willingness to work, as well as for their love of animals. This, of course, may be peculiar to the CBSG network, but it is also possible that global social innovation networks are largely peopled by this type of person and fueled by the excess energy that remains when normal "working hours" are done.

Much like the knowledge workers that Peter Drucker argues are the wave of the future, such individuals measure organizations by their capacity to meet their professional needs. Therefore, they are not wedded to any organization in the traditional sense, but search for organization as a vehicle for self-actualization. Hence, the network form may be inherently more empowering, or more attractive, to empowered people wishing to engage in effective action. It would be interesting to compare the response of networked individuals with that of community-based individuals in their response to chronic disasters.

An Intense Excitement
With the CBSG Approach

Certainly, the respondents overtly express an appreciation of the structures and processes that Seal and CBSG have developed. They are articulate in their awareness of the unusual nature of CBSG as an organization and as an approach to established problems. I share the strong feeling that many of the organizations, institutions, and structures that have been built up have become the problem instead of the solution. CBSG work offers the chance to break some of the shackles and do something in spite of the structures—so that anyone with a trace of anarchist in him or her, or a desire for progress, feels rewarded. In an age of exploding communications and travel, lots of people see the anachronisms, feel that the old structures are clearly drawn too narrowly, and do too little.

Some of the motivation, therefore, comes from the sense of taking part in an experiment, of being part of a process where action is more important than custom and where communication is more important than hierarchy. Because most of the core group of CBSG members works in traditional, often hierarchical organizations, participation in CBSG gives the members an alternate identity, alternate roles, and a kind of freedom of thought and expression they may feel they have to inhibit elsewhere.

For those working in professional bureaucracies, as researchers or scientists, in contrast, CBSG processes offer not so much an alternative to hierarchy as an alternative to competitive, individualistic orientations:

> CBSG simply cuts through the crap and provides written guidelines put together by experts that, if implemented, will help conserve a rare species. It provides "organization" in a field that is inherently unorganized because of self-interest spawned by having accessibility or ownership of rare specimens. It also brings science to the forefront making it practical and useful. Before these strategies were available, chaos reigned. Territoriality was rampant, zoos were strictly competitive and no species benefited. For scientists, there was less justification for their existence. Basic science in a zoo was seen as a luxury. CBSG breaks down the territoriality and re-emphasises the importance of the scientific method and basic research. In addition to offering organization, it mandates cooperation not just locally, but internationally. This is the only way to affect [*sic*] real conservation change.

Here, the emphasis is on the breaking down of old boundaries, thought, and practice in order to effect "real conservation change." As mentioned earlier, this is viewed partly as a radical new approach and partly as getting back to basics. After all, as one scientist reported, "That's why most of us became scientists . . . to work together to make things better."

Whereas the first two categories (the emotional impact of working with animals and the satisfactions of relationships within the CBSG network) may be said to be emotionally based motivations, the second two (the love of the work and the excitement of CBSG's approach) may be said to relate to intellectual and ego needs, the need to work well and productively, and the recognition and appreciation of new and successful methods for achieving goals. The final motivation, potentially the most interesting, has to do with moral or spiritual concerns. These statements were the most common of all and have to do with a sense of duty and responsibility that is unusual, but clearly deeply felt.

A Profound Sense of Duty and Responsibility

As an article of faith, members of CBSG felt strongly that biodiversity was a "good." This was a belief that could be defended intellectually, but it was also deeply felt. It was strong enough to represent the kind of conviction that provides an unquestioned guidance for action and effort. As one respondent said, "We have no RIGHT to extinguish other species." To destroy species was linked closely to destroying both life itself and certainly an important part of the beauty and wonder that was an essential ingredient of creation:

> The natural world is the work of millions and billions of years of unique evolution. The idea of trading such marvels, forever, for one more ephemeral gas station, housing development or even farm seems outrageous. Worse, species are far less replaceable than human art works—we can make good reproductions of the Mona Lisa, but not of elephants.

As regards this treasury of marvels, CBSG respondents had developed a sense of duty and obligation. It was this sense of duty that kept them going, rather than any sense that victory or success was imminent. "It is as if you are lost in a snowstorm," said one respondent. "You have to keep going, even if it isn't very likely that you are going to survive." Some even expressed this sense of duty and responsibility as a spiritual or religious trust:

> I do not believe for a moment that we are going to win. I do not openly say this . . . instead I make up slogans about "winning the war on wildlife" but it is not going to happen. There are too many people who do not have a dominant gene for picking up a piece of paper. Even if everyone got it overnight, it would still be difficult. I continue to work because, even if the desired result is not forthcoming, I have still done my duty . . . I have done whatever I could to bring it about, irregardless of anything. This is important to me spiritually.

However, CBSG members were not unconscious of the chronic disaster nature of the problem. Species are never saved for all time. The problem is endless, and probably hopeless. Apparent in many of the statements made by members, however, was an interesting symbolic device for dealing with the unbounded nature of the problem. It was the concept of "watch," a means of placing an arbitrary, comprehensible frame around the problem, setting the limits to be the lifespan of each individual:

> Ethically, the idea of passing on a permanently impoverished world is also pretty distasteful to me—it feels like things are going bad on my "watch." One current phrase reacts with "No more prizes for predicting Floods . . . prizes only for building Arks." As a friend of mine said, instead of wanting to go down in history, our ambition is NOT to go down in the geological record—i.e., NOT to mark our time stratum with the very last of the rhinos, etc, as a near-eternal monument to one generation living stupidly.

In this rich statement are a number of themes that are critical to the ability of CBSG members to find motivation to continue in the face of a chronic disaster.

The first is the notion of finite responsibility. We are not responsible for saving endangered species, only for saving them on our watch. Our responsibility ends when our productive lifespan ends. The future is the watch of others. A second theme is an emphasis on action. Knowledge is seen as valuable only if it is translated quickly and effectively into restitutive action. The image of the ark is widely used among this group of conservationists, and it is a dramatic symbol. In this flood, however, the water is the wave of human population, drowning out all other species. Finally, there is the notion that individual quests for fame, linked as they are with the philosophies of competition, dominance, and individualism, are no longer appropriate in a time of crisis and flood. For too long, human individuals have distinguished themselves by "making a mark." Now, a generation must be distinguished for *not* making a mark, for conserving rather than destroying or producing.

Most critical, however, from the point of view of Erikson's chronic disasters, is the psychological value of framing the sense of responsibility and duty, and for selecting milestones for progress that become grounds for optimism. As one respondent noted:

> Although the big picture looks pretty hopeless, we do win small battles. Most of the species on which we work will be lost, but my efforts might secure the future of a species that took millions of years to evolve and that plays important roles in the ecosystem. That makes it all worthwhile.

CBSG, as mentioned earlier, *has* been associated with saving (at least for the moment) a number of species (or at least with a "major, beneficial revamping of conservation efforts"), including the Florida panther, the black-footed ferret, and the Kenya black rhino. Each recovery can be treated as a milestone. For some, the milestones are defined even more minutely:

> I do get discouraged when people don't appreciate the world around them or become disgusted when I talk to them about the beauty of jumping spiders. But when at least one person is changed, I feel good. When another species is saved, I feel good. This business is replete with discouragement and hopelessness, but if I weren't a little bit of an optimist, I would have given up a long time ago.

Hence, the notion of bounded duty and of interim milestones helps to make a sense of duty and responsibility bearable, in the face of a nearly hopeless dilemma. Nevertheless, CBSG members describe themselves as "honour bound to give our best." Their best is certainly considerable, but to whom are they honor bound? There was little reference to any specifically religious motivations. However, a number of the North American respondents mentioned having participated in the Scouts as children, and it is interesting that much of the language, the concepts of "watch" and "duty," and terms such as *honor bound* seem reminiscent of the scouting movement. For all that it has lost much of its earlier momentum, the scouting movement was perhaps particularly attractive to those with strong biophyliac tendencies. It taught a love of nature and a harmonious coexistence with nature, and it certainly contained a concept of duty to community and the world that is rarely taught in children's group or community activities today.

As Seal himself reported, "We didn't have organized sports . . . what we had were the community churches and the scouts." Both of these organizations demanded commitment and responsibility to others and to the world (whether social or natural). Whatever its origin, a strong sense of duty, it appears, is considerable protection against the apathy, depression, numbness, and alienation of chronic disasters. Moreover, once committed to a community, once permitted to "taking the world seriously," this sense of duty in CBSG members seems to be less tied to a specific community and more to a sense of inner direction. This allows members to operate at the more abstract level of the global community as well as at the specific, physical community in which they find themselves. It certainly results in a mental toughness and an intense dedication to life itself:

> Yes, I feel exhausted, discouraged and hopeless most of the time, but at least you know you are alive. Most everything in my life has come the hard way and I wouldn't be here if I were easily discouraged. You have to want and believe you can make a difference to continue at the pace that it takes to be involved in so many things. If it helps in any small way than [sic] it is worth it. The alternative is to say that I can't or don't have time to make a difference. I personally think that attitude is terrible.

SUMMARY AND CONCLUSIONS

The Beauty and Genius of a Work of Art May Be Reconceived Though Its First Material Expression May Be Destroyed; a Vanished Harmony May Yet Again Inspire the Composer. But When The Last Individual in a Race of Living Beings Breathes No More, Another Heaven and Another Earth Must Pass Before Such a One Can Be Again.

This quote, written on the memorial stone of Gerald Durrell—novelist, conservationist, and founder of the Jersey Wildlife Preservation Trust—is a fitting epitaph for a man who was a pioneer in the fight to preserve endangered species. I have argued in this chapter that the CBSG network is peopled by many who share Durrell's inspiration, commitment, and determination. As a social organization, CBSG indeed represents a global social innovation. It is a loosely structured, value-driven, but ongoing (as opposed to temporary) network organization, operating on little money, volunteer time, and the ingenuity and commitment of a core group all over the world. Its processes are designed to fundamentally address some of the contradictions of global problems, such as the need to operate simultaneously on a global and local level; to find a unity of perspective and purpose while simultaneously allowing for diversity and variety; and to marry the technological sophistication, relative resource richness, and power of the North to the traditions and local knowledge of the South. To operate such processes requires great skill in process design, conflict management, and cross-cultural sensitivity. Each workshop mounted is very labor intensive, drawing heavily on the time and energy of the organizer. And ultimately, this dedication, skill, and commitment can be but a drop in the bucket compared with the enormity of the problem, a "vast wave of destruction sweeping over the planet," as one respondent described it.

This chapter represents an exploration of some of the reasons why CBSG, whose only real resource is the talent, knowledge, and energy of its members, has operated so successfully in the face of the chronic disaster represented by the rapid extinction of species and the diminishing biodiversity of the planet. It suggests that, in fact, an important element of humanity is moved by biophyliac tendencies, as Wilson argued.

It also suggests that although such individuals are particularly sensitive to the chronic disaster of extinction, they have found, in CBSG, certain tools and resources that protect them against the demoralization described by Erikson. They also bring certain dispositional resources to CBSG, which strengthens their sense of resolve and purpose. From the point of view of Erikson's theory of a new species of trouble, CBSG's new species of solution offers the following insights:

1. The hopelessness expressed by the representatives of Erikson's chronically traumatized community is a reaction not only to a fundamental destruction of the environment but also to the sense of lack of empowerment. His cases describe laypeople who do not have the tools to discern and

represent the threats they face. CBSG democratizes tools and gives people the chance to feel that they can act productively, as individuals, in response to their emotional and intellectual concerns.

2. The boundaryless aspect of the CBSG network provides a structure that may be said to fit with the boundaryless nature of chronic disasters. In this sense, it is an appropriate organization for such problems and seems more immune to demoralization than do traditional, bounded communities.

3. Because of improvements in communication technology, the sense of connection, both instrumental and affective, is strong in the CBSG network. Hence, it satisfies emotional needs for contact, as well as moral aims and professional competencies.

4. The CBSG members bring to the network an intense love of their work. They are people endowed with unusual amounts of energy and competence. The network form of CBSG is a vehicle that allows them to use this energy in effective action. Traditional communities and organizations think of individuals as members, subservient to the community as a whole. They see their contract as one of integrating, regulating, and caring for members in return for loyalty; they do not see the contract as one of providing environments and materials that provide exciting opportunities for those motivated to turn expertise to action. Hence, traditional communities may fail to provide such vehicles.

5. Erikson's case describes communities that become disorganized as a result of a threat, with the subsequent loss of the experience of trust and goodwill that is the basis of that community. Most people in the CBSG network experience profound disorganization, even chaos, as part of their efforts to work for conservation. However, in their case, the disorganization is viewed as a beginning of a new form of organization, as opposed to the ending of an old; of an experiment and a pioneer effort in their field, instead of the loss of valued order. This suggests that optimism may be a function of an innovative organizational form, and of the interpretation of disorder that is associated with innovation.

6. Erikson describes the debilitating effects of the fact that chronic disasters do not have a beginning and an end, and that although they are the result of human error, blame is hard to allocate. CBSG network members bring

a profound sense of duty and responsibility to the cause; they handle the need to assign responsibility by assuming it themselves, voluntarily. They balance this with the concept of "watch," a symbolic attempt to frame and subdivide the problem into manageable units and milestones. Their concepts of duty are deeply held and unquestioned, and they act as an effective bulwark against depression. Nevertheless, it would appear that for unbounded problems, some psychological "limiting" devices are necessary for successful functioning.

For scholars interested in GSCOs, this case also offers a number of interesting insights. First and foremost, it underlines the need to do more research around the affinity between the network form and the type of social problem. Erikson's work suggests that unbounded problems, such as what he describes as chronic disasters, have qualities that seem to undermine human beings' inherent problem-solving abilities. Perhaps an organizational form that is equally unbounded can counteract this tendency.

However, although the network may be theoretically unbounded—in the sense that it is without a center, exists on a worldwide basis, and has no planned limits to growth—it nevertheless has important emotional significance for members. On the level of finding role models, points of reference for adult identity, and intense friendships, the CBSG strikes me as certainly a highly personal environment, containing clanlike qualities that many organizations would envy. I have attributed some of this to the availability (and indeed emphasis) on communications within CBSG. But this relationship is one that deserves more study, as does the role of affect in general.

Finally, I would argue that the case of CBSG demands that we rethink the tendency to view organizations as actors in the interorganizational domain and see them more often as vehicles—resources for people who are anxious to put their expertise to work. From a psychological viewpoint, the CBSG respondents represented in this chapter are highly inner directed and value driven. This dedication is not produced by CBSG; rather, CBSG offers them an exciting vehicle for putting their dedication to work. This may be true of networks generally and suggests that maybe it is not only the form that makes them effective, but also that the form provides a better vehicle than does hierarchy for a growing and highly effective part of the population.

5

GLOBAL CHANGE AS
CONTEXTUAL COLLABORATIVE
KNOWLEDGE CREATION

RAMKRISHNAN V. TENKASI
SUSAN ALBERS MOHRMAN

Until very recently in history, people have responded to global change phenomena as if they were local and linear; as if they did not require any transboundary learning, organizing, or action (Cooperrider & Bilimoria, 1993).

A good illustration of this line of thought is reflected in the domain of international technology transfer studies, a discipline that has concerned itself with issues of global change over the past 30 years by seeking to transfer knowledge and innovations both technical and social from developed to developing countries. Examples include studies of diffusion of agricultural innovations (Howes, 1980; Rogers, 1983); birth control methods (Jacobson, 1988); disease control and eradication programs, such as smallpox (Fenner, Henderson, Arita, Jezek, & Ladnyi, 1988) and poliomyelitis (Wright et al., 1991); and social technologies, such as management by objectives (MBO; Hofstede, 1984).

Traditionally, international technology transfer has operated under the predominant assumption that effecting change is primarily an issue of knowledge transmission from the expert source to the nonexpert receiver (Tenkasi & Mohrman, 1995). If there were difficulties (or impedance) with the transmission, then it was regarded as a problem of nonunderstanding by the user that could be remedied by better channel management (Reddy, 1979) and/or strategies such as guidance by an expert (Rogers & Kincaid, 1981; Williams & Gibson, 1990) to put this transferred knowledge to effective use in the recipient settings.

The stance that we take here is that this knowledge transmission model may be inadequate to facilitate the required alterations in environmental and human systems necessary to foster global change because knowledge is not value free. This is particularly the case with technologies that directly intervene into human systems, as it has been observed that even so-called pure technologies are not value neutral (Moore, 1980). We posit that global change may be best viewed as a process of "contextual collaborative" knowledge creation between different communities of knowing that embodies mutual learning.

The rest of the chapter is organized in the following manner. We briefly review the traditional knowledge transmission models of change and point out the implicit assumptions underlying these traditions that rely on an objectivist conception of the nature of knowledge. Next, we propose an alternate set of assumptions that underscores the contextual and social nature of knowledge and provides the rationale for looking at global change as a process of contextual collaborative knowledge creation. Then, we locate mutual perspective taking as the basis of such collaborative learning, examine potential issues around mutual perspective taking, and conclude by discussing some ways of facilitating such learning.

TRADITIONAL MODELS OF KNOWLEDGE TRANSMISSION

The conventional models of knowledge transmission for change in international technology transfer ventures can be classified into three major approaches: the appropriability model, the knowledge dissemination model, and the currently popular knowledge utilization model (Williams & Gibson, 1990).

The *appropriability model* follows the logic that good knowledge as embodied in good technologies sells itself because it appeals to the rational self-interests of the users. Once the researcher develops the right idea and makes the results available through various forms of mediated communication, people will automatically accept it, and therefore, additional, purposive transfer mechanisms are unnecessary (Kozmetsky, 1990). A classic example of the appropriability model is evident in the early attempts at controlling the Third World population explosion (Waldrop, 1992). The standard approach at that time tended to place a heavy reliance on economic determinism coupled with standardized campaigns for people to practice birth control. To achieve its optimum population, all that a country had to do was give its people birth control devices and the right economic incentives to use them in order to control their reproduction. The logic was that they would automatically follow their own rational self-interest in using these devices. The economic determinism approach was heavily sponsored by the United Nations in the early 1970s.

The *knowledge dissemination* approach popularized by Everett Rogers (Rogers, 1983; Rogers & Kincaid, 1981) takes the view that diffusion of innovations is best facilitated when experts inform and train potential users of the technology (Williams & Gibson, 1990). The guiding assumption was that "once the linkages are established, the new technology [knowledge] will flow from the expert to the non expert much like water through a pipe once the channel is opened" (Williams & Gibson, 1990, p. 15). A good example of such an approach is documented by Moore (1980), who noted that international mariculture experts trained Malaysian fishermen in the use of mechanized fishing trawlers and advanced fishing apparatus.

The *knowledge utilization* model is an increasingly popular view of change reflected in much of the current literature (Szakonyi, 1990; Zacchea, 1992). It represents an evolutionary step in that it focuses on strategies to put knowledge to effective use in the recipient settings (Backer, 1991). In this model, there is more of an attempt to understand the local context to which the knowledge is being transferred, the best solution given the local conditions, and the various barriers that can get in the way of the local populace putting this knowledge to effective use. Howes (1980) has illustrated such an example: Nigerian ecological conditions were simulated in an artificial laboratory environment to find the single and most suitable food crop that could realize the highest yields in the shortest period of time.

Although there is an appreciation of the complexities of knowledge transfer, it has been argued that the knowledge utilization model suffers from a linear bias (Dimancescu & Botkin, 1986). The stated or implicit notion is that basic knowledge moves from the researcher to the client, in one direction, with some minor modifications to accommodate local conditions. This model reduces the transfer process to chronologically ordered one-way stages, "whereas practice shows the process to be interactive and complex" (Williams & Gibson, 1990, p. 15).

UNPACKING THE OPERATIVE ASSUMPTIONS OF THE TRADITIONAL MODELS OF KNOWLEDGE TRANSMISSION

The major arguments against the predominant transfer approaches is that they entail a one-way transmission of information, from source to destination or from originator to receiver. Although this is a valid criticism, we posit further that the one-way transmission of information is essentially a manifestation of three interrelated theses about the nature of knowledge. The three conjoint operative assumptions about the nature of knowledge are that (a) knowledge can be objectively realized, (b) knowledge is applicable across contexts, and (c) knowledge is complete.

Knowledge Can Be Objectively Realized

The assumption behind this thesis is that truthfulness of knowledge can be empirically determined. There are universal constants and "true" models of the world that correspond with the world as it is and that can be empirically realized. Such knowledge that has been empirically determined is objective, has validity, and represents the implications for universal action. An example would be where a research finding, such as "high performers are driven by the need to achieve," is taken as truth and used to guide action. Another example would be theories of neoclassical economics that suggest that all human beings are driven by rational self-interests.

Knowledge Is Applicable Across Contexts

An interrelated postulate is that knowledge that has been objectively determined will apply uniformly across contexts and time. An example would be the belief based on the previously mentioned research that, regardless of the country or subculture, people trained in achievement motivation will perform better or that economic incentives will control the human reproduction rate.

Knowledge Is Complete

The assumption here is that knowledge can be created in its complete form by people who have the expertise. Advocates of this approach act as if a single individual or group can hold all of the requisite knowledge necessary for productive action, and the issue is one of transmission of this knowledge so that users can put it to productive use. This assumption would be embodied in approaches to the diffusion of technology that involve "packaging" or "instrumenting" the technology. Following the previous example, this assumption might lead the generators of the knowledge that high performers are driven by the need to achieve to base selection tests, training, and counseling interventions on this "truth," or the United Nations to advocate the development of standardized programs of economic incentives for population control.

These operating assumptions about the nature of knowledge are well reflected in the appropriability and the diffusion models of transfer. In the first model, the users simply absorb the knowledge/technology "as is" based on their rational self-interest, and in the second instance, the absorption of knowledge is facilitated through instructions by an expert. One can infer that these one-way transmissions of knowledge are guided by the implicit frames of objectivity, universal applicability, and completeness of knowledge theses.

In the knowledge utilization model, there is an element of two-way communication. However, as Doheny-Farina (1992) and Dobrin (1989) argue, the two-way communication is primarily oriented toward maneuvering around the communication barriers between the originator group and the user group. The assumption still is that there is "a body of information, of objective facts, just lying there waiting to be communicated" (Dobrin, 1989, p. 60). The underlying tenet is that knowledge is an object that exists independently, is valid, is complete, and has universal applicability, and this basic knowledge moves from the researcher to the client, with some modifications to accommodate local conditions. It is the job of the implementers to transfer the knowledge correctly through the appropriate channels. If there are problems with the user group adopting this knowledge, it is because its members do not understand. This would entail finding better ways of managing those channels to achieve better dissemination or diffusion of knowledge.

If the foregoing assumptions about knowledge (objectivity, universal applicability, and completeness) were true, then the traditional modes of knowledge transmission are most appropriate. Change would be a simple process of moving knowledge/innovations from the source to the receivers.

However, there are several examples from international development projects that suggest that the change process is not so simple, and the foregoing assumptions about knowledge may not be accurate.

Some of the early attempts at population control in Third World countries that relied on the appropriability model, which included a combination of economic incentives for not producing children and generous distribution of birth control devices, are illustrative of the fallibility of the "objectivity of knowledge" theses. As summarized by Waldrop (1992), "[It was puzzling as to] why rural families were still producing an average of seven children apiece, even when modern birth control was made freely available—and even when the villagers seemed perfectly well aware of the country's immense overpopulation and stagnant development" (p. 26). This finding came as a shock to some of the economists studying population control—the idea that human beings will not respond to abstract economic incentives even though it was in their best self-interests. Furthermore, these studies showed that one could not settle upon a universal, deterministic theory of human fertility. Instead, what they found was that fertility rates were part of a self-consistent pattern of folkways, myths, and social mores—a pattern, moreover, that was different for each culture.

Other attempts at change that rely on these traditional assumptions about knowledge have demonstrated negative impacts on the user community. Moore (1980) has documented a case of the knowledge dissemination approach, in which fishermen in some Malaysian fishing villages were trained in the use of new fishing methods and apparatus in place of traditional fishing practices. This included the replacement of traditional fishing vessels by mechanized fishing trawlers. However, the new fishing methods and apparatus introduced wiped out the local population's fishing reserves in a short period of time. For one, the new apparatus and methods failed to distinguish between mature and immature fish. In addition, the trawlers' nets cut the fish and drained their blood, and because consumers did not like the taste, cut fish did not sell in the market.

Similarly, Howes (1980) describes the use of the knowledge utilization model in certain parts of Nigeria in the replacement of multi-cropping systems of certain food crops with the mono-cropping of a high-yielding variety of a single crop. This crop was developed based on simulating Nigerian agricultural conditions in laboratories in the West, using Western scientific understandings of the ecological system in Nigeria. The idea behind the simulations was to determine the most economically viable crop that fit the local ecological dynamics. Although the introduction of a single crop was a success in the short run, producing higher yields and higher cash return per acre of farmland cultivated, in the long run, it proved to be a disaster. The intensity with which a given unit of land was exploited increased tremendously, showing decreasing returns over time. Furthermore, the mono-crops were more susceptible to invasions from pests. The mixed cropping systems of earlier times included several plant species with different stem lengths that showed varied degrees of resistance to various pests and served to optimize ecological stability and long-term productivity of the land. In retrospect, the scientists realized that they should have obtained some local perspectives of the ecological dynamics instead of just relying on the perspectives of the researchers from the laboratory, which limited their understandings of ecology to a specific model.

Based on this and several other examples (Brokensha, Warren, & Werner, 1980), we believe that a different set of theses about the nature of knowledge is better able to capture and manage the complexities of technology adoption and global change. This alternate set of assumptions presents us with a rationale to understand global change as a process of contextual knowledge creation through collaborative learning. In the next section, we examine this alternate set of assumptions and provide case examples to illustrate how they may guide attempts at global change more accurately.

AN ALTERNATE SET OF ASSUMPTIONS
ABOUT THE NATURE OF KNOWLEDGE

In contrast to the generally accepted views of knowledge, we posit that three different assumptions can provide a more relevant set of operating assumptions to comprehend the global change process: (a) Knowledge is subjectively constructed and may be subjectively consumed, (b) knowledge requires contextual adaptation, and (c) knowledge is incomplete. These are described below.

Knowledge Is Subjectively Constructed
and May Be Subjectively Consumed

Knowledge is a belief or set of beliefs about a segment of reality that is socially constructed by a community of knowing. It is based on a set of assumptions about the nature of such a segment of reality. Distinct communities of knowing develop unique social and cognitive repertoires that guide their interpretations of their world. It is through these socially situated judgments of reality that individual and social knowledge is constituted.

Fleck's (1935/1979) concept of "thought worlds" is one such notion that refers to the unique interpretive repertoire of a distinct community of knowing. A community's thought world is characterized by two aspects: (a) their "fund of knowledge," or what they know; and (b) their "systems of meaning," or how they know. What is already known influences the method and content of cognition. A thought world evolves in a community of knowing as an internally shared system of meaning that provides a readiness for directed perception.

Barnes (1983) also underscores the social nature of knowledge and learning. He argues that knowledge is socially constituted and that learning in a community is always mediated by its social process. To learn is to classify, and to classify is to employ the specific classifications of some community or culture. Concept acquisition and application, or knowledge, is a social activity that is determined by this culturally given classification of reality. Cognitive operations of classification and concept formation are shaped by the unique linguistic operations of a culture or community.

The subjectivity of knowledge theses—that the nature of knowledge is based on a culturally given classification of reality—has been illustrated in several domains (Brokensha et al., 1980). A telling example is a study conducted by Burton and Kirk (1980) on the ethnoclassification of body parts among three cultures. Their central thesis was that different cultures construct different models of the body, which in turn determine belief systems concerning disease, conception and contraception, and mental illness. For example, the Gourma tribe of Upper Volta (Swanson, 1980) visualizes the human body as an amalgamation of ancestor soul, communal soul, guiding spirit, god consciousness, and personal destiny, and their approach to healing locates the origin of the disease within this broader social context of the afflicted individual (Howes, 1980). Likewise, the Dutch phenomenologist Van Den Berg (1974) has vividly illustrated that the Europeans and Chinese, because of their differing conceptions of the human body, have invented two divergent forms of medicine, allopathy and acupuncture, that are equally valid in their own right.

Because each community of knowing bases its definition of reality on its unique interpretive conventions, any information or knowledge, regardless of how well it is empirically determined by an outside authority, may still be subjectively consumed in reference to the community's interpretive repertoire. It has been observed that even within a distinct community of knowing, there could be subcommunities that have their distinct interpretive conventions (Brown & Duguid, 1991). Kuhn (1970) calls this barrier to mutual interpretation the "incommensurability" of meaning systems among different communities of knowing, whereas Fleck (1935/1979) addresses this as the "inherent tenacity" of thought worlds.

Dougherty (1992), drawing on Fleck, has examined this incommensurability of meaning systems within organizational communities. A fund of knowledge, for example, can be primarily conceptual (such as research and development)—acquired through education, training, and laboratory experimentation—or it can be practice based (such as marketing)—acquired through direct interaction with customers. Complex ideas cannot be shared easily across thought worlds with different funds of knowledge and systems of meaning. People in different thought worlds will attempt to interpret each other's ideas based on their unique thought worlds. If such interpretation fails, then they may view the other's central issues as esoteric, if not meaningless.

There are several examples of this subjective consumption of received knowledge and its technological embodiments in international development projects. Moore (1980) describes the construction of overhead water storage tanks in villages in Indonesia. The tank water was purer and more convenient than the traditional pond water. However, the villagers did not accept it. To them, the tank water was not "the real water which fell from the sky." Furthermore, the ponds served as social meeting places, performing a function that the overhead tanks could not fulfill.

Another example can be drawn from the experiences of medical personnel from the World Health Organization (WHO), who attempted to start disease eradication programs in the Gourma tribe of Upper Volta. The physicians from WHO tried, unsuccessfully, to convince the community that the disease was really due to infection by germs. Because the Gourma tribe's view of the human body was meshed into the social context, all forms of individual diseases were also attributed to relationships in the social context, and the germ theory went against such attributions (Howes, 1980).

Knowledge Requires Contextual Adaptation

For a community of knowing to adopt an idea, information, or knowledge from a different community of knowing, the information or knowledge may have to be reconfigured or adapted to fit in with the recipient community's meaning system. External ideas that may not fit in with one's system of meaning may be rejected outright (Fleck, 1935/1979).

Gidden's (1974) theory of structuration provides insights on the nature of such meaning systems and the process of such reconfiguration, or "appropriation" (Poole & DeSanctis, 1994). The theory of structuration essentially argues that human understanding and behavior are contextual. Knowledge, cognition, and behavior in any social system are guided and constrained by the contextual rules and resources resident in the social structures. Actors use these rules to make sense of their own acts and those of other people. The structurational conventions that condition human understanding, behavior, and practices are constituted by three interdependent structures, what Giddens (1974) terms as the "modalities of structuration." These interdependent structures are interpretive schemes, norms, and power relationships.

Interpretive schemes are standardized, shared stocks of knowledge and beliefs that actors in a setting draw upon to interpret behavior and events. Norms are the rules governing sanctioned or appropriate conduct. Power enters into human interaction by providing humans with the capabilities to accomplish outcomes, and most social systems are marked by an asymmetry of power distribution. Frequently, there is a defined pattern of power relationships within a social system.

Technology, or, for that matter, any external knowledge or information, may be appropriated by a social system within the context of its structurational conventions. The structurational conventions can mediate the appropriation process. If an idea is too antithetical to a system's structurational conventions, then the system could reject it. So the task becomes one of either reconfiguring the knowledge or its technological embodiments to fit the situational contextual requirements, or changing the structurational conventions of the recipient group.

Holzner and Marx (1979) offer specific insights into how local knowledge systems interact with received knowledge. Their argument is that societies use a set of "epistemic criteria," or truth tests, that is socially accepted by the community and integrated into their daily practices to ratify experience as knowledge. These epistemic criteria can be interpreted from two perspectives: At one level, they are the knowledge forms or objects of knowledge of a community of knowing (including being storehouses of knowledge), and at another level, they can also be employed as criteria to validate or reject any received wisdom and knowledge.

According to Holzner and Marx (1979), a wide variety of epistemic criteria can be distinguished. However, just like the modalities of structuration, they are not distinct categories but intermingle with each other. The following are major examples of epistemic criteria in any community of knowing.

1. *Ritualistic/superstitious* criteria for truth are commonplace in most societies, including high-technology Western societies. Barley (1988) identified a variety of problem-solving routines used by radiological technicians that were purely ritualistic, in the sense that they reflected a blind faith that a given action has a beneficial consequence (e.g., banging on a machine in a particular way). The actual efficacy of such procedures need not be demonstrated; they are part of the common stock of knowledge because they are simply there.

2. *Authoritative criteria* are best exemplified in religious beliefs. The basis for justification of a great many beliefs in many societies is simply that a trusted, respected, or feared individual says that this is the "truth."

3. *Pragmatic criteria,* or practical experience, is a major source of knowledge in any social group. Success is the critical test for many kinds of knowledge. Frequently, pragmatic criteria are based on the efficacy of demonstrated procedures without understanding why they work. Mulkay (1984) offers the example of a British surgeon using strips of paw-paw fruit to clear up a postoperative infection after a kidney transplant. The doctor could not explain why the tribal remedy worked, but he had seen it work before, and that was enough.

4. *Scientific criteria,* especially in the Western world, have a strong grip on scholars and scientists (Kuhn, 1970). In contrast to pragmatic criteria, scientific criteria seek for explanatory theory. This is the case for both Western science and ethnoscience. The term *ethnoscience* is viewed as the set of concepts, propositions, and theories unique to each particular cultural group in the world—its particular ways of classifying its material and social universe. Thus, Western science is one of a number of types of ethnoscience of culture groups throughout the world (Meehan, 1980).

Stefflere (1972), a cognitive anthropologist, found evidence that supports Holzner and Marx's thesis. He found that the acceptance of new knowledge or innovation by a local community would vary depending upon the innovation's location in a knowledge space consisting of local cultural objects of knowledge of varying degrees of similarity to the proposed innovation. He predicted that people would behave toward new objects or received knowledge in ways similar to how they behave toward existing cultural objects that were judged to be similar to the new objects. Thus, received knowledge is often evaluated in terms of existing ritualistic, pragmatic, authoritative, and ethno-scientific criteria, and, based on similarity conditions, either accepted or rejected. The earlier illustration, in which locals in villages in Indonesia rejected the overhead water tanks set up to replace traditional pond water, is a case in point (Moore, 1980). According to local beliefs, the tank water was not real water that fell from the sky and therefore was not pure enough. Furthermore, the tanks could not perform the practical function that the ponds did of serving as social meeting places.

Stefflere provides the example of how all efforts by Peace Corps volunteers to introduce social change programs in some parts of Peru were met with resistance. As the Peace Corps people realized subsequently, the reason was that the only Western people with whom the natives had previously come into contact were a fundamentalist religious group that had tried to convert them, a process that violated all of their conceptions of truth. The Peace Corps group was identified with this fundamentalist religious group, and pragmatic criteria, based on prior experience, indicated that any association with the strangers could be detrimental to the community.

However, there are several examples of presenting knowledge in ways that complemented local truth wclaims. The global campaign to eradicate smallpox is a good example of such contextual adaptation, where received knowledge was reconfigured to conform to the local epistemic criteria (Joseph, Tenkasi, & Cooperrider, 1994).

Smallpox, a dreadful disease known to humankind since the 12th century B.C., was successfully eradicated globally. As the result of a 10-year effort spearheaded by the smallpox eradication unit instituted by WHO, the last case of smallpox was detected in Somalia in 1977. However, the technology (in the form of a vaccine) to eradicate smallpox had been in existence for more than 177 years. In fact, several earlier attempts to combat the dreadful disease failed: "A century and a half of vaccination attempts yielded only modest results" (Fenner et al., 1988, p. 1346). One of the major barriers to the earlier campaigns was that in many countries, the indigenous system of medicine held beliefs and advocated practices that interfered with the concept of vaccination.

The earlier programs tried to force the vaccination technology or explain the benefits of vaccination using Western scientific criteria without understanding or acknowledging these local belief systems. However, in the case of the successful campaign, some of the WHO personnel, along with the local leaders, recognized this problem and made an attempt to present the vaccination technology as complementing the local knowledge and belief systems in almost every country. The new knowledge was configured within the context of rituals, authoritative local leaders, and ethnoscientific or causal knowledge.

For example, in India, the folk goddess of smallpox was a deity named Shitala Mata. She was represented as riding on a donkey with a basketful of grain on her head. In one hand, she had a pitcher of water, and in the other, a broom. The belief was that when she shakes her head, the grains that spill turn into smallpox pustules. The victim survived if she cleaned the spilled grain with water, but did not if she used only the dry broom. To incorporate the vaccination technology within this local meaning system, hundreds of large posters were created where the water in the goddess's hand was replaced by a large syringe containing the vaccine. As observed by Holzner and Marx (1979), and as illustrated in the example, epistemic criteria or forms of knowledge intermingle with each other. The smallpox deity had symbolic-ritualistic significance, while, at the same time, it also represented causal knowledge of smallpox.

There are other examples of successful contextual reconfiguration of received knowledge within the context of local epistemic criteria. The previously cited example of the Gourma tribe in Upper Volta is a case in point. The WHO personnel were initially unsuccessful in their attempts to convince the tribe about the germ theory of disease because the local community located the causes for disease within the broader social context of the afflicted individual. Subsequently, however, both types of explanations were assimilated. With the help of local elders, the germ agent was reinterpreted as constituting another part of the individual's social context, and the diagnostic and healing practices associated with both systems were employed (Horton, 1967; Howes, 1980).

Bruce and Peyton (1990) argue that such reconfiguration of received knowledge is essential for successful innovation adoption. They posit that the so-called distortion of innovations is, in reality, the adaptation of innovations to suit the local context. These perceived distortions are an integral part of "appropriating" the knowledge, or fitting it to the situational context of the transfer domain. This might well be a prerequisite for successful adoption of an innovation.

Knowledge Is Incomplete

Frederich Hayek (1945) has argued that the knowledge necessary for productive action rarely resides in any one place, person, or group but is divided throughout society. The knowledge challenge that society faces is how best to tap into and integrate the additional knowledge distributed throughout society that is required for effective action.

Likewise, adaptive systems theory (Ormrod, 1974) argues that the greater the universe of perspectives, the greater the opportunity for productive solutions to be found. A multiplicity of problem definitions, solutions, and experiments can lead to eventual answers. Knight (1980) uses an adaptive systems framework to analyze the negative aspects of the replacement of traditional agricultural practices in many countries by modern, Western technologies. He concludes that "we [must] view traditional practices as a source of innovation, it is clear that they greatly enhance potentials for local agricultural improvement, as well as multiply the numbers of potential "solutions" to the world-wide food supply problems" (p. 212).

There is considerable local knowledge to be taken into account and used. As Lévi-Strauss (1966) tellingly observed, the thirst for knowledge is one of the most neglected aspects of the thought of the people we call "primitive." Even if it is not directed toward facts of the same abstraction or their interconnections as those with which Western science is concerned, ethnoscience or local causal knowledge implies comparable intellectual application and methods of observation. In both cases, the universe is an object of thought, at least as much as it is a means of satisfying a specific community's need. Knight's (1980) conclusions are similar: "In spite of dissonance between these systems [ethnoscience and formal Western science], there exists commonality that is the basis for comparison" (p. 222).

Formal, Western science and ethnoscience share a lot of common characteristics. They are both based on a common "quest for explanatory theory" and an accounting for the apparent diversity, complexity, disorder, and regularity in the environment (Knight, 1980). Both systems contain theory that builds a wider causal context than just pragmatic criteria or common sense. Both systems also abstract, analyze, and synthesize, frequently with analogies providing the basis for explanation. However, ethnoscience can differ from formal science in some respects (Horton, 1967). Frequently, ethnoscience may attach a magical attitude toward its explanations. This is because ethnoscience can be occasion bound rather than built from ideas to further ideas. In other words, ethnoscience does not address the nature of its own thought processes. It does not have a philosophy of its own science and is therefore a relatively closed system. However, ideally, formal Western science is supposed to be open with respect to the acquisition of new knowledge, but it seldom is. It clearly reflects the interests, motivations, and attitudes of the society in which it is embedded (Kuhn, 1970).

This premise implies that knowledge for effective action requires a fusion of received knowledge with local knowledge, and mere contextual reconfiguration of received knowledge may not be enough. As Dougherty (1992) found in her research, thought worlds can selectively filter information and insights. Because of different funds of knowledge, a certain thought world is likely to best understand certain issues and further ignore information that is equally essential to the total task. Relying on such partial knowledge may result in ineffectual contextual adaptation.

There are several examples of fusing received knowledge with local causal and pragmatic knowledge to produce instances of enduring change. In a project by Richards (1975) on preservation efforts of some plant species in the Philippines, it was revealed that locals had superior ethnobotanical knowledge. An average adult could identify a staggering 1,600 species—400 more than previously recorded in a systematic botanical survey. Similarly, other projects have suggested that indigenous observers had superior empirical understanding of the localized ecosystem as a whole (Barker, Oguntoyinbo, & Richards, 1977). In this particular instance, local elders could accurately predict the attack by a particular type of grasshopper on a certain type of cassava crop that had been introduced. Furthermore, they could provide detailed knowledge on cyclical ecological changes.

Another interesting example is the case of bamboo tubewells, which appeared first in Bihar in India and rapidly spread both nationally and internationally (Dommen, 1975). Faced with the problem that the water supply from canals was unreliable, the government scientists introduced iron tubewells. However, the iron tubewells were expensive and tended to rust. Confronted with this problem, the local farmers came up with an ingenious solution. Their alternative, which was much cheaper and reliable, was to use locally available bamboo shoots that were nailed together with iron rings and covered with bamboo coir.

These examples attest to the fact that effective contextual adaptation was best achieved when there was a creative synthesis of distinct knowledge domains. Successful change efforts, as in the case of bamboo tubewells, involved a fusion of the conceptual knowledge of the scientists and the practice-based knowledge of the farmers that bamboo shoots can be a good conductor of water.

The Problem With Soft Technologies

The subjectivity of knowledge and the need for contextual adaptation, as well as the need to fuse received knowledge with local knowledge, take on more acute proportions with soft or disembodied technologies. Soft technologies, such as procedures or systems, can be conceived of as essentially social practices that may reflect a specific system's structurational conventions about how to organize, work, or manage people. They are more abstract than hard technologies, the developer's contextual assumptions behind the nature of the technology have to be explicated, and their relevance has to be examined in light of the contextual background of the recipient. This combined approach may result in creative approaches to contextualize the technology productively.

Hofstede (1984) extends an interesting example of how attempts to introduce management by objectives (MBO) to some other countries failed miserably. He argues that MBO presupposes that subordinates are sufficiently independent to negotiate meaningfully with their boss, and that performance is seen as important by both. When MBO was first introduced in France in the 1960s, people expected that this new technique would result in long-overdue improvements in productivity. However, by 1970, MBO was severely discredited in France. The reason, argues Hofstede, is that the French culture encourages dependency relationships among superiors and subordinates. The traditional hierarchical structure protects against anxiety, whereas MBO generates anxiety.

As Hofstede (1984) elucidates:

> The reason for the anxiety in the French cultural context is that MBO presupposes a depersonalized authority in the form of internalized objectives; but French people, from their early childhood onward, are accustomed to large power distances, to an authority that is highly personalized. And in spite of all attempts to introduce Anglo-Saxon management methods, French superiors do not easily decentralize and do not stop short-circuiting intermediate hierarchical levels, nor do French subordinates expect them to. (p. 325)

PERSPECTIVE TAKING AS THE BASIS
FOR COLLABORATIVE LEARNING

This alternate set of assumptions about the nature of knowledge provides us with a different view of change. If innovations have to be adopted successfully, then knowledge has to be contextually adapted, which could entail the creation of new knowledge. Collaborative learning is necessary for purposes of reconfiguration of received knowledge to fit within local meaning systems, as well as to enable new insights and new knowledge through the creative synthesis of distinct knowledge domains.

The basis of collaborative learning rests in a process of mutual perspective taking. It is a process whereby distinctive individual knowledge, values, meanings, assumptions, and beliefs are exchanged, evaluated, and integrated with those of others (Duncan & Weiss, 1979; Shrivastava, 1983). Knowing what others know is a necessary component for coordinated action to take place. Much of social behavior is predicated on the assumptions that an actor makes about the knowledge, beliefs, and motives of others. And as Brown (1981) observed, understanding another requires that the point of view of the other be realistically imagined. The fundamental importance of taking the other's point of view into account is seen in Mead (1934), who referred to it as taking the attitude of the other and equated our ability to be fully human with our ability to maintain an inner conversation with a generalized other. This is the essence of the process of perspective taking (Bakhtin, 1981; Clark, 1985; Krauss & Fussell, 1991).

Issues in Perspective Taking

Mutual perspective taking of each other's knowledge and background into account is fundamental for collaborative learning. However, it is a complex process and can frequently break down. There are two principal and interrelated issues to mutual perspective taking. First, knowledge and meaning systems of a community of knowing are often tacit and taken for granted. Frequently, such tacit knowledge is housed in the various expressive and instrumental modes unique to a community of knowing (cultures) that are employed for making sense of their social and material universe. These modes could range from formal education to folk tales, music, debate, drama, dance, tales, visual representations, rituals, and mime (Compton, 1980). Second, because such knowledge and meaning systems are tacit and taken for granted, and one's interpretive procedures are so automatic, most people assume that the rest of the world's perspectives are more similar to their own than they actually are. This tendency to focus on one's own perspectives may be further compounded by the belief that one's knowledge system is superior to the other.

Knowledge as tacit and taken for granted. At least part of the knowledge, beliefs, meaning systems, and norms that form the interpretive conventions of any group or community of knowing are tacit in nature. Understanding and interpretation involve a great deal that is not explicit or explicable, that is framed and embedded in communal conventions, and that one is not aware of in the daily conduct of life (Brown & Duguid, 1991).

There are at least two levels of consciousness in any social system; *discursive* consciousness, which involves knowledge that actors are able to express at the level of discourse, and *practical* consciousness, which involves tacit stocks of knowledge that actors are normally not able to formulate discursively, but draw upon in the constitution of social conduct (Giddens, 1974). And many times, it is only when the rules go wrong that a community of knowing examines the nature of their interpretation. "Otherwise, our giving of meaning to objects—our interpretative practices are so automatic that we do not notice that any interpretation is involved" (Collins, 1983, p. 90).

This issue is further compounded in many non-Western societies. Knowledge in such communities is not a rational product or process that is represented formally, as in the canons of Western science (Howes, 1980). Ethnoscientific knowledge, whether ritualistic, authoritative, pragmatic, or explanatory, has different forms of organization than is found in Western societies. Formal acquisition and storage of knowledge, as in classroom instructions and books, is not prevalent in many other parts of the world. It is frequently stored in folk arts, stories, tales, and other narrative modes (Compton, 1980).

For example, in Africa, the telling of folk tales is the primary medium through which cultural knowledge is transmitted between individuals and to succeeding generations. Village storytellers, who are the repositories of cultural knowledge, develop their skills over a number of years through an apprenticeship arrangement between an elder and young aspirant. Similarly, folk dance has often been observed to transmit knowledge on themes such as agriculture, occupations, courtship, marriage, religious observance, and war strategies (Compton, 1980).

Therefore, for mutual perspective taking to succeed, not only should mutual tacit knowledge be made explicit, but the storehouses of such tacit knowledge have to be identified. The unique modes of knowledge acquisition, storage, and transmission practices of each culture or subculture also have to be understood in order to draw out this knowledge.

False assumption that others' knowledge and meaning systems are more similar to one's own than they actually are. Because a group's knowledge and meaning systems can operate outside the bounds of day-to-day consciousness, there is a tendency to automatically assume that others' worldviews are more similar to one's own than they actually are. Fleck (1935/1979) calls this the "inherent tenacity" of thought worlds to focus on their own perspectives.

The false consensus effect, in which subjects assume that others are more similar to themselves than is actually the case (Ross, Green, & House, 1974), is a form of bias particularly relevant to the perspective-taking process. Steedman and Johnson-Laird (1980) have proposed that "the speaker assumes the hearer knows everything that the speaker knows about the world and about the conversation, unless there is some evidence to the contrary" (p. 129). This heuristic should lead to overestimates of the extent to which a speaker's knowledge is shared by others.

Denzin (1989) explains how this false consensus effect can get in the way of designing effective social change programs:

> In social life there is only interpretation. That is everyday life revolves around persons interpreting and making judgments about their own and others' behavior and experiences. Many times these interpretations and judgments are based on faulty, or incorrect understandings. Persons for instance mistake their own experiences for the experience of others. These interpretations are then formulated into social programs that are intended to alter and shape the lives of troubled people. . . . But often the understandings that these programs are based on bear little relationship to the meanings, interpretation, and experiences of the persons they are intended to serve. As a consequence there is a gap or failure in understanding. The programs don't work because they are based on a failure to take the perspective and attitude of the person served. (p. 11)

Others have suggested that the failure in perspective taking is not due to a false consensus bias, which may be well intentioned, but rather a form of knowledge arrogance. Although knowledge arrogance can be a trait present in many world cultures, Western societies in particular have been criticized for taking a unidirectional approach toward issues of knowledge. Howes

(1980) summarizes the knowledge arrogance notion in his analysis of many agricultural development programs, including the green revolution. His primary observation is that the overall Western philosophical position rests on the unilateral perspective that knowledge is to be transmitted from the researchers in the West to the farmers elsewhere. If this simplified model breaks down, as it frequently does, then questioning the validity of the model is not the response. This unidirectional model, with a tendency to denigrate indigenous knowledge, he adds, is not simply one of ideology but also reflects fundamental patterns of economic inequality, "which in turn has been responsible for the destruction of indigenous knowledge, and the reduction in the number of options open at the grass root level" (p. 354).

The surfacing of mutual tacit knowledge can help overcome the false consensus bias of automatically assuming that others' worldviews are more similar to one's own. However, the additional implication is to try and create conditions of openness where different cultures can explore and understand each other's worldview without quick evaluation of the veracity or legitimacy of the other's knowledge claims.

Creating Contexts for Collaborative Learning

Facilitating perspective taking requires what we will summarily term as *interpretive spaces* for mutual learning and joint meaning making. According to Denzin (1989), interpretation or the act of interpreting creates the conditions for understanding. Thus, interpretive spaces are interactional mechanisms that create the conditions for understanding by intervening at the level of knowledge structures, interpretive schemes, or thought worlds and bringing them to conscious awareness and facilitating their exchange in a process of mutual dialogue. They provide for the opening of one's preconceptions, assumptions, and meaning systems to oneself and to others (Habermas, 1979). Becoming aware of tacit consciousness requires self-reflexivity on the part of the actors. In Schutz's (1964) terms, reflexivity is the ability to periodically suspend our natural attitude. Interpretations normally given in a matter-of-course, taken-for-granted, natural way should be suspended so that one will be able to notice the assumptions, beliefs, and meanings that are the basis of our knowledge. Perspective taking happens best when individuals interact with each other at the level of interpretive dynamics and approach each other with a sense of nonjudgmental openness and a desire to broaden one's horizon of knowledge.

Comprehensive mutual understandings of a situation can be developed best by making it possible for individuals to portray their original understandings of a situation, self-reflect, reexamine these displays in the process of exchange with others, and come away from these reexaminations with different interpretations and perspectives of what they might mean (Weick, 1990). There are some examples of such interpretive spaces that can be gleaned from various intellectual traditions.

Cognitive anthropologists in international development studies have experimented with various knowledge elicitation and knowledge exchange techniques that use local modes of knowing as the primary medium. One creative example is where a local African board game called Ayo was used to understand and exchange knowledge on farming problems and issues on environmental preservation (Barker, 1980). The process resulted in genuine dialogue and mutual learning between the farmers and research workers. Similarly, in the smallpox eradication program (Fenner et al., 1988), WHO personnel made special efforts to gather local folklore concerning smallpox and its causes. They also creatively used skits and other local traditions of storytelling to communicate their knowledge of smallpox and how it can be prevented. Frequently, these sessions led to the genuine exchange of perspectives and sharing of mutual knowledge, which led to new insights.

Paulo Freire (1973) is well noted for his dialogical method of mutual education. Freire's work is concerned with radical social change. His approach attempts to make people aware of the broader historical and social contexts in which they are embedded and the power of existing institutional arrangements over their taken-for-granted practices and beliefs. By highlighting the arbitrary nature of these arrangements, he indicates that people need to find ways to modify the cognitive, material, and social foundations of these overarching contexts that inform their actions. His dialogical method opens up a reflexive attitude on the part of the various parties involved in the interchange. His premise rests on a process of mutual perspective taking within or between communities where, through dialogue, individual differences in ideologies, values, and asymmetrical distribution of resources and their relationship to unique beliefs and behavior are brought to the fore. An understanding of these significant individual differences and the nature of the background assumptions that guide these differences opens up the possibilities for alternative social orders that can eradicate conventional patterns of domination and hierarchy.

Search conferencing is an interesting approach for mutual perspective taking that has shown impressive effects in many cultures (Emery & Purser,

1996). A community development approach developed by Weisbord (1987), search conferencing is a powerful method to "excite, engage, produce new insights, and build a sense of common values and purpose" (p. 285). It is an exercise in learning, awareness, understanding, and mutual support.

Frequently in a search conference, all parties who are stakeholders to a decision are brought together, representing the whole system to the extent possible. Next, the groups go through a series of activities to examine their present and past, with a specific emphasis on laying bare their understandings, assumptions, beliefs, and meanings to themselves and one another. Participants use different devices such as stories, pictures, and skits to help them explicate their tacit understanding to oneself and to others. The whole system looks at this information, interprets what it finds, and draws conclusions for action for the future. Successful search conferences uncover shared values, open new possibilities, and enable congruent action plans for the future.

Appreciative inquiry (Cooperrider & Srivastva, 1987) is another promising approach that attempts to promote mutual understanding and learning across cultural contexts (Cooperrider & Bilimoria, 1993). Used extensively as a methodology for studying global social change organizations, appreciative inquiry is based on the philosophical premise that mutual valuing and appreciation is essential for collaborative learning and social transformation. As a process, it establishes ground rules that promote an uncritical viewing of the other's perspectives without critical evaluation of the veracity or legitimacy of the other's knowledge claims.

Interpretive interactionism (Denzin, 1989) is an approach to social research that strives to clarify meanings. By capturing and producing meaningful descriptions and interpretations of social processes from the subjective point of view of different actors, interpretive interactionism attempts to create conditions for understanding and "translate what is said in one language into the meanings and codes of another language" (p. 32). It is a mode of research that can expose and reveal the assumptions that support competing definitions of a problem where key individuals from different cultures can act as "semiotic brokers" (Lyotard, 1984).

The interpretive researcher(s) uses naturalistic inquiry methods such as case studies and biographical approaches to identify different definitions of a problem and competing models of truth that may operate in an interactional setting. Armed with these rich data, the researcher then facilitates the process of mutual perspective taking and collaborative learning among the different parties.

CONCLUSION

In this chapter, we have called for a reorientation of our understanding of global change, especially in relation to international technology transfer. This shift is based on a different set of assumptions about the nature of knowledge —that knowledge is subjectively constructed and consumed, that knowledge may require contextual modification to be adopted in the new context, and that effective contextual adaptation may warrant a creative synthesis of different thought worlds to produce new knowledge. This mindshift implies a move away from the traditional knowledge transmission approaches that rely on a universalistic theory of knowledge to one that appreciates collaborative learning through a process of perspective taking as a fundamental component of global change. We identified some potential issues in perspective taking and provided some examples of interpretive spaces for mutual learning, knowledge sharing, and joint meaning making, which is the essence of perspective taking.

A deeper understanding of the dynamics of perspective taking and ways to enable it represents an important area of future research, especially across cultural contexts. Within this overarching framework, several additional issues stand out. One issue of interest is to understand the unique modes of knowledge acquisition, storage, and transmission practices of each culture. Another issue is to explore under what conditions different cultures can overcome the inherent tendency to focus on their own perspectives and openly explore and try to understand each other's worldviews. We believe that the whole domain of perspective-taking research and its relationship to global change is particularly timely because, as a global society, we are becoming more interdependent than ever before.

PART

II

COLLABORATION AND PARTNERSHIP ARRANGEMENTS

The Structures of Global Change

6

SOCIAL CAPITAL, MUTUAL INFLUENCE, AND SOCIAL LEARNING IN INTERSECTORAL PROBLEM SOLVING IN AFRICA AND ASIA

L. DAVID BROWN
DARCY ASHMAN

A central aspect of the global changes now under way is increasing interdependence among a wide variety of actors—regions, nations, cultures, classes, ethnic groups, and organizations, among others. These interdependencies often make it possible for a wide range of resources and perspectives to contribute to solving social, economic, and political problems—but they also make possible destructive competition and conflict. This chapter examines cases of successful cooperation among actors from different institutional sectors—grassroots groups, nongovernmental organizations,

This chapter is based on a long-term research program carried out jointly by the Synergos Institute, the Society for Participatory Research in Asia (PRIA), the African Association for Literacy and Adult Education (AALAE), and the Institute for Development Research (IDR), and in cooperation with Grupo Esquel, the Highlander Research and Education Center, and Interaction Associates. The authors greatly appreciate the support to this program from the Rockefeller Foundation, the UN Development Programme, and the International Institute for Sustainable Development.

government agencies, and international donors—concerned with solving development problems in Africa and Asia. It seeks to identify factors associated with increasing social capacity to solve complex problems.

The scale and complexity of the social, political, and economic problems that challenge many developing countries daunt even the most optimistic. A large fraction of humanity is currently condemned to extreme poverty; little political voice; little access to education, health care, or other basic services; and ecological conditions that limit the possibilities of improving their living conditions (UNDP, 1992). Although the past 50 years have seen unprecedented improvements in the lives of many people all over the world (Patel, 1992), the same period has produced unprecedented increases in the differences between the rich and the poor. In 1960, for example, the richest fifth of humanity had incomes 30 times those of the poorest fifth; by 1990, that difference had doubled, so the incomes of the richest fifth were 60 times those of the poorest (UNDP, 1992, p. 1).

For many people in the bottom fifth, their disadvantages—poverty, lack of employment, poor education, ill health, environmental decline—interact in positive feedback loops that make climbing out of the morass extraordinarily difficult (Ackoff, 1974; Chambers, 1983). Problem-solving activities that do not take into account the systemic "mess" that preserves and reinforces the status quo may treat symptoms rather than causes and be vulnerable to feedback loops that damp out long-term improvements. They may also fail to mobilize the kinds of information and resources required to improve the situation, because those resources are often held by many different actors who do not cooperate.

Significant long-term improvements in many of these complex development problems depend on joint action by many different actors who, together, have the knowledge, resources, and potential for long-term engagement required for sustainable changes. In some circumstances, the interaction among such actors—from different institutional sectors, unequal in power, with very diverse interests and perspectives—leads to startling improvements (e.g., Uphoff, 1992); in many others, the results are conflict, power struggles, or disintegration of the alliance well before it has any long-term impacts (Gray, 1989).

This chapter seeks to identify ingredients associated with successful cooperation across differences in sector and power to solve development problems. It examines 13 cases of multiparty cooperation in 12 countries in Africa and Asia, with special attention to social capital resources, patterns of conflict and mutual influence, and learning at several levels of analysis.

We begin by providing an overview of the conceptual background of this analysis. The possibilities of intersectoral and interorganizational cooperation to solve problems have drawn a good deal of attention in recent years because researchers and practitioners have recognized that many urgent problems are beyond the capacities of single organizations (e.g., Gray, 1989; Trist, 1983). Next, we discuss the cases, the methods by which case data were collected and formulated, and our approach to comparative analysis. Then, we present the results of this analysis. Finally, we consider the implications of these results for policymakers and for social capacity building.

CONCEPTUAL BACKGROUND

Cooperation among diverse organizations has emerged over the past decade as an important way of dealing with problems too large or complex for single organizations to handle. Interorganizational cooperation has helped resolve problems as diverse as improving urban schools (Waddock, 1993), articulating national policies for coal production and use (Gray & Hay, 1986), enhancing urban leadership networks (Brown & Detterman, 1987), promoting regional economic development in declining areas (Trist, 1986), and enhancing national capacity to compete in the semiconductor industry (Browning, Beyer, & Shetler, 1995). But it is often difficult to create cooperation among diverse organizations, especially when they have histories of conflict or see their interests as divergent, even when it may be in their long-term interest to work together.

In this analysis, we will be particularly concerned with differences associated with institutional sectors and inequalities in power. Organizations from the state sector, such as legislatures and government bureaucracies, have interests and concerns that differ substantially from organizations from the market sector, such as manufacturers and banks, or organizations from the civil society, such as neighborhood groups, churches, or nongovernmental development organizations (Brown & Korten, 1991). Actors who differ in power may find their relations characterized by communication problems and explosions of unexpected and difficult-to-resolve conflict (Brown, 1982).

Differences in power and culture are inevitable when cooperation involves grassroots groups, international agencies, nongovernmental development organizations (NGOs), and government agencies, as in the cases discussed here. Multiparty cooperation in problem solving is possible in developing countries, as these cases illustrate, but it is not common. Increasing recognition that the state cannot solve many important development problems by itself sets the stage for more intersectoral cooperation in the future. This analysis will seek to understand factors involved in successful cooperation across differences in power and culture, as well as their implications for the abilities of organizations and societies to learn in the face of social diversity and turbulence.

Earlier analyses of some of these cases (Brown, 1998; Brown & Tandon, 1993) have identified some factors associated with successful cooperation across power inequalities and sectoral differences. Three sets of factors in particular will be examined in more detail here: (a) preexisting "social capital" that supports cooperation among key actors, (b) mutual influence among parties in spite of sector and power differences, and (c) learning processes that enable new behavior by organizations and interorganizational systems.

First, the concept of *social capital* refers to relationships among social actors that enable joint action. Some definitions focus on the social capital available to individuals, such as interpersonal relationships characterized by trust and reciprocity (e.g., Coleman, 1990, pp. 300-321). Individuals with large stocks of social capital can call on extensive networks of trusting relationships to help them accomplish their goals, and so they have significant advantages over individuals with less social capital. Other definitions focus on the stocks of social capital available to a society, in the form of high levels of voluntary associations, strong norms of reciprocity and inclusion, and high degrees of social trust (e.g., Fukuyama, 1995; Putnam, 1993). Societies with high stocks of social capital are able to mobilize the widespread civic engagement associated with responsive government and rapid economic development (Bratton, 1992; Putnam, 1993).

We are interested here in a kind of social capital in between that of individuals and that of societies. We are focusing on social capital in the relationships of trust and reciprocity that connect stakeholders who are critical to understanding and solving specific social problem domains—in other words, social capital that bridges differences in sector and power to enable joint action by diverse groups and organizations. We want to examine the extent to which such bridging of social capital, preexisting or created, affects the success of cooperation across sector and power differences.

Second, we will examine the patterns of *mutual influence* among key actors in the course of decision making about problems and solutions. We are particularly interested in the extent to which mutual influence is possible across power differences among government agencies, international donors,

NGOs, and grassroots groups. Differences in sector and power can easily produce disagreement and conflicts of interest. Such disagreements can escalate into destructive conflict or oppression (Brown, 1982; Paige, 1975). But such conflict can also be constructive when all of the stakeholders can influence decision making and see possible joint gains (e.g., Paige, 1975; World Bank, 1994). This analysis will also examine how conflict and mutual influence are related to successful intersectoral cooperation.

Finally, we are concerned with the *social learning* processes by which groups of stakeholders develop new perspectives, goals, and behaviors. Milbrath (1989, pp. 92-93) argues that social learning advances from the accumulation of knowledge, response to new technology, and expanding communications. Together, these factors reshape the capacities of social systems to deal with their environments. The issue of organizational learning has become a focus of attention in response to rapid technological and environmental changes (e.g., Argyris & Schon, 1978; Haas, 1990; Huber, 1991; Senge, 1990). The notion of social learning has received less explicit attention (e.g., Finger & Verlaan, 1995; Milbrath, 1989), but the need for rapid learning and innovation that serves larger social units than the organization is also increasingly apparent as nations and regions become more richly connected and interdependent. So, this analysis will also examine factors associated with social learning in these cases.

CASES AND METHODS

Because cooperation across sectors and power inequalities to solve social problems is not well understood, this study is necessarily exploratory. On the other hand, because initial analyses have been carried out, this analysis can focus on key elements in the creation of such cooperation. The availability of a number of cases in Asia and Africa makes it possible to compare cases across regions and across outcomes to identify factors associated with success.

The cases were chosen to represent a wide range of problems and countries in Asia and Africa. They all involved cooperation across sectors, usually among community groups, NGOs, government agencies, and international donors, and they all achieved some level of success in solving problems. Table 6.1 describes briefly the problem for each case.

These cases cover a variety of problems, from health services (Bangladesh, Sudan) to income generation programs (India Workers, Malaysia, Lesotho) to the improvement of economic productivity (Zambia, Uganda, Indo-

Table 6.1   Intersectoral Cooperation Cases in Africa and Asia

---

Africa

> *Kenya Cookstove Program:* to promote environmental protection through distribution of new fuel-efficient cookstoves (Houghton, 1994).
>
> *Lesotho Credit Union Program:* to improve rural poverty conditions by making sources of credit available (Braimoh & Sets'abi, 1994).
>
> *Sudan Popular Health Program:* to improve the availability of health services to the urban poor refugees in Khartoum (ElSheikh & Wangoola, 1994).
>
> *Uganda Fishing Program:* to revitalize fishing villages in northern Uganda (Odurkene, 1994).
>
> *Zambia Integrated Rural Development:* to promote food security, market access, and reduced emigration from North Western Province (Machila, 1994).
>
> *Zimbabwe Water and Sanitation:* to expand the number and quality of water and sanitation facilities available in Gwanda District (Nyoni, 1994).

Asia

> *Bangladesh Immunization Program:* to provide an expanded immunization program for children throughout the country (Hussain, 1991).
>
> *Indian Biogas Program:* to build biogas plants for poor rural families in the state of Orissa (Bezborua & Banerjee, 1991).
>
> *Indian Workers Initiative:* to revive and make profitable a "sick" industrial plant closed by its owners (Chadha, 1991).
>
> *Indonesian Irrigation Program:* to turn responsibility for maintenance and control over small irrigation systems to local water users (Purnomo & Pambagio, 1991).
>
> *Malaysian Youth Technology Centers:* to encourage youth in rural villages to undertake local economic activities (Rahim, 1991).
>
> *Pakistan Urban Sanitation Program:* to build sewage systems in Karachi slum areas (Rashid, 1991).
>
> *Philippines Urban Upgrading:* to improve housing and other facilities in Manila slum areas (Rosas-Ingnacio, 1991).

---

nesia) to the improvement of physical infrastructure (Pakistan, Zimbabwe, Philippines). Although the cases were all successful to some degree, they vary considerably in the reach of their activity and the nature of their activities, as might be expected from such a diverse set of problems. This sampling strategy does not allow detailed comparisons across similar projects, but it does allow comparisons to identify major factors that distinguish between more general measures of success.

We chose to develop case studies as an approach that would provide detailed information about a wide range of factors that might influence the success of cooperation among such diverse partners. We did not believe that the more focused data collection by surveys would provide access to the complex description possible in detailed studies of multiple cases (Miles & Huberman, 1994; Yin, 1984).

The cases were written by casewriters selected for their access to the parties to the case, especially the communities and the NGOs, in addition to their skills in writing analytic case studies. We expected that it would be particularly difficult to collect valid information about the perspectives of relatively low-power participants, and so we sought casewriters who would have good access to those participants. Casewriters used a common set of questions to examine the evolution of cooperation, and they sought to capture the perspectives and experiences of many different parties.

Although the casewriters in both Asia and Africa used the same basic set of questions to collect data and write the cases, the two regions designed their studies to reflect regional concerns and priorities. In Asia, the casewriting and analysis process was coordinated by the Society for Participatory Research in Asia (PRIA), in close cooperation with the Institute for Development Research (IDR). Cases were selected after wide consultations that identified examples of relatively successful intersectoral cooperations, and then casewriters were recruited in consultation with national organizations knowledgeable about the cases. PRIA and IDR project leaders cofacilitated a workshop attended by casewriters and by other members of the international consortium to review initial outlines of the cases and to agree on a final set of questions to be asked. Then, casewriters took 6 months to prepare drafts, which were discussed at a case conference that brought together casewriters, coordinators, consortium members, and representatives of key actors in the cases to try to identify similarities, differences, and important lessons of the cases. Several analyses were grounded in the cases, and these discussions were written over the next year (Brown & Tandon, 1993; Schearer, 1993; Tandon, 1993).

In Africa, the African Association for Literacy and Adult Education (AALAE) coordinated the data collection and analysis process and used its own regional network to identify cases and recruit casewriters. AALAE organized a casewriters' workshop at which they agreed to use a protocol of questions that supplemented the Asian topics with others relevant to the African setting. The African conference first focused on African perspectives and analyses of the cases and invited members of the international consortium to participate in a subsequent discussion of regional conclusions and outsider perspectives. A summary report of the findings of the conference was prepared by AALAE (Nyambura, 1994), and a review of the cases and findings of the international consortium discussions is also available (Nyambura et al., 1995).

In both regions, casewriters were encouraged to explore multiple perspectives on case events and to provide as rich a description of those perspectives as possible in telling the story of the case. Those descriptions were discussed and elaborated during case conferences, and casewriters revised their cases on the basis of feedback from those conferences. Those revised cases are the basis for this analysis.

Comparative analysis of the 13 cases has posed a daunting task. We have sought to identify critical ingredients and patterns in the evolution of cooperative problem solving without losing sight of the unique stories of each case. To do so, we have engaged in an iterative process of data display and analysis that has produced a series of matrices of data from the 13 cases (Miles & Huberman, 1994). We began by examining information about the effects of cooperation in each case on its initiating problem, and we found that the cases could be distinguished on a rough index of "success" based on the number of people directly affected and the commitment of various constituencies to continuing the cooperation. The resulting clusters of "clear," "potential," and "questionable" successes have been used to identify factors associated with success.

It is difficult to identify simple causes in events as complex as these cases. There are too many variables for easy identification of sufficient causes; events are almost always determined by a number of factors; and causes and effects often interact over time, so one period's effect is another period's cause. Nevertheless, factors and patterns may be identified that help to explain complex events, and those explanations may be of use in planning and implementing future actions.

ANALYSIS AND FINDINGS

This analysis begins with an assessment of the success of cooperation and then examines factors and patterns associated with that success. It will focus on two clusters of factors that appear to affect success: social capital that preexisted or was created by the project, and patterns of decision making within the project.

Cooperation Success

Table 6.2 portrays the cases on two dimensions of success and then orders them in three rough groups by their level of success. Because the cases focused on quite different problems, they are not directly comparable in terms of

Table 6.2 Outcomes of Cooperation

Cases	Reach of Solution Effects	Resources for Sustainability
Clear success		
Lesotho Credit Unions	Wide: 70+ credit unions with 19,000 members affect lives of 200,000 people.	High: GO supports program; NGO key supporter; GROs committed.
Pakistan Urban Sanitation	Wide: 6,000 lanes organize to build 64,000 latrines to affect 250,000 people.	High: GO cooperates; NGO expands role; GROs expand.
Philippines Urban Upgrading	Wide: Establish ownership; improve 90% of dwellings for 170,000 residents.	High: GO reluctant support; NGO key promoter; GROs mobilized.
Bangladesh Immunization	Wide: National immunization from 2% to 80%; child mortality down 20%.	High: GO approves; NGOs support expansion; GROs want more.
Sudan Popular Health	Wide: 40+ new clinics serve estimated 1.6 million clients in Khartoum.	High: GO wants help; NGO is committed; GROs want service.
Potential success		
India Biogas Program	Wide: Built 45,000 biogas plants, affecting more than 200,000 people.	Medium: GO program; NGO expanding; GROs not involved.
Indonesia Small Irrigation Systems	Medium: New policy transfers control of irrigation systems to water users.	Medium: GO needs policy; NGOs support; GROs not organized.
Uganda Fishing Program	Medium: Technical assistance and gear to 10,000 fishermen and 300 self-managed groups.	Low: GO support not clear; no local NGOs; GROs not viable.
Zimbabwe Water and Sanitation	Medium: Built 50 new wells, 300 dams, 7,000 latrines for 30,000 people.	High: GO initiated; NGOs support; GROs support program.
India Workers' Initiative	Narrow: Restart plant; reemploy 600 workers; set precedent for future.	Medium: GO wants change; NGO starting; GROs interested.
Questionable success		
Malaysia Youth Centres	Narrow: Start 30+ youth centers with 3,000-4,000 members; encourage new efforts at income generation.	Low: GO committed; NGOs not involved; GROs weak interest.
Zambia Integrated Rural Development	Narrow: Provide technical assistance to 200+ new groups and 5,000+ farmers.	Low: GO limited support; NGOs not involved; GROs few viable.
Kenya Fuel-Efficient Cookstoves	Narrow: Initial group distributes 5,000 cookstoves; inspires 22 new groups.	Low: GO little support; NGO little support; GROs not viable.

NOTE: GRO = grassroots organization; NGO = nongovernmental organization; GO = government organization.

solutions. We have chosen to compare them on two quite general variables in this table: (a) the reach of problem solutions in terms of people directly affected, and (b) constituency commitment to sustaining that solution.

Reach of problem solutions refers to a rough calculation of the number of people affected by the program: Programs rated as having "wide reach" have affected more than 100,000 people; programs rated "medium reach" have affected from 10,000 to 100,000 people; and programs rated "narrow reach" have affected fewer than 10,000 people. The assignment of cases to categories is *not* a statement about their present or future potential; some programs with narrow impact today may have wide impact tomorrow. But the capacity to affect large numbers of people is an important issue. The problem of "scaling up" has not been solved by many otherwise successful programs (Rondinelli, 1983; Tendlar, 1989), and expanding program impacts to affect hundreds of thousands of people is critical to widely disseminating useful solutions.

Resources for future sustainability include the energies, skills, financial support, and policy commitments that can be mobilized to sustain the improvements introduced by the project, especially as resources from external donors are withdrawn or focused in other areas. A rating of "high" resources for sustainability in the second column reflects substantial support from all three constituencies—government agencies (GOs), nongovernmental development organizations (NGOs), and grassroots organizations (GROs)—for continuing the program. A rating of "medium" indicates that two out of three constituencies support continuation, whereas a rating of "low" indicates that one or fewer constituencies supports its continuation. Although international agencies were important to starting these cooperations, sustainability will depend on resources within the country, so international agencies are not included in this analysis.

On the basis of these dimensions, we can divide the cases into three groups. Some programs expanded to affect hundreds of thousands of people and generated commitment from all three constituencies to support their continuation. We have clustered five such *clear successes* in the first half of the table—three from Asia and two from Africa. Three other cases, one Asian and two African, produced relatively narrow impacts and displayed limited success in building constituency commitment to support the future program. Although these cases have produced some desirable outcomes, it is not clear that these programs can survive without heavy, ongoing investment by external donors or government funders. We have labeled these cases *questionable successes* and placed them at the end of Table 6.2. The other five cases, three Asian and two African, have achieved less impact than the clear successes but more than the questionable successes. They also vary considerably in the extent to which they mobilize resources for sustainability. We have labeled these cases *potential successes* to reflect the possibility that they might move in either direction over the longer term.

Wide reach and resources for sustainability appear to be linked in these cases. This is consistent with other findings that have suggested the importance of integrating project implementation with the concerns and resources of local institutions (e.g., Cernea, 1987; Morss, Hatch, Mickelwaite, & Sweet, 1976). It is not too surprising that cooperations that solve problems affecting hundreds of thousands of people will also generate wide support for continuation. But it is also increasingly recognized that sustainability is anything but a foregone conclusion, even when such widespread support exists.

Social Capital

Social capital in the form of relationships of trust and reciprocity can be particularly valuable when it bridges the social chasms created by sector and power differences. There is evidence that intersectoral partnerships in industrialized settings (Waddock, 1993) and sustainable development projects (Cernea, 1987) both depend in large part on such social capital. More specifically, Table 6.3 examines two aspects of these cases that reflect the presence or absence of social capital that enables such bridging: (a) the existence of local organizations and networks, and (b) the existence of relationships or contacts among the parties.

The existence of local organizations, which reflect bonds of trust and common interest within grassroots populations, supports dialogue with other actors by creating a coherent voice from grassroots interests that often speak in an unorganized cacophony and make it difficult for even the most interested listeners to respond to their concerns. Without organizations to represent their interests, grassroots populations become recipients or implementors of programs with relatively little influence on design decisions that shape project goals, plans, and outcomes. In these cases, two forms of local organization were active participants in projects. In many cases, GROs, like credit unions or lane organizations, spoke for their members, often on the basis of a specific locale. In some cases, networks of grassroots organizations (GRNs), such as the Zone One Tondo Organization (ZOTO) or the Credit Union League, represented the views of many GROs in different locales. The first column of Table 6.3 describes the extent to which GROs existed or were created in the

Table 6.3   Existing Social Capital

Cases	Grassroots Organizations and Networks	Intersectoral Contacts
Clear success		
Lesotho Credit Unions	GRO: Created. Credit unions become viable GROs. GRN: Created. Credit Union League (LCCUL) negotiates with government and donors.	High: National University (NUL) uses links to international agencies and GoL; rural workers link university and local groups.
Pakistan Urban Sanitation	GRO: Created. Lanes organize to build latrines. GRN: Created. Lanes work with OPP to negotiate with government agencies.	Medium: OPP founder has credibility with elites; OPP builds close relationships with lanes; OPP avoids contact with GoP.
Philippines Urban Upgrading	GRO: Existing. GROs organized at start. GRN: Existing and created. ZOTO already operating; UGNAYAN created as larger alliance.	Low to Medium: Little link at outset; ZOTO and UGNAYAN build contacts with bank and GoP insiders for information.
Bangladesh Immunization	GRO: Few. GROs organized for other purposes participate. GRN: None.	High: Large NGO leaders and ADAB have extensive links to INGOs, government, and grassroots groups.
Sudan Popular Health	GRO: Few. Communities choose to invite clinics. GRN: None.	High: IARA and HIKMA contacts with GoS, Islamic, village elders, business leaders, and medical establishment.
Potential success		
India Biogas Program	GRO: Few. Families contribute to build biogas plants. GRN. None.	Medium: Gram Vikas founder has links to GoI officials, state officials, and grassroots leaders.
Indonesia Small Irrigation Systems	GRO: Created. Water user associations take over irrigation in pilot tests. GRN: None.	High: LP3ES oversees pilots and workshops to help GoI and water user associations work together for new policy.
Uganda Fishing Program	GRO: Created. Organize fishing, credit, and self-management groups. GRN: None.	Medium: ACORD has GoU sanction and trains local organizers to work with communities but is an expatriate agency.

Table 6.3　Continued

Cases	Grassroots Organizations and Networks	Intersectoral Contacts
Zimbabwe Water and Sanitation	GRO: Existing. Many local associations already active. GRN: Existing. ORAP represents interests of associations.	Low to Medium: Links of GoZ to ORAP vary with level of political and tribal conflict at time.
India Workers' Initiative	GRO: Existing. Kamani Employees Union guarded plant for years without pay. GRN: None yet.	Medium: Union leaders key figures in pleading case to GoI and Supreme Court while preserving worker loyalty.
Questionable success		
Malaysia Youth Centres	GRO: Existing. Youth groups are prerequisite to establishing Centers. GRN: None.	Low to Medium: Minister of Youth & Sports is key actor, but few contacts with other sectors.
Zambia Integrated Rural Development	GRO: Few. Effort fails to create independent ongoing GROs. GRN: None.	Low to Medium: GTZ cooperates with GoZ but has little contact with other sectors except as project implementors.
Kenya Fuel-Efficient Cookstoves	GRO: Few. Keyo successful early but not viable for longer term. GRN: Existing. But women's network not viable as voice.	High: Many contacts among GoK, KENGO, ITDG, MYW but no central bridging agency emerges to coordinate.

course of cooperation, and the extent to which GRNs existed or were created to play active roles in these projects.

A second important element of social capital is the existence of intersectoral contacts, through individuals or organizations with relationships across sectors and power differences, that enabled credible communications among actors. Without such bridges, it is more difficult to develop a shared understanding of the problem or to recognize common or complementary interests that diverse actors have in problem solving. Again, the emphasis is on identifying such bridges and assessing whether they existed at the outset or merged during the course of interaction across sectors. In the second column of Table 6.3, a rating of "high" indicates extensive and credible intersectoral contacts by bridging organizations and individuals; "medium" indicates contacts across sectors but some problems of credibility; and "low" reflects relatively little credible and enduring cross-sector contact that enabled communication and joint action. In some cases, the amount of intersectoral contact changed significantly over time and will be represented by a changing rating (e.g., "low to medium").

The first three clear successes were marked by the presence of strong GROs and GRNs; the other two had less involvement of GROs and little sign of active GRNs. On the other hand, the latter two displayed high levels of intersectoral contact, in contrast to somewhat lower levels of such contact among the first three. It may be that some forms of social capital are substitutes for one another in expanding initial efforts to reach many people: A strong grassroots voice (as in the Pakistan, Philippines, and Zimbabwe cases) may compensate for low levels of intersectoral contact and credibility, and effective bridging organizations may compensate for low levels of grassroots organization (as in the Bangladesh, Sudan, and Indonesian cases).

Where social capital to support cooperation is not well developed, project sustainability may be questionable. Thus, the Malaysia and Zambia cases display relatively low levels of the local organization or intersectoral contacts that appear to be associated with clear success. Success may also be undermined if existing social capital does not link actors who are central to effective problem solving on the specific problem. In the Kenya case, for example, moderate levels of local organization and high levels of intersectoral contacts were unable to compensate for competition and conflict among potential bridging organizations.

Decision Making

The success or failure of cooperation is also shaped by the processes of decision making and mutual influence that frame problems, set directions, articulate plans, and guide actions. Whatever expectations or preferences the parties bring, the actual practice of decision making shapes their future expectations and actions. Table 6.4 summarizes two aspects of decision making and mutual influence in these cases: (a) level of conflict, particularly among unequal parties; and (b) grassroots participation in decision making.

Although these projects emphasize cooperation, experience suggests that conflict is also an important aspect of multiparty relations (Brown & Tandon, 1993). In the first column of Table 6.4, the cases are rated on levels of conflict displayed among the parties: "Low" conflict suggests few reports of disagreements or tensions among the parties; "moderate" conflict reflects clear in-

Table 6.4   Decision Making

Cases	Level of Conflict Among Parties	Grassroots Participation in Decision Making
Clear success		
Lesotho Credit Unions	Moderate to Intense: Credit unions and network resist GoL takeover plans; reject donor leadership nominations.	High: Credit unions participate in LCCUL policy setting; LCCUL influences GoL and donor decisions about credit union governance.
Pakistan Urban Sanitation	Moderate to Intense: OPP and Department of Public Works struggle over control of expanded sanitation program.	High: OPP works with lane organizations to define and implement sanitation program; OPP and lane organizations plan and implement expansion with GoP and donors.
Philippines Urban Upgrading	Intense: ZOTO and UGNAYAN GRNs challenge GoP and World Bank plans for urban redevelopment.	High: Neighborhood organizations participate in ZOTO and UGNAYAN decisions; they influence GoP and World Bank to define and implement program.
Bangladesh Immunization	Moderate: Friction among GoB and NGO staffs in carrying out immunization campaign.	Low to Moderate: Grassroots groups bring children for vaccination but do not participate in program decisions; NGOs and GoB jointly implement program.
Sudan Popular Health	Low: Minor conflicts are resolved among professionals in HIKMA and IARA.	Low to Moderate: Communities decide to accept clinics, but do not participate in other program decisions; NGOs influence GoS and donors in developing program.
Potential success		
India Biogas Program	Moderate to Intense: State government agency and Gram Vikas fight over compensation for plants constructed and program expansion.	Low: Individuals help build plants but do not influence program decisions; NGOs influence state agencies on policy.
Indonesia Small Irrigation Systems	Low: LP3ES careful about offending GoI agencies and is criticized by other NGOs for cooperating too much.	Moderate: Water user associations demonstrate that they can manage irrigation systems; LP3ES helps interpret research and articulate new policy; GoI has final say.
Uganda Fishing Program	Low to Moderate: Local government officers resent higher pay of ACORD rural workers; seek to control program resources.	Moderate: ACORD trains local leaders and rural workers to increase local control and self-reliance.

(continued)

Table 6.4   Continued

Cases	Level of Conflict Among Parties	Grassroots Participation in Decision Making
Zimbabwe Water and Sanitation	Moderate to Intense: GoZ bans some activities of ORAP in response to national political instabilities in mid-1980s.	Moderate: ORAP emphasizes member participation in Association decisions; ORAP influences donors and GoZ on some issues.
India Workers' Initiative	Moderate: Some tensions between workers and union executives over plant management. (Intense struggle with old owners resolved by Supreme Court.)	Moderate to High: Union emphasizes membership role in decision making; joins with management in rehabilitating plant.
Questionable success		
Malaysia Youth Centres	Low: Little conflict among parties, especially when they differ in power and status.	Low to Moderate: Youth clubs invited to participate in starting centers; more active in program implementation than in design.
Zambia Integrated Rural Development	Low: Limited dialogue among the parties; little overt conflict reported.	Low: Program largely defined for region by GTZ; local participants largely in role of project implementors.
Kenya Fuel-Efficient Cookstoves	Low to Moderate: Conflict among NGOs over program responsibilities; tensions among DOs, NGOs, and GRO.	Low: Program formulated by GTZ for implementation by KENGO, and formulated by KENGO for implementation by Keyo.

stances of friction and disagreement that do not threaten to escalate into destructive relations; and "intense" conflict refers to strong disagreements and escalated tensions associated with active opposition and efforts to frustrate each others' intentions or interests.

Mutual influence is an essential element of interorganizational cooperation but one that may be difficult to achieve when the partners are unequal. Grassroots participation in decision making becomes important in the analysis of these cases, and the second column of Table 6.4 summarizes levels of participation by grassroots groups. In this analysis, "low" participation indicates relatively little influence on problem definition, goal setting, or action planning; "moderate" participation involves an active role in some stages of decision making; and "high" participation reflects active grassroots roles in many decisions and a demonstrated capacity to successfully oppose powerful actors on important issues. Low levels of participation involve consultation, information sharing, and work to implement others' plans; high levels involve strengthening the capacities and roles of low power groups and increasing their ability to influence and control resources directed at their problems.

Four of the five long-term successes report moderate to intense levels of conflict among actors in the cooperative projects, whereas the three questionable cases report low to moderate conflict. Only in the Sudan case is long-term success associated with low conflict, perhaps because the expert-driven character of health services requires little participation from low-power groups and because the shared commitment to Islam allowed for informal mediation of differences. In general, however, these cases indicate that successful and sustainable cooperation can coexist with moderate or even intense conflict.

There is considerable variation on how much grassroots groups participate in decision making. The first three cases in Table 6.4 exhibit high levels of participation, as might be expected from the high levels of GRO and GRN activity reported in Table 6.3. In contrast, the next two cases—also clear successes—report low or low-to-moderate levels of participation, much like the three questionable cases. Is participation actually irrelevant to success in cooperation?

We believe that two factors produce this result. First, the problem defined for the Bangladesh and Sudan programs required less active grassroots mobilization than did the first three cases, so creating strong local organizations was not essential to expanding their impacts. Second, the interests of grassroots groups in those cases were addressed in part by the active participation of NGOs and NGO networks in project decision making. In the questionable cases, in contrast, low grassroots participation in decision making was combined with problems whose long-term solution required active local participation and organization, so solutions were undermined by a mismatch between problem demands and resources mobilized.

The dimensions of conflict and participation appear to interact: High levels of participation are associated with moderate to intense conflict, and low levels of participation are associated with low conflict. Partnerships that mobilize the resources of grassroots groups to solve problems are likely to be stormy, with grassroots actors challenging government and donor organizations when their activities violate local interests—as in the Lesotho, Pakistan, and Philippines programs. But those cooperations also produce long-lasting programs that mobilize many resources in the support of problem solving—

often, resources such as grassroots energy and creativity that would not otherwise be available.

Social Learning

Social learning is not a well-understood process, however important it may be to responding to the challenges faced by modern societies. Table 6.5 focuses on two aspects of these cases that contribute to the capacity to social learning about intransigent problems: (a) evidence of learning processes at different levels; and (b) catalyst roles played by different actors, organizations, and individuals who have fostered a search for new perspectives and solutions to these problems.

The learning processes described in the first column of Table 6.5 describe evidence that learning may have occurred in the course of these activities as actors sought to define, analyze, and solve problems. It has been argued that organizational learning, although it depends to some extent on learning by its individual members, must include changes in organizational-level patterns of behavior (Fiol & Lyles, 1985; Swieringa & Wierdsma, 1994). Social learning, by the same token, may depend on individual and organizational learning but include changes in societal institutions and patterns of behavior that persist after specific individuals and organizations move on. The table describes learning at three levels. *Program learning* enables the parties to deal with the specific issues involved in carrying out the program, such as giving immunizations in Bangladesh or running a cooperative in Lesotho. *Organizational learning* indicates changes in specific organizational actors, such as increased capacity of the Association of Development Agencies of Bangladesh, the NGO charged with coordinating hundreds of NGOs involved in the campaign. Finally, *social learning* in this context indicates changes in interorganizational arrangements that enable multiple organizational actors to understand and work together effectively. Each form of learning is rated as "+" when clearly present or "?" when absent or not clearly present.

The second column reports on catalyst roles played by organizations and individuals in the course of these cases. Learning in these cases was often largely the result of actions taken by key individuals and organizations who pressed for better solutions, encouraged parties to engage with each other, fostered the examination of multiple alternatives, and facilitated problem-solving activities when cooperation efforts ran into problems. These actors were not necessarily the sources of solutions to problems, but they were often

Table 6.5 Social Learning

Cases	Learning Activities	Catalyst Roles
Clear success		
Lesotho Credit Unions	*Program +:* Systematic efforts to learn about credit unions. *Organizational +:* Many parties (e.g., unions) develop new capacities. *Social +:* Many parties learn about and continue to adapt to each others' concerns.	*Organization:* National University of Lesotho Extension Service; St. Xavier University in Canada.
Pakistan Urban Sanitation	*Program +:* Systematic creation of new sanitation technology and programs. *Organizational +:* NGO develops new Research and Training Institute. *Social +:* New configuration of GROs, NGOs, donors, GoP in urban change.	*Organization:* OPP initiates research and organizing to define project with BCCI support; WHO and World Bank help preserve participation emphasis. *Individual:* Founder has reputation that launches and protects OPP.
Philippines Urban Upgrading	*Program +:* "Reflective organizing" as GRO learning strategy. *Organizational +:* ZOTO builds capacity for national campaign. *Social +:* New linkage of ZOTO, World Bank, GoP for joint learning and action.	*Organization:* ZOTO mobilizes communities to resist initial definition of program and represents them in negotiations with GoP and Bank.
Bangladesh Immunization	*Program +:* Evaluation of pilot programs results in expanding NGO role. *Organizational +:* NGOs, GoB build capacity to deliver rural services. *Social +:* NGOs, GoB build attitudes and precedent for large-scale joint action.	*Organization:* Large NGOs are initial mediators between GoB and NGO community; ADAB later coordinates campaign.
Sudan Popular Health	*Program +:* Shift from curative to preventive in response to new data. *Organizational +:* HIKMA learns to promote and support program. *Social?:* Little evidence of interorganizational learning.	*Organization:* IARA establishes initial concept and then creates HIKMA to mobilize communities for health care. *Individual:* The leader of HIKMA has been particularly important in building its links with many other institutions.

(continued)

Table 6.5   Continued

Cases	Learning Activities	Catalyst Roles
Potential success		
India Biogas Program	*Program +:* Improve quality of biogas plants and building process over project. *Organizational +:* NGO builds capacity for large-scale program delivery. *Social +:* Attitudes and arrangements between NGO, GO altered by program.	*Organization:* Gram Vikas key agency in working with local communities to plan and implement biogas construction. *Individual:* Founder of Gram Vikas has credibility with many agencies required to make program work.
Indonesia Small Irrigation Systems	*Program +:* Action research to support management by water user associations. *Organizational +:* NGO, GoI, water user associations build new capacities. *Social +:* Expanded capacity for GoI, NGO, and associations to work together.	*Organization:* LP3ES central to interpreting action research, examining policy alternatives, and developing training programs for government officials and user associations.
Uganda Fishing Program	*Program +:* Systematic efforts to promote action learning for local groups. *Organizational +:* GROs, NGOs learn new capacities to carry out programs *Social +:* Increased capacity for rural workers, GROs, and NGOs to learn from each other.	*Organization:* ACORD is driving force in conceiving, financing, and implementing project in a process that makes heavy use of local leaders and rural development workers.
Zimbabwe Water and Sanitation	*Program +:* Reflections on experience build association capacity. *Organizational +:* NGO develops new capacities from experience. *Social?:* Agencies independent and learn little from each other.	*Organization:* GoZ ministries are major actors in defining and implementing the program and involving other agencies.
India Workers' Initiative	*Program +:* Major effort to plan, organize, and build skills for takeover. *Organizationalal +:* New union, GoI relations; Supreme Court changes law. *Social +:* Union, co-op, and GoI agencies share perspectives; Court changes law.	*Organization:* Kamani employees' union supports workers, develops plans, and advocates changes in law and policy. *Individual:* Union leaders develop credibility with GoI officials, new plant managers, and workers for program.

Table 6.5   Continued

Cases	Learning Activities	Catalyst Roles
Questionable success		
Malaysia Youth Centres	*Program +:* Initial employment programs modified to fit local needs and interests. *Organizational +:* GoM builds economic programs and capacities for youth. *Social?:* Little evidence of capacity for parties to learn together.	*Organization:* The Ministry of Youth is the primary actor in making these centers a reality. *Individual:* The Minister was in large part responsible for promoting the concept of the centers.
Zambia Integrated Rural Development	*Program?:* Limited learning by grassroots groups involved in program. *Organizational?:* Not clear organization learned from experience. *Social?:* GTZ remains responsible; other actors not fully engaged.	*Organization:* GTZ takes the lead in formulating the program and in coordinating its implementation.
Kenya Fuel-Efficient Cookstoves	*Program +:* Active local learning on developing cookstove technology. *Organizational?:* GRO remains unaware of key issues, such as marketing. *Social?:* Actors pursue centrifugal interests and do not learn together.	*Organization:* Many catalysts with diverse agendas (KENGO, ITDG, Maendeleo wa Wanawake, GTZ, GoK) create confusion about goals and implementation steps.

key to enabling communication or developing new knowledge that led to solutions. To play such a role requires not only commitment to the cooperation idea but also the skills, contacts, and credibility to bring different parties together and facilitate joint learning.

The learning activities in the first column of Table 6.5 suggest that learning about programmatic issues was widespread, as might be expected when selection criteria emphasized successful problem solving. Almost all of the cases displayed some signs of organizational learning as well. The pattern of changes in interorganizational relations, however, indicates that social learning was less common, especially among the questionable successes. This finding suggests that expanding and sustaining initial success turns, in part, on the capacity of the parties to institutionalize new arrangements for working across the gulfs of wealth, power, and perspective—to combine program and organizational learning into enduring changes in interorganizational structures and expectations.

Many different actors played catalyst roles in these learning processes. They included a variety of NGOs (universities, research NGOs, operational NGOs); GRNs; government agencies; international NGOs; and donor agencies. It is quite striking that the catalyst organizations associated with the clear successes are, without exception, indigenous NGOs or GRNs, and the catalyst individuals are all NGO leaders. The catalyst organizations for the three questionable cases, in contrast, are a government ministry, an international donor agency, and a collection of competing international and indigenous agencies, and the catalyst individual mentioned is government ministry. This result may reflect the importance of involving indigenous actors—NGOs, networks of GROs, well-known NGO leaders—who are trusted by grassroots actors as well as by government and international agencies as catalysts for these kinds of projects, even when other organizations (such as Deutsche Gesellschaft für Technische Zusammenargeit [GTZ] in Zambia or the Ministry of Youth in Malaysia) play a central role in starting up the project.

DISCUSSION

These cases demonstrate that interorganizational cooperation across sector differences, power inequalities, and cultural differences can improve the quality of life of poor populations. In some settings, such joint efforts can affect the lives of hundreds of thousands of people, so the stakes of intersectoral problem solving can be high.

Table 6.6 summarizes the findings of this analysis. The first two columns summarize the success of cooperation in terms of reach and resources for sustainability, as described in Table 6.2. The next two columns describe the GRO and intersectoral contacts forms of the social capital described in Table 6.3, and the following two columns report conflict and mutual influence in decision making from Table 6.4. The last two columns describe levels and catalysts for social learning from Table 6.5.

Some patterns of behavior appear to be generally linked to the success of interorganizational cooperation. Social learning, for example, appears to be associated with clear and potential success: Four of the five clear successes and four of the five potential successes showed signs of change in intersectoral patterns of behavior, whereas none of the questionable successes showed such

Table 6.6 Summary Matrix

	Impacts		Social Capital		Decision		Learn	
Cases	Size	Sustainability	GRO/GRN	Intersectoral Contacts	Conflict	Participation	Learning:Program/ Organization/Social	Catalyst
Clear								
Lesotho Credit Unions	+	+	+/+	+	0/+	+	+/+/+	NGO
Pakistan Sanitation	+	+	+/+	0	0/+	+	+/+/+	NGO
Philippines Upgrading	+	+	+/+	-/0	+	+	+/+/+	GRN
Bangladesh Immunization	+	+	0/-	+	0	-/0	+/+/+	NGO
Sudan Popular Health	+	+	0/-	+	-	-/0	+/+/?	NGO
Potential								
India Biogas Program	+	0	0/-	0	0/+	-	+/+/+	NGO
Indonesia Irrigation	0	+	+/-	+	-	0	+/+/+	NGO
Uganda Fishing	0	-	+/-	0	0	0	+/+/+	INGO
Zimbabwe Water	0	+	+/+	-/0	-/0	0	+/+/?	GO
India Workers' Init.	-	0	+/-	0	0	0/+	+/+/+	GRO
Questionable								
Malaysia Youth Centres	-	-	+/-	-/0	-	-/0	+/+/?	GO
Zambia Rural Development	-	-	0/-	-/0	-	-	?/?/?	DO
Kenya Cookstoves	-	-	0/+	+	-/0	-	?/?/?	?

Key: + means Wide High Yes High Intense High Yes
0 means Med Med Med Med Mod Med ?
– means Narrow Low No Low Low Low No

161

signs. There were also indications that some degree of conflict and grassroots participation is associated with successful cooperation. A third common pattern is the role of indigenous NGOs as catalysts of social learning in successful cooperation, as contrasted to international NGOs, government agencies, and international donors.

This analysis also suggests the existence of two quite different patterns of success. One form, illustrated by the Lesotho Credit Union Program, the Pakistan Urban Sanitation Program, and the Philippines Urban Upgrading Program, emphasizes the role of GROs and GRNs in program decision making and implementation. These grassroots-centered cooperations depend on local resources and information to solve problems. Where the programs cover large areas, networks that represent many GROs are needed to deal with large agencies from other sectors. Participatory decision making is important to mobilizing grassroots energy and resources, and decision making often involves moderate to intense conflict as grassroots groups express interests that might not be voiced in other circumstances.

The other pattern of success, illustrated by the Sudan Popular Health Program, the India Biogas Program, and the Bangladesh Immunization Project, emphasizes the role of NGOs as mediators among donors, government agencies, and grassroots populations. These NGO-mediated cooperations focus on delivering services and technical assistance to less organized grassroots constituencies. The services delivered by these projects depend less on local resources and organizations and more on the technical capacities of service agencies, such as NGOs or government agencies. Such projects make fewer demands for grassroots participation in decision making and require less management of conflict among parties with diverse interests.

Why do NGO-mediated initiatives succeed in some circumstances, and grassroots-centered cooperation in others? In part, the different patterns may reflect the stakes at issue: immunizations, health services, and family biogas plants provide incentives for individual or family rather than community action. The development of neighborhood sanitation systems, slum rehabilitation programs, or credit unions, in contrast, has impacts on larger social groups. In part, the patterns may reflect the need for grassroots resource investment, such as labor, money, or commitment, in order to solve problems successfully. It does not require sustained and organized community investment to gain the benefits of immunizations, family biogas plants, or curative health services; it does require systematic community participation to build and maintain sanitation systems with local resources, rehabilitate slum communities with sweat equity, or build successful and sustainable credit unions.

NGO-mediated initiatives may be easier to launch and maintain. They do not require GROs or GRNs, and they are less likely to produce conflict among diverse participants or demands for mutual influence. On the other hand, they do require individuals or organizations who can bridge the differences among the parties, and they are most useful for delivering narrowly defined services. Over the long run, they generate fewer resources from within the constituencies served, and they are less likely to generate local organizations that will take on other activities.

Different forms of social capital are central in the development of the two patterns of cooperation. GROs and GRNs were key actors in grassroots-centered cooperation but were often absent or unimportant in NGO-mediated cooperation. Where a clear and coherent voice for grassroots interests and mobilization of local resources is central, effective GROs and GRNs are vital. In contrast, bridging individuals and organizations with extensive contacts across sector boundaries was central to NGO-mediated cooperation but less critical to grassroots-centered cooperation. Social capital in the form of individuals and organizations trusted by many parties is critical to NGO-mediated cooperation when other vehicles for representing grassroots interests are not available.

In some cases, the needed forms of social capital existed prior to the project, such as the neighborhood organizations and networks in the Philippines or the NGO networks in Bangladesh. In other situations, social capital had to be created, as in the development of the HIKMA Popular Health Program as an NGO in the Sudan, the creation of the League of Credit Unions in Lesotho, or the mobilization of neighborhood organizations in Pakistan.

The social capital available may influence the definitions of problems, the forms of cooperation, and the solutions deemed relevant. Where bridging NGOs exist, they may encourage NGO-mediated cooperation—possibly at the expense of grassroots participation in problem definition and provision of local resources. Where GROs exist, they may shape problem definitions and solutions around their interests. Where the needed organizations do not exist, they may have to be created for sustainable solutions. Policymakers who want to promote intersectoral cooperation can find or support the creation of needed bridging organizations or grassroots groups.

Decision making in intersectoral cooperation involves integrating the interests and perspectives of diverse participants. In grassroots-centered cooperation, decision making involves negotiation and joint decision processes in which grassroots representatives have substantial voice. These decision-making processes put a premium on the capacity of the parties to deal with conflicts of interest and foster participatory decision making. Thus, the successful grassroots-centered cooperations were characterized by moderate to intense conflict and high levels of grassroots participation and mutual influence among the participants.

In NGO-mediated cooperation, lower levels of overt conflict among actors and lower levels of grassroots participation are possible because the NGOs mediate the expression of differences. Such cooperation puts less emphasis on direct negotiation of differences among diverse parties and more emphasis on the role of NGOs as decision makers who take the interests of all parties into account. Although shared norms and systems for mutual influence and power balancing among unequal participants are essential for grassroots-centered cooperation, in NGO-mediated cooperation, the NGOs span differences with less explicit conflict and participation. Thus, NGO-mediated cooperation may be particularly appropriate when some parties are unwilling or unable to negotiate directly across social and political differences.

Social learning produces enduring changes in the institutional arrangements that enable future intersectoral action. Evidence of such social learning appeared in most cases of successful cooperation, although the learning processes may vary in different patterns of cooperation. In grassroots-centered cooperation, social learning may emerge from the clash of perspectives reflected in higher levels of overt conflict and grassroots participation. There appears to be a link between conflict and social learning: In seven of eight cases, the demonstrated social learning was characterized by moderate to intense conflict; all five of the cases with little social learning were characterized by low or low-to-moderate conflict. In NGO-mediated cooperation, however, clear success may be achieved without much overt conflict, as in the Sudan Health Program, because learning may occur within the NGO rather than among the parties—*organizational* learning rather than intersectoral learning.

Social learning emerges from interaction among parties with different perspectives in settings that enable constructive use of those differences. Not all conflict has constructive outcomes, of course: The Kenya project, for example, suffered from conflict that undermined learning and performance. Intersectoral learning depends on the creation of social settings in which participants can explore their differences, learn from each other, and synthesize solutions that create mutual gains. Creating shared expectations, norms, and rules to organize constructive interaction among diverse parties becomes

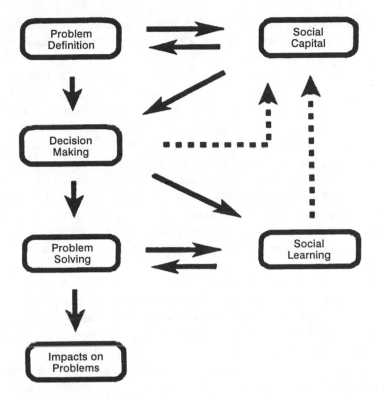

Figure 6.1 The Mountain Forum

a key issue for fostering social learning (e.g., Brown, 1998; Browning et al., 1995; Ring & Van de Ven, 1994).

Figure 6.1 suggests possible relationships among these variables. It suggests that the definition of the problem and the existing social capital influence one another: The definition of the problem suggests what sorts of social capital are needed, and the social capital available can shape the definition of the problem. The need to reach grassroots groups focused the attention of Bangladeshi immunization officials on NGOs; the NGOs redefined the problem as one of mobilizing families to bring their children for vaccination.

Both problem definitions and available social capital affect the interaction among participants, as well as the extent to which conflict, participation, and mutual influence are at work in problem solving and social learning. Redefining the Philippines project as urban upgrading and the mobilization of neighborhood organizations set the stage for mutual influence in project planning and implementation.

This decision making directly affects problem-solving activity and its impacts. Decision-making processes can also produce social learning that reshapes future interactions among the organizational participants. Cooperation to plan and build slum sanitation systems in Pakistan changed the sanitation situation in Karachi. It also created effective GROs; strengthened the capacities of the mediating NGO; and built relationships among grassroots groups, NGOs, government officials, and international donors. So, the project produced social learning and new social capital, as indicated in the dotted arrows of Figure 6.1, that could be used in efforts to solve future problems.

Because grassroots-centered cooperation encourages constructive engagement among more diverse participants, it offers many opportunities to mobilize new resources and catalyze significant social learning from the integration of diverse perspectives. On the other hand, NGO-mediated cooperation may be more practical in circumstances where problems do not require substantial investments by local groups, GROs do not yet exist, or participants cannot handle overt conflicts and mutual influence. NGO-mediated cooperation may sometimes set the stage for grassroots-centered cooperation by creating GROs and more relationships across sectoral differences. Movement toward more grassroots-centered cooperation appears to be emerging in subsequent developments of the Bangladesh Immunization, India Biogas, and Indonesian Irrigation cases. Participation in either form of cooperation may have an educational impact that can build a base for future joint action (Brown, 1998; Hadenius & Uggla, 1996).

Global changes are placing high premiums on societal capacities to recognize, assess, and creatively solve complex social problems. Individuals and organizations have invested in building capacities to learn rapidly in a turbulent world, and there is evidence that "network learning" across organizational boundaries is critical to meeting the challenges of rapid change and intense competition (Browning et al., 1995; Powell, Koput, & Smith-Doerr, 1996). We are only beginning to foster interorganizational and intersectoral social learning capacity that enables societies to deal with rapid change.

These cases suggest that cooperative problem solving is possible across sector boundaries, power inequalities, and vast differences in interests and perspectives. But that problem solving depends on the existence or creation of social capital, mutual influence, and intersectoral learning for widespread and long-term success. Societies that want to enhance their capacities for such problem solving may have to invest in creating social capital that will allow for communication among diverse parties, enabling participatory decision making and constructive conflict management, and creating institutional arrangements that foster exploration across interests and perspectives. If social learning is important to building a sustainable world, creating the social capital and mutual influence that enable cooperation among key stakeholders is a fundamental priority.

7

TRANSNATIONAL AND INTERNATIONAL SOCIAL MOVEMENTS IN A GLOBALIZING WORLD

Creating Culture, Creating Conflict

MAYER N. ZALD

The idea of cooperation across national boundaries to achieve desirable social goals has intuitive appeal. We live in an era of increasing global interaction marked by lower costs of transportation; increased international trade; the rise of multinational corporations; the emergence of international nongovernmental organizations mobilizing resources and people to effect positive social change; and, facilitated by both the mass media and electronic means of communication, an increased awareness of what is occurring around the world and an increased ability to communicate with people in distant places. Cooperation across national boundaries to alleviate hunger and starvation, to contain and eliminate the spread of AIDS, to combat environmental degradation, and so on, are representative of these cooperative endeavors to achieve high-consensus goals. The organizational form of these cooperative ventures may vary—from one-time campaigns to achieve very specific goals,

I am indebted to Jane Dutton for her comments on an earlier draft of this chapter.

to long-term networks of peoples and organizations, to new international organizations and international agreements signed by governments.

But there is an apparent paradox here: Some of the same large trends that promote cooperation in the service of agreed-upon goals also create the conditions for large-scale conflicts. Groups and cultures that were once fairly isolated from each other are now brought into contact, and the practices and norms of one society may be challenged by members of other societies. Moreover, organized cooperation and coordination across national boundaries creates conflict with groups and organizations with opposing priorities, goals, and values. For instance, as corporations from Western capitalist states do business in formerly command economies, they band together and attempt to use international agreements to change the practices of the host country. Or, for an example more relevant to this chapter, the contemporary women's movement draws upon participants and resources from many countries, but the movement conflicts with states, religions, and communities that oppose the goals of the movement. Somewhat ironically, the movements that create and escalate conflict also contribute to the creation of a global shared culture. Movements such as the women's movement, the environmental movement, and the population movement spread a discourse about their domains that helps to create a worldwide shared definition and understanding of the condition of humankind.

In contrast to many of the chapters in this volume, which assume that organized action across national boundaries is in pursuit of largely agreed-upon goals, this chapter explores the ways in which globalization affects the bases of social conflict; in particular, how globalization contributes to the internationalization of collective action and social movements. I focus on two large and interrelated questions. First, how do globalization processes—the growth of a world polity and economy and the accompanying changes in population distribution and mass and personal communications—internationalize the resources used in social movements, the definition of social movement goals, and the instrumentalities of movement (i.e., the policies and agencies through which goals are achieved)? Second, how are these disparate elements combined into collective action across national borders, into more or less coordinated attempts to change societies or specific practices, often at great cost or with great conflict? Although it will receive less attention, I also explore the implications of these social conflicts for creating a larger global culture.

This chapter not only attempts to understand the increasing globalization of conflict, but it also attempts to help change the focus of the theory and research on social movements. That theory has largely focused upon movements and social conflicts within communities or within the nation-state (for an exception, see Mendlovitz & Walker, 1987). Yet obviously, many social movements are international or transnational phenomena. Focused movements, such as the women's suffrage movement, the movement to abolish slavery, and the environmental movement, have a global dimension. They rise and decline in many nations during overlapping time periods. Moreover, for some enduring movements, such as the peace movement, cycles of mobilization and demobilization recur several times in all of those nations sharing common threats of war. Whereas the proximal targets of peace movements tend to be the policies of national governments, the threats to peace occur in an international context.

Large ideological transformations also do not recognize national boundaries. For instance, the decline of absolutism and the rise of representative government; the growth of the ideals of social democracy; the emergence of fundamentalist reactions to modernity and secularism, both political and religious—all transcend national boundaries. We need to examine how the internationalization of the context of social movement action changes how mobilization and social conflict occur.

Moreover, because of the academic division of labor between sociology and political science, historically, the analysis of social movements tended to end at the edge of the state. That is, once social movement issues moved into legislative and party politics and into the bureaucratic practices of agencies, sociological analysts left the implications of state involvement to political scientists. This division of labor is now seen as inadequate even for national movements, and those scholars who emphasize the role of political opportunity and structure in shaping movements take the state seriously. Taking the state seriously is fundamental for studying movements with an international component. For many issues—from the abolition of slavery to the modern environmental movement, although pushed and cajoled by nongovernmental organizations and private citizens—state actors, authorities, and their agents play an important role in pushing other states and international agencies to act. We need to have a capacious view of social movements, one that includes the state as an ally or agent of social movements. Finally, in thinking about social movement success or outcomes, we need to ask, How does the international or cross-national context shape outcomes? How do the norms of national sovereignty and the difficulty of penetrating social structures buffered by national governments and national boundaries affect the tactics and outcomes of global social movements?

This chapter attempts to sketch the role of social movements and collective behavior in generating culture change and conflict across national boundaries. To do so, it describes in short compass the internationalization of social movements and collective action. My purpose is to show how some of the same processes that lead to organized cooperation for consensual goals paradoxically also lead to organized cooperation within groups that leads to conflict between groups. More descriptive than theoretical, the chapter uses key categories and variables of the modern theoretical synthesis on social movements (see below) to lay out the range of processes involved in creating transnational social movements.

First, I discuss the aspects of globalization that are the background conditions for the internationalization of social movements. These include the increasing dispersion of national populations through migration, the increased awareness of social conditions around the globe that has been created by the mass media, and the growing interdependence of economic and sociopolitical life that both creates conflicts and changes the venues for the resolution of those conflicts (Boli & Thomas, 1995; Rosenau, 1990; Smith, 1994). Second, I examine how international and transnational movements emerge, mobilize, and have an effect across national boundaries: What are the diffusion and mobilization processes within and between nations that facilitate international movements? How is this diffusion and concurrent mobilization hindered or helped by technological and institutional mechanisms? How does the national and international context of movements affect the relative success of movements? Why is it that some movements are relatively successful in achieving their goals, whereas others flounder at national borders? Finally, in the conclusion, we suggest that social movements have a dual edge: On the one hand, they are mechanisms for the spread of a global discourse and culture; on the other hand, they produce conflict, that is, they polarize domestic politics and increase conflict between national societies.

ASSEMBLING RESOURCES AND THE INTERNATIONALIZATION OF TARGETS

Social movements—or more precisely, social movement organizations (SMOs)—assemble resources (e.g., money, personnel, and facilities) from constituencies (i.e., institutions and individuals who support the goals of the SMO) to attempt to change behavior, attitudes, and ideologies, as well as policies and allocations of individuals, states, and organizations. Increasingly, resources are drawn from outside the local community and nation. Globalization affects the location of the resources and defines grievances or injustices outside of the local scene. International migration changes the distribution of populations and creates expatriate communities interested in the politics and policies of home communities. Moreover, the increasing scale of mass communications (connecting populations with little previous awareness of events and conditions in other countries) and the ability of the mass media to vividly portray misery and problems make available a pool of potential sympathizers that transcends national boundaries and can be converted into constituencies. Finally, the increasing interdependence of the world polity and economy creates a nexus of targets, or levers for change, beyond national borders. That is, the increasing interdependence creates conflict issues beyond national borders and also changes the location of the government and other organizations that must be implicated to resolve the conflicts.

Migration and the Distribution
of Mobilizable Constituents

Over the past two centuries, the declining costs and increasing speed of transportation have led to an unprecedented linking of populations, once far removed. International migration, whether the result of a search for economic opportunity or the escape from political turmoil or oppression, has led to the creation of expatriate communities around the globe. The development of these expatriate communities extends the reach of social movements. Where the expatriate communities are located in affluent capitalist societies, they usually have higher incomes than their parallel communities at home. Moreover, these affluent host nations are often removed from the national conflicts and are less authoritarian; thus, they are less likely to suppress political and social mobilization.

From the Sikh community in Canada; to the Irish in Boston and in the rest of the United States; to the Armenians in Los Angeles; to the Muslims in France, Germany, and elsewhere in Europe and the United States; to Jews in the United States and elsewhere, expatriate or diasporan communities become resource purveyors and sites of conflict. Members of the diasporan community send money to the homeland in support of ethnic minorities involved in nationalist conflicts. Some members of the diasporan community may have their identities as ethnic minorities sharpened and focused in the diaspora, leading them to take active roles in the movement (Anderson, 1994; van der Veer, 1995). Moreover, the internal policies and external relations of the host nations to these expatriate communities become implicated in social movement conflict. Philanthropic donations, arms shipment policies, and foreign policy alliances and agreements become part of the social movement/conflict context. Host nation policies are conducted in two games at once—the game of domestic politics and the game of international relations (Evans, Jacobson, & Putnam, 1993). Thus, for instance, the relationship between the United States and England is affected by the conflict over Northern Ireland; or, our relationship with Turkey is affected by Armenian revanchism.

The development of an international higher education system adds a different dimension to the relationship of international migration to social movements. As students move to regional and global centers of higher education, whether in Pakistan, England, the former Soviet Union, or the United States, they are exposed to the ideologies and discourse of the metropole, or they are reinforced in ideologies that already predisposed them to social movement activism.

From the point of view of global conflict and cooperation, the distinction between social movements and national or ethnic movements may be relatively unimportant. Because we are discussing how the distribution of populations affects international relations, we should note that the boundaries of ethnic identity do not correspond with the boundaries of geopolitical units. The Kurds in Turkey, Iraq, and Iran (Nagel, 1980), the existence of distinct groups in Angola, the contest over control in the former Yugoslavia—all exist in places where ethnic mobilizations deeply implicate foreign policy and international relations. Events affecting part of the ethnic population in one nation have mobilizing potential for those in the neighboring population (Nagel & Whorton, 1992).

Transforming Role of Media

Not only is there an unprecedented intermingling of the world's population. The movement of news over the Pony Express, the development of the electrical transmission, the spread of radio transmission, the development of television and satellite transmission—each in turn expands the potential bystander publics far beyond the site of the production of news. Each increase in scale of public awareness and dramatization of grievances leads to a possible transformation of bystander publics into adherents and contributors well beyond national borders (Ganley, 1992; Rosenau, 1990). Thus, television's portrayal of the events in Tiananmen Square was riveting and brought the student-led uprising into homes around the globe. Moreover, the leaders of the uprising adopted tactics to appeal to international audiences, at the same time that they mobilized within China.

International reporting of events in the mass media is not a new thing. Nor is it new for social movements to be bolstered through such reporting. The transformation of T. E. Lawrence, a British colonial officer, into Lawrence of Arabia, a romantic figure known throughout the Western world as a leader and fighter for the Arab nationalist cause during World War I, was in large part a function of the growth of international journalism and the rise of the mass newspapers. The growth of mass circulation newspapers linked by cablegrams allowed daily reporting of events around the world to reach mass audiences. Both the size of the audience and the immediacy of reporting were changed by technology. These possibilities have only intensified and multiplied, given the insatiable demand for news and the globalization of communications technology. Although the production routines of the media continue to shape what is broadcast, and although a determined state can attempt to erect barriers to global communication, the spread of satellite systems, inexpensive VCRs, personal computers, cellular phones, and fax machines ever decrease the costs and make more difficult the suppression of global news. These changes in the media of communication not only make it possible for people far away to view social conditions and social conflict, but they also make it possible for adherents and activists to communicate with their counterparts in other countries.

The Internationalization of Venues and Grievances

In a world in which national economies are relatively independent and in which people pay attention to events and problems in their own communities or nations, the problems for resolution are close to home, and local and national governments are seen as the appropriate venues for resolving those conflicts. Moreover, the targets and grievances of social movements often are created by state action (McAdam, 1982; Tilly, 1978). The passing of a law, the imposition of a tax, or the carrying out of state policies rewards some groups and punishes others. In a world where national economies are increasingly interdependent and problems transcend national boundaries, the problems of interest are no longer just local issues. Here are some examples: The behavior of tobacco companies in Eastern Europe is relevant to those who think tobacco is a major health risk and must be contained. The labor policies of multinational corporations in Thailand are relevant to American labor unions. Environmental practices in the Amazon are relevant to American environmentalists. Global warming cannot be affected just by the policies of one government. Moreover, where international agencies, such as the International Monetary Fund or the World Health Organization, or international nuclear regulatory agencies are vested with real powers, it is no longer just the agents of the state that are the provocateurs of grievances but the agents of the international polity. Because national policies are often harmonized in regional alliances, the policies of the alliance become the policies of the participating units. Social movements then respond in the local arena to policies generated at the international level (Tarrow, 1995a).

The prime case is, of course, the waves of the peace and antinuclear weapons movements since World War II (see Wittner, 1988). Each wave of the movements is precipitated by perceived changes in the strategic balance between the "West" and the Soviet Union and the military/armament policies adopted by the Western alliance, although led by the United States. The peace movement in the Netherlands or in Great Britain is aimed at local participation in the alliance; but that local participation is, in fact, the result of a larger, historical, geopolitical process.

If, as is likely, international relations and international agreements increasingly penetrate local polities—from economic agreements about foreign trade, such as the North American Free Trade Agreement, to agreements about the rights of women, such as the attempts to eliminate clitoridectomies in Africa—local mobilization will increasingly respond to grievances created by the actions of international agencies. Those agencies, in turn, develop their policies in response to pressure groups, including social movements, from other nations (Rucht, 1997).

It is clear that these changes in the international context of social movements and collective action increase the possibilities for mobilization for conflict across national borders. But there are many unanswered questions. We know very little, in a systematic and comparative way, about how much difference internationalization makes. For instance, although it is clear that diasporan communities contribute resources (both money and personnel) to ethnic nationalist conflicts, we do not know how many resources they contribute, nor do we know why, in one community, only money may be contributed, whereas in another community, a whole cadre of militant activists may be developed.

Similarly, although the mass media obviously generate large audiences for dramatic events, whether the policies of the authorities or the extent of the social movement are affected by that international portrayal is not well studied. Rucht's (1996) study of German audience responses to "distant" issues is one of the first quantitative studies of responses to such issues. How much did the media portrayal of the events in Tiananmen Square affect the behavior of the Chinese authorities? Does extensive portrayal of mass starvation in Africa affect the awareness and readiness to act of television viewers in Germany? In the United States? Nor do we know much about how the changing venues of international relations affect the opportunities for mobilization. Still, it should be clear that globalization changes the possibilities for social conflict and social movements. In the next section, we look directly at the processes of mobilization in a globalizing world.

COLLECTIVE BEHAVIOR, ORGANIZATION, AND TACTICS IN A TRANSNATIONAL ENVIRONMENT

In the summer of 1992, immediately following the not-guilty verdict in the trial of police officers for the beating of Rodney King, riots, protests, and street vandalism broke out, not only in Los Angeles, but in other cities in the United States and in major cities in Canada and western Europe. In 1848 and 1871, fears of insurrection and civil disorder spread throughout western Europe, even though there were few linking SMOs. In 1968, student-led protests paralyzed institutions in many nations; were sometimes linked to "terrorist" actions; and culminated in crackdowns and repression, on one hand, and institutional reforms on the other. Beginning before the Russian Revolution, but accelerating after it, an international socialist movement, and then a communist/Russian-led movement, coordinated (sometimes loosely, sometimes tightly) the activities of socialist and then communist organizations around the globe. Before World War I, and between the two world wars, members of the International Chamber of Commerce advocated international trade agreements and international institutions as a means to peace through world trade (Ridgeway, 1938). In recent years, an amalgam of voluntary associations, philanthropic organizations, government bureaus, and international agencies have created international movements in areas as diverse as human rights, population control, environmental preservation, and women's rights. How can we explain these diverse manifestations of international collective action? How do people around the globe sometimes come to act in concert? For short-term collective actions, such as riots and street vandalism, or collective expressions of emotion, such as periods of mourning following the assassination of well-known respected figures, little coordinated activity or cross-national institutional structures need be involved. For longer term campaigns and for sustained pursuit of goals, organizations, networks of actors (both state and nonstate), and conferences and conventions knit together actors and actions for collective goals.

I begin with the simplest case: demonstration effects and collective action with little intentional coordination. Second, I analyze social movement campaigns increasingly composed of formal organizations (SMOs and other nongovernmental organizations) and state-led agencies. Third, because transnational movements often lead to the creation of international agencies and international agreements, I discuss the role of such agencies and agreements in social movements. Finally, I probe the limits of transnational social movements as they encounter opposition and the difficulties of penetrating local cultures and national politics.

Our analysis is guided by modern social movement theory, especially the writings that focus on resource mobilization, political opportunity, and cultural framing. Resource mobilization theory focuses on the ways in which social movements overcome free-rider problems, collect money and personnel, sometimes cooperate and sometimes conflict with other SMOs and social movements, and use strategy and tactics to effect social change. Political opportunity theory focuses upon the ways in which political structure and coalitions facilitate or repress social movement action. Framing theory focuses on the way that symbols and ideologies are used to interpret meaning, goals, and opportunities (McAdam, McCarthy, & Zald, 1996; Tarrow, 1995b).

Demonstration Effects and Simple Diffusion Processes

Demonstration effects occur when individuals or groups that are not in interaction model their own behavior on that of another individual or group. Thus, for instance, prisoners in one prison hear of a riot in another prison and decide to riot themselves. A demonstration effect presumes that the mimicking or copying groups perceive themselves as similar in some important regard to the group being mimicked; they may share important social identities or values and ideological commitments. Students copy other students, not prisoners, usually. But not all students or all campuses had protests during the student movement of the 1960s; nor do all prisons have riots following other riots. We assume, first of all, that it is not just structural equivalence that leads to copying but the elaboration of a perception of similar grievances and parallel situations. Many students were not supportive of the anti-Vietnam War movement. Furthermore, many campuses would have been relatively quiescent, whereas others had histories of activism. A protest on one campus would be more likely to have a demonstration effect on an activist campus than on a quiescent one. Moreover, the flow of information is important: In the 1960s, the American student movement had received a great deal of attention in European media, whereas European student issues were less well known in America. It is unlikely that collective action in Europe would have been copied by collective action in the United States. Similarly, leaders of the student movement in the United States were aware of Mao and the Red Guards movement in China. We have no reason to think that the student movement in the United States helped generate the Red Guards.

Demonstration effects can lead to parallel movements at different sites within a nation as well as between nations. In the purest case, there is no coordination or direct contact between participants at the different locales. National boundaries per se play no role in inhibiting demonstration effects unless political authorities are able to suppress the flow of information or unless the national boundary also is coterminous with different levels of mass media development, so that events in one nation that might be very salient to the population in another are not even communicated. Even when parallel groups react to events elsewhere, differences in institutions and political opportunities may shape perceptions of the relevance and risk of collective action repertoires. Thus, for example, even though neo-Nazis in Europe may be aware of Ruby Ridge or Waco, their own behavior is more likely to be responsive to the action of the state in their own countries than to the actions of the U.S. authorities.

Demonstration effects can sustain parallel movements as long as high mobilization and/or hard grievances persist. When energies wane, however, and the attention of potential adherents wanders, copying behavior declines as adherents and activists focus upon events closer to home and the relevance or engagement of the shared object of attention declines. Cycles of demonstration effects might occur if there are cycles of mobilization and grievance across nations, as in the post-World War II peace movements, yet transnational movements persist even when mobilization is at a lower ebb. What are the mechanisms?

The Development of Transnational Social Movements: NGOs and State-Sponsored Forms

The first phase in the development of international social movements is the identification of harms, problems, and injustices in many countries. Moral entrepreneurs, such as Wilberforce, Frances Willard, Betty Friedan, Rachel Carson, or Simón Bolívar, need not be the first to identify a problem but become the spokespeople for an emerging awareness of a widespread issue. Assuming that voluntary associations are locally permissible or that networks of activist/dissidents are not suppressed, this growing awareness of problems becomes the base for local action. However, as parallel movements develop, it is likely that awareness of counterparts in other nations will also develop. Following lines of transportation, communication, and cultural/linguistic similarity, contacts between neighboring movements are likely. If no shared action is entailed, say, for the passing of national voting laws, the most likely form of international collaboration is through some direct interaction among activists. McAdam and Rucht (1993) document the linkages between American student leaders and those in western Europe and especially Germany during the student-led antisystemic movements of the 1960s. Because specific targets differ and local strategic considerations vary, parallel movements can develop in different countries with only the loosest of linkages as long as there are shared diagnostic and prognostic frames, that is, shared interpretations of the causes of problems and shared ideas of strategies and tactics for solving the problems (Snow & Benford, 1992). In the case of the student movement, for example (and much oversimplified), the diagnostic frames centered upon military-industrial bureaucracies and elites perpetuating repressive state policies; prognostic frames centered upon student-led uprisings that would draw the masses into system overthrow. Students in France, Germany, and the United States shared the general diagnoses and prognoses, although their immediate contexts were quite different.

A movement develops an international formal structure through formal meetings or congresses. International congresses or conferences may bring together single-purpose organizations dedicated to movement goals (SMOs).

However, not all countries facilitate the dedicated SMO form (Garner & Zald, 1985). Instead, the organizational carrier may be other kinds of organizations, such as political parties, religious organizations, or voluntary associations that pursue social change objectives alongside other goals. Thus, in many countries, specific movements, such as women's rights, the environment, or peace, may be carried by a variety of organizations that have diverse general functions. International congresses may then bring together delegates or members who represent very different kinds of organizations and organizational linkages.

International congresses may also develop coordinating mechanisms beyond the hosting of periodic meetings. Secretariats and coordinated policy initiatives may be developed. Earlier, I mentioned the role of the International Chamber of Commerce, which linked national chambers of commerce, in pursuing world peace. Those efforts required direction and coordination among groups from many countries. Ever since the outbreak of the cold war and the rise of authoritarian ex-colonies, the international labor movement, as a confederation of national labor unions, has supported democratization movements. The strategy has been to nourish and support labor union adherents in countries that are antiunion and antidemocratic, and to implore their own governments to promote prolabor and prodemocracy policies in these countries.

Although popular imagery visualizes social movements as grassroots or citizen's organizations, transnational social movements may have a strong element of state direction. The Soviet Union clearly had a large impact, although exactly how much is still debated, on communist parties around the globe. Ronald Reagan's policies were concerted with those of the Catholic Church to support the dissidents in eastern Europe, including the large social movement initiated in Poland under the name of Solidarity. The Iranian government supports Islamic antiwestern or anti-American groups, financially and strategically, wherever Islamic antiwestern groups emerge. Because state-supported movements are able to draw upon state revenues, offices, and platforms, compared with many movements, they are able to be sustained without the ebb and flow of support so typical of most movements.

The extent of state direction and external state support is of course variable. In some cases, national movements and conflicts would continue even without support from other nations, state or NGO provided. In other cases, state support may be so vital that local conflicts may be quickly resolved, or at least continue at a much reduced scale, once external supports are removed. Nagel and Whorton (1992) discuss the contribution of military support and international politics to ethnic conflicts in Iraq and Angola.

Social Movements and the Growth of International Agencies and Action

Transnational social movements may attempt to effect changes in many nations, or they may attempt to change the international agreements and actions of nations as they relate to each other. Moreover, as international agencies have developed dealing with issues on a cross-national basis—the alphabet soups of Geneva, Paris, Washington, and New York—these international agencies become the fulcrums for effecting changes in local policies. The abolition of slave trading, trading in prostitutes (the white slave movement), and piracy on the high seas are all the results of international agreements—in these cases, international agreements backed up by military power. But other movements have also used international agreements to spread social movement goals (Brysk, 1993; Keck & Sikkink, 1994; Sikkink, 1993). Organizations that now appear staid, such as the International Labor Organization, were initiated as part of the international labor movement's attempt to humanize industrial work around the globe. In more recent times, the environmental movement has attempted to expand its horizons globally through using the auspices of state agencies, which were established at an earlier time in national legislation (Frank, 1994). Thus, for many purposes, social movement analysis must implicate national politics and bureaucratic imperatives as it attempts to understand the international impact of movements. Students of social movements must join students of international organizations if they are to trace the impact and limits of transnational social movements.

The Impact of Transnational Movements

In recent years, social movement scholars have recognized, as all of policy analysis has, that the mere passing of legislation or the creation of an agency does not mean that the goals of policy or movements have been achieved. The achievement of policy aims requires an analysis of the bureaucratic and incentive structures designed to promote, channel, and monitor behavior, whether of government officials or private citizens. Thus, social movement analysis extends into the bowels of the state. Do bureaucratic agencies promote or inhibit the attainment of legislative goals? Are policy instruments adequate to the tasks at hand? (Kitschelt, 1986; Mazmanian & Sabatier, 1983) Transnational movements, in which the movement is largely based outside of the countries that are targets of the movement, have even more difficult problems in attaining their goals.

Transnational campaigns and social movements are sometimes success-ful. Nadelman (1990) documents the extent to which "global prohibition regimes" have eliminated unwanted behavior. Compacts between nations, backed up by overwhelming military power, have essentially eliminated slave trading between nations and severely constrained slave trading within na-tions—although some forms of indentured servitude and near-peonage still exist. Piracy on the high seas, once a major problem for international shipping and trade, has been largely eliminated, even though there may be an upsurge in small-scale piracy related to tourists and small craft. Supported by the interests of international business, hundreds of compacts have regulated the flow of goods and property, at least within the capitalist world market.

Yet in many areas, transnational movements may be quite ineffective. First, to the extent that the target of the movement is behavior that is not easily controlled by domestic regimes, transnational movements find it difficult to penetrate local practice. For example, the women's movement will find it hard to eliminate clitoridectomies in Africa, no matter how much international agencies and movements protest, because the local populations will resist and the states are weak. Similarly, the environmental movement will find it difficult to penetrate economies where the local environmental movement is weak and the domestic regime depends upon groups opposed to international policies. Second, and obviously, local regimes may completely oppose the changes. It is hard to imagine many Islamic regimes in the current mood buying into the international feminist movement's attempt to change the status of women. Similarly, very poor countries may find little local support for labor and health policies that substantially raise the costs of production. Thus, although transnational movements may affect some nations' policies and even create international agencies and compacts, the cartography of impact will be mediated by the resistance of local regimes and local populations.

This section has been written in an assertive mode, as if we knew a lot about the operation of transnational social movements. We have briefly discussed demonstration effects across national boundaries, the emergence of transnational movements and organizations, the role of international agencies and agreements, and the impact of transnational movements. On a descriptive level, we probably do know a lot about these processes and organizational forms. Histories of particular movements have been written, or scholars interested in a particular policy issue have described the process by which an international agreement has been achieved. Yet on a comparative and theoretical level, much remains to be done. The walls between disciplines have sealed off analysts of social movements from the analysis of international relations and the study of bureaucracy; similarly, political scientists have rarely studied the impact of social movements on international relations and agencies (but see Willetts, 1982). We have few studies of the impact of transnational social movements. Yet the trends in globalization will inevitably lead to more transnational social movements and a more complex interweaving of conflict and cooperation.

CONCLUSION: CREATING CULTURE, CREATING CONFLICT

This chapter has sketched the mechanisms through which social movements transcend national boundaries. As the costs of transportation and communication decline, as ethnic diasporas are created, and as global communications create shared images of grievances and conditions, the possibilities for transnational movements are facilitated. Moreover, increasingly, problems such as environmental ones spill over national boundaries, and international compacts and agencies themselves create targets of protest; thus, the manufacture of grievances occurs from collective international processes, not locally disaggregated ones. In some ways, the internationalization of social movements is a direct function of the integration of world politics and economics (Boli & Thomas, 1995).

There is a paradox in all of this: On one hand, the globalization processes spread a common culture; on the other hand, the spread of a common culture creates conflict as it spreads. Transnational movements, such as the women's movement (Berkovitch, 1994), the population control and family planning movement (Barrett, 1995), and the environmental movement (Frank, 1994), publicize the issues that then get spread around the world. This very act of defining the issue creates the issue as part of a common worldwide discourse and becomes part of a global rationalizing environment (cf. Meyer, 1994, pp. 28-54). Each movement is both partially generated by and must come to terms with the dominant institutions and discourse of the world system (e.g., the feminist movement ties to liberal notions of the individual and individual rights dominant in Western societies). Population control has ties both to a discourse about children and their rights and to a discourse about population as a resource of the nation. Each large, new transnational movement is initially in tension with the status quo but becomes rationalized to the larger civilizational discourse. Moreover, as the international or global movement takes off, networks of cooperation spread as individuals, nongovernmental organizations, and states develop common policies, strategies, and compacts. Yet in framing the issue, movements also create conflict over them. For example, the feminist movement embodies a Western egalitarianism that is anathema to societies that have long traditions of separate spheres and of patriarchy. Or, again, environmentalism seems irrational in a society promoting economic growth and individual wealth above all else. The seedbed of countermovements is found in the actions of movements. That dynamic should give pause to any notion that globalization is inherently a recipe for cooperation.

8

THE DEVELOPMENT OF GLOBAL ENVIRONMENTAL REGIMES

Organizing in the Absence of Authority

BARBARA GRAY

onflicts over rights to and appropriate use of environmental resources around the world are not only growing in number but are becoming increasingly important as the last of precious natural resources are being threatened worldwide (Cairncross, 1992; Gore, 1993; Postel, 1992; Wade, Tucker, & Hamann, 1994). These conflicts cut across sovereign borders; are tightly interwoven with economic, political, and social issues; inextricably link the North to the South; and pose complex challenges to all parties involved (Porter & Brown, 1991).

> Negotiation of international environmental issues is especially difficult because of complex linkages with underlying economic, political, and social issues; scientific uncertainties; and, solutions that require the participation of many nations, as well as agreement and implementation of differential and symmetrical obligations. These issues require commitments that affect the way sovereign States use their own natural resources, affect neighboring country resources and the international commons. (Scott & Trolldalen, 1993, p. 45)

Conflicts ranging from the construction of a hydroelectric dam between Czechoslovakia and Hungary (Wood, 1992), acid-rain negotiations between the United States and Canada (Golich & Young, 1993), or destruction of natural watersheds in the Everglades or the Brazilian Pantanal raise critical questions about how to balance ecological, political, and economic concerns. Although the conflicts just mentioned may have only regional implications, other issues, such as destruction of tropical rain forests, global warming, depletion of the ozone layer, pollution of the oceans, and reduction in biodiversity, can effect either regional or global consequences (Fleagle, 1994). In the environmental arena, global changes can produce different local impacts (e.g., sea-level increases from global warming, coupled with other geophysical changes, can differ by locations); conversely, regional problems can induce global consequences (e.g., deforestation in Brazil contributes to global warming) (Fleagle, 1994). To manage the myriad of environmental changes that are forecast requires organizing at both the local and global levels. For example, according to Fleagle (1994), rising sea levels associated with global warming are predicted to have a heavy impact on Puget Sound, affecting marine businesses, fisheries, and private landowners. Response efforts will involve local, state, and federal agencies; regional utilities; and public interest associations. Organizing these stakeholders to generate a joint response is the sensible thing to do. But generating collaborative versus many cross-cutting, unilateral actions presents a formidable challenge.

A good example to illustrate the need for both global and local mechanisms of organizing concerns implementation of the Bruntland Report. The report of the World Commission on Environment and Development, prepared in 1987 and commonly known as the Brundtland Report, legitimized the concept of sustainable development and gave impetus to redefine development to include future as well as present needs. The Report argued for "a rapid transition to sustainable systems of renewable natural resource management and a global accord to stabilize world population at the lowest possible level" (Porter & Brown, 1991, p. 30). However, concrete steps to execute the concept are still in their infancy and, although vital to our global future, have been referred to as the "flimsy machinery of international agreement" (Cairncross, 1992, p. 149). The United Nations Conference on Environment and Development (UNCED) in Rio de Janeiro in June 1992 represents a first step in focusing collective attention on "the true nature of the global environmental crisis" (Gore, 1993, p. xi). A central message of the summit was the inexorable link between economics, politics, and environmental concerns worldwide. The Rio Conference succeeded in joining a diverse range of parties in a participatory negotiation process on many issues linking economics, politics, and environmental concerns worldwide. However, criticism of UNCED for its failure to go far enough (Cairncross, 1992; Porter & Brown, 1991; Susskind, 1994) highlights the obstacles that are inherent in negotiating global agreements about the environment.

The purpose of this chapter is to review what is currently known in organization theory about organizing to address multistakeholder disputes and to investigate current organizing efforts pertaining to global environmental issues in light of this theory. The use of theory enables us to identify obstacles that impede progress in organizing these domains, understand better why these obstacles arise, and also recommend some steps for surmounting the obstacles.

The chapter is organized as follows. First, a classification of global environmental disputes is presented. Second, the critical stakes in global environmental disputes are introduced. Third, a theory of organizing in underorganized domains is presented. Fourth, several alternative approaches for organizing to achieve sustainable development are proposed along with illustrative case examples. Fifth, several obstacles to organizing these domains are identified. The chapter concludes with some suggestions for dealing with these obstacles in future regime organizing efforts.

CLASSIFICATION OF ENVIRONMENTAL DISPUTES

Before trying to understand the challenges of organizing around global environmental issues, it is useful to distinguish them structurally because, as we will see later, different models of organizing are appropriate for different kinds of problems. Four classifications of environmental problems have been identified: (a) commons, (b) shared natural resources, (c) transboundary externalities, and (d) linked issues (Young, 1994, p. 19). Each is described below.

Commons

One type of environmental problem is the commons, stemming from the "tragedy of the commons" (Hardin, 1968). "Commons are physical or biological systems that lie wholly or largely outside the jurisdiction of any of the individual members of a society but that are valued resources for many segments of society" (Young, 1994, p. 20). One of the traditional problems with commons is their shrinking availability as more and more users claim their rights to tap what the commons have to offer.

Shared Natural Resources

"Shared natural resources are physical or biological systems that extend into or across the jurisdictions of two or more members of international society" (Young, 1994, p. 21). Typically, these link contiguous nations, but noncontiguous states may also be involved, as in the case of migratory birds or fish that traverse the waters of several states.

Transboundary Externalities

Transboundary issues occur when activities within one state produce adverse effects for others. Acid rain is an obvious example. Another is a shift in agricultural products in one country that results in contamination of a boundary river between it and a bordering state. If these issues involve two or three states, they are typically international in scope, but if more stakeholders are involved, they can become global in scope. Young (1994) suggests that the destruction of the city of Dubrovnik during recent hostilities in the former Yugoslavia created global externalities because of its value as a world heritage site.

Linked Issues

Linked issues involve relationships between environmental preservation/ destruction and nonenvironmental issues, such as economic development or trade. They arise when regimes for addressing an environmental problem create unintended consequences for other types of regimes. In the area of trade, for example, can states restrict the import of products whose production was environmentally deleterious? Many such battles are under way between environmentalists and free-trade advocates.

We now turn our attention to the underlying issues or "stakes" that infuse global environmental disputes. The issues are indeed complex. They interlace economic growth, access to resources, quality of life (now and for future generations), biological diversity, political sovereignty, and even global extinction. More important, perhaps, they pose the ultimate question: Who gets to decide the answers to these questions for whom?

WHAT IS AT STAKE?

As developing countries struggle to achieve a higher standard of living, they consume more resources and generate more pollution per capita. Although the developed countries argue that population growth should be curtailed and pollution controls enacted in the Third World, they continue to consume at much higher per capita rates. Compare average per capita fuel consumption for a person in a developing country (the equivalent of 1 to 2 barrels of oil per day) with 40 barrels per day for U.S. residents. The fundamental question is, Who should sustain the reduction in GNP to reduce energy consumption? Cairncross (1992) puts it baldly: "Why should they [developing countries] be forced to rein in and restrict their future growth to accommodate the past misdeeds of the rich?" (p. 166).

Conflicts over deforestation represent a good illustration of competing interests. Stripping of forests to generate fuel for indigenous people and the creation of grazing lands and agricultural space for increasing numbers of subsistence farmers pit national interests of African, Asian, and South American countries against global concerns (primarily by environmental groups in the North) about the buildup of greenhouse gases and the reduction in biodiversity resulting from deforestation. Exacerbating the problem are economic interests in the North who harvest timber for export and for developing-country governments that benefit from these exports (Trolldalen, 1992). Water access and preservation represent an equally complicated and dicey arena— one that is at the heart of many intra- and international political disputes (Carroll, 1986; Postel, 1992). At the global level, when developing countries increase agricultural yields through water diversion and fertilization, this restricts water availability and generates pollution for downstream users. Whereas these issues pit economic development interests of the Third World versus global environmental concerns, reduction of CO_2 emissions by industrialized nations pits northern economic interests against global environmental safety. And industrial interests in the United States blocked the U.S. signing of an international agreement to reduce CO_2 emissions at the Rio Conference (Gore, 1993).

Finally, security issues are not exempt from consideration in formulations of global environmental change. Increasingly, national security and environmental issues are intertwined in international environmental negotiations (Mathews, 1989; Piddington, 1989; Ullman, 1983). Such was the case when the United States tried to enforce the International Whaling Commission's ban on whaling by refusing imports of Icelandic fish. Iceland retaliated by threatening to close the U.S. military base at Keflavik, a move that forced the United States to withdraw the embargo. The relationship between the environment and security is succinctly stated by Porter and Brown (1991): "Damage to ecosystems, population pressures, and depletion of natural resources can contribute to political instability in developing countries as well as to local political turmoil or regional political or military conflicts" (p. 110). For example, environmental degradation can contribute to mass migration, and serious threats to national security are posed by large groups of displaced peoples (Trolldalen, 1992). The most deleterious connection, of course, involves the threat of nuclear war. Nuclear testing poses clear hazards, and maintenance of nuclear arsenals and storage of nuclear waste create enormous threats to the planetary environment (Alvarez & Makhijani, 1988; International Atomic Energy Agency, 1981).

What is at stake in promoting sustainable development worldwide is whether or not we preserve the ecological system. The more fundamental question that ignites conflict is, At what costs to whom? Negotiations over global environmental issues are at the core of economic and political divisions between nations and regions. "Global environmental negotiations seek to achieve effective international cooperation under circumstances in which the environmental interests of states diverge" (Porter & Brown, 1991, p. 17). As a result, what is at stake are national sovereignty (Mathews, 1989; Piddington, 1989; Ullman, 1983) and the future economic well-being of various regions. According to Golich and Young (1993), "International pollution agreements must address the tension between these competing forces—to yield sovereignty in order to achieve broadly based mutual interests, or to re-assert sovereignty in order to achieve narrowly conceived national interests" (p. 65). While the scientific and research communities stress the planetary harm inherent in failure to act expeditiously, national and regional interests are focused on claiming or preserving their rights to the benefits of economic development. These questions form the firmament of current debates about global environmental change.

The next section begins with a review of theoretical perspectives on collaboration and negotiation. These theoretical insights provide a vantage point for understanding the challenges of organizing global environmental regimes and inform efforts for structuring current and future regimes.

THEORETICAL BACKGROUND

Organizing metaregimes presents a supreme challenge for international relations and organizational scholars in particular. These regimes represent underorganized systems (Brown, 1980) par excellence. Identifying the boundaries of such systems is extremely problematic (Alderfer, 1976; Stern & Barley, 1996).

Organizing in the Absence of Boundaries

Consideration of how to organize in underorganized (Brown, 1980) or underbounded (Alderfer, 1976) settings has received some attention from organizational scholars despite the general dissuasion accorded such work within the organization sciences (Stern & Barley, 1996). For example, Trist (1983) has characterized these settings as problem domains. A problem domain consists of all the actors who have a stake in a particular problem. Whereas some domains may be highly organized, that is, actions among the stakeholders are highly coordinated (e.g., the network of health care delivery in the United States), others have little or no connections among the stakeholders. In underorganized domains, diverse stakeholders act in uncorrelated ways to deal with a problem that affects them all (Perlmutter & Trist, 1986; Trist, 1983). Under these circumstances, no party or group of parties has sufficient power to force unilateral decisions (Gray, 1989).

Establishing Negotiated Orders Through Collaboration

Some organizational scholars have conceptualized the problems of domain organization in the absence of authority. Underorganized domains are considered turbulent fields in which stakeholders act disuniformly (Trist, 1983). Collaboration has been proposed as one mechanism for coordinating stakeholders' actions and reducing the turbulence (Gray, 1989; Perlmutter & Trist, 1986; Trist, 1983). According to Gray (1989), "Collaboration involves a process of joint decision making among key stakeholders of a problem domain about the future of that domain" (p. 11). Through dialogue and negotiation, stakeholders seek to hammer out a consensus on how to manage the domain. Achieving collaboration, of course, requires that the relevant stakeholders are identified and that they agree to work together. Voluntary participation in a negotiated process involving the relevant players is required.

But creating the auspices under which stakeholders can seek a collaborative solution is a major task during the early stages of any effort to reach a collaborative solution to environmental disputes.

Political scientists frame the question in much the same way it has been framed by organizational collaboration scholars. At the core of these decisions is how to govern without government (Young, 1994, p. x).

Governance arises as a social or societal concern whenever the members of a group find that they are interdependent in the sense that the actions of each impinge on the welfare of others. Interdependence is likely to become a source of conflict when the efforts of individual members to achieve their goals interfere with or impede the efforts of others to pursue their own ends. It will be seen as a basis for cooperation, on the other hand, when opportunities arise to enhance social welfare by taking steps to coordinate the actions of the individual members of the group (Young, 1994, p. 15). And although the actors are interdependent, the mechanisms by which these interdependent actors come to engage in dialogue about their collective plight and generate rules to govern their individual and collective responses to it raise fascinating questions and very real practical dilemmas about how to organize in the absence of authority.

The Negotiation Stakes

Logsdon (1991) identified two preconditions for participation in a collaboration: high stakes and high interdependence among the parties. The stakes in global environmental disputes include economic interests (e.g., increase or preserve living standards), political interests (such as sovereignty) and social and psychological issues (e.g., self-preservation). Stakes may also be classified as efforts to gain or preserve efficiency, stability, and legitimacy (Logsdon, 1991; Oliver, 1990). Low-power stakeholders, for example, often have not been included in past decision making about the domain. Even when they mobilize and put pressure on existing governments, their legitimacy to be at the table is often questioned (Brown & Ashman, 1995). Recognition of these groups as legitimate may disrupt stability in the domain and challenge the efficiency of existing resource distributions.

Environmental disputes are problematic because they frequently address issues with high stakes for all of the parties and because the parties' efforts to secure their stakes interfere with one another. Long-standing differences in the power of the North versus the South in the global arena are at the root of many of these disputes. And as southern stakeholders have begun to realize their interests in the resources they possess, the stakes for them have gone up. As they increasingly resist northern exploitation, they build countervailing power and increase the interdependence among the stakeholders. Coping with these inherent power differences is fundamental to the design of global regimes.

Organizing Mechanisms

Brown (1980) has identified four mechanisms for organizing domains: leadership, culture, structure, and technology. While these mechanisms jointly contribute to domain organization, they do not necessarily play equal roles. Some mechanisms may be more salient in certain domains than others.

Leadership

Whereas in tightly organized systems, leadership roles are well-defined and imbued with legitimate authority, in underorganized domains, these roles are underdefined and must be negotiated. Leaders influence domain organization by creating the auspices within which the various stakeholders can begin to negotiate the terms of their joint efforts to coordinate the domain (Gray, 1989). In this sense, leaders are properly called "conveners" because they enjoin a dialogue among the stakeholders of the domain. In some cases, conveners may serve as bridging agents (Brown, 1993; Westley & Vredenberg, 1991) who mediate between stakeholder groups, often between groups that differ substantially in power (Brown, 1993). In other cases, they may be facilitators who encourage parties to engage in a dialogue (Gray, 1989).

Four types of convening of interorganizational collaboration have been identified (Gray, 1996; Wood & Gray, 1991): legitimization, facilitation, mandate, and persuasion. Legitimization and mandate require formal authority on the part of the convener—situations that are nonexistent in the global arena. Conveners who use facilitation are invited by the parties because of their credibility, influence, and knowledge. Conveners whose mode is persuasion also rely on credibility, influence, and knowledge but use knowledge of stakeholder relationships and personal charisma to attract others to the table in addition.

In the history of alternative environmental dispute resolution in the United States (which spans the past 15 to 20 years), conveners are frequently government agencies (or their designees) who have some statutory authority over the issues in dispute (Purdy & Gray, 1994). Conveners must identify the relevant parties who have a stake in a problem and persuade them to participate in a collaborative process to solve the problem. The approaches, although consistent across cases, are still fairly ad hoc, requiring a strong convener and a timely intervention (Gray, 1989; Kaufman & Duncan, 1990; Susskind & Cruikshank, 1987; Wood & Gray, 1991). What little institutionalization has occurred in this field is the evolution of a number of third-party organizations that are linked contractually with government to provide convening and mediation services (Purdy & Gray, 1994).[1]

Culture

The second organizing mechanism identified by Brown (1980) is culture. Establishing a shared culture for the domain creates norms and rules that govern the stakeholders' interactions and prescribe appropriate behavior (Pettigrew, 1976). For global environmental problems, this requires the creation of "metaregimes" in which the meaning of international principles such as "good neighborliness," "equal access," and "sustainable development" can be thrashed out among the critical parties (Golich & Young, 1993, pp. 86-87; Porter & Brown, 1991; Spector, Sjostedt, & Zartman, 1994; Young, 1994). Through cultural norms, stakeholders begin to regulate their domain-relevant actions and their interactions with other stakeholders.

Structure

The third organizing mechanism proposed by Brown (1980) is structure. While tightly organized systems often suffer from too much structure, underorganized domains lack formal, routinized means of exchange and interaction. Structuring, or creating a systematic form of interaction among stakeholders is often critical to collaboration (Trist, 1983). Frequently, in underorganized domains, stakeholders have had little or no interaction, or their relationships are characterized by high levels of mistrust. Attempts to impose structure prematurely may be seen as power plays and meet with resistance, especially if some stakeholders are excluded from participation.

A useful conceptualization of the evolution of structure in interorganizational domains is to conceive of them as negotiated information orders (Gray, 1989; Heimer, 1985). According to Heimer (1985), a negotiated information order occurs when a group of interrelated organizations agrees on a system of criteria for determining the social sufficiency of information that guides their joint decisions. Gray (1989) goes further to suggest that the stakeholders must also agree on the extent of risk that they will collectively incur and rules for governing stakeholders within the domain. For collaboration to be successful, stakeholders must recognize their interdependence and devise methods for sharing responsibility for the domain-level outcomes—that is, sharing control over the domain (Gray, 1989). If this involves ongoing governance activities, then authorization of some stakeholders to act on behalf of the others will be necessary. Trist (1983) refers to this as structuring. To achieve this level of domain organization requires what Giddens (1994, p. 93) calls "active trust," that is, trust that is gradually negotiated through interaction.

As noted above, conflicts among domain stakeholders typically involve power differences (Brown & Fox, 1996; Gray & Hay, 1986; Gricar & Brown, 1981; Hardy & Phillips, 1998). When power is unequally distributed among stakeholders, Heimer (1985) contends that the more powerful stakeholders will determine the negotiated order for the domain. When power differentials are substantial, change to the domain is likely to be minimal and will occur only if the dominant stakeholder(s) agrees (Hardy & Phillips, 1998). Until the stakeholders develop roughly equal or countervailing power, it is not likely that significant change will occur.

Technology

The fourth mechanism for organizing is technology (Brown, 1980). When technology is highly rationalized, tighter organization is necessary to gain efficiency. Within environmental domains, technology is frequently an area of contention because of the uncertainty of predictions (e.g., differing forecasts regarding global warming) or because of differing risk perceptions associated with its use (Porter & Brown, 1991; Thomas, Swaton, Fishbein, & Otway, 1980; Van Liere & Dunlap, 1980). When agreements about the use and impact of technology can be reached, as in the Chlorofluorocarbon Treaty (to prevent ozone degradation) in March 1988, technical provisions can contribute to domain organization.

Types of Regimes

International negotiations in which the parties establish a system of norms and rules that govern behavior among the players with respect to a particular issue (e.g., limiting dumping of hazardous waste in the oceans) are called international regimes. Typically, a regime consists of a multilateral legal instrument that prescribes agreed-upon principles, norms, and goals. Historically, efforts to create international regimes on global environmental issues occur at two levels: framework conventions and protocols. The latter impose binding obligations on the signatories, whereas the former articulate general principles and expectations with which compliance is voluntary. Some regimes specify consequences for organizations or states that violate their provisions, whereas others rely on goodwill and voluntary compliance by signatories and nonsignatories.

An example of a regime in which obligations and sanctions are prescribed is the London Dumping Convention of 1972, which governs dumping of certain hazardous materials in the sea and enables coastal states to punish violators. In contrast, Agenda 21, signed at the Earth Summit, provides guidelines for environmental protection and sustainable development for the next century but contains no enforceable provisions or sanctions for nations that do not comply with its provisions. The evolution of these provisions over time through ongoing negotiations will be required. Regimes typically start out as framework conventions and, over time, formulate binding obligations. For example, the regime for reducing ozone depletion that began in 1985 as the Vienna Convention for the Protection of the Ozone Layer was amended twice to become the Montreal Protocol, which sets specific targets for reduction in chlorofluorocarbons by the year 2000. The importance of the extended ongoing negotiations is highlighted by Spector et al. (1994):

> International agreements are not generally hammered out at the negotiating table at a single blow. Many are the product of the convention protocol approach in which broad, often vaguely worded statements of principles are established, followed by multiple agreements that elaborate on the details. Thus, a continuous negotiation process is established that must be implemented, managed, adjusted and sustained by some mechanism, which in many cases are regimes. During the formative and operative stages of agreement implementation, regime mechanisms are needed to foster a sense of cohesiveness, common purpose, and continuity among a set of nations that have agreed to abide by common objectives and standards. (p. 3)

For example, the Rio agreement produced some preliminary foundations for a regime on sustainable development, but it did not go nearly as far on climate change, biological diversity, technology transfer, and financial assistance, and it only marked the need for negotiations to start on deforestation and desertification (Spector et al., 1994).

We now turn our attention to the forms that international environmental regimes can take. Examples from several different environmental disputes illustrate these different forms

SOME ALTERNATIVE MODELS OF GOVERNANCE

The difficulties in organizing for global environmental change are formidable, indeed. Some claim that they are the most difficult changes the world has ever faced (Gore, 1993). Some progress in designing forums for the resolution of environmental conflicts has been under way in the United States both locally and nationally, as well as in Canada (Bingham, 1986; Crowfoot & Wondolleck, 1988; Gray, 1989; Shaftoe, 1993), and these forums have demonstrated some adaptability to international arenas, particularly for multilateral agreements (Golich & Young, 1993; Synergos Institute, 1993; Trolldalen, 1992).

At the global level, although progress on establishing some environmental regimes has occurred, it has been slow in coming, often requiring a decade or more to move from framework conventions to protocols (Young, 1989). Looking to the future, scholars vary in their optimism about the likelihood of significant progress. Four general approaches for "creating and strengthening the needed global environmental regimes over the next decade" (Porter & Brown, 1991, p. 144) are considered.

As Table 8.1 indicates, some governance systems are more suited to certain environmental problems than others. Restricted common property options can be used to solve commons problems, as can assigning one state national jurisdiction, whereas joint management regimes are appropriate for shared resource problems. Global governance systems have a role to play in dealing with linked issues and commons problems, and they may create general rules for transboundary issues for which monetary partnerships and technical assistance transfers may also be advantageous. Each form of governance is examined in more detail and illustrated by example below. The advantages and problems associated with its use are also delineated.

Joint Management Regimes

Although not global in scope, regional joint management regimes support regional progress on an environmental issue, promote education (particularly in developing countries), and build experience among stakeholders in how to

Table 8.1   Types of Environmental Issues and Corresponding Governance
Approaches

Commons	Deep seabed minerals, electromagnetic spectrum, geostationary orbit, stratospheric ozone, global climate system, outer space, high seas	Global governance, national jurisdiction, restricted common property
Shared resources	Pools of oil, straddling stocks of fish, migratory animal stocks, ecosystems that cross national borders (e.g., rivers or seas)	Joint management regimes
Transboundary externalities	Destruction of world heritage sites (with amenity value), tragic accidents, deforestation, acid rain	Global governance, joint management regimes
Linked issues	Environmental standards within free-trade agreements	Global governance, partnerships

reach collaborative agreements that wed environmental preservation with economic improvement. They focus on regional environmental issues that may or may not have global implications. Many of these efforts occur under private, rather than governmental, auspices. Where global changes are expected to have differential regional effects (as in the Puget Sound example above), collaboration at the regional level to plan for and cope with the impacts will be necessary (Fleagle, 1994). Although such efforts need not be global in scope, learning from one region may clearly profit others. The Chimalapas Coalition illustrates negotiations at the regional level in a conflict over deforestation, whereas energy development efforts would be better addressed by a joint management regime.

A major controversy over construction of a hydroelectric dam and highway through the Mexican rain forest, Chimalapas, in southern Mexico, was resolved through a collaborative initiative known as the Chimalapas Coalition. The coalition included the states of Oaxaca and Chiapas (where the rain forest is located), the federal legislature, and several ministries, environmental nongovernmental organizations (ENGOs), human rights groups, and international organizations. The convening role was performed by the Synergos Institute, a U.S.-based partnership-building group that enlisted participation of groups reluctant to join the coalition. Synergos also served as a bridge to organize and facilitate discussions among groups that had no formal relationships, secure outside funding to assist in organizing indigenous peoples (the Campesinos) to participate, and create a structure for the Coalition.

The Coalition has assumed a variety of organizational forms over the past 4 years, ranging from a tightly organized formal partnership to a loosely coupled affiliation of independent groups (Synergos Institute, 1993, p. 8). The Coalition's efforts have produced several positive outcomes: (a) resolution of long-standing land tenure disputes, (b) community plans for use and conservation of the forest, (c) state government commitment to upgrade public works and improve services to communities, (d) agreement not to build the hydroelectric dam and highway, (e) creation of a loan fund for small projects, and (f) plans for a Campesino-controlled biosphere reserve within the rain forest.

Joint management regimes certainly have their place, especially in dealing with shared resource situations and transboundary externalities. Regional agreements generally illustrate what some scholars have referred to as the incremental change approach (Mathews, 1991; Porter & Brown, 1991). That is, it addresses environmental change on a case-by-case basis. This is the predominant approach on our planet to date. It denies the fundamental interdependence among economic, political, and environmental issues at the global level and presumes that "reasonable progress can be made on global environmental challenges within the parameters of existing global political institutions, diplomatic practice, and socioeconomic realities" (Porter & Brown, 1991, p. 145). It might include efforts to generate framework conventions, but they would not bind the signatories to compliance. Individual nations might generate their own targets and timetables for reducing or eliminating hazards, but it would not fundamentally alter existing economic distributions or lifestyles among nations in the North. The consequences of the incremental change approach have been aptly summarized by Porter and Brown (1991, pp. 146-147).

1. The problem of the industrialized states' reluctance to divert major resources to developing countries for participation in global environmental agreements would remain unresolved.

2. Climate change, deforestation, and biological diversity conventions would fall short of what is needed to reverse those threats.

3. Isolation of environmental issues from larger North-South economic development issues would continue.

4. No change in domestic economic structure or lifestyle would be demanded.

5. Modest progress toward effective regimes would be traded for assumptions that sufficient progress will evolve over time.

Another example of a regional agreement is the Air Quality Agreement between the United States and Canada signed in 1991 to deal with acid rain. Although a bilateral agreement, it does include several environmental principles evolving at the global level for previous international regimes about the environment; however, there are a few to which it does not subscribe, such as the polluter pays principle and *res communis*, which designates the environment as part of the common heritage (Golich & Young, 1993).

Global Partnership Approach

Although the task of promoting environmental change is daunting on a global scale, some progress has been made using the global partnership approach, particularly in dealing with regional issues. Global partnership approaches generally require that industrialized states display a new willingness in all international forums to address the primary economic concerns of developing states as well as the objective obstacles to environmental and resource management in all countries (Porter & Brown, 1991, p. 148). A few examples will be provided here as models that create hope.

GEF

The Global Environment Facility (GEF) project began as a $1.3 billion joint effort between the World Bank, the United Nations Development Program (UNDP), and the United Nations Environment Program (UNEP) to support environmentally sensitive Third World development. GEF funds projects in developing countries that "address environmental problems of global significance and nature including reduction of greenhouse gases, pollution of international waters, preservation of biodiversity, and prevention of ozone depletion" (Trolldalen, 1992, p. 179). Thus, GEF serves as a forum for project-by-project decisions regarding Third World development. GEF provides funds only to nations that have signed the Montreal Protocol. According to Trolldalen (1992), "GEF seems to be one of the most important means available for the UN system and the Bretton Woods institutions in management of IEC's [international environmental conflicts]" (p. 180). Others have argued that support for GEF is paltry and that efforts to link environmental demands with technology transfer agreements and monetary support for development require considerably more finances (Porter & Brown, 1991).

The purposes of GEF were reviewed and strengthened during UNCED. GEF was viewed as a means of financing (in part) the implementation of Agenda 21. Critical to the UNCED agreement to back GEF, however, were changes in its decision-making procedures. These involved reallocation of voting rights to reduce the influence of developed countries and give greater input to NGOs (Susskind, 1994). These changes were consistent with the views of Mostafa Tolba, UNEP's executive director, on global partnerships "in which all countries have an equal say in resource allocation" (Starke, 1990, p. 173).

CSD

Another agreement stemming from Rio was the formation of the Commission on Sustainable Development (CSD). CSD, charged with monitoring progress in implementing Agenda 21, is constituted as a commission within the United Nations Economic and Social Council. Formation of CSD was fraught with representation issues, as well as concerns about sovereignty infringement of the South by the North in data collection and the role of NGOs in the assessment (Susskind, 1994).

Debt-for-Nature Swaps

Debt-for-nature swaps represent another form of global partnership and begin to address North-South issues, albeit on a project-specific basis with private resources. These transactions use northern donors to purchase the debt of a developing nation at greatly reduced rates in exchange for conservation efforts by that country. Three parties from the debtor country are usually involved: the government, the central bank, and a conservation organization that receives the funds (von Moltke & DeLong, 1990). NGOs in creditor nations raise the funds for the swap, but to avoid concerns about imperialism, these organizations must transfer responsibility for administration of the conservation efforts to an NGO in the developing country. Creditor NGOs transfer title of the debt to conservation organizations in the debtor country.

In the first debt-for-nature swap, Conservation International paid 15% of face value for Bolivian debt. Funds were then used to enlarge and manage a biosphere reserve for which the Bolivian government agreed to provide legal protection. Other swap rates have varied from 12% to 55% (von Moltke & DeLong, 1990). Perhaps the most important consideration in making these swaps successful is taking the interests of all of the parties into account. These agreements require careful negotiations among all of the parties to ensure that donors are assured proper use of the funds and tax credits, debtor nations are truly committed to environmentally sustainable projects, good relationships ensue between banks and debtor nations, and conservation efforts actually materialize. Debt-for-nature swaps require local, not generic, negotiations. Although they "have had a small impact on foreign indebtedness by the debtor nations, the resulting conservation programs have had a major impact on environmental protection" (von Moltke & DeLong, 1990, p. 10).

More grandiose partnership schemes have been envisioned, such as exchanging reductions in energy consumption in the North for population stabilization in the South. Expanded versions of GEF or debt-for-nature swaps could be used as inducements for national plans for pollution control, reduction of deforestation, and so on. If First World governments entered debt-for-nature swaps, protection of rain forests might be possible.

Skepticism about the partnership approach has been aptly expressed, however. A global partnership approach to regime creation would require a level of political will to address global environmental issues that does not appear to exist now. There is still strong resistance in the United States, Japan, and Germany to these kinds of resource transfers, and removal of protectionist barriers is still blocked by special interests throughout North America, western Europe, and Japan (Porter & Brown, 1991, p. 152).

Global Governance Approach

The final approach to global environmental change is even more ambitious. It proposes new international structures to overcome veto power and speed up compulsory action by all nations. Proponents of this approach advocate the creation of an international structure that can legislate and enforce environmental regulations worldwide. Thirty nations support a document proposing such an institution, but opposition from the United States, the former Soviet Union, Great Britain, China, and Japan stymied it from serious consideration. Criticism of the approach from a transaction cost perspective has also been proffered.

Other suggestions that fall under this heading include Vice President Gore's (1993) proposal for a "global Marshall Plan" and the creation of a system of global environmental taxes (Mathews, 1991). The overarching goal of the former includes "establishment, especially in the developing world—of the social and political conditions most conducive to the emergence of sustainable societies" (Gore, 1993, p. 307). Achieving consensus, particularly among the political powers, remains unlikely, and political efforts to do so may siphon energies that could be directly applied to environmental problems (Porter & Brown, 1991). Mathews (1991) notes that the incremental approach and global governance (what she calls the quantum leap approach [p. 311]) are not mutually exclusive, and "what qualifies as a quantum leap today may seem little more than a sensible next step in a year or two" (p. 310). Nevertheless, serious obstacles to this approach remain to be addressed.

CHALLENGES TO ORGANIZING

Despite some progress in creating alternative governance modes, several challenges to the successful resolution of global environmental dispute remain. According to Young (1994), "Those engaged in interactive relationships commonly fail to solve collective-action problems, even when the mutual losses to be avoided or the joint gains to be reaped from doing so are substantial" (p. 18). Three major challenges to forging international regimes on highly contested environmental issues warrant attention here: framing the problem, dealing with power differences, and selecting a convener. All three of these become significant early in the problem-setting phase of regime formation (Gray, 1989).

Framing the Problem

Problem setting (Gray, 1989) refers to activities that precede negotiations in which preliminary organizing of the relevant stakeholders occurs and initial efforts to define the problem are set forth. How the problem is framed can be critical to the success or failure of efforts to bring stakeholders to the table (Mather & Yngvesson, 1980-81; Spector et al., 1994). Young (1994) suggested that framing the issue of global climate change in terms of the link between environment and development was crucial to moving it forward—because both the North and the South need to adjust their consumption patterns. If either the North or South claims only one of these issues, the other will feel blamed, and negotiations will break down. In addition to framing the issues, reaching agreement on several process issues is also critical to the problem-setting phase of collaboration. These include deciding how decisions will be made among the stakeholders, how dispute resolution will be handled within the regime, and how free riders will be dealt with (Spector et al., 1994).

Dealing With Power Differences

The ability of the various actors to wield power has a profound effect on regime formation. Four power issues, critical during the problem-setting phase, are addressed here: standing of the parties, infringement of national sovereignty, resource sharing, and veto potential.

Standing of the Parties

Standing refers to one's right to participate in negotiations and the degree to which stakeholders are considered legitimate and equal players (Gray, 1989). Although all nation-states currently have a place in UNCED negotiations, questions regarding the role of NGOs remain problematic. Susskind (1994), for example, notes that although the NGOs often create the impetus for issues reaching the table, they themselves are not permitted to join the actual negotiations. At Rio, for example, NGOs held their own, parallel conference while national delegates met for formal negotiations. The ability to exclude critical stakeholders is clearly an exercise of power (Bachrach & Baratz, 1963).

Infringement of National Sovereignty

In international disputes, problem setting immediately raises jurisdictional issues, such as sovereignty and property rights with respect to the global commons for some stakeholders (Golich & Young, 1993; Mathews, 1991; Sebenius, 1992; Soros, 1986). According to Susskind (1994), a major reason that UNCED failed to arrive at specific agreements stemmed from some states' unwillingness to accept certain constraints on economic development activities. Where questions of equity are concerned, Young (1994) contends that regime formation efforts have fallen short. For example,

> The U.S. (and several other important players in a more circumspect fashion) backed away from key provisions of the 1982 Law of the Sea Convention precisely because they became dissatisfied with provisions in Part XI on deep

seabed mining that seemed likely to benefit members of the group of developing countries. (p. 49)

Equity issues in the negotiations on various aspects of the New Economic International Order (during the 1970s and 1980s) resulted in no agreement because the advanced industrialized nations were unwilling to accept concessions. Similarly, despite limited concessions (including compensation) to the developing countries in the ozone regime, compliance with the agreement, especially by China and India, remains suspect (Young, 1994). In the Rio talks, the North's refusal to reduce consumption patterns and the resistance of political leaders around the world to conserve now for the sake of future generations thwarted agreement (Susskind, 1994, p. 222).

Resource Sharing

A more immediate power issue in the aftermath of UNCED involves the resistance of several nations to exchanging scientific data at the next regime meeting. Current provisions for data collection on Agenda 21 depend on the good-faith efforts of each nation to provide the necessary information. Susskind (1994) argues that southern nations may forestall progress by resisting northern technical standards for data collection, thereby making cross-region comparisons impossible. Even though UNCED participants agreed to data collection efforts in the areas of biological diversity and climate change, no penalties for nations that fail to comply were instituted, nor were specific details of how the North would generate support for the Convention of Biological Diversity.

Veto Potential

Power is also exercised through veto of agreements by those states that stand to lose the most on the issue. In virtually all global environmental issues, some nation or coalition has veto power over the issue and has compelling reasons to sabotage organizing efforts by refusing to come to the table. "Veto coalitions constitute potential obstacles to effective international cooperation on environmental issues, and their role is central to the dynamics of bargaining and negotiation in global environmental politics" (Porter & Brown, 1991, p. 18). A good example concerns the potential power of Brazil, India, and China to scuttle any attempts to reach an international agreement on reduction of fossil fuel usage. Any of these three countries may be unwilling to forestall the rate of its national development for the sake of limiting CO_2 production, thus jeopardizing global efforts to reverse global warming. Young (1994), however, believes that concessions from the North (such as technology transfers, technical training, and financial support for industrial processes that reduce greenhouse gas production) may be more likely in climate change negotiations because the developing countries have considerable bargaining power behind their threats to push industrial development at the expense of environmental degradation. The key to success in these negotiations is taking the environment/development linkage seriously by all parties (Young, 1994).

Selecting a Convener

Another obstacle is finding a convener who has sufficient credibility to entice the necessary players to the table (Gray, 1989). In international disputes, the problem of convening is particularly difficult because there is no international organization with statutory jurisdiction over the parties involved. The fundamental issues include how an issue becomes salient enough to get on the global agenda (Porter & Brown, 1991), how the parameters of a dispute are shaped, who the relevant parties are, how to get them to the table, and who can serve as a convener. Moreover, the parties themselves represent kinds of organizations—various representatives of nation-states (representing environmental, security, and economic development interests), national or international NGOs, multinational corporations, and multilateral financial institutions (such as the International Monetary Fund, the World Bank, and the Asian Development Bank), as well as numerous United Nations agencies. The convening role can be performed by virtually any of these stakeholders, but frequently, it is the environmental NGOs that elevate an issue to the level of urgency and generate pressure for international negotiation on the topic (Porter & Brown, 1991), even though, ironically, they are rarely invited to the table (Susskind, 1994).

For major global disputes, the convening role frequently falls to the United Nations. For example, UNEP has served as convener for several conventions, including those on endangered species (1973), maritime dumping (1972), ozone depletion (1985, 1987) and transboundary movement of hazardous waste (1989). More recently, however, other UN agencies have usurped this convening role. Typically, the UN's role can be classified as persuasion, but it may shift to mandate if protocols are established granting the UN agency some authority within the regime.

Although UNEP effectively performed a convening role for several regimes during the 1970s and 1980s, its credibility was contested during the 1989 negotiations on transboundary movement of hazardous wastes when UNEP's director, Mostafa Tolba, was accused of capitulating to the interests of the North by the Group of 77, a coalition of developing countries that asserted that UNEP's agenda favored northern issues. Since then, UNEP's role in international environmental negotiations has been reduced, and other UN organizations, including the General Assembly, have adopted the convening role for environmental concerns (Porter & Brown, 1991). This dispersion of the environmental agenda to a more diverse set of organizations (including the Food and Agricultural Organization [FAO], UNDP, United Nations Children's Fund [UNCF] and the General Assembly [UNGA]) aligns environmental issues with other UN priorities, such as population growth, trade, and security issues.

Aside from the United Nations, a few other groups may have the clout and legitimacy necessary to convene certain disputes. One of these is the World Bank, which, along with other multilateral development banks, has been criticized by the NGO community for environmental indifference (Porter & Brown, 1991) and by the South for its intrusion into the policies of individual countries (Susskind, 1994). The credibility of the World Bank to deal with environmental issues has been questioned by the NGO community because the World Bank's role is primarily economic and financial. Since 1987, the World Bank's environmental track record has been checkered. It increased its environmental staff but continued to be ambivalent about its energy policies (vacillating between supporting coal plant and natural gas development). Trolldalen (1992), arguing in favor of the World Bank's credibility as a convener, claims that

> the Bank does have the necessary staff resources to gain access to appropriate scientific information and expertise, and is therefore able to separate the issues as a basis for efficient conflict resolution. . . . The Bank could play an increasingly important role in the resolution of IECs involving compensation for transboundary negative externalities. (pp. 23-24)

A major initiative that enhanced the World Bank's role as a global change agent was the creation of GEF, although, as noted above, challenges to the World Bank's role were raised during UNCED.

CONCLUSION

If we hark back to the notion of regimes as negotiated information orders (Gray, 1989; Heimer, 1985), several predictions about how the organization of regimes will evolve can be drawn from organization theory. First, conveners will need to urge inclusive, integrative framing of problems in order to entice parties to the table. This means continually looking for ways to link issues that allow for trade-offs among the parties (Susskind, 1994). As noted above, unless environmental and economic development consequences are joined in the framing of regimes, insufficient maneuverability exists for either side to offer concessions.

A second prediction from organization theory concerns interdependence. Until the players from the North and the South realize that they cannot operate independently of each other, little progress will ensue. In some cases, worsening of the common predicament in which all the parties find themselves may be necessary before concessions will be made on either side. That is, parties will need to conclude that the consequences that ensue from a negotiated agreement will ultimately serve their interests better than the consequences of failing to reach an agreement.

Third, as Heimer (1985) argues, the burden of innovation in cases of unequal power falls on the low-power stakeholders. Although it may appear that southern nations have less power, given their veto power in some global disputes, it is not always the North that has the power edge. In any case, the dependent group will have to make adjustments or find new, creative solutions in order to shift away from a stalemate.

Fourth, the entrance of new players can alter the power balance in a regime. In critiquing the two-step, convention protocol process of regime formation, Susskind (1994, pp. 230-232) has proposed strengthening the role of NGOs in regime decision-making processes. Should NGOs press for greater participation in decision making within regimes, the balance of power may shift and/or new coalitions may emerge to break some of the current logjams.

A fifth solution already in use (as illustrated by the Chimalapas Coalition) is the generation of regional solutions. Parties affected by a particular ecosystem, for example, can convene their own collaborative forums and begin to create solutions unburdened by the political posturing of their own governments in global regime deliberations. Regional-level projects can also begin to develop pockets where active trust among the parties is generated. As cross-sectoral social capital formation is built, these trusting relationships among institutions can transcend specific locales (Westley, Gray, & Brown, 1996).

Finally, another solution is to develop methods for local participation in technological problem solving and implementation (Evans, 1996), as well as local monitoring of those agreements that are reached in international forums. If local stakeholders realize the tremendous power they can exercise over corporate and governmental actors and begin to leverage it toward collective ends, institutional actors will be forced to make adjustments (Brown & Fox, 1996). Such processes will become increasingly important and necessary as international development agencies incorporate environmental protection and management into their agenda for development projects (Scott & Trolldalen, 1993; United Nations Environment Program, 1989; World Commission on Environment and Development, 1987).

It is not my intention here to recommend the most propitious approach to global environmental change. Rather, I have tried to outline the scope of the problem and assess the political hurdles that impede easy resolution of even the most straightforward environmental issues. No consideration has even been given here to the technological feasibility of addressing many of the issues—such as providing adequate water supplies or cleaning up repositories of hazardous nuclear waste. I have focused only on creating organizational forums within which to search for collaborative solutions to what may be life-threatening or life-giving issues. Regardless of which approaches are taken, it is clear that organizational scholars can make a contribution by helping the various stakeholders to appreciate the dynamics in which they are embedded and by fostering exploration of creative new means for organizing environmental domains.

NOTE

1. The practice is most developed within the Environmental Protection Agency, which uses third parties to convene and facilitate regulatory negotiations (Fiorino, 1988).

9

INTERNATIONAL NETWORKING

The Role of Southern NGOs

JULIE FISHER

We are a conspiracy in a true sense of the word. To conspire means to breathe together. We know that there are already large numbers of such conspiracies all over the world. They have grown independently, but they are united by a common vision to give birth to a new culture, a culture based on ecological principles. The knowledge of these conspiracies and their interrelatedness gives us courage and strength.

> —A Swiss sociologist who organized an
> environmental movement in Switzerland after
> visiting Chipko, a women's environmental
> movement in India (Bahuguna, 1988, p. 13)

NONGOVERNMENTAL ORGANIZATIONS AND GLOBAL CHANGE STRATEGIES

The United States in the late 19th century was not unlike global society today. As immigration lowered labor costs and production techniques were simplified, cutthroat competitive pressures grew and investments in labor productivity declined. After the Civil War, securities manipulation became increasingly common. Yet these changes also began to empower workers to organize and to reap the long-term benefits of industrialization (see Hall, 1989, pp. 222-223).

Today, the international private sector is marked by breathtaking changes—currency manipulation by out-of-control young traders, skyrocketing numbers of multinational corporations, the beginnings of trade liberalization, and, above all, revolutionary changes in global communication. Although this global marketplace bears some resemblance to the activities of the robber barons and will make the few very rich, like the industrialization of the United States, it also offers potential opportunities for the many. In rural Honduras, for example, elementary classrooms are using textbooks printed with publishing software (Annis, 1992, p. 590).

The international intergovernmental sector is, of course, even weaker than was the government of the United States in the 19th century. Although the peacekeeping role of the United Nations has expanded, even its most basic function of preserving order is beset with financial and political obstacles just as ethnic hatred, environmental deterioration, population growth, and poverty escalate into what has been called the "new world disorder." Official regional organizations face similar pressures but are often weaker than global ones. Even a wealthier organization, the World Bank, is finding it difficult to move away from top-down bureaucratic decision making, beholden as it is to the narrowest political exigencies of member governments.

Yet because of the revolution in global communications, something is happening internationally that was confined to local spaces in 19th-century America. Despite the accuracy of Alexis de Tocqueville's observations on voluntarism in America, the independent sector in the United States did not begin to have a major impact on the national dialogue about how people should live together and order their lives until the mid-20th century. Even then, it was, at least initially, more the product of philanthropic investments by the corporate establishment than of grassroots organizing (Annis, 1992, p. 590).

In contrast, the international independent sector, composed of international, northern (developed), southern (developing), and now "eastern" nongovernmental organizations (NGOs), is already affecting global society. NGOs are influencing not only the global dialogue but also intergovernmental relationships, if not yet multinational corporations. NGOs are demanding, and successfully organizing, consultative roles at major global events; they are also becoming players at the annual meetings of international financial institutions.

Global institutional change is driven by the urgency of the global agenda. The end of the cold war highlighted the need for new institutional strategies to confront rising fears engendered by the multiple, interlocking, environmental and humanitarian catastrophes that threaten to become even numerous in the future. This chapter focuses on the role of southern NGOs in global networking but places the topic within the larger context of the "organizational dimensions for global change" by using a strategic typology for global change developed by Morgan, Power, and Weigel (1993). This typology consists of the following:

- *Global issue regimes* on problems such as ozone depletion or debt restructuring, described as the "creation or reconfiguration of international institutions that are issue-based, functioning as both think tanks and conduits for . . . institutionalization of new global norms" (p. 1916).

- *More developed country governments (MDCs) as initiators of change.* This strategy includes domestic changes on environmental issues, as well as foreign assistance on issues such as global poverty.

- *Less developed country governments (LDCs) as initiators of change.* Examples include domestic policy reform or the Group of 77.

- *Alternative institutional strategies* that focus on the international and national roles of the voluntary or independent sector.

- *Strategies that focus on the adjudication of international conflict,* usually by intergovernmental institutions.

- *Strategies focused on global value transformation.* Examples include the World Order Models Project and the *State of the World* reports by the Worldwatch Institute. They may also emerge from a process such as the sustained dialogue that transformed the Israeli-Palestinian relationship.

Although the main purpose of Morgan and her colleagues is to categorize and assess change strategies within this typology, the typology can also be used to assess the role that actual institutions play in implementing, as well as thinking about or planning, global change. Thus, Morgan et al. use the World Resources Institute to assess the potential effectiveness of a think tank's focus on global values transformation.

If, however, we move beyond individual organizations or institutions to the global equivalents of the three sectors of national society—government, private for-profit, and the Third or independent sector—then the typology becomes useful in a way not completely foreseen by Morgan et al. Strategies initiated by MDCs or LDCs belong in the intergovernmental sector, as do most adjudications of international conflicts and global issue regimes, such as the Montreal Treaty on ozone depletion. Although Morgan et al. do not focus on the international for-profit sector, multinational corporations are not always oblivious to the long-term consequences of global trends.[1] Indeed, international organizations such as the Business Council for Sustainable Development could fit into an additional strategic category. Another example is the Technical Information Pilot Service, which collects and disseminates information about trade and technology among 2,200 LDC users, mostly small and medium businesses (Gifford, 1993, p. 62).

The impact of a growing international independent sector, on the other hand, fills, but also spills over, the "alternative institutional" strategic category. For one thing, NGOs, foundations, and think tanks are helping to shape global issue regimes, global value transformation, and, in some cases, strategies focusing on the adjudication of international conflict.[2] Not only have international networks that include NGOs progressed beyond the think tank stage, they are also networking with each other and proliferating at an astounding rate. For another thing, the domestic activities of NGOs can affect the ability of MDC and LDC governments to initiate change.

This chapter focuses on that part of the alternative change strategy directed by Third World or southern NGOs as they increase their international networking with each other. To understand and define these South-South parameters, however, we need to touch on the relationships that comprise both South-South and North-South networks and on the spillover of the alternative change strategy into the other typologies of global change. To do this, we need to define different types of NGOs more precisely.

DEFINITIONS

The rapid growth of the independent sector in the Third World is increasingly defined by partnerships between two types of NGOs: grassroots support organizations (GRSOs) and grassroots organizations (GROs).[3] GRSOs are nationally or regionally based development assistance organizations, usually staffed by professionals, that channel international funds to GROs and help communities other than their own.[4] There are at least 35,000 to 50,000 active GRSOs in the Third World (Fisher, 1993, p. 7).[5] Although some GRSOs are counterparts to international NGOs (INGOs) or northern NGOs from the developed countries, the vast majority are indigenous. In addition to building linkages with GROs, GRSOs are also uniting with each other.

GROs are locally based groups that work to improve and develop their own communities through communitywide or more specific memberships, such as women. Although many have been promoted by GRSOs, they have also become more active on their own. There are probably more than 200,000 of these in Asia, Africa, and Latin America. Faced with the deterioration of their environment and increasing impoverishment, both traditional and newly created GROs began organizing horizontal networks among themselves. In some cases, they have created GRSOs from below by hiring their own expertise (Fisher, 1993, p. 7).

The term *southern NGO* is used here to include GROs, GRSOs, and their national and subnational networks. The term *northern NGO* will be used to describe organizations that are based in a northern country but work directly in the South, sometimes supporting the work of southern NGOs.

An INGO, on the other hand, "has its own international governing body made up of representatives from many countries" (Hall, 1993, p. 11). Thus, Save the Children Federation in the United States is a northern NGO but is also a member of the International Save the Children Alliance, an INGO that includes Save the Children organizations from other countries. INGOs are, in other words, international networks. Among the other prominent North-South INGOs are the International Planned Parenthood Federation and the International Red Cross. Although Hall (1993) argues that some INGOs are too centrally controlled to also be considered international networks, they increasingly face pressures to internationalize their staffs and work through southern NGOs. Many INGOs were originally northern NGOs that discovered the virtues of an international staff and increasing autonomy for their field offices. Other INGOs—the focus of this chapter—are exclusively southern in membership and may be limited to one region or have representation from more than one continent.[6]

Although many INGOs were founded before the communications revolution, they are now proliferating more rapidly because of computers, faxes, and modems. Boulding (1990) points out that in 1909, there were an estimated 176 INGOs, compared with 18,000 in 1988. By 1994, the total number of INGOs had increased to an estimated 20,000.[7]

In addition to the broad human rights, human welfare, and development agendas, some INGOs are international professional networks or clearinghouses for scientific research (Hall, 1993). Many of these, such as the World Engineering Partnership for Sustainable Development, are also beginning to focus on global issues. As the line between global information exchange and implementation blurs, computer networks promote a broad global agenda, increasingly accepted by NGOs and other kinds of organizations.

EXPLORING INTERNATIONAL
NETWORKING AMONG NGOs

This chapter explores two types of international networking among southern NGOs within the alternative change strategy:

1. Intraregional INGOs or networks (hereinafter called regional networks) that operate in more than one country with headquarters and work centered in one region of the Third World (see Diong, 1994, p. i). Although some northerners have helped found them, most are organized by people from the Third World.
2. Interregional South-South INGOs or networks. These are defined as networks that span at least two of the three major regions of the Third World. Some of these focus very generally on sustainable development. Others—such as the Vetvier Network, which focuses on a grass that prevents soil erosion—are extremely specialized (Grimshaw, 1993, p. 64).[8]

Before examining these two patterns in detail, we should note that southern NGOs also participate in other patterns of international networking. For example, southern NGOs participate in some mixed networks that may also include governments or other organizations, such as universities and academies of science. The Third World Network of Scientific Organizations, founded in 1988 by 15 ministers of science and higher education and 30 heads of science academies and research councils from 36 developing countries, promotes science-based economic development. With headquarters in Trieste, Italy, at the Third World Academy of Science, it has 121 members, including government ministries, science academies, science councils, and 20 other organizations (including NGOs) from 69 countries. Among many other projects, it has collaborated with the Third World Academy of Science to establish a network of centers dedicated to research and training in the high-tech and environmental sciences critical to sustainable economic development.[9] The Academy also houses the Third World Organization for Women in Science, which provides travel and publication grants.

Unlike the Third World Academy of Science, however, most mixed networks are intraregional. A new INGO, EarthCare Africa, was founded after the Rio Conference by African governments, private academies, and NGOs to prepare Africans to participate in the global environmental movement (*Brundtland Bulletin*, 1993, p. 38). The Regional Network of Environmental

Experts (ZERO), based in Zimbabwe, mobilizes African experts on energy issues from governments and NGOs in eight countries of eastern and southern Africa (Diong, 1994, pp. 8-9).[10] The Caribbean Network for Integrated Rural Development at the University of the West Indies in Trinidad links governments to GRSOs (Towle & Potter, 1989, p. 59). The Latin American Network for Child Welfare, with a regional data bank, has more than 1,000 members from NGOs, governments, international organizations, and children's movements (FAO/FFHC, 1987, p. 102).

Mixed networks that include governments can be characterized as merging global issue regimes and LDC government strategies. The South-South Partnership for Population Action, for example, was founded by 10 countries after the Cairo Conference in 1994 to match institutional needs with the expertise of other participants and to share models for promoting family health, family planning, and women's education. The first board meeting, held in 1995 in Zimbabwe, included NGOs and private sector providers.[11]

A second networking pattern is for southern NGOs to become an integral part of the larger process of NGO networking within the intergovernmental system, with a spillover effect on global issue regimes, LDCs as initiators of change, and MDCs as initiators of change. Beginning with the enormous media impact of women's NGOs at the Nairobi Women's Conference in Kenya in 1985, NGOs increased their influence on the conference process. During the preparatory commissions (PrepComs) for the Cairo Population Conference in 1994, NGOs sucessfully lobbied for the central importance of educating women to reduce fertility, although NGOs had been excluded from the PrepComs in previous years. It may be that the poor treatment of the NGO forum during the Beijing women's conference in 1995 was a reaction by a fearful government to the growing power of the international NGO movement. NGOs are also lobbying specialized international agencies. In 1993, for example, the Food and Agriculture Organization (FAO) approved the composition of a Consultative Group to strategically guide the Tropical Forestry Action Plan. Although their real power and influence still remain in question, NGOs have seven self-nominated representatives from the North and South out of 36 Consultative Group members (*Brundtland Bulletin,* 1993, p. 20).

Finally, southern NGOs are part of global or North-South NGO networking, which can affect global value transformation. Cause-related INGOs or networks (also called "transnational social movement organizations") target both governments and official international institutions and governments (see Smith, Pagnucco, & Romeril, 1994).[12] The International Green Cross, for example, promotes ecological law and disaster prevention.[13] Other organizations use a quieter, more scholarly approach; for example, Civicus, the World Alliance for Citizen Participation, serves as an advocate for stronger voluntary sectors, promotes research, and identifies models of voluntary action. Global NGO networking, including southern NGOs, also informs global issue regimes on internal-external issues such as migration, trade, and pollution (Shaw, 1994, p. 143).

Now that we have sketched, in simplified form, the range of networks that includes, but is not limited to, southern NGOs, we turn to the major focus of this chapter—international networking among southern NGOs.

THE INTRAREGIONAL LEVEL

Although it is difficult to assess how many international networks do more than hold occasional conferences, intraregional networks have proliferated rapidly since the 1960s, spurred by four major historical trends. The first, documented elsewhere (Fisher, 1993), is the proliferation of southern NGOs. A second, related trend, increased international support for southern NGO networking, is described below, as are two others—NGO networking surrounding major United Nations conferences and the rise of computer and communications technologies.

International support is often an important, if not essential, precursor of South-South networking. The Organization for Economic Cooperation and Development, for example, began promoting regional research networks in the 1960s. The Council for the Development of Economic and Social Research in Africa (CODESERIA), which had 56 member organizations from 29 countries by the late 1980s, holds workshops on women, population, agriculture, and industrialization (Cordoba-Novion & Sachs, 1987, p. 10). Then, in the early 1970s, the Freedom from Hunger Campaign of the FAO helped create general transnational networks of NGOs. Finally, in the early 1980s, the United Nations Environment Program (UNEP) created the Environmental Liaison Center International (ELCI), which includes national networks of NGOs and large international NGOs, such as Greenpeace (*IFDA Dossier,* 1987b, p. 33). In 1982, ELCI carried out surveys of GROs and GRSOs working on food, energy, water, and shelter in a number of countries and helped connect donors and NGOs through the creation of the African NGOs Environment Network (ANEN). UNEP also helped found the Environnement et Developpement Action-Tiers Monde (ENDA), which trains African NGO leaders.

Networking may also be advanced by INGOs that evolve into regional NGO networks. The Central American Environment Program (PACA) is a field-based network of three northern NGOs—the Cooperative for American Relief Everywhere (CARE), The Nature Conservancy, and Conservation International—as well as universities and national NGOs. It focuses on five core endangered areas, promotes sustainable activity in the buffer zones, and is involved in policy analysis and environmental education.

Northern influence, however, is often more indirect. Central American environmentalists, who began studying in the developed countries after Earth Day 1970, founded a network of environmental NGOs, called the Regional Network of NGOs for Sustainable Development in Central America (REDES-CA), with the help of the International Conservation Union (Barzetti & Rovinski, 1992, p. 103).

Since the mid-1980s, the global NGO networking surrounding U.N. conferences and the spread of computer technology to Asia, Latin America, and Africa have further accelerated the pace of regional networking. A Central American NGOs Network, for example, was further activated by the preparations for the United Nations Conference on Environment and Development (UNCED) held in Rio in 1992. Coordinated by the Nicaraguan NGO Federation and the Movimiento Ambientalista Nicaraguense, it represented environmental NGOs at the Central American Committee on Environment and Development at the United Nations, the Pan American Health Organization's project on Environment and Health in the Central American Isthmus, the Central American Forestry Action Plan, and the Central American Inter-Parliamentary Commission on the Environment (*Brundtland Bulletin*, 1991, p. WP 4).

The NGOs that participated in the Rio Conference rejected the idea of creating a central infrastructure to promote the environmental treaties that emerged from UNCED. Rather, the Global NGO Forum encouraged intra-regional networks to convene meetings on the treaty process, act as caretakers, determine their interests in continuing to coordinate the treaties, identify new questions, and distribute the treaties (*Network '92*, 1992, p. 17). In addition to the established regional networks that were part of the Rio Conference, a network called the Southern Networks for Environment and Development (SONED) was created at the conference to promote interregional networking. The Africa region of SONED is promoting five "green" colleges for capacity building, information collection and dissemination, an African environmental bank, and mechanisms to mobilize intra-African trade (*Brundtland Bulletin*, 1993, p. 47).

Intertwined with the PrepComs and the Global NGO Forum that paralleled the Rio Conference, computer networks permitted ever-larger numbers of organizations to become active, particularly on specialized topics. For example, the *Instituto Latinoamericano de Servicios Legales Alternativos* has ongoing legal service contracts with 1,500 groups in Latin America and other regions. Its activities include seminars, work with law schools, a data bank, research publications, and the legal registration of GROs.

NGOs also sponsor specialized databases with a Third World perspective on such topics as employment, deforestation, and multinational corporations. Among those generated and operated by NGOs in Latin America are the following:

- BIREME, a Latin American and Caribbean Health Sciences Network
- CLAD, the Latin American Public Administration Documentation and Information Network
- CLASCO, a network of social scientists
- DOCPAL, a Latin American network on population
- ILET, the Institute of Transnational Studies
- LATINAH, a human settlements data network
- PEPIDISCA, a network for sanitary engineers and environmental sciences
- PLACIEX, information on trade and support for foreign trade
- REDUC, or Information and Documentation Network on Education for Latin America and the Caribbean
- RIALDE, Latin American Association of Development Finance Associations[14]

Intraregional Networks: A Cook's Tour

In Latin America, FAO support led to the creation of the Latin American Association of Promotional Organizations (ALOP), located in Quito, and Solidarios, based in the Dominican Republic. With a membership of 34 NGOs as of 1994, ALOP supports microenterprise development, although its General Assembly has taken positions critical of the "prevailing neoliberal economic model" (*Monday Developments*, 1994, p. 2). In 1993, ALOP created the Latin American Development Fund (FOLADE) in Costa Rica. To support FOLADE, 16 members agreed to identify and channel resources to populations neglected by traditional financing (*IFDA Dossier*, 1987a, pp. 65-67; *Monday Developments*, 1994, p. 11).[15] Solidarios provides management services for its members and brokers assistance from international donors. Among the other Latin American networks are FAZENDA, an informal forum of leading

GRSOs, and the Latin American Environment Network in Montevideo, Uruguay (Theunis, 1992, p. 235).

There are also a number of exclusively Central American networks:

- REDES-CA, the Regional Network of NGOs for Sustainable Development in Central America, was created after the first Action on the Environment Conference held in Managua in May 1987 (see the section titled "The Intraregional Level," earlier in this chapter). It focuses on water quality, loss of species, appropriate technology, and deforestation (*IRED Bulletin*, 1988, p. 18).
- CRIES, the Regional Coordinator of Socioeconomic Studies, studies conflict situations in the region and promotes exchanges on mutual problems.
- CRES, the Regional Committee of Emergency and Solidarity, assists GRSOs and others with communications training and refugee settlement.
- ALFORJA, the Regional Coordination Program for Popular Education in Costa Rica, provides other organizations with support teams to spread nonformal educational methods (Lopezllera Mendez, 1988, p. 5; Theunis, 1992, p. 117).
- *Concertacion*, based in Costa Rica, is a forum on GRSO-GRO ties in Central America. It focuses on ties with other Central American and Latin American NGO networks, including ALOP, the Latin American Evangelical Commission of Christian Education, the Regional Commission of Economic and Social Investigation, the Commission to Defend Human Rights in Central America, ALFORJA, and the Regional Association of National Networks for the Support of Refugees, the Displaced and Repatriates. *Concertacion* sponsors institutional development workshops, organizes regional seminars on peace in relation to the Esquipulas Peace Plan, lobbies the EEC on export issues, publishes extensively, and has a regional pilot program on basic grains for small farmers (Theunis, 1992, p. 117; Uvin & Miller, 1995).

In Asia, there are many networks that span the entire region. For example, the Asian NGO Coalition for Agrarian Reform and Rural Development, based in Manila, promotes study tours on topics such as strategic management and environmental problems and holds specialized training courses on specialized topics, such as sericulture. Its members include GRSOs, national networks of GRSOs, and other regional networks. The Asia-Pacific People's Environment Network lobbies governments and the United Nations and holds regional seminars on sustainable development for GRSOs and environmental organizations from Japan, Australia, and New Zealand. Among other Asian networks are the Asian Cultural Forum on Development (ACFOD; see the section "Staying in Touch With the Grassroots"), and Approtech Asia, which trains its member organizations in environmental analysis (*IFDA Dossier,* 1984, p. 77; *NGO Management,* 1986a, p. 13; *NGO Management,* 1986b, p. 11.

On a subregional level, the South East Asia Association of NGOs, sponsored by the NGO Management Network, with headquarters in Pakistan, draws its membership from other regional networks, GRSO networks, GRSOs, and GROs in South Asia. The South-East Asian Forum for Development Alternatives concentrates on participatory development research, training, and information exchange.

Because there are a number of grant-making foundations in Asia, Asian networks have funding opportunities rarely available in other regions. But despite well-established NGO networks and rising foundation interest in NGOs, connections between Asian philanthropists and NGOs appear to be weak. An observer at the Conference on Development of NGOs and Philanthropy in Asia, held in Osaka in late 1994, reported that foundations and corporate givers talked in sessions about how philanthropists could promote NGOs, as if thousands did not already exist in Asia. In fact, almost no NGOs had been invited to attend.[16]

In Africa, there are several continentwide networks, despite linguistic and financial barriers. One of these is the Forum of African Voluntary Development Organizations (FAVDO), founded in 1987 at a Dakar, Senegal conference of 100 African GRSOs from 23 countries.[17] FAVDO's board includes representatives from all five African subregions. Yet at its second conference, held in Khartoum in 1988, participants recommended that effective national networks and subregional cooperation should receive priority over continentwide networking (Diong, 1994; Sudan Council of Voluntary Agencies, 1988).[18]

Another Africa-wide network, ANEN (see the section titled "The Intraregional Level," earlier in this chapter), has 530 member organizations from 45 countries and works with GRSOs linked to national and international policymakers through the linguistic subregions of the continent. It holds training seminars on environmental management and planning for GRSO project officers, supports an African network of environmental journalists, and publishes a widely distributed magazine called Eco-Africa. ANEN has devised a new form of participatory research based on GRSO experience that is being disseminated widely; it also provides small grants for community-based environmental and population projects. Close ties to the scientific and technical research communities give ANEN the resources to promote specialized local GRSO networks on desertification, food production, energy provision, and genetic resources conservation.[19] However, as of 1994, ANEN was planning to reorganize itself on the basis of a survey of African NGOs. Because its director, Mazide N'Diaye, is also the President of FAVDO, this information may allow it to extend its ties beyond its own circle.

Another way to do this is for ANEN to strengthen its ties to African networks established by women. Among those active both internationally and regionally are the African Women's Association for Research and Development (AWARD), the International Committee for African Women for Development (CIFAD), and the Women, Environment, and Development Network.[20] CIFAD coordinates exchanges between African GRSOs, promotes a "North South Dialogue on women in development," and sponsors an international network for development projects that identifies organizations capable of financial or technical support (IWRAW, 1987, pp. 5-6; *NGLS News*, 1987, p. 3). The Women, Environment, and Development Network grew out of the first African Women's Assembly for Sustainable Development, held in Harare, Zimbabwe in 1989. Its 200 workshop participants from 20 countries discussed topics such as deserts, forests, and woodlands. One of the major recommendations of the conference was that tree seedlings be given to women's groups, because local women's groups tend to be environmentally conscious and are more capable of managing reforestation than are governments.[21]

Yet another way that the entire continent is being linked is through a network of national networks. Thirteen African Councils and NGO networks met in 1994 in Entebbe, Uganda to discuss their role within the African NGO movement. Hosted by the Development Network of Indigenous Voluntary Associations of Uganda, the meeting focused on the role of NGOs in civil society, including codes of conduct (*Brundtland Bulletin*, 1994, p. 35).

Nevertheless, those who would unify the entire continent must confront the fact that most African networks are subregional, with a disproportionate number located in Dakar or Nairobi. Subregional networks may not be able to afford the time and money needed for Africa-wide activism. They also face political problems, such as nonrecognition by governments. Even if governments recognize subregional networks, they may refuse to accept NGO members of these networks from their own country.

In West Africa, the Reseau Africain pour le Developpement Integre, located in Dakar, works on women's issues, irrigation, health, small business, and agriculture with NGOs from Mali, Guinea, and the Central African Republic (*Brundtland Bulletin*, 1994, p. 35). In Burkina Faso, the Centre d'Experimentation et d'Etudes Sociale et Economique Pour L'Afrique Occidentale (CESAO) trains NGO personnel in agriculture and health and has developed widely used correspondence courses. The Institut Africain pour le

Développement Economique et Social (INADES), founded more than 30 years ago in the Ivory Coast, provides training in agricultural technology, natural resources protection, management, and communications, mainly in French-speaking Africa. However, with a staff of 255, it has begun to expand its operation and, as of 1994, had national offices in 14 countries.

In East Africa, the Nairobi-based African Center for Technology Studies supports scientific and technological research on sustainable development, policy sciences, and publications management. The East African Environmental Network, founded in 1990, promotes environmental awareness and education. And the Kenya Energy and Environment Organization (KENGO) is a national NGO network that has begun to play a regional role.

Networking in southern Africa began with the formation of an intergovernmental organization called SADCC (Southern African Development Coordination Committee) in the 1980s and has accelerated with the dramatic political changes in South Africa. Among the SADCC-related NGO networks are the Southern Africa Energy Network (SAN), SADCC Food Security Network, the NGO Management East and Southern Africa (NGOMESA), and ZERO (Diong, 1994, pp. 8, A-15; Sawadogo, 1990, p. 66; see also the section titled "Exploring International Networking Among NGOs," earlier in this chapter).[22]

Networking is less common in Central Africa. One exception is the Association Congolaise pour l'Environnement et le Developpement en Afrique Centrale (ACEEDAC), founded in Brazzaville, Congo in 1987. ACEEDAC focuses on capacity building, support to churches involved in grassroots development, environmental training, and direct assistance to grassroots groups in Central Africa.

Yet another way to link the continent would be to link regional research and information networks to each other and to networks that train NGOs and work in the field, such as CESAO and INADES. However, most research networks are only beginning to establish linkages with community health, agriculture, and population networks.

In the Middle East, networking is much less extensive than in Asia, Latin America, and Africa. However, the Cairo-based Arab Network for Environment and Development (RAED) works with more than 50 NGOs in 17 countries. Before the Rio Conference, RAED emphasized consultation on environment and development issues. Since Rio, it has focused more on information exchange through existing publications such as *Ecoforum* and *Mediterranean Newsletter.* It also issues environmental reports for each country (*Brundtland Bulletin,* 1993, p. 35). There is also an Arab Women Solidarity Association based in Egypt.

Specialized Intraregional Networks

Specialized regional networks, more numerous than the general NGO networks described previously, began to emerge during the 1970s and 1980s as a result of the proliferation of southern NGOs. Most specialized networks are continentwide because they rely primarily on research and communications within a particular field.

In Latin America, for example, INFOREDES (Information Networks) is an international team that specializes in fostering communication among other networks. Other specialized Latin American networks include the following:

- The Latin American Adult Education Council and The Women's Training Program link adult education programs in a number of countries.
- CELADAC, the Latin American Ecumenical Center for Development and Communitarian Education
- CORPI, the Indigenous People's Regional Coordinator
- CLADES, the Latin American Consortia on Agroecology and Development, unites eight appropriate technology centers, supports member advocacy, and lobbies donors to improve collaboration with NGOs, governments, and academics based on comparative advantage (Farrington & Bebbington, 1993, p. 167; *IFDA Dossier,* 1990b, p. 101).
- The Latin American Social Ecology Center (CLAES) in Montevideo, founded in 1989, runs the Latin American Social Ecology Network and an information system on commerce and the environment. By 1991, it had 50 participants in 12 countries (*IFDA Dossier,* 1991, p. 101).

Among the more specialized Asian networks:

- The Asian Council for People's Culture sponsors regional meetings, workshops, cultural festivals, and training in building networks (*IFDA Dossier,* 1991, p. 97).
- Action for Rational Drugs in Asia (ARDA) promotes essential drugs and education about harmful ones. ARDA has developed materials for doctors and a charter of patient rights (*IFDA Dossier,* 1990a, p. 110).
- The Asia Pacific Desertification and Deforestation Control Network enables forestry organizations to communicate with each other through a computer-based information system.
- Approtech Asia promotes appropriate technology and assists Asian GRSOs with strategic planning. It emphasizes environmental analysis, including the social, political, and economic milieu within which GRSOs have to operate.

In Africa, the specialized networks include the following:

- The Nairobi-based Climate Network Africa focuses on information sharing through a publication called *Impact.*
- The African Water Network (AWN), also based in Nairobi, assists NGOs in research and capacity building through exchange visits and training programs. It also has some linkages with NGOs in southern Africa and West Africa. AWN is one of several specialized networks established by ELCI; among the others are the Pesticides Action Network and the Seeds Action Network.
- The East African Wildlife Society publishes several magazines and works on reforestation and wildlife habitat.
- A nonformal educational theater network has members drawn from eight countries, holds international meetings, and has received support from the International Theater Institute and UNESCO to promote local playwrighting about development (Eyoh, 1985/6).[23]
- The Settlements Information Network Africa (SINA), coordinated by the Mazingira Institute in Nairobi, promotes the exchange of information on self-help housing projects. By the late 1980s, it had more than 300 members in 26 African countries.
- The Association pour la Promotion des Initiatives Communitaires Africaines in Cameroon promotes appropriate technology.
- The African Association for Literacy and Adult Education (AALAE) coordinates data collection and case writing on cooperative problem solving used in international workshops (Brown & Ashman, 1995, p. 5).
- GERDDES-Africa, the Study and Research Group on Democracy and Economic and Social Development in Africa, organized in Cotonou, Benin in 1990, unites African NGOs focused on democracy building.

Staying in Touch With the Grassroots

A general dilemma faced by regional networks is the risk of losing touch with the grassroots organizations and communities that ultimately determine the impact of any GRSO. However, some international networks are promoting networking among GROs.

For example, ACFOD, founded by a group of Asian intellectuals in 1976, has stated its purpose as "bringing . . . the grass roots to the international level." A program to train development workers led to the creation of the Integrated Action Program, including GROs as well as GRSOs. ACFOD has helped fishermen from seven countries organize an international network, and it also supports peasant networks and a regional women's program (Sabur,

1986). ACFOD also promotes international exchanges between GROs. One of ACFOD's first projects was to encourage exchanges among rural theaters in different countries.

In fact, Asian networks seem to be particularly focused on the need to strengthen their ties to local communities. Some examples of these international-local connections are initiated from below:

> There is a remarkable woman in Papua New Guinea named Matarina, who as an illiterate teenager founded the Gavien Women's Development Group in her village. At age 28 she is now the coordinator for four GROs, trains leaders at the local government center, arranges transport and training for leaders from neighboring villages, produces educational cassettes on development, travels to other provinces for similar activities, and is recognized at the national level, where she shares her ideas and training programs with universities, GRSOs and the government. She has created an informal international network on women in development. It includes a Fiji network, feminist academics from the University of the South Pacific, the Women and Development Network of Australia, the Australian Council of Churches, aboriginal communities in Australia, and women's development leaders in Fiji, Tonga, Samoa, and Vanuatu. (Cox, 1987, pp. 22-23)

In Latin America, the related trend of international networking among indigenous GROs is exemplified by the Caribbean Organization of Indigenous People, set up in 1988 by GRO representatives from Guyana, Belize, Dominica, and St. Vincent and also by the Purepechas tribe of Michoacan, Mexico, which hosted 49 other indigenous groups as part of the International Group for Grassroots Initiatives. Another major player is the Coordinating Body for the Indigenous People's Organizations of the Amazon Basin (COINCA), made up of the heads of the major indigenous federations of Bolivia, Brazil, Colombia, Ecuador, and Peru, who represent more than one million people. At a 1990 meeting with North American environmentalists, COINCA's president, Evaristo Nukuag, declared,

> I am encouraged that environmentalists are seated at the bargaining table with the heads of South American governments, the international lending agencies, and the timber and cattle magnates. But the time has come for the indigenous peoples of the Amazon—the people who have always lived there—to take a place at the table as well. (Arena-DeRosa, 1990, pp. 1-2)

Remarkably, one tribal elder paddled for 1,000 miles to get to Iquitos, where COINCA held an international conference in May 1990. A major recommendation of the conference was that debt-for-development schemes be replaced with debt for indigenous stewardship. Also attending were dozens of international environmental organizations, as well as indigenous GRO networks. A permanent committee of environmental and indigenous organizations established in Washington, D.C. in 1990 has expanded contacts beyond environmental organizations (Arena-DeRosa, 1990, pp. 1-2; *Oxfam America News*, 1989).

In Africa, two regional NGOs/networks promote grassroots ties. The West Africa Rural Foundation in Dakar connects donors to grassroots organizations. It promotes participatory research; links research grants for individuals and GRSOs to sustainable development; and provides grants for strategic planning, monitoring, and advice (Diong, 1994, p. 10). The Six S Association (Se Servir de la Saison Seche en Savanne et au Sahel) focuses on agriculture and water conservation. Founded by a Burkinabe sociologist in the 1970s, it makes horizontal grassroots networking among village organizations a condition of its assistance in Burkina Faso, Mali, Mauritania, and Senegal (see Diong, 1994; Fisher, 1993, pp. 200-201).

INTERREGIONAL SOUTH-SOUTH NETWORKING

Historically, the development of interregional networks began in the 1970s. One of the first South-South networks was the International Liaison Committee for Food Crop Projects (CILCA), founded in response to the high cost of technical assistance from developed countries. CILCA's founding institutions were Plan Puebla in Mexico (which is linked to the Graduate Agricultural College at Chapingo and the International Wheat and Maize Improvement Center) and a large Sri Lankan GRSO, Sarvodaya Shramadana (Morganthau, n.d., p. 6). Then, in 1978, CILCA expanded to pilot projects in six African countries, and international exchanges between Sri Lanka, Mexico, and Africa strengthened team training in agricultural development techniques. In Mali, for example, the Toko village used help from Sarvodaya to start preschools and kitchen gardens.

Some African networks have also gone global. Even before ELCI opened offices on other continents, it was helping regional networks such as ANEN become linked to each other. In fact, a Malaysian consumer leader, Anwar Fazal, was elected as ELCI chairperson.[24] By 1987, ANEN, with ELCI's help, linked 233 organizations from 66 countries and had a computerized database on 7,000 NGOs (International Tree Project Clearinghouse, 1987, pp. 52-53). According to the Center for Our Common Future, ANEN was, as of 1993, the largest network of southern NGOs; with new regional offices in Central America and India, it was sharpening its focus on improved relationships between NGOs and intergovernmental organizations (*Brundtland Bulletin*, 1993, p. 11). Another UNEP offspring, ENDA, has branch offices in India, Colombia, the Dominican Republic, Zimbabwe, Mauritius, Bolivia, Morocco, Mali, Guinea Bissau, Tunisia, and France. It has an NGO study and exchange network, and it sponsors participatory environmental projects in Dakar and Rufisque, Senegal; Bogotá, Colombia; La Paz, Bolivia; and Bombay, India. After the Rio Conference in 1992, ENDA helped formulate the Desertification Convention (Cordoba-Novion & Sachs, 1987, p. 11; Diong, 1994, pp. 6-7; A10-A11).

Among the other South-South networks are the following:

■ The Third World NGDOs (nongovernmental development organizations) Task Force, based in the headquarters of DESCO, a Peruvian GRSO, promotes both institutional and functional networks and runs regional training courses (Padron, 1986).

■ Honey Bee, based in India, is a global network founded on the idea that poor people should not become poorer after sharing their insights. With members in 57 countries, the network has provided multilingual documentation of more than 600 indigenous innovations in plant protection, veterinary medicine, animal nutrition, farm implements, and horticulture (Gupta, 1993, p. 65).

■ El Taller is an 80-member global NGO network based in Tunisia. Its 1991 conference in Chile attracted NGO leaders from 44 countries. El Taller develops courses for different regions through a system of sabbatical exchanges (*Impact*, 1992, p. 22). By the mid-1990s, it was pioneering ties between the Third World and the transitional countries of central and eastern Europe.

■ Development Alternatives with Women for a New Era (DAWN), founded in 1984 in Bangalore by women's groups from India, Bangladesh, Africa, Morocco, Brazil, Mexico, and the Caribbean, sponsors research centers, publications, and training. Its international newsletter on advocacy concentrates on one theme and identifies women already researching it.

■ The International Women and Environment Network was created in Managua in 1989 by 1,200 participants from 60 countries attending the Congress on the Fate and Hope of the Earth (*DAWN Informs*, 1989, p. 6).

- SONED was founded at the Rio Conference to promote intraregional networking (see the section titled "The Intraregional Level," earlier in this chapter).
- The Colombia-based Information Exchange Service for Non-Formal Education and Women for Latin America (SINENFAL) has strong ties to INADES in the Ivory Coast, Michigan State University, and Los Banos University in the Philippines. With the assistance of UNICEF's Office of Non-Governmental Affairs, SINENFAL created FINDESARROLLO, an international network that connects GRSOs to sources of financing.[25]
- A housing network in Bogotá is linked to ENDA in Senegal.

In addition to like-minded networks focused on similar methodologies or issues, some southern-dominated networks have northern members. One good example is Development Innovations and Networks (IRED), based in Geneva, which had more than 1,000 mostly southern members by the late 1980s. Another is the Appropriate Technology International Information Services (SATIS), which had 27 members as of 1989, one fourth from developed countries (Baquedano, 1989). Most South-South networks, however, have not attracted or do not want to attract members from the developed countries, except as donors.

Despite the vast nature of all this activity, a major barrier to effective networking is that intra- and interregional southern NGO networks are less likely than are other international players to have access to advanced computer and communication technologies. Therefore, we now turn to the potential role of regional networks in a virtual global community.

A VIRTUAL GLOBAL COMMUNITY

Although international computer networks with strong NGO participation have begun to erase the line between "North-South" and "global," the results of this technological quantum leap are still unclear. On one hand, many national networks have acquired basic word and data processing capabilities. Despite the explosive growth of the Internet, computers, modems, and Internet providers remain expensive for southern NGOs and limit their access to sophisticated international networks (such as Internet rings) such as INTERDOC (the International Network of NGOs), founded in 1984; GEONET, a private European data communications service; ECONET in California; GREENet in Europe; and the Association for Progressive Communication (APC).

The barriers to international computer networking, now partially over-come by the Internet, are exemplified by the history of ALTERNEX, the Brazilian node of INTERDOC and APC, organized by the Brazilian Institute of Social and Economic Analysis (IBASE). In 1990, IBASE was already an established NGO network, skilled in the democratization of databases, desk-top publishing, and statistical analysis, yet it had only 150 users. NGOs did not understand the potential benefits of being on-line, had difficulties assimi-lating new technologies, and, in any case, could not afford to purchase computers and phone lines, either of which can cost more than $2,000 in Brazil. At this point, IBASE created "community e-mail agencies" in 25 of the largest Brazilian cities, each handling an average of 25 user organizations each. These centers were equipped with computers connected to ALTERNEX and were also open to GROs. GRO participation is facilitated by a revolving loan fund established by a group of large GRSOs (Afonso, 1990; Cruz, 1990; Puliatti, 1990).[26] By 1995, IBASE had overcome many difficulties, so that Brazilian NGOs only needed a computer, modem, and phone to become a part of ALTERNEX (Eberlee, 1995, p. 17).

Yet the initial problems that ALTERNEX confronted in Brazil are worse in poorer, less technologically developed countries. Although APC and its regional and country-based nodes had 17,000 organizational subscribers in 95 countries as of 1995, networks such as this are still limited to southern NGOs that can afford computers and modems and that have access to good telephone service. It seems likely that the vast majority of Third World NGOs still lack this Internet access.[27] Only a small percentage of the tens of millions of e-mail users worldwide live in Latin America, Africa, or the poorer countries of Asia.

Fortunately, there are several interesting international efforts to address inequality in the virtual global community. The Canadian International De-velopment Research Centre (IDRC) supports the Pan Asia Networking Pro-gram (PAN) and, as of April 1995, had also developed 12 nodes in Africa. Because the cost of creating an African node has come down to 10,000 to 12,000 Canadian dollars, including equipment and operator training, IDRC's goal is to help create one for every country on the continent. Each node can support 100 to 200 user groups on a self-sustaining basis (Eberlee, 1995, p. 17). A second promising effort has been launched by the Together Founda-tion for Global Unity, which sponsors Togethernet. For a $15 connection charge and a $10-per-month user fee, Togethernet provides unlimited access and no per-minute charges within the local calling area of host systems in Caracas, Venezuela and Rio; it also plans to expand to other Third World cities. A third effort began in 1993 when the UNDP helped set up the Sustainable

Development Network Pakistan (SDNP) to serve as a model for 15 other Internet access networks. "In addition to using the Internet system to provide timely and crucial information to various users in Pakistan . . . SDNP provides free consultancy services and public domain software to various organizations in setting up databases and electronic mail facilities" (Daudpota, 1995, pp. 26-28). Because SDNP includes most of the commercial e-mail in the country, it has the long-term potential to be privately financed.

Despite such progress, the most formidable barrier to the further spread of computer networking remains the telephone. Because telephones are so costly in many countries—LDCs have only 12% of the phone lines in the world—some have suggested imposing a surcharge for northern users, sharing leased lines, and editing the volume of information in electronic conferences. A more promising trend is the spread of cellular phones to the Third World. The fastest growing cellular market in the world is Latin America, where only 7% of the population has access to a regular phone (Engardio, 1994, pp. 47-49). As of 1995, there were 500,000 cellular phones in Thailand, and all of the 300,000 lines that Vietnam plans to install will be optical fiber, with digital switching.

Unfortunately, the economic conditions of all but a handful of people in rural areas make it unlikely that the demand for cellular phones can provide the incentive needed to install switching centers. Without such connections, it is unlikely that most rural GROs will be brought into the virtual global community. And if only a few urban GROs are included, the risk will grow that computer networking, even among high-minded GRSOs, will become an end in itself, rather than a means to promote sustainable development that benefits people at the grassroots.[28]

Africa faces some additional barriers. Because commercial satellites cost 250 million to 400 million U.S. dollars, and governments use them as a way to generate revenue, a one-page fax can cost $30 in Mali (Clement, 1993, p. 60; C. Clement, personal communication, February 13, 1995).[29] Because of the present Internet structure and billing regimes, African nodes have to pay for both incoming and outgoing e-mail that they cannot control (Eberlee, 1995, p. 17).[30]

One possible high-tech answer to the cost problem is illustrated by a project being carried out by a U.S. NGO called SatelLife, located in Cambridge, Massachusetts. SatelLife uses a $1 million (U.S.) satellite the size of a basketball to link the Health Net User's Association (HNUA) in the Cameroon to similar centers in Ghana, with linkages planned for other African countries. The government of Cameroon has licensed HNUA to operate a ground station that can communicate with its Ghanaian counterpart and libraries in developed countries, provide electronic bulletin boards from leading medical journals, and offer e-mail consultations from such institutions as the Harvard School of Public Health. Eventually, more mini-satellites could lower the costs of communication so that GROs (such as, in the case of SatelLife, small, village-run clinics) could be included.

CONCLUSION

The expanding role of southern NGOs within the exploding universe of international networking is difficult to catalogue, let alone comprehend. However, what is clear is that the successful promotion of sustainable development through regional and global networking is as dependent on grassroots empowerment as any small development project within one country. New technologies offer enormous promise—the ability to trade expertise, communicate "what works" to thousands of development practitioners around the world, and share information that can challenge narrow power monopolies. Fulfilling this promise, however, must depend on more than just the goodwill of the well-educated and well-motivated leaders of southern NGOs. It must also depend on democratizing the communications revolution so that isolated hamlets and poor urban neighborhoods in the Third World become a part of the global village.

The new role of NGOs within the intergovernmental system entails the same risk. Intergovernmental decision makers are "advocating dialogue and joint activities with INGOs: but on whose terms? Until there is greater democracy within such agencies, the danger of cooptation will remain, with the implication that NGOs would become . . . increasingly divorced from their own constituencies" (Shaw, 1994, pp. 141-142).

Although there can be no technological fix for this challenge, cellular telephones, community computer access, and mini-satellites offer great promise for the future, provided the international community recognizes the need for up-front financial support. The Internet has strengthened the tendency for democratization to coincide with the declining importance of the state in relation to civil society in much of the world. The real issue is whether the emerging institutions of civil society will continue to be aware of their own dependence on the grassroots within each country, and of the importance of that relationship to sustainable development and democracy throughout the world.

NOTES

1. They argue that "compelling robust strategies" should rank high on "fit" with the international environment, specificity (definitive guidelines for policymakers), reach efficiency (means suited to ends), and multidimensionality (taking account of relevant data within the policy environment).

2. Among the examples are the Carter Center in Atlanta, the Kettering Foundation in Dayton, Ohio, and the Institute for Multi-Track Diplomacy in Washington, DC.

3. For a discussion of the role of NGOs within the larger independent sector in many Third World countries, see Fisher (1993, pp. 98-111).

4. Bratton (1994, p. 48) points out that "southern or national NGOs" concentrate their headquarters and field operations in one country and have permanent staffs composed of nationals of that country.

5. The United Nations Development Program (1993) has estimated that there may be as many as 50,000.

6. A very recent phenomenon are South-East networks attempting to link the developing countries to the transitional countries of Central and Eastern Europe. See the discussion of El Taller in the section titled "Interregional South-South Networking," in this chapter. Among the other types of INGOs not considered here are North-North networks.

7. In 1993, the Union of International Associations confirmed Boulding's estimate of 1,300 "fully international" NGOs (Union of International Associations, 1993, p. 2), approximately equivalent to Boulding's estimate of 1,530 (8.5% of the total) in 1988. By figuring out what Boulding included and left out, I have updated her estimate, using the *1994-5 International Yearbook of Associations*. I would guess, however, that many southern NGO networks are not yet included in this estimate.

8. Three thousand people in 80 countries receive the Vetvier newsletter, and the network provides seed money for NGO demonstration projects.

9. Information obtained from pamphlets put out by the Third World Network of Scientific Organizations and the Third World Organization for Women in Science.

10. Some regional NGOs that are not NGO networks also interact with governments. A good example is the African Center for Technology Studies in Nairobi, which trains government officials from many countries and sponsors research and publications on sustainable development.

11. The Statement was obtained from the interim Secretariat, located at the Rockefeller Foundation. The permanent Secretariat was established in one of the partner countries in September 1995 and is closely linked to the U.N. Fund for Population Activities. The countries included are Thailand, Bangladesh, Indonesia, Egypt, Tunisia, Morocco, Kenya, Zimbabwe, Mexico, and Colombia.

12. Some of these are primarily advocacy organizations, whereas others, such as OXFAM and Friends of the Earth, are also engaged, at least through partner organizations, in development. Although Greenpeace's membership remains largely northern, the other organizations studied have members or affiliates in the Third World.

13. The International Green Cross was founded in 1993 in Kyoto during a global forum of parliamentary and spiritual leaders. Mikhail Gorbachev is an active participant.

14. NTC/NCT Newsletter, special issue on South/North Exchange on New Communications Technologies, cited in Hall (1993). Many of these networks have obtained support from the International Development Research Center in Canada.

15. ALOP is also promoting closer ties to Asian and African networks.

16. Interview with Yuko Frost, January 24, 1995.

17. Forty northern, five non-African southern NGOs, official representatives of official international organizations, and government officials from many countries also attended (*DevCom Bulletin,* 1987).

18. A subregional international network has developed in the Indian Ocean area. The Center for Research and Documentation for Indian Ocean Training promotes policy-oriented research and information sharing. It produces a directory of grassroots support organizations in the Comoros, Seychelles, Madagascar, Mauritius, and Reunion (see *IFDA Dossier,* 1989, p. 88).

19. Executive Director Jimoh Omo-Fadaka is a specialist in the interface between environment and development. ANEN operates out of the administrative facilities of the Kenya Energy and Environment Organization (KENGO), which also grew out of an ELCI project. Much of KENGO's experience has been incorporated into the design of ANEN.

20. AWARD was, as of 1990, one of 30 transnational networks of women addressing development issues (see Boulding, 1990, p. 39).

21. There are also some promising efforts to computerize women's networking and indigenous knowledge in Africa, supported by ELCI, the IDRC, and York University in Toronto.

22. Mwelekeo Wa Non-Government Organizations, initiated by the Ford Foundation office in Nairobi, is planning to move to Harare. It focuses on information exchange and research on participatory development, civic education, policy advocacy, and NGO management.

23. For more on the use of theater for community empowerment, see Fisher, 1993, p. 106.

24. Anwar Fazal is also among the founders of several global consumer networks, including Consumer Interpol on hazardous waste, Health Action International on pharmaceutical issues, and the Pesticides Action Network (*IFDA Dossier,* 1987c, p. 81). The International Organization of Consumer Unions has developed a network to promote preventive medicine and encourage the rational use of pharmaceuticals (*IRED Bulletin,* 1986, p. 38).

25. SINENFAL had data on 4,000 institutions involved in nonformal education in Latin America as of 1984, and there were plans to include 6,000 more (Hauzeair, 1984).

26. The Brazil office of UNDP and the Institute for Global Communications in San Francisco have assisted ALTERNEX, the Brazilian international computer network that supplemented a national network established in the early 1980s (see Garrison, 1989, pp. 48-49).

27. These included, as of 1993, ALTERNEX in Brazil, Chasque in Uruguay, NICARAO in Nicaragua, MANGO in Zimbabwe, WORKNET in South Africa, ESANET among East African universities, and networks in Ethiopia, Kenya, Uganda, Tanzania, Zambia, Ghana, Senegal, Thailand, India, the Philippines, the Caribbean, Chile, Peru, and Colombia. Another large international computer networks is HURIDOCS, a human rights information network. *HURIDOCS News,* a quarterly, reaches 1,300 organizations, many of which describe themselves as active in development and environment, as well as human rights issues (Thoolen, 1990, pp. 88-89; see also Eberlee, 1995, p. 17). APC focuses on peace, human rights, and environmental preservation.

28. Global computer networking also challenges some of the older, established global networks, such as the Society for International Development chapters for development professionals in 34 LDCs. Some international networks, such as the International Foundation for Development Alternatives (IFDA) in Nyon, Switzerland, have not been able to obtain sufficient funding to continue (*Compass,* 1993, pp. 21-24).

29. The satellite was funded by the IDRC, the NEC Corporation of Japan, and the International Physicians for the Prevention of Nuclear War.

30. As of 1995, only 12 of Africa's 54 countries were linked to the Internet. Yet by skipping investments in copper wiring and going straight into fiber optics and wireless communications, the continent may eventually enjoy some of the advantages of the latecomer (see French, 1995, p. A14).

10

CONSTRUCTING AND DECONSTRUCTING GLOBAL CHANGE ORGANIZATIONS

JOHN D. ARAM

This chapter is part of a volume that aspires to bring the organizational sciences to bear on global change issues, advancing the organizational dimensions of global change. I take two broad approaches to this project. An initial section discusses several theoretical approaches to understanding global organizations. In this regard, I argue that the numbers and strength of organizations that deal with global issues should make a significant revision in the ways that we think about organizational relations. As discussed by Perrow (1986), theories of exchange, efficiency, and transaction costs dominate our thinking about organizations, and concepts of opportunism and free riders pervade mainstream thinking about public policy development. Organizations involved in global change constitute a counterpoint to these ideas that should be taken seriously.

In place of concepts of rational choice, I suggest that Granovetter's (1973, 1982) theory of weak ties in sociological network theory casts an important light on the nature of global change organizations. This theory explains how a social system organized by a greater number of acquaintances (weak ties) rather than close friends (strong ties) will exhibit greater aggregate innovativeness, cohesiveness, and adaptability. The decentralized, diffuse nature of membership in most global change efforts, especially aided by modern electronic communications, builds issue-oriented, low-density organizational networks. I suggest that this aspect of social network theory offers a productive avenue for understanding the growth and resiliency of global issue organizations.

In addition to this brief glimpse of global organizations from a theoretical perspective, I suggest several assumptions and values underlying the apparent wide interest in global organizations, paying attention to what may be internal contradictions within this "movement" and perhaps to significant theoretical issues involved in building an organization theory in this area.

My second purpose here is to examine the wider context and the larger forces that will affect the survival and success of global organizations. As an example, we should include discussion of ways in which economic globalization may be affecting social stability and cohesion. In this vein, the chapter briefly examines several global phenomena that affect social issues: a resurgence of ethno-nationalism, the internationalization of crime, and conflicting views of justice that circumscribe the efforts of global change organizations.

First, what do we mean by a "global organization in the nonprofit field"? Let us begin with Elise Boulding's (1988) definition of international nongovernmental organizations (INGOs) as "transnational voluntary associations covering the whole range of human interests from sports, occupations, civic affairs, science, and commerce, to culture and religion" (p. 118). The organizations I would like to discuss are not necessarily voluntary, although they often may be so in large part. More important, the global change organization of interest here is problem, or improvement, oriented, where the problem or issue is perceived to transcend established organizational or political boundaries. Thus, a global change organization is an affiliated collection of people across various countries who share a common perception of a transcending problem and a commitment to altering its consequences.

A COUNTERPOINT TO THE UTILITARIAN
BIASES OF ORGANIZATION THEORY

First, we note that global organizations offer an exception and a contrast to the dominant self-interest assumptions of management theory. Barnard (1938) and Etzioni (1961) were among the first organization theorists to examine normative power as one basis of organizing and to understand the moral involvement of lower participants in organizations. In current parlance, it may be more precise to designate normative organizations as public or collective goods organizations. The matters of concern to members of global change organizations are value issues—human rights, environmental protection, biodiversity, women's rights, community development. The organizations aim to include, not exclude, others from the created benefits. Thus, members seek to conserve natural resources, ensure political freedoms, enhance the social roles and property rights of women, or strengthen the economic base of a community regardless of whether the people benefiting from these actions contributed to the effort. The members' aim is to commonize benefits, not privatize them, as we would assume is the case with more utilitarian or instrumental organizations. They are willing to accept personal costs associated with their actions simply because they care deeply about the issues.

This orientation challenges the dominant assumptions of management and organization theory and practice where, at best, organizations are seen as utilitarian inducement/contribution (contract) systems, where hierarchy and control (even self-control) are designed to minimize shirking and agency costs, and where opportunism is assumed to prevail (cf. Perrow, 1986). Nor have scholars applying concepts of ethics, social responsiveness, and corporate social performance established uncontested alternatives to the utilitarian paradigm of management theory.

Conceptually and practically, global change organizations provide an alternative to the dominant cost-minimization, benefit-maximization paradigm in the management sciences. Costs rather than gains are privatized in global organizations, and access to benefits is intentionally nonexclusive. In terms of the influential theory of collective action (Olson, 1965), these behaviors should not be evident where large numbers prevail and group membership is heterogeneous, conditions present in most global issue organizations. The theory of collective action has been challenged in particular circumstances (Oliver & Marwell, 1988; Oliver, Marwell, & Teixeira, 1985); however, the enormous magnitude of the global change movement demonstrates the widespread prevalence of a different set of behavioral principles.

Positive selective incentives may be present in many global change organizations, but, in light of the large numbers of such organizations, their enormous numbers of participants, and their relatively loose administrative systems, it would be difficult to argue that global organizations depend on selective incentives. Nor do nonprofit global organizations depend on rent-seeking capability for their existence; a great deal of global change organizing may depend on the contribution of external resources from public and private bodies. Nor is the public goods aspect of these organizations diminished simply because the organizations may play specialized roles—such as those involving environmental quality, health, peace, and so on—in a larger organizational community. From the standpoint of theory development, one challenge is to build concepts in which the self-sacrificing quality of people and organizations that create public goods is the central, as opposed to a peripheral or tangential, issue.

The presence of a strong alternative to the utilitarian assumptions of management theory carries significance for the intellectual traditions of management. Our behaviors in organizations and society are dictated by our mental models and beliefs about organizing. Maybe we have too readily accepted thinking about organizations as utilitarian, instrumental, self-interest-seeking systems, and by neglect, we may have discouraged thinking about organizations as collective action systems and vehicles for public goods creation. Some of the literature on organizational culture approaches this realization but again falls short of being a consistent empirical alternative to the utilitarian assumptions of management thinking. I believe that the organizational significance of the global change movement lies in the incontrovertible and widespread evidence of public goods behavior.

GLOBAL ISSUE ORGANIZATIONS
AS NETWORKS OF WEAK TIES

We have said that global issues transcend the boundaries of established organizations and political units. Local and national organizations addressed to issues are tied together by common values and a commitment to reform. From an organizational standpoint, global change organizations are loosely structured networks of relatively autonomous, decentralized units. These organizations are more associational than hierarchical, and core activities of the central office lie more with coordination and development than with direction and control.

Sociologist Mark Granovetter's (1973) theory of weak ties yields some surprising and paradoxical results that may help us understand the growth and resiliency of global issue organizations. Granovetter describes communities in terms of low-density and high-density networks. Acquaintances characterize the former and close friends the latter. In a high-density network, my friends are close friends of each other; together, we form a strong or dense network. In contrast, where my close friends do not know each other, the network has a greater number of weak ties, or lower density.

Granovetter hypothesizes that social systems or communities characterized by greater numbers of weak ties have several attractive features. First, new ideas and innovations will diffuse more rapidly through the system. High-density systems are more "lumpy," that is, information has a more difficult time getting transferred between strong networks. Second, weak ties at the micro level of a society allow more cohesion at the macro level. Where strong ties predominate at the micro level, the community as a whole is likely to experience greater fragmentation. Low-density network communities have, for example, greater capability to organize themselves and act as collectivities. Finally, Granovetter hypothesizes that leadership is more likely to arise in low-density network communities. Leaders are trusted where members have the "capacity to predict and affect their behavior" (p. 361). A prospective leader has greater difficulty making connections with members of the community where strong ties predominate. Where the community is segmented into tightly knit groups with few connections to other groups, there will be a relative lack of intermediaries to give assurance to the populace that the leader is trustworthy and to present the interests and desires of the people to the leader. Network fragmentation reduces the potential connections between leaders and followers, diminishing leadership potential.

Nine years after his original article, Granovetter (1982) summarized support for his ideas from direct and indirect evidence. For example, weak ties played significant roles in helping people who were looking for work to obtain job information and locate a new position. Weak ties also explained the diffusion of information and the structure of scientific communication patterns. In another example, a children's psychiatric hospital with more than 200 staff people discouraged tight, exclusive cliques and was able to achieve a high level of organizational integration. A different study of community change concluded that most reform leaders occupied marginal positions with respect to community social networks, and that weak-tie reform groups were more successful in their efforts than were strong-tie groups.

The evidence suggests that network theory and the strength of weak ties may help explain the phenomenal growth and increasing influence of global change organizations. Although the application of these ideas is necessarily speculative at this time, the application of these concepts to global organizations seems to merit further development.

CULTURAL/INTELLECTUAL INFLUENCES
ON GLOBAL CHANGE MOVEMENT

Members of global change organizations are generally oriented toward value-driven social change. It may be easy for sympathetic observers, such as the contributors to this volume, to become swept up in the enthusiasm and commitment of this movement and to idealize these organizations. It may be useful, therefore, to try to get outside of our cultural "set" and examine the nature and limitations of the social constructions with which we are working. What might be some of the less frequently examined assumptions of proponents of global issue organizations? An effort to deconstruct assumptions of the global change movement may contribute to a sound theoretical basis for understanding the dimensions by which participants act organizationally.

Although not true for all global organizations or their members, the following values and influences appear to play significant roles in the global change movement.

Rational and Progressive

Perceptions of global "problems" and efforts to organize for their "solutions" convey a belief in progress and the power of reason. The principles of natural ecosystems, for example, can be "discovered," and public policies can be informed, by accumulated knowledge and scientific effort about the environment.

Similarly, social and political systems can be understood, influenced, and controlled by superior information and understanding. Change and development become legitimate academic activities for which knowledge, technology, and experts exist. Incentive structures for human action or inaction can be logically described, studied, and influenced, and the behavioral sciences can be applied to change system functioning. We even believe (apparently) that contributions to human progress occur by bringing these organizations into the "science" of management.

Advocacy of Human Rights

A shared assumption among those associated with global change organizations is the belief in the dignity and autonomy of individuals. The rights of the traditionally less powerful—women, children, and minority populations—are often at political risk. A number of global issue organizations seek to define political, social, and economic rights; expose their violations; apply international pressure on governments that fail to respect these rights; and work to bring about necessary internal social and political changes. The cultural assumptions underlying these efforts are democratic and secular.

Internationalist

Another cultural influence on the global organization movement is a professed allegiance to internationalism. We see that economics and technology have made the world highly interdependent and interconnected. Managing this interdependence calls for expanding the boundaries of our consciousness, accepting global responsibilities, creating multicultural communities, and forging new transnational institutions. Following Bellah, Madsen, Sullivan, Swidler, and Tipton (1991), the institutional context of behavior matters. Like Bellah et al., we seek to graft Tocqueville's enlightened, civic participation onto a postindustrial age. In a global context, these values mean that American "ideals of freedom and justice require a broad commitment to international cooperation" (p. 249).

Communitarian

The internationalism of global organizations is communitarianism writ large. Proponents of global change may often define the world as a human community; they reassert human, ecological, and social functions over the individualistic biases of market capitalism; and they seek to forge communities of interest against commercial and technocratic processes. Philosophically, the mission of global change organizations connects with American communitarianism, which is engaged in a moral mission emphasizing the importance of personal and collective responsibilities in sustaining individual liberties (Etzioni, 1993). I would also see the movement as sympathetic to the desire for spirituality and caring as an alternative to cynicism and greed in shaping institutions and political discourse.

Cosmopolitan

People affiliated with global issue organizations generally travel widely and may live in places other than their home societies. They often depend closely on laptop computer, e-mail, and fax capabilities. They typically value multiculturalism, as well as racial, religious, gender, and ethnic tolerance and diversity. Anthony D. Smith (1991), a British writer on national identity and the new nationalism, argues that the "global culture" consists of mass commodities, a patchwork of ethnic styles and motifs, general ideological discourses on human rights, and a standardized language of communication and appraisal, "all underpinned by the new information and telecommunications systems and their computerized technologies" (p. 157). Global change organizations are both an expression of and a stimulus to an internationalist, cosmopolitan culture.

Social Reformist

If global organizations represent social change efforts, members and proponents of global change organizations are, by definition, dissatisfied with aspects of the status quo. Whether gradualists or radicals, social reform is a shared value. On the level of emotional orientation, the global change movement distrusts centralized authority and existing political institutions. This emotional stance may often be articulated as a rational approach to interdependent, transnational problems, and it may be enhanced by appeals to universal human values.

The reformist nature of the global change movement also allows potentially conflicting individualistic and communitarian values to coexist. A community of reformers is needed to restore individual rights from oppressive regimes or to alter the damage to people, plants, and animals waged by the commercial world. If the "community," however, is thought to encompass larger numbers of people and more ideologically diverse interests than the members of the global change movement, many people may feel that community interests require sacrifices to their individual freedom.

Messianic/Evangelical

The field of management shows a distinct appreciation for the role of charismatic leaders and the organizational hero. We appreciate transformational leaders who mobilize energies and enact visions—messiahs who will lead the way. They inspire us to commitment and responsibility and imbue us with the potential for mending and restoring the world. We look for transformational leaders to ignite our global change efforts—inspiring us toward world peace, social justice, political leadership, or ecological transformation.

Finally, am I wrong to perceive an evangelical strain among many advocates of global change? Global issues can be a new religion of believers. Proponents point to the day of salvation when the world's interdependencies will be respected and its wrongs will be righted. They show the road to well-being and contentment in the indefinite future. And we are reinforced in these beliefs by our communities of like-minded reformers.

Implications

These are hypothetical and quite speculative statements. A useful focus of research would be to identify the central assumptions and values of people involved in the global change movement and to analyze variations among and between different organized groups. However, a number of these qualities, if valid, may be difficult to reconcile. A tension between individual and communitarian values is suggested above. Also, differences between the rational and scientific approach and the messianic and evangelical element may be difficult to integrate and may lead to differing streams of organizations, change strategies, and leadership styles. In other words, underlying patterns of values may be an important element in organizational theory building in this area.

Moreover, other large-scale forces may compete culturally with global change organizations and may even pose threats to their existence. Disproportionate numbers of people today are not internationalist, communitarian, or cosmopolitan. Isolationist, unilateralist views are strong and may even predominate in the world today. Many people may believe that solutions to the world's problems lie in returning to religious fundamentals and nonsecular political regimes than in valuing rationality, progress, secularism, and democracy. It might be easy for us, a number of like-minded people thinking about global change, to insulate our awareness from the larger social and political context and the wider constellation of forces and ideas in the world that will shape the prospects of global change organizations. Theorizing about global issue organizations may benefit from analysis and discussion about the larger forces that influence the prospects and outcomes of these organizations. The following sections attempt to elaborate several of these issues.

GLOBAL FORCES CONTENDING
FOR INFLUENCE ON HUMAN BEHAVIOR

Few people would dispute that economics and technology foster interdependence and integration in today's world. Electronic communications integrate financial markets and facilitate interaction among widely dispersed people and organizations. International capitalism increases the frequency of interactions across societies and encourages convergence in thinking, behavior, and language. George Herbert Mead once wrote that economic transactions require that buyers understand the role of sellers and vice versa (i.e., the role of the other). Following this thought, increasing international trade and investment may promote sociocultural understanding and integration.

Market economics may be disintegrative in a different sense, however. In many cases, economic growth correlates with growing wealth disparities globally and within countries, increasing social fragmentation and segmentation. Also, economic expansion, alone, may perpetuate or reinforce traditional gender roles and undemocratic political regimes. Industrialization, by itself, imposes environmental costs in pollution, unsustainable resource use, and loss of biodiversity. By the logic of gross domestic product (GDP) growth, per se, human distress is good because events such as illnesses, divorces, earthquakes in populated areas, and massive toxic spills increase gross economic transactions that show up as a larger GDP (Cobb, Halstead, & Rowe, 1995). In this view, natural resource depletion is also good (until a crisis occurs), and people make positive economic contributions when they eat food they do not want or need and then pay for dieting solutions to try to lose weight.

By calling for greater conservation and equality, and by valuing non-economic activities such as family time and community service, global change organizations seek to remedy perceived unwanted by-products of economic/industrial development. By-products such as environmental degradation and community disintegration transcend national boundaries. Thus, global change organizations serve as integrators in their own right, binding together people across political borders in common concerns. Although advocates of particular issues often see themselves in opposition to economic forces, the global change movement may bear a symbiotic relationship to economic change in the sense that the justification and need for the work of these organizations is a function of the social by-products of economic growth.

Advanced communication capability also allows global change organizations to be more effective integrators. Telephonic and electronic communications are ideally designed for networks based on weak ties. A recent news article reported on wide use of the Internet among social activists in Latin America, specifically Brazil (Epstein, 1994). Human rights activists, environmentalists, and a variety of social reformers exchange information and provide needed support through worldwide electronic communication.

In different ways, and largely with different participants, international capitalism and global change organizations act as international integrators in today's worldwide society. They both utilize and increasingly depend on electronic communication.

But these developments do not constitute the whole story. Another set of forces is at work throughout the world circumscribing, if not counteracting, the integrative forces of market economics and the presence of global change organizations. Three such forces are ethnicity as a global phenomenon, the globalization of crime, and conflicting views of justice. Each of these developments at least challenges forces for international integration. Consequently, they are important contextual dimensions of global change organizations.

Ethno-Nationalism as a Global Phenomenon

It is easy to associate the rise of ethnicity as a political force in the modern world with the fall of the Soviet empire. However, the origins of this development appear to go far deeper. Scholars were observing the rise and political significance of ethno-nationalism in world affairs in the early 1980s. For example, political scientist John F. Stack, Jr. (1981) was writing about conflicting trends toward global interdependence and toward increasing political fragmentation before the disintegration of the USSR. "With the establishment of Afro-Asian states in the late 1950s and early 1960s," he writes, "two concurrent trends have characterized world politics: the steady increase in systemic interdependence; and the progressive fragmentation of the world along political, cultural, and ideological lines" (p. 23). Let us briefly consider several ways in which ethnic consciousness may be associated with political fragmentation.

Economic and technological changes often increase social disparities and make them more evident. In virtually all countries, socioeconomic differences are associated with ethnic differences, and perceived differences in wealth and opportunities between ethnic groups may heighten in-group consciousness, raise expectations, and foster social and political conflict.

Stack also suggests that the forces of industrialization and of transnational institutions, such as the European Union, no matter how well justified in terms of economic well-being and international peace, may be accompanied by a loss of local and personal control. The demands for labor flexibility and mobility undermine communities and the associational fabric of private life, leading to little sense of belonging, a weak sense of commitment, and social insecurity (Dahrendorf, 1996).

An upsurge of ethnic consciousness may arise in reaction to these developments, attempting to cope with life in a postindustrial and economically integrated age as people attempt to place themselves in smaller, more intimate communities. Smith (1991) discusses territorial, economic, political, and psychological dimensions of nationalism. For example, he comments on the role of national identity in a changing world:

> A sense of national identity provides a powerful means of defining and locating individual selves in the world, through the prism of the collective personality and its distinctive culture. It is through a shared, unique culture that we are enabled to know "who we are" in the contemporary world. By rediscovering that culture we "rediscover" ourselves, the "authentic self," or so it has appeared to many divided and disoriented individuals who have had to contend with the vast changes and uncertainties of the modern world. (p. 17)

The basis of this shared culture is often found in ethnicity—a sense of belonging based on race, religion, common historical experience, or language.

Following Stack (1981), the renaissance of ethnic consciousness on a global scale counteracts the integrative forces of economics, and thus global change organizing, by generating political fragmentation. Autonomy, sovereignty, and self-determination comprise the ideology of the modern political state. This ideology became a powerful attraction to many ethnic communities as the vestiges of colonialism were rejected in the 1950s and 1960s, as the arbitrariness of existing state boundaries became apparent to many with the demise of the cold war and the Soviet empire, and as ethnically divided countries began to face the tasks of self-governance. A recent study (Gurr, 1995) identified 292 different communal groups that were either regionally concentrated communities challenging the political legitimacy of the state in which they found themselves or communities that accepted existing state authority but wanted to change their socioeconomic or political status within that state. Ethnic conflict is an explosive global issue and deeply challenges the values of cooperation. Olzak (1992) studied the surge of ethnic violence at the turn of the 20th century, in which violence toward African Americans, Chinese Americans, and European immigrants surged under conditions remarkably similar to those today—rapid economic change and dislocation, increases in immigration pressures, and populist politics. The increase of racial and ethnic conflict caused by increased ethnic contact and competition a century ago does not bode well for social stability in many of the world's nations today.

Globalization of Crime

Global change organizers seek to reform societies from the bottom up. Their methods aim to empower grassroots movements; their ideology is democratic and populist. The accountability inherent in democracy leads, it is believed, to more equitable and sustainable transnational policies involving economics, environment, and human rights. It is no accident that Elise Boulding's book about our interdependent world is titled *Building a Global Civic Culture* or that social analysts such as Ralf Dahrendorf (1996) believe that "individualized conflict"—unorganized theft, property damage, personal attacks, and other illegal activities—are manifestations of social disintegration, anomie, and deep insecurity.

Other ominous trends appear in the widespread organization of terrorism and crime that also transcend national boundaries. The significance of these developments is difficult to ascertain; their opposition to a global civic culture, however, seems clear. Where global change organizations seek to enhance democratic processes, international crime thrives on weakening democratic institutions. Where global issue organizations want to build social confidence and participation, crime syndicates feed on fear and intimidation.

Stack argues that disaffected terrorist groups use the same forces toward global communications and transportation that are vitally important to an integrated world economy and, by inference, to global change organizations. Widespread access to the mass media gives terrorists a cheap, effective way to gain visibility and to place their demands before a global audience. Moreover, our use of jet transportation allows terrorists to strike anywhere and gain instant attention around the world. Terrorist incidents by one group in support of the cause of another group, such as the Lod Airport massacre in 1972 by the Japanese Red Army in support of Palestinian liberation, leads Stack to coin the term of "psychological immigration," where images and self-perceptions replace traditional ethnic identity based on a common historical experience. One only has to reflect on the growth of armed militias in the United States, or domestic incidents of bombing terrorism, or the torching of nearly 40 predominantly African American churches in the South over a 2-year period to sense how social fragmentation may be expressed in physical danger.

The internationalization of crime may be a trend that threatens efforts to build a global civic culture. It would seem to be a rare country today in which organized crime and corruption are not significant threats to institutional integrity and social stability. Yet an apparent increase in international crime syndication may be an even more dangerous development (cf. Sterling, 1994). Recently, the U.S. Congress received testimony about the growing internationalization of crime, linking criminal organizations in the United States, Russia, South America, China, Italy, and Japan (Dillin, 1994). Grounded in the enormously profitable drug trade, international crime groups now target banks, private businesses, and governments. The ability to combine brutal intimidation for noncooperation with lucrative payoffs for cooperation can pose a significant threat to legitimate institutions.

The precise nature and strength of the internationalization of crime may not be known, or at least publicly disclosed. However, it would seem to comprise a distinct threat to the civic model of internationalism envisioned by the global change movement. These considerations suggest that, indeed, there are limits to cooperation. At a very minimum, a conference devoted to the activities of such public interest organizations may well take into account the numbers and strength of organizations that seek to extract private gains at the expense of society's legitimate institutions.

Conflicting Justice Claims

The public goods intentions of global change organizations allow proponents to claim a high moral ground in world affairs; yet the high ground remains contested in a broad ideological conflict. What seems absolutely sensible and right to proponents of particular global issues seems misguided and wrong to people looking at the world differently. And, as with all ideological struggles, the debate is the thing; there is no external reference point to which to appeal.

This point stands out in a recent issue of the *Journal of Social Issues* in which social psychologist Susan Clayton (1994) examines how both pro-environmental and anti-environmental proponents appeal to justice in public debates on environmental issues. In general terms, environmental debates pit advocates of justice for the individual (microjustice) against advocates of justice for the larger group or society (macrojustice). The former conception defines fairness in largely procedural terms (i.e., whether the resources and rewards are allocated by merit); the latter defines fairness in substantive or distributive terms, relying on assessments of equality and need. Microjustice advocates more readily break down interests into competing subgroups (spotted owls vs. jobs), which leads them to stress individual entitlements and rights, especially property rights. Proponents of macrojustice principles tend to think in terms of the connected parts of larger societies or ecosystems and responsibilities and obligations to the whole. Their concerns lie more in social relations, whereas the microjustice view generally favors economic concerns. People favoring macrojustice may be more willing to impose restrictions on individual actions in the interest of the community as a whole. People favoring microjustice feel a greater need to defend individuals from social control and state regulation.

Clayton found empirical support to show a relationship between the type of justice argument and the strength of pro- and anti-environmental positions. She showed that appeals to procedural justice were relatively stronger when connected to an anti-environmental stance. In addition, people's attitudes on the issues are quite predictable; Clayton reports studies that show that women, Democrats, social science majors, people from collectivist cultures, and people in a good mood favor macrojustice principles. Men, Republicans, natural science majors, people from individualistic cultures, and people in a bad mood rely to a greater extent on procedural justice claims and microjustice.

The point is that advocates of global change do not alone lie on the side of goodness. Other contestants may also argue their views from a stance of justice or fairness, and global issue proponents cannot assume that they will occupy an uncontested high ground. A realistic view of global change organizations needs to recognize the likely presence of a polarized ideological environment that may define and to some extent constrain their roles and consequences.

UNPACKING THE THEME: ORGANIZATIONAL DIMENSIONS OF GLOBAL CHANGE: NO LIMITS TO COOPERATION

This chapter seeks to make three types of contributions to the overarching themes of this book. First, Granovetter's theory of weak ties that has been developed and applied in the sociological literature appears to offer an effective conceptual handle by which to explore the organizational dimensions of global change. This analysis lends itself to exploring why some global change organizations grow more rapidly than others, adopt innovations more quickly, or are perceived to be more effective than others. It also allows us to hypothesize that when ties are weak, as defined by Granovetter, greater geographical extension is correlated with organizational effectiveness, members will experience stronger collective identifications and loyalties, and strong leaders will arise more frequently.

I have argued that the significance of global change organizations to management theory goes beyond a new theoretical approach, however. The size and magnitude of the global change movement suggests the need for a wholesale rethinking and revision of management assumptions and concepts. This movement provides a strong counterpoint to the dominant assumptions of instrumental self-interest embedded in many management theories, and it reverses a great deal of conventional wisdom. For example, in the traditional framework, loose ties between organizational units may increase transaction costs, lend themselves to opportunism, and create problems of coordination. From a revisionist perspective, by contrast, loose ties in the context of global change organizations may accelerate innovation diffusion, reinforce an ethic of public goods creation, and reduce costs. The question is, How can we build management theory that takes into account the larger variety of motivations, gratifications, and structures actually present in the world of organizations? Can we build conceptual understandings that parallel the actual diversity and richness of organizational life?

A preliminary attempt to "deconstruct" global change organizations suggests the potential utility of examining their different values and ideologies. I have argued that the global change "movement" is large and diversified, and that serious inquiry into the organizational dimensions of this movement should be founded on a specific understanding of the many cross-currents affecting these activities. It may be too easy to romanticize or idealize global change and to pay insufficient attention to the internal contractions of this class of organizations. A finer grained and less romantic approach may yield payoffs in the utility of the resulting organization theory.

Finally, I have drawn attention to the fact that there are countervailing forces, also on a global level, to the objectives and aspirations of global change advocates and their organizations. Three such forces, the rise of ethno-nationalism, international crime and corruption, and conflicting ideas of justice, have been discussed briefly. In my view, sociopolitical forces such as these must be accommodated in developing a true understanding of the role of global change organizations in creating the future. More than any other factor, awareness of factors that may lead to violence, injustice, and oppression are just as important as understanding the sources and expressions of appreciation and goodness. In fact, to an independent eye, it may not always be entirely clear which is which. The implication of this analysis for the themes of this volume may be to realize that there are realistic limits to cooperation.

CONCLUSIONS

This discussion has sought to discuss global change organizations from several unconventional perspectives. First, the extensive participation in these organizations and their considerable influence on social and political developments make a convincing case against the universality of the widely accepted utilitarian models of management and organization. Taking this realization seriously may encourage us to reconsider how to enhance our understanding of the normative basis and moral aspirations of our concepts of organizing.

I have argued that global change organizations, qua organizations, deserve to be understood as networks of weak ties. Mark Granovetter has convincingly argued about the superiority of communities organized by low-density networks in innovativeness, cohesion, and ability to engage in collective action. Realizing that the strength of organizations, such as those engaged in global issues, may lie in their networks of weak ties opens the way for fresh ideas and perspectives for organizational research and theory building.

I have also speculated about some of the cultural assumptions embedded in the global change movement. My intention was not to disparage the inferred values of this movement but to indicate that these values may not be internally consistent or universally valid. We should moderate a tendency to idealize or glorify global issue organizations, recognizing that they are, as are all organizations, part of a larger and more diverse cultural context.

Part of the recognition of the culture and context of global change organizations involves exploring countertrends in the international environment. Here, I have suggested that ethno-nationalism, the internationalization of crime and corruption, and disputed views of justice are also global phenomena that circumscribe the aspiration for a civic global culture and a desire by global change advocates to claim the high moral ground. These trends seem to me to work against the integrative force of global change organizations, and they may well diminish the focus and support for these organizations' goals. Exploring forces toward global fragmentation and conflict, as well as the integrative and constructive consequences of global change organizations, may ultimately help us understand the challenges of organization and management in the wide context in which their roles will be decided.

PART

III

SOCIAL CONSTRUCTIONISM
AND GLOBAL CHANGE

11

GLOBAL ORGANIZATION AND THE POTENTIAL FOR ETHICAL INSPIRATION

KENNETH J. GERGEN

In many respects the chaotic crush toward global organizing can be viewed with alarm. In previous centuries, only the emperor, the Pope, the king, or the Führer possessed sufficient power and resources to imagine globalization—the possibility of extending indefinitely the perimeters of influence, ownership, imprimatur, and/or self-aggrandizement. With the 20th-century development of low-cost technologies of communication and transportation, the potential for globalization has become available to virtually all—from youth activists in Tiananmen Square, to the wine maker in rural Argentina, to the paper towel manufacturer in a small city. Because of essential needs for an expanding market and low-cost labor and materials, the most aggressive thrust toward globalization has, of course, been that of the business community. And it is the multinational corporation in particular that has been subjected to the most intense critique. Globalized business expansion has been variously excoriated for its exploitation of foreign workers (and women in particular), ruthless destruction of natural resources, disregard for the safety of its working conditions and products, marketing of inessential products, and

This chapter represents a revision of a previous article, "Global Organization: From Imperialism to Ethical Vision." *Organization, 2,* 519-532 (1995).

its destruction of local cultures. For a chorus of critics, multinational corporations have been singled out as worst case examples of ethical consciousness (e.g., see Lavipour & Sauvant, 1976; Levitt, 1970; Tavis, 1982; Tugendhat, 1972; Vernon, 1977).

Such criticisms have scarcely gone unanswered. Defenders point to the effects of the multinationals in increasing employment opportunities for thousands of otherwise impoverished peoples, creating an entrepreneurial infrastructure in Third World nations, contributing to the democratization of otherwise autocratic nations, and even contributing to the end of apartheid in South Africa. Furthermore, in the mushrooming of international voluntary organizations (Cooperrider & Pasmore, 1991), commentators point to the potential of globalization for altruistic and life-giving ends. However, much of the argument on behalf of globalization, particularly in the corporate sector, has remained defensive. Strong attempts are made to generate ethical guidelines and avoid undesirable publicity (through the development of public relations offices). But the general posture remains one of quiet reserve toward the ethical dimension of globalized expansion.

I wish to open discussion here on what I see as the potential for global organizations to reverse the playing field. Rather than the apologetic and defensive postures of the past, I believe the time is at hand for global organizations to nurture the potential for ethical leadership. An enormous lacuna in ethical leadership now exists on the international level. I believe that global organizations, and multinational corporations in particular, are now poised for assuming this role. To pursue this argument, I shall first consider the failure of other potential contenders for ethical inspiration. Then, I shall focus on the shift from modern to postmodern forms of organizing. As I shall argue, it is within the postmodern organizing process that we can locate the impetus for reconsidering the ethical potential of the global organization. The ethical potentials of postmodern organizing are realized most particularly in relational process. Finally, I shall demonstrate the ethical potentials of such practices by drawing from recent work in a multinational pharmaceutical corporation.

THE ETHICAL CHALLENGE OF GLOBALIZATION

It is first essential to place the problem of organizational ethics within the global context more generally. This précis will act as a prophylactic against any self-satisfying simplification of good and evil—for example, pitting malignant expansionists against innocent Third World cultures. More important, we shall find that the globalizing process itself thrusts issues of the good into unparalleled prominence. To appreciate these points, it is important, first, to consider the social origins of ethical presumptions. Virtually any form of social organization embodies an internally shared ontology (a consensus view of "the real") and ethical sensibility (quotidian commitments to what is collectively deemed worthy and desirable as opposed to improper or reprehensible). Agreements on the nature of reality and on the value of certain activities as opposed to others are essential for the very formation of organizational culture (Weick, 1995); without such agreements the organization would cease to be effective. More generally, beliefs in the good are community achievements (MacIntyre, 1984).

To the extent that organizations are fully integrated into local communities, organizational ontologies and ethics pose little problem. When community constructions of "is" and "ought" are fully reflected in the practices of its businesses, governmental offices, churches, and so on, the expansion and strengthening of these institutions simply contributes to the shared sense of the good within the community. However, as organizations expand, drawing members from disparate communities or spanning several communities, so is there a tendency for the constructed character of the world within the organization to deviate from the surrounding community. The organizational understanding of the good may come into sharp conflict with local understandings (consider the frequent conflict between family and corporation in terms of the hours a young executive should work).

In these terms, globalization represents an enormous intensification of ethical conflict. As organizations expand into foreign locales, so do they import alien constructions of the real and the good. From their standpoint, their actions seem reasonable, even commendable; local traditions seem parochial, backward, or even reprehensible (surely in need of change). From the local standpoint, however, the ways of life favored by the globalizing organization often seem invasive, insensitive to local customs and community, and even deeply immoral (consider the reaction of Muslim fundamentalists to many Western corporations and products). There is an important sense in which much of the invective directed against the multinational corporation is derived from just this condition—with the corporation evaluated by standards that are largely alien or are differentially construed from within as opposed to outside the organization.

As we see, however, the globalizing process represents an enormous expansion in the field of ethical conflict. The problem is not that of ruthless and colonizing organizations seeking world dominion; "ruthlessness" and "colonization" are the epithets of the outsider. Rather, the problem is that of multiple and competing constructions of the good. And without means of solving these conflicts, we face the problem of deterioration in relations, legal warfare, and even bloodshed (consider the bombing of the Trade Towers, the murder of priests in Africa, the ransoming of business executives in Colombia, and the assassination of Russian officials concerned with Mafia-like business practices).

THE PROBLEMATICS OF PRINCIPLES AND SANCTIONS

From the present standpoint, we find that problems of ethical conduct are not essentially problems of malignant intention. We should not think in terms of the evil practices of the multinationals as against the purity of traditional culture (or vice versa). Rather, ethical problems result primarily from the clashing of community (or cultural) standards of action. In these terms, however, the rapid shift toward globalization invites an enormous expansion in the domain of ethical conflict. Wherever an organization coalesces and expands, so does it enter territories where its mission destabilizes and violates accepted standards of the good. As we confront a world of globalization without limit, what resources are available for adjudication, rectification, or coordination? How are we to proceed?

There is first the long-standing attempt to generate binding ethical principles, to articulate a set of standards or ideals to which all parties can (or should) aspire. This is the territory of philosophers, business ethicists, and human rights specialists concerned with instilling universal goods or values. Yet I find little reason for optimism in this domain. At the outset, after 2,000 years of moral philosophy, there is, as yet, no broad consensus—even in Western culture—on matters of the good. As MacIntyre (1984) characterizes such deliberation, it is both "interminable and unsettleable" (p. 210). When such standards move across cultures, the conflicts are even more profound. For example, Western principles of women's rights generate harsh antagonism in Islamic culture. Under these conditions, who is legitimated to "call the ethic" for all? Even multination attempts to hammer out a universal slate of human rights have not been impressively successful. Not only are such platforms resented by governments feeling that they are being used to undermine their power, but abstract principles seldom dictate specific actions in concrete circumstances (see Gergen, 1994).

Given the problematic of generating and instilling ethical principles, most problems of disagreeable conduct are simply treated pragmatically. Thus, in the sphere of global organization, international trade commissions, international tribunals, United Nations policies, and sanctions and policies within various nations are typically used to prevent egregious violations of situated senses of the good. Although such efforts have been useful, they are also limited. By and large, such sanctioning efforts are reactive; they are activated only when problems emerge. In this sense, they are always chasing demons already on the move. There is little opening for positive visions of the future. Furthermore, they generate a schism between "we" and "they"—between ruling and assessing organizations, on one hand, and those whom they judge. The result in the latter organizations is the emergence of a strategic sensibility: All actions are acceptable as long as they do not arouse the suspicions of the sanctioning body.

In the case of both moral principle and pragmatic sanction, perhaps the major problem is that of extrinsic origin. That is, in both cases, efforts toward the good originate outside the organization itself. The organization must instill the principles or act according to rules generated elsewhere. They must acquire a special sensitivity that is not inherent in the routinized activities of the organization itself. If a broadly shared sense of the good is to be achieved, the more optimal solution would lie in the internal practices of the organization—practices valued by the participants in terms of their own sense of mission. It is precisely this set of practices that emerges in the transition from the modern to the postmodern organization.

THE MODERN ORGANIZATION: ETHICAL AND PRAGMATIC SHORTCOMINGS

With the field of ethical conflict exponentially expanding, and attempts to instill ethical principles and legislate the good both found wanting, what other sources are available? It is here that I wish to propose that the globalizing organization itself may provide the most promising alternative. I am not speaking here of self-policing organizational policies, of the adoption of specific ethical codes of conduct for the globalizing organization. Such standards would inevitably be "local," in the sense of representing internal conceptions of the good. Rather, I am speaking of forms of organizational practice that, indeed, are just those practices best suited to the viability of the globalizing organization. Such a proposal may initially seem ironic. After all, it is the globalizing process itself to which we have traced the problem of ethical conflict. However, as I shall hope to demonstrate, such conflict is largely derived from the expansion in a particular form of organization. Ultimately required is a transformation in the organizing process itself. Let us turn our attention, then, to contrasting conceptions of the organization.

There is now a voluminous literature on the changing nature of the organization in the 20th century, with much of this commentary focused on the major transformations of the past few decades. There are numerous ways of indexing these changes, with terms such as *postindustrialization, the information age, chaos management,* and *postmodernism* among the more prominent. To sustain coherence with a number of previous offerings (Gergen, 1991; Gergen & Whitney, 1995), I shall use the term *modern* to refer to an ideal form of organization, approximated in varying degree by most major corporations (along with military, educational, and governmental estab-lishments) in Western culture for more than a century. We may then refer to the emerging processes of organization as *postmodern.* In what follows, then, I shall briefly characterize major features of the modern organization, along with its vulnerabilities—both practical and ethical—within the context of globalization. This will prepare the way for a discussion of the ethical potentials of postmodern organizing.

There is a burgeoning literature on the modern organization (e.g., see Berman, 1982; Clegg, 1990; Crozier, 1964; Frisby, 1985; March & Simon, 1958). Of specific relevance to our present concerns, we may characterize the modern organization as one committed, at the outset, to a hierarchical view of relationship. In more primitive form, the single, rational agent takes command (responsibility, control) over a group of subordinates. In expanded form, a policy-making committee, informed by subordinates responsible for collecting relevant information, dictates organizational action. Directives flow from top to bottom, and information (or feedback) flows in the opposite direction. In this sense, the organization is monological; a single, coherent rationale (strategic plan) dominates all sectors of the organization. The model is also committed to an individualistic basis of action, wherein single indi-viduals serve as leaders or followers, are assigned responsibilities, are sub-jected to evaluation, and rise upward in the hierarchy (or are thrust out) accordingly. The organization itself is also framed in the individualist meta-phor, with firm boundaries recognized between what is inside versus outside the organization, and organizations are typically viewed as locked in a competitive struggle for position in a hierarchy from which they may be discarded.

In the present context, it is also important to point out that the modern organization represents a major incitement to ethical conflict. Although modern organizations inevitably generate a shared sense of the good, an internal justification for their policies, they do so in relative independence of their social surrounds and with their own prosperity or well-being foremost in view. Thus, as the modern organization becomes globalized, it essentially attempts to replicate itself (through its subsidiaries) throughout the world. The monologic rationality and ethical sensibility ideally prevail throughout. In effect, the organization becomes an alien intruder that functions primarily to fortify (and justify) its own hegemonic ends.

It is not simply that the modern organization is flawed with respect to the ethical necessities of a pluralistic world. Rather, in my view, as the modern organization globalizes, its capacity for effective functioning is also diminished. In significant degree, such losses result from the availability of the very technologies that have made globalization possible. I am speaking here primarily of this century's advances in communication and transportation technology. Through such innovations as the telephone, video recording, the microchip, high-speed computers, and satellite transmission, on one hand, and massive highway systems, rail systems, and jet transportation on the other, it is possible to move information, opinions, people, and products across the globe with ever-increasing speed and efficacy. However, the global expansion of the modern organization is also accompanied by a range of new challenges and adjustments, each of which undermines its viability. Among the more prominent alterations are the following:

Dispersion of intelligibilities. As the organization expands, a strong tendency toward specialization occurs. The company is divided into functional areas; individuals are hired and evaluated as specialists in different domains (e.g., research, production, marketing). Differing specialties are housed in separate buildings and sometimes in different geographical locations. With further expansion, the organization is reproduced in miniature in other parts of the world. Within each segment, shared conceptions and values develop differentially. Most important, what is obvious, rational, and valuable in one part of the organization is seldom duplicated in others. In effect, a multiplication of realities is generated, reducing the intelligibility and the rhetorical efficacy of the singular "voice from the top."

Disruption in chains of authority. Because there are few decisions within a functional domain that do not affect other domains, and because most major initiatives require the coordinated input from diverse functional specialties, increased reliance must be placed on time-specific teams from across specialty areas. The result is first a blurring of the modern organizational structure in terms of the orderly distribution of responsibilities. The clear assignment of responsibilities to individuals or distinctive functional units is subverted. Furthermore, the command structure is undermined as unit chiefs lose the power to control and evaluate the work of members operating in multiple team contexts.

Erosion of rationality. With the availability of high-speed information transmission, information can be rapidly accessed or collected from a variety of sources and speedily transmitted across broad networks. Thus, decision makers are confronted with ever-increasing amounts of information relevant to various decisions. Because the organization is increasingly segmented, this also means that there is increasing differentiation in the sources of information available. There are more "kinds" of information to process. And because information continuously accumulates, new factors are continuously identified, and new developments continue to take place, the half-life of available information is reduced. Yesterday's statistics are all too often a summary of yesterday. Although statistics are the benchmarks most frequently used in strategic planning, few guidelines exist for evaluating when information is useful and when it has outlived its relevance. In effect, not only is reliance on a single center of rational planning reduced, but the very concept of rationally based policy is thrown into question.

Reduction in centralized knowledge. The same technological advances stimulating global expansion of the organization also mean that centralized authority is progressively cut away from the context of decision making. Subsidiary decision makers are more intimately acquainted with the contexts in which they operate; their knowledge base is richer and more fully nuanced. Furthermore, windows of opportunity are suddenly and unpredictably opened (e.g., by a local election, an invention, a shift in interest rates, a merger) and shut. As a result, decisions from a distance—from the spatio-temporal remove of headquarters—prove relatively slow and insensitive. Increased dependency must be placed, then, on local representatives to respond within the context of application.

Communication technologies have simultaneously permitted a broad expansion of interested audiences—groups involved in the control, purchase, or use of a product or service—not only in terms of sheer numbers but in variety as well. Such audiences will also vary in characteristics and requirements from one culture to another. Furthermore, as the media, the government, and various interest groups become players in decisions affecting the organization, the organization must be able to communicate with differing content and emphases to multiple audiences. The potential of a centralized authority to communicate effectively across all target audiences is minimal, most particularly when this group operates at a geographical remove from the target. Again, the result is increased reliance on local, contextually embedded decision makers.

Undermining of autonomy. Because the media are increasingly the major sources of public information, their power to shape an organization's future is augmented substantially. In effect, media professionals—news analysts, commentators, science columnists, news writers—operate as gatekeepers of national reality. Because their views are typically presumed to be unmotivated—and thus objective—they often seem more authentic than do the views issuing from the organizations themselves. In this way, organizations lose a certain capacity for autonomous self-direction. Their voices lose authority in the public sphere. Increasingly, the views of outside opinion leaders must be taken into account prior to decisions—in effect, giving such leaders a voice within the organization. The boundary between "inside" and "outside" the organization is blurred.

This erosion in autonomy is furthered by the fact that available technologies increase the capacity for various concerned audiences to identify themselves and their goals and to organize action. This is not only true in the case of political parties and governmental offices, but also for various groups that recognize the economic potentials in organizing (e.g., consumer and labor groups), and for various grassroots interest groups (e.g., environmentalists, feminists, associations of retired people) who now take a keen political interest in global organizations. Not simply passive observers, such groups are actively engaged in information searches relevant to globalizing practices. In effect, the global organization is placed under unprecedented scrutiny, the effects of which may spill into the media at any time. Again, there is a diminution in the capacity of the organization for self-direction.

As we find, the technologies of globalization place the modern organizational structure in jeopardy, with the capacity of central authority to maintain intelligibility, command authority, make rationality claims, accumulate knowledge for local decision making, and make autonomous decisions all diminishing. As David Freedman (1992) summarizes the case,

The traditional scientific approach to management promised to provide managers with the capacity to analyze, predict, and control the behavior of the complex organizations they led. But the world most managers currently inhabit often appears to be unpredictable, uncertain, and even uncontrollable. (p. 26)

RELATIONAL PROCESS AND THE ETHICS
OF POSTMODERN ORGANIZING

As I am proposing, the 20th-century process of globalization is accompanied by a decline in the capacity of the modern organization to sustain itself. Yet as we have seen, ethical conflicts are born of just this capacity of the modern organization for self-exportation and global duplication. In effect, ethical conflict is derived from a form of organization that ceases to be functional. In this sense, organizations seeking to bolster top-down authority, to control local operations, and to be increasingly self-determined are not only operating against their self-interests but do so at a cost of ethical anguish. Given this condition, we now confront the challenge of envisioning practices of organizing that are at once beneficial for the organization and ethically productive. Can we, then, elucidate processes of postmodern organizing that simultaneously benefit the organization and favor a globalized condition of ethical well-being?

It is here that we enter the sphere of postmodern organizational theory. Although this literature is undergoing robust development (e.g., see Bergquist, 1993; Boje, Gephart, & Joseph, in press; Cooper & Burrell, 1988; Crook, Pakulski, & Waters, 1992; Hage & Powers, 1992), it is far too early to draw confident conclusions regarding ethical potentials. However, the central place occupied by social constructionist dialogues within the postmodern literature (e.g., see Kvale, 1992) does provide some useful leverage. In particular, social constructionist analyses typically favor a relativistic stance concerning ethical premises. Thus, they stand as a bulwark against any potentially hegemonic articulation of the good. Simultaneously, constructionism places a strong emphasis on relationships as the font of both ontology and ethics (see Gergen, 1994). In doing so, they shift the focus from individuals or social structures to processes of ongoing interchange, processes we may characterize as relational. In the present context, I wish to propose a conception of relational process as a pivotal metaphor for achieving the dual ends of organizational sustenance and ethical well-being. Let us explore.

At the outset, an emphasis on relational process abandons two central features of the modern organization, namely, the assumption of self-contained units and of structural solidity. From the relational standpoint, the primary concern is not with recognizable units (e.g., headquarters, subsidiaries, the marketing division) and their structural arrangement, but with continuous processes of relationship. By foregrounding relationship, we call attention to the domain of interdependence, the forms of coordinated activity from which the very conceptions of headquarters, subsidiaries, and marketing division derive. In this sense, there are no single individuals making autonomous decisions, but forms of relationship out of which actions that we index as decisions become intelligible. An individual, then, is the common locus for a multiplicity of relationships. His or her intelligibility (capacity for reasoned action) is chiefly dependent on participating in processes of relational coordination.

To the extent that parties to a relationship continue to communicate, they will generate an internal domain of intelligibility (a sense of "the true" and "the good," as indicated earlier). Thus, as organizations segment relationships in various ways—geographically, functionally, hierarchically—so do they generate multiple centers of intelligibility. We may view organizational configuration, then, in terms of a range of relational nuclei, each striving to coordinate internal meaning. As internal meanings are stabilized, so is the internal efficacy of the nucleus enhanced. However, as its intelligibilities ossify, so is its capacity for coordination with other nuclei potentially reduced (see Gergen, 1994). A premium is thus to be placed on avoiding closures of intelligibility, that is, allowing any construction of the true and the good to become sedimented, or simply "common sense." Within the nuclei, multiple logics should be encouraged, and a healthy appreciation for incoherent policies should prevail. Furthermore, all decisions and policies may be construed as contingent, formalizations of "the conversation at this moment." In this way, space remains for a continuation of the dialogue and a revisioning of policies and practices.

Finally, and most important for present purposes, we see that the adequacy of a decision or policy does not rest on the intellective capacity of the single decision maker (or decision-making group). Rather, maximal reliance must be placed on relational processes linking those responsible for the decision or policy to those who will be affected. This is not to recapitulate the modern presumption that effective decisions should be based on information about target characteristics (e.g., attitudes, motivation, cultural habits, income). Rather, it is to say that "the targets" should optimally join in fashioning the character of those decisions. The decision-making process, then, should be permeable, interactively embedded within the context of consequence. In effect, relational nuclei within the organization should be multiply enmeshed with other nuclei, engaged in dialogues in which multiple intelligibilities share, interpenetrate, modify, concatenate, or act with critical reflection on each other. Similar processes should characterize relations with various "target audiences" of concern to the organization.

Outlined thus far is a vision of postmodern organizational process, one in which the chief emphasis is placed on relational process. Its contours have been importantly fashioned by conversations with managers across the globe concerned with organizational viability. More will be said about the efficacy of this vision of organizational process. However, we must finally return to our major challenge, that of envisioning globalizing organizations as positive forces for ethical generativity. Specifically, in what sense does relational process furnish a basis for ethical vision? On what grounds can it be argued that relational process is intrinsically ethical? The answer to this question can be traced to the earlier proposal that ethics themselves are communal creations; conceptions of the good emerge in the process of relationship. In this sense, an organization in which relational process of the present kind is preeminent is also one in which the generative conditions for ethical sensibility are continuously restored. That is, no preconceived conception of the good enters the relationship unchallenged; no voice of the good—developed from afar—remains inviolate. The preexisting relations offer resources from which participants will surely draw; but the offstage ethics are not binding within the new context. Conceptions of the good are thus born and reborn within their specific contexts of usage.

TOWARD ETHICALLY GENERATIVE PRACTICE

What I am proposing here is essentially a shift from a conception of ethical principles from which proper practices are derived, to forms of ethically generative practice—practices that give rise to conjoint valuing and the synergistic blending of realities. By shifting the emphasis to practice, we avoid the endless contestation on the nature of the good, stripped from history and culture. There is no ethical a priori from which, indeed, springs the very sense of the evil other. Rather, the focus is on developing relational practices that are themselves the sources of the communal sense of the good. Can we, however, offer a blueprint for ethically generative practices, a set of criteria or activities that will guarantee the emergence of a collaborative sense of the good? In my view, such a temptation is to be avoided, for to do so would be to again close out the possibility for broad participation. Every practice will necessarily favor certain groups, skills, or traditions. Rather than articulating such practices in bold script, I am drawn rather to a process by which we as scholars join with practitioners to develop a range of potentials—concepts, visions, metaphors, stories—that may encourage the development of ethically generative practices on sites of local action.

In this context, I wish to share a number of "stories" growing out of organizational development work conducted by Mary Gergen and myself with Sandoz Pharma, an extended, multinational pharmaceutical company. In this project, we deliberated extensively with managers in wide-ranging locales concerning optimal management practices for the future (Gergen & Gergen, 1994). In particular, we asked them to identify what they were now finding to be the most effective communication practices. Would such practices reflect the traditional, or modernist, conception of optimal communication (stressing centralized authority, top-down flow of policies, and the upward flow of information)? Interestingly, the answer was almost univocally in the negative. Repeatedly, we were told of management experiences that were relational in character and that emphasized dialogic process, multiple logics, and permeable boundaries within organizational spheres and between the organization and its external context. It is this same set of practices that, in my view, possesses ethically generative potential. Consider the following:

- In one organizational restructuring project, top management avoided the usual "independent study" of its operations by outside consultants and instead turned the task over to the organization itself. Fourteen teams, representing all sectors of the company, carried out broadscale interviews, met periodically with other relevant teams to explore the total operations of the company, and deliberated on the demands and skills necessary for future success. Finally, they contributed to a seven-volume summary containing their research and recommendations concerning personnel reductions, training, and the organization of work. A steering committee, headed by the CEO, eventually adopted some 75% of the recommendations. In effect, virtually all sectors of the company were given voice in molding the future of the company.

- The company was placed under sharp critical attack for its research on genetic engineering. An information campaign, mounted to inform the public of the positive effects of such research, did nothing to dissuade an increasingly vocal organization of dissenters. The company then shifted to a relational orientation, in which they proposed to the opposition that they work cooperatively to create a public exhibition informing the public of their diverse views on these complex and emotionally charged issues. After much active discussion, the various participants agreed on a set of informative exhibits that were subsequently displayed at a city cultural center. The exhibition was praised for its balance and open design. Company representatives felt that there had also been an informative exchange of opinions with the opposition; both sides had developed more differentiated and appreciative views, and the public had been exposed to the multiple issues involved.

- Pharmaceutical companies in general are placed under close and critical scrutiny by the press. Traditional company policy was to protect internal information and decisions against press intrusion, as well as to plan information campaigns designed to sway the public through the press. However, the relationship thus spawned between the organization and the press was strategic and adversarial. In two countries under study, this policy was abandoned in favor of a collaborative relationship with the press. Press representatives were called in to attend internal briefings within the company; company representatives met frequently and informally with the press for exchanges of views and information. The results, in both cases, proved highly satisfying; distrust and misunderstanding receded.

These several instances are only illustrative of practices that have ethically generative potential. Also resonant, however, were the development of an international research team, in which young researchers from six nationalities devoted 6 days to working on issues of mutual understanding and respect; an Asia Pacific workshop in which representatives of 14 countries met to hammer out business policies for the future; and a meeting of Eastern and Middle European region representatives to consider future markets. Relational process was also evident in the company's communication with numerous "target audiences." In one initiative, for example, the company worked cooperatively with both international and local agencies to develop organ donor programs; in another, a Third World subsidiary set up a program to train youth in technical specialties within the company.

Interestingly, the result of many of these efforts has also been an incorporation of outside values into the corporation itself. For example, rather than seeing ecology activists as a threat to profitable enterprises, the chemical division developed EcoVISION, an internal program dedicated to environmental protection; rather than simply letting unused drugs end up in landfills or in the hands of children, French managers took an active role in developing a drug recycling program; and rather than viewing bioethics as an infringement on research rights, the company took an active role in championing an international policy of bioethics. In effect, external ethical concerns were now incorporated into company policies.

CONCLUSIONS

As I am proposing, it is the globalization of a particular form of organization, termed modern, that furnishes the primary incitement to invectives of immorality. Yet, as we also find, the unlimited expansion of this organizational form is detrimental to its own existence. Ethical conflict and a deterioration in organizational efficacy are linked. However, as we scanned the postmodern terrain, we located a range of specifically relational practices that offered promise for both a reinvigorated organization and the coordination of world peoples. Both the instantiation and efficacy of such practices were illustrated in the work of a multinational pharmaceutical company. Although there remain myriad questions to be explored, we find here possible hope for the globalization process. The relational practices of the postmodern organization may serve as a positive force for livable ethics.

12

GLOBAL TECHNOSCAPES AND SILENT VOICES

Challenges to Theorizing Global Cooperation

RAZA A. MIR
MARTA B. CALÁS
LINDA SMIRCICH

> The fundamental political conflict in the opening decades of the new century, we believe, will not be between nations or even between trading blocs, but between the forces of globalization and the territorially based forces of local survival seeking to preserve and to redefine community.
>
> Barnet and Cavanagh (1994, p. 22)

In a globalized world, where symbolic and cultural aspects of multiple societies have been liberated from the territorial, imperatives for global cooperation present themselves in a variety of urgent ways. Issues of environmental degradation, the inability of capitalist businesses to fulfill their designated role as trustees of society, and the failure of modernization projects in bringing about global welfare, among others, have been invoked within the theme of this book to demonstrate how existing institutional arrangements are hopelessly inadequate for answering to such predicaments on a worldwide scale. In addressing these issues, most chapters in the volume emphasize the need for organizations to discover their cooperative potential within meta-institutional arrangements, bringing together multiple constituencies and serving their common interests—that is, a new paradigm for global cooperation.

Interestingly, however, a cursory examination of the term *cooperation* in the history of organization theory helps us quickly discern that those calls for a *new paradigm of cooperation* are not new, and in fact, they seem to echo, with little modification, from a not-too-distant past. Classical organizational theorists often invoked cooperation in defense of their ideas and strategies, as we illustrate in Table 12.1. Yet *cooperation,* as a term, served to homogenize not only the theorists' apparent epistemological and ideological differences— all clearly rooted in Western liberal humanism—but, more important, the expected, desirable behaviors of organizational members. Furthermore, in these writings, the ability to cooperate became a sign of progress and development in organizational knowledge. All in all, we are disturbed by the possibility that the assumptions informing today's calls for "global cooperation" may be too close to the assumptions that drove cooperation in early organization theory.

Indeed, the language of cooperation—and its ideological acolytes—in organization studies have not altered much over the years. Consider, for example, the following passage.

> We live in an age haunted by the specter of world destruction, in a world where physical and natural phenomena appear more controlled and orderly than their human users, at a time when unpredictable change destroys old values before new ones are developed. These world conditions implicate (theorists) as never before (Bennis, 1963, p. 127).[1] Given this profoundly changed relationship between the human world and the planet, the call to the social sciences is clear: To effectively understand and craft responses to global environmental change, social scientists must make a significant contribution (Bilimoria et al., 1995, p. 73), applying social knowledge to create more viable social systems (Bennis, 1963, pp. 157-158).

(continued)

Only in the past 5 years have the human dimensions of global change been brought into scientific focus (Bilimoria et al., 1995, p. 73). We are now in a much better position today to assess the results and the potentialities of applied social sciences precisely because there are more complete reports and more analyses available to us (Bennis, 1963, p. 129). The massive scientific projects being developed all over the world to respond to the ecocidal crisis cry out for collaboration between the social and natural sciences (Bilimoria et al., 1995, p. 73). There is a growing disenchantment with the moral neutrality of the scientist (Bennis, 1963, p. 128).

Notice (however), a growing concern with normative planning, with new forms of social architecture, with "realistic" and "vivid" utopias, with more radical assumptions about social value, point(ing) toward an emerging action role for the behavioral scientist (Bennis, 1963, p. 126) (in contributing) to positive global change through research on the organizational dimensions of global change (Bilimoria et al., 1995, p. 72).

This seemingly coherent piece was constructed, by us, through splicing together two texts that are more than 30 years apart (Bennis, 1963; Bilimoria et al., 1995). In one, Warren Bennis, writing about a new role for the behavioral scientist in 1963, suggested that social science was uniquely poised to effect social change, a change that had been rendered urgent because of potential science-led ravagement of the world, and a change that had become possible due to new theoretical sophistication in the social sciences. In the other, the current themes of global cooperation, as expressed by organizers of the conference from which this volume emerged, echo Bennis's concerns and expectations.

The similarities in these discourses are unmistakable; the apparent seamlessness of many aspects of the two arguments a matter for some introspection. How different from its intellectual predecessors is the call for global cooperation that resonates in this book? How likely is it that *global cooperation* is another attempt at social engineering, which will homogenize a diversity of concerns and ideologies under the banner of common interests? How likely is *global cooperation* another instance of paying homage to dominant ideolo-

Table 12.1 Classical Management Quest for Cooperation and Collaboration

F. W. Taylor (1911)	M. P. Follett (1925/1940)	C. I. Barnard (1938)	E. Mayo (1939)
Scientific management will mean, for the employers and the workmen who adopt it . . . the elimination of almost all causes for dispute and disagreement between them. What constitutes a fair day's work will be a question for scientific investigation, instead of a subject to be bargained and haggled over. . . . More than all other causes, the close, intimate cooperation, the constant personal contact between the two sides, will tend to diminish friction and discontent. It is difficult for . . . people whose interests are the same . . . to keep up a quarrel. (pp. 142-143)	THE REASON WE ARE HERE STUDYING HUMAN RELATIONS IN INDUSTRY IS THAT WE BELIEVE THERE CAN BE A SCIENCE OF CO-OPERATION. BY THIS I MEAN THAT CO-OPERATION IS NOT, AND THIS I INSIST ON, A MATTER OF GOOD INTENTIONS, OF KINDLY FEELING. IT MUST BE BASED ON THESE, BUT YOU CANNOT HAVE SUCCESSFUL COOPERATION UNTIL YOU HAVE WORKED OUT THE METHOD OF CO-OPERATION—BY EXPERIMENT AFTER EXPERIMENT, BY A COMPARING OF EXPERIMENTS, BY A POOLING OF RESULTS. IT IS MY PLEA ABOVE EVERYTHING ELSE THAT WE LEARN HOW TO CO-OPERATE. (PP. 123-124)	*The morality that underlies enduring cooperation is multidimensional. It comes from and may expand to all the world; it is rooted deeply in the past; it faces toward the endless future. As it expands, it must become more complex, its conflicts must be more numerous and deeper; its call for abilities must be higher, its failures of ideal attainment must be perhaps more tragic; but the quality of leadership, the persistence of its influence . . . all express the height of moral aspirations, the breath of moral foundations.* *(p. 284)*	The art of human collaboration seems to have disappeared during two centuries of quite remarkable progress. . . . How can human capacity for spontaneous collaboration be restored? It is in this area that leadership is most required. . . . What is wanted is knowledge, a type of knowledge that has escaped us in two hundred years of prosperous development. How to substitute human responsibility for futile strife and hatreds, this is one of the most important researches of our time. (p. 5)

gies, under the guise of an alternative, that will deny various peoples in the world their rights to preserve and to redefine community?

GLOBAL COOPERATION AND ORGANIZATION THEORY: AN INVITATION TO "SELF" REFLEXIVITY

Theorists of global cooperation make, indeed, a compelling case for the notion of "no limits to cooperation." It is undeniable that we live within the specter of a world that has become integrated, if only through a common environmental predicament. Under these conditions, it is perhaps only fitting that one consider the possibility of a narrative of global cooperation as a way of reconfiguring, at a minimum, the socioeconomic landscape. Such a project, Bilimoria et al. (1995) argued in the article that preceded the conference, may entail us having to "examine our assumptions about knowledge itself, acknowledging and accessing multiple ways of knowing" (p. 77).

Yet it is precisely at this point, when we traverse a path that questions *knowledge assumptions,* that we come across a number of seemingly unresolvable inconsistencies in the current call for no limits to cooperation. In our view, this call rejects the very possibility of the global cooperation it seeks to enact—that is, how global are the knowledge assumptions that undergird global cooperation? Whose views of the world do they represent? In particular, we find at least three major discrepancies in this later version of global cooperation, and we believe that this bears some further scrutiny. Said differently, global cooperation cannot, and should not, be celebrated without reflecting first upon its own epistemological priorities.

A critique of science that obscures the cooperative links of science and capitalism. The notion of no limits to cooperation, as articulated by Bilimoria et al., questions the anthropomorphic stance of modern Baconian science that has led to the formulation of the conquest of nature as a measure of progress. However, Baconian science, or the commitment to positivist truth that it represents, has not only led to the wanton destruction of ecological resources, but has been a cornerstone of the entire industrial-technical establishment as it exists in the Western world (Bajaj, 1988). It is questionable then, whether we can theorize a non-Baconian (anti-Baconian) approach to science without having to also confront the industrial superstructure that rest on its premises.

A holistic notion of cooperation that is Eurocentric. The holistic notion of human interaction that has to accompany any argument in favor of limitless cooperation carries within itself an ultimately Eurocentric assumption of "universal emancipation"—remnants of the Romanticism that opposed the Enlightenment's conception of knowledge (e.g., Jones, 1969). This holism is closer to Hegel's and, in particular, to Schopenhauer's, than to any non-Western form of thought, and it might carry little relevance for most non-Western peoples' contemporary concerns (Ashcroft, Griffiths, & Tiffin, 1995; Mohanty, 1991; Prakash, 1995). Although Bilimoria et al. acknowledge that Eurocentrism is implicated in our contemporary worldwide predicaments, they do not pursue the logical extension of this issue. That is, that any project that calls for universal cooperation is already crafted along Eurocentric terms and notions of humanity, *which may be incommensurable* with a variety of non-Western thought systems and interests.

An essentialist rhetoric of human cooperation. Furthermore, when one theorizes cooperation without taking into account the fact that actions, issues, and events can be interpreted in multiple and often unavoidably conflicting ways by various peoples in the world, it is easy to fall prey to an essentialist assumption that there is such a thing as "the human propensity to cooperate" (Bilimoria et al., 1995, p. 82). Regardless of our possible sympathy for a less conflictual and more collaborative global future, we cannot avoid noticing that this is a Western humanist rhetorical strategy, supported by the ontological assumption of an original human essence rooted in cooperation, from which unqualified "goodness" would emerge. This rhetoric has at its core an ideal transparency, a ghost, that when rendered knowable would reveal nothing but our common "closer to nature" humanity—*ourselves undressed,* in Michele Rosaldo's (1980) terms. The dangers of such a rhetorical move are many. At a minimum, consider that any statement proposing—unproblematically—an inherently cooperative humanity would render inhuman those who resist cooperating (e.g., resisting collaboration with "the enemy"), whereas it would extend a humanizing mantle even to those who have cooperated in horrendous crimes against humanity, such as the Holocaust (Bauman, 1989). It is this narrative of essential humanism and common consciousness that legitimizes Western discourses of knowledge—in this case, the possibility of a science of global cooperation—by leaving outside humanity precisely those "uncooperative/ unknowable others" they also claim to represent.

Thus, as one notices these and other inconsistencies in the epistemic stance of global cooperation, it is a matter of major concern that theorists promoting such notions resolve their contradictions by asserting that the seemingly fundamentally conflicting views are, in effect, "interdependent and complementary" (Bilimoria et al., 1995, p. 78), or that they can be subsumed under a common rubric of "participative epistemologies" (Bilimoria et al., 1995, p. 79). Such assertions make their arguments ultimately cooperative with nothing other than traditional organizational scholarship. That is, their arguments treat epistemic contradictions as communication problems; dilute the political implications of these differences; theorize a fictive common ethical dimension to these issues; and, concurrently, neglect the power relations that mediate the legitimation and dominance of some epistemological positions over others.

Our challenges to the possibility of global cooperation as an epistemological enterprise require further elaboration. Simply put, we are asserting that a new paradigm of global cooperation is unrealizable unless there is a *fundamental rethinking* of the ways through which this new knowledge is to be created. For these purposes, knowledge creation cannot be thought of as an unproblematic collaborative enterprise, or even as a neutral territory. Rather, the process of knowledge creation for global cooperation needs to be recognized as emanating from, and theorized as, the very contested ground *that it always already is.* An example may clarify this point. Regardless of good intentions, the call for papers for the conference from which this volume emerged was positioned, a priori, as fostering an epistemology of cooperation and a holistic value system. Yet this positioning, of necessity, was a totalizing gesture that left "outside the text" (of the call for papers and of the conference)—silencing, muti(lati)ng—most, if not all, of the epistemic arguments that might problematize the conference's aims.

Less immediately apparent, however, is the function, in all of this, of arguments—such as ours—that are invited to participate under the guise of resisting the conference's epistemic stance. In this case, the act of writing this chapter (and our presentation in the conference) introduces our work into a particular realm of knowledge (i.e., an instance of alternative organizational discourse). As such, our own oppositional activity does not detract from the tradition of disciplinary discourse. Rather, traditional disciplinary power becomes enhanced by our participation in the discourse as an addition to the modernist mythology of the progress of knowledge, further enhancing the modernist tradition of "truth making" through falsification. In other words, knowledge creation, in the Western mode, is always a contested terrain in the form of a power/knowledge network that appears as a seamless fabric only through well-crafted representations—after the opposition, or negation, has been either silenced by omission or selectively voiced by permission.

Perhaps more important, these power/knowledge networks become actualized, formed, and transformed through practices of subjectification (Foucault, 1977b, 1978, 1988), that is, as particular subjectivities become enacted through their "self" recognition in discourses of knowledge. For example, by participating in the discourse of "scholarship" articulated in this volume, we are paradoxically subjects of and subjectified by this discourse as we call attention to and reenact the limits of that discourse. Furthermore, when trying to perform oppositional practices—in the very act of resisting the discourse—we produce power effects that get inscribed and reinscribed both in the scholarly discourse and in the materiality of our bodies as "scholarly resistors." Thus, the modern Western episteme renders invisible all but those capable of recognizing themselves as subjects of/in its discourses—the rest does not exist in knowledge.

This latter observation offers a particular twist to our arguments. We are asserting the impossibility of leaving behind the modern/Western/epistemic stance if we want the power to speak "knowledge" to and in the West. However, by analyzing this epistemic stance as a contested territory, we are recognizing the existence of interstices in the power/knowledge network—not a seamless, solid fabric but a web(bing) full of holes—where fragments of other voices, so far silenced, might appear as they try to negotiate/resist/ re-create a space in the West/rest relations of power. It is in these spaces that other epistemologies and other subjectivities might come to be articulated, not as positive and final alternatives to modern/Western/knowledge, but as transient, hybrid voices, emerging and reemerging from contemporary relations of power. In our view, then, the challenge to theorizing "no limits to cooperation" can be met only by a different epistemological position that is capable of listening to and recognizing—*as knowledge*—those fleeting, "strange" voices that until now represented only silences in the discourse. Such is the challenge we are trying to address in this chapter.

Yet if we are to articulate knowledges and subjectivities that have hitherto been excluded from the boundaries of the dominant epistemology, we have no option but to be rebelliously uncooperative. The inclusion of such voices demands the breaching of boundaries of disciplinary discourses in multiple ways, disturbing norms and mores, practices and power relations themselves.

Unavoidably, on breaching the boundaries of discourse, we are actively engaging in confrontation and conflict, which can scarcely be termed an act of global cooperation.

To fulfill this agenda, we first introduce a specific example: the marketing of portable ultrasound scanners in India and their potential impact in perpetuating female feticide. We use this situation as an exemplar of the global terrain where multiple discourses and subjectivities intersect in a manner that renders cooperation impossible. Second, we examine the implications of this example for contemporary discourses of global cooperation. Issues of voice/silence, representation, and strategic choices for those outside these discourses are examined. We conclude that silences find their own voice in a variety of ways that are untheorizable within the boundaries of limitless cooperation, as proposed by the theme of this book. Yet it is in these silences, *including the silence in theory,* that we may find the more relevant implications of global change for contemporary organizational knowledge.

ORGANIZATION THEORY AND FEMALE FETICIDE: A CURIOUS (POWER/KNOWLEDGE) INTERSECTION

In the modern age, new forms of domination are increasingly embodied in the social relations of science and technology which organize knowledge and production systems. The divergent voices and innovative practices of subjected peoples disrupt such cultural reconstructions of non-western societies. By listening to polyphonic tones challenging dominant themes, and attending to lives conducted in shadowy recesses as well as under the spotlight, anthropologists can disclose myriad aspects of our modern condition. (Ong, 1987, p. 221)

Consider the following: In 1993, General Electric Company (GE) announced a selection of key strategic moves to invest heavily in its operations in India, China, and Mexico. Hailed by the popular business media as a move of great entrepreneurial wisdom (Smart, 1993), this move was targeted toward ensuring that GE increases the international component of its sales revenues to more than 50% of its total revenues (currently estimated at $60 billion per annum).

> **"WE'RE A COMPANY WITH GREAT INFRASTRUCTURE STRENGTHS AND, THEREFORE, A COMPANY TO GO WHERE GROWTH IS. . . . IT'S CLEAR TO ANYONE THAT THE GROWTH WILL BE IN THE PACIFIC RIM, INDIA AND MEXICO."**
> **GE CHAIRMAN JACK WELCH (SMART, 1993, P. 66)**

A major area for expansion is the market for diagnostic imaging equipment in India—a $16 million market that is growing at 20% per annum (Engardio, 1993)—where GE hopes to emerge victorious in a battle of dominance with other multinational giants such as Siemens, Phillips, and Toshiba.

> **"IF YOU AREN'T IN ASIA . . . IN 10 OR 15 YEARS YOU MIGHT AS WELL BE NOWHERE" [JOREM MALM—PRESIDENT OF GE MEDICAL SYSTEMS' ASIA OPERATIONS]. INDIA SLIPPED FROM GE'S SIGHT ONCE BEFORE. IT WON'T HAPPEN AGAIN.**

One of the marketing innovations planned by GE is the development of a 20-pound ultrasound scanner—a device that could fit into the backseat of a car—because technology for imaging then could be made accessible to the Indian hinterland. Aside from developing this machine, GE plans to work with local finance companies to help make these machines accessible to remote areas. These ultrasound scanners have vast imaging possibilities but are primarily used to monitor the development of a fetus in a womb. Among other benefits, this technique is known to have a powerful accuracy in predicting the sex of the fetus by the middle of the first trimester of pregnancy.

> GE's showpiece in India is its 50%-owned medical systems venture, which is based in the southern city of Bangalore. Hardly a factor in India two years ago, GE is coming on strong in ultrasound devices, used from everything from detecting gallstones to monitoring the development of a fetus in a womb.
>
> Smart (1993, p. 6)

Contrast this information with another Indian story; in August 1994, the Indian government banned fetal sex determination tests, recognizing their role in the perpetration of selective female feticide.

The availability of the [ultrasound] machines, though, while boosting infant health, has created some unintended consequences. In India as in other developing countries, the technology is often used to determine the sex of a fetus—which in turn often leads to abortion of females. While some women's groups in India criticize the machines' new availability, Wipro GE President says that sex determination is a "very, very small percentage of their usage."

Smart (1993, p. 68)

"*Our society is absolutely male-dominated. It is the men who decide how many children they will have, and whether any of them will be girls. That is the condition of our country.*"

Geeta Mukherjee, a women's rights campaigner in India (Burns, 1994, p. 5)

The government's move has been prompted by the revelation of some sobering statistics; in the decade 1981-1991, the female-to-male ratio in India has dropped from 934 females per 1,000 males in 1981 to a ratio of 927 in 1991. In some states of India, the sex ratio is as low as 875 (Burns, 1994; see also Kishwar, 1987). In sheer numerical terms, this implies that there are now 60 million fewer women than men in India, and that this numerical disparity between men and women has further increased by about 3 million in the past decade alone!

Although a number of practices—such as differential access to nutrition, failure to address female-specific health issues, and the selective impact of poverty on the female members of society—may be cited as major causes of this disparity, one troubling practice that has emerged recently has been that of selective female feticide, whereby sophisticated technologies such as ultrasonography are used to determine the sex of the fetus, and female fetuses are aborted. Hard data on this issue are difficult to come by, yet it is estimated that between 200,000 and 400,000 female fetuses are aborted every year following sex determination tests (Arora, 1996). Interestingly, the ban extends to all clinics that administer prenatal sonographic tests to determine the sex of the fetus but does not extend to any control on the production and sale of diagnostic equipment.

"Of course, the women want only a boy. . . . If we tell them it is a girl, they will feel very sorry, there will be a sadness in their face, and they will be looking as though they will have a nervous breakdown. And the husband will be saying right away, 'O.K., you are going for an abortion.' "

Banarsi Dass, a male physician in India (Burns, 1994, p. 5)

But as the new law passed through Parliament, many women's groups were divided. For one thing, India's uphill battle to overcome the poverty that traps more than 40% of its people is linked closely to the failure to curb the birth rate.

(Burns, 1994, p. 5)

"All you are doing with this new law is giving the police a new potential for extorting bribes. Now, instead of extorting from street hawkers, they will be extorting from doctors."

Madhu Kishwar, editor of an Indian women's right journal (Burns, 1994, p. 5)

The failure of the government to support the ban on clinics and hospitals with any control on the sales of these machines, or even the provision of mandatory registration of such machines, in effect means that the law will remain unenforceable. All the clinics need to do to circumvent this law is to stop recording the sex determination tests as such and convey the information verbally.

This story is indeed very complicated, yet there is another twist to it. The practice of feticide, which is a recent phenomenon, mirrors an earlier practice, that of female infanticide, a story that is characterized by a similar polyglot of opinions. Indian knowledgeables, Western knowledgeables, and affected subjectivities have very diverse readings of the situation.

> It is a sieve of prickly bush
> and the heart is filled with grief

> Among the women who sing this song are those who have been resorting to female infanticide to save the babies from a heartless, dowry seeking man's world waiting to crucify them when they grow up.
>
> *The Hindu* (1994, p. v)

> Infanticide is a longstanding and widespread practice. Female infanticide among humans—its motivations, methods, and determinants—has a long history. . . . Long-term scholarly interest in the subject . . . however . . . yields surprisingly little dependable information. It is difficult to obtain firsthand, carefully confirmed data . . . and the social variables related to infanticide, in sufficient quantity to allow theory testing.
>
> *Economic and Political Weekly* (1992, p. 1153)

> The tragedy is that female infanticide has become almost an acceptable practice only during the last 10 or 15 years and it was not prevalent earlier.
>
> *The Hindu* (1994, p. v)

> The villages in which female infanticide occurs tend to be even more remote and have less educated populations than the villages with no cases of female infanticide.
>
> *Economic and Political Weekly* (1992, p. 1155)

> The chilling and incredible part of the story is that even educated parents resort to female infanticide. The young wife of a graduate had to submit to the demands of her husband to kill the first baby girl since otherwise she would have been rejected by her husband.
>
> *The Hindu* (1994, p. v)

> The option of sterilisation by women who have obtained the desired number and gender composition in their offsprings may significantly reduce the number of unwanted female births. Other government policies related to raising the status of women may also have beneficial impact: scholarships for women students.
>
> *Economic and Political Weekly* (1992, p. 1155)

> Will the spread of education end this evil? One cannot be sure. Several graduates and post-graduates in the area are jobless. . . . Government by depositing Rs. 1,000 on the day of the birth of a girl child . . . would give [her] a lump sum at the age of 21 . . . sufficient for her to get married. . . . The only solution would be to make the women economically independent.
>
> *The Hindu* (1994, p. v)

Is there any relationship between GE's entry into India and the sex determination laws? At face value, the comparison seems quite ludicrous. On one hand, we see a corporation seeking to test its mettle in an inviting, if competitive, market. On the other hand, we observe sedimented, unenlightened practices reincarnating themselves in a modern avatar. Progress and its exact opposite are not supposed to be related.

We argue, however, that it is precisely in this relationship between "liberating" global technology and entrenched patriarchy that we may find the limits to cooperation. Undoubtedly, there is no linear causal relationship between modernity and its discontents, but their relationship is far more complicated than our theories of cooperation would let us imagine. In the next section, we attempt to make sense of the multiple relationships that characterize this issue, not in the spirit of finally unravelling these connections, but in an attempt to show how such a terrain renders the issue of cooperation hopelessly problematic.

THE INADEQUACY OF THEORY AND THE IMPOSSIBILITY OF GLOBAL [EPISTEMOLOGICAL] COOPERATION

Science speaks a language of universal authority. Diverse women express their gender consciousness and the core meanings of reproduction in polyglot, multicultural voices. . . . At stake is the cultural negotiation of gender and parental practices in a world shaped by both social diversity and scientific hegemony. . . . Until we locate and listen to the discourses of those women who encounter and interpret a new reproductive technology in their own lives, we cannot evaluate it beyond the medical model. . . . It cannot be settled by recourse to a universal explanation, as if all women held similar interests in the problems. (Rapp, 1991, p. 392)

The issue of female feticide illustrates what must be a troubling conundrum for theorists of global cooperation. First, there is the dominant global industrializing enterprise that may be seen as represented by GE. On the other hand, this company is certainly not a totally foreign power in India; rather, GE is in India at the behest of a second force, the Indian government, which actively sought and lobbied for GE's investment largesse. Indeed, the Indian government is proud of having attracted the Foreign Direct Investment (FDI) made by GE into India, and it has embarked on a project of aggressively soliciting more international investment in its economy (Engardio, 1993).

Contributing to this state of affairs, there is a constituency of scholars that addresses the globalization of the Indian economy from a neoliberal perspective and renders the problem of feticide and the concerns of India's industrialization as independent issues (see Arora, 1996). From these perspectives, the liberalization of the Indian economy should be allowed to run its course as the "natural" path toward progress and prosperity, whereas government's law-and-order related measures should be the key to curbing those usually unrelated instances where feticide and industrialization might intersect. In other words, if feticide is to be stopped, it should be done by stopping those who partake of it, rather than blaming those who manufacture the instruments used in its perpetration.

This motley crew of elites, comprising local and global interest groups, including "knowledge-creating" interests, would view the technologization of the Indian hinterland as an unqualified benefit for its "teeming millions," and it would consider the practices of feticide and infanticide as external aberrations. That is, the problems are conceptualized as a result of preindustrial ignorance, and even of entrenched patriarchy, which development may help dispel. In such a setup, the instances of selective female feticide and infanticide might be understood in several, but very reductionist, terms—as an educational problem; a religious problem; a population control problem; and even a human resources problem, if one considers the need of multinationals for (cheaper) female labor.

Others have expressed the linkages between patriarchal and capitalistic practices in more critical terms. According to the "Forum Against Sex Determination and Pre-selection," an Indian nongovernmental organization, "Society has hitherto looked to gods and supernatural powers to realize its desire for male progeny; it has now turned to the practitioners of modern medicine" (Shiva, 1992, p. 78). This statement fully captures the irony of the linkage between GE and the sex ratio in India; the liberation that was promised by science and technology has not only been belied, but technology has helped turn patriarchy into a finer art. The simplicity, the "elegance," and the accuracy of sex determination techniques are only one side of the story. More difficult to pin down is the sense of legitimacy they bring to the process. These instruments are not merely instruments of feticide; they also detect gallstones, help save lives, and ride a promise of development and emancipation through foreign direct investment. In short, they offer an invitation to a global collectivity and a threat of inevitability, implying that those outside the ambit of this imagined collectivity are outsiders forever.

For this promise to be accepted, the linkage between technology and patriarchal practices needs to be suppressed. This suppression is carried out in a variety of different ways. The mystification of technology helps construct a discourse of emancipation around the issue. For example, when viewed in terms defined by Western liberal tradition, these technologies may be theorized as bringing long-awaited and delayed reproductive freedom to women. Social arguments cast the issue in the context of family-planning targets for the nation, meaning, for instance, that reproductive freedom may lead to solving the population problem. Finally, the discourse of eliminating birth disabilities, in that the use of ultrasonography to detect fetal abnormalities ensures a "healthy output" of babies, casts the mother in the role of a mere carrier of the fetus and subjects the process of birth to the rhetoric of quality control (Arora, 1996).

This rhetoric, however, has not gone uncontested. Several feminist theorists level strong critiques against reproductive technologies as a means of medicalizing pregnancy, technologizing the body, and being a microcosm of repressive transnational practices, politics. and policies (Ginsberg & Rapp, 1995; Haraway, 1997). Viewed through the lens of such a critique, one may term the use of ultrasound imaging in perpetrating female feticide as a classic case of the manner in which state, corporate, and patriarchal powers intersect in effacing the centrality of women to reproduction, even in those aspects that affect female bodies directly.

Debates on the relationship between technology and women's bodies continue to be fought frequently. Yet in presenting these comments, we are not trying to argue which discourse is right or wrong: the neoliberal argument of technological rationality, or the feminist critiques. Rather, it is our argument that using imaging as a reproductive technology has not been a silent issue, but one that appears—as our examples reiterate—to rest on very contested grounds. These contested grounds stem from the complexity of the issue, the power interests that define the nature of the problem, and the multiple disciplinary discourses that attempt to provide legitimate voices to articulate the situation.

Furthermore, despite the shaky grounds on which these arguments rest, each of these discourses presents its own understanding as if it were constructed over a seamless space of knowledge; a space without fissures, an all-inclusive voice able to speak the truth but which, paradoxically, in order to do so, must silence several subjectivities that it claims to represent. Thus, it is from this reflection that we must ask, *Would a discourse that sets store by an assumed, a priori, limitless collaboration do any better?* Put simply, can we accept the assertion that there are, indeed, no limits to cooperation when faced by the concrete existence of feticide and infanticide in the context of the growing market for portable ultrasound equipment? Very clearly, in instances such as this, the question of participative epistemologies is fraught with problems. The problems, at the end, are not due to lack of explanations; rather, they have to do with what is understood, who has to understand, and for what purposes.

In particular, can the discourse of "no limits to cooperation" theorize a space where patriarchal society, elitist self-interest, and affected subjectivities—whose bodies constitute the site of the cutting edge of the technological discourse—exist in harmony? Should we visualize an emancipatory tomorrow reminiscent of the "vivid utopias" that Bennis had visualized in 1963? Even if we were to visualize a cooperative discourse, who would be the participants in this discourse, and whose purposes would this participation serve?

For example, if we go back to the textual excerpts discussed earlier, we would notice not only their contrasting voices—often engaged in quite oppositional arguments—but also the different positions from which they are speaking. Who authorizes these voices? Who should one believe? Should one believe the Indian experts? The claims made by Smart (1993)? From the perspective of the theme of limitless cooperation, should these voices be reconciled, and turned from polyglot to symphony?

Far more important, in our estimation, is the question of the absence of voices of those women who were actually subjected to, or engaged in, feticide. What do they have to say? How would they say it? Although we could engage in endless speculation over this issue, our intention is not to provide a resolution to this matter but to point to the naiveté of participative epistemologies when we are facing the reality of a world of contested meanings.

Indeed, it is this contestation of meaning above all that renders the notion of cooperation most profoundly problematic: What subjectivities are representable in this epistemological roundtable? Whichever way we answer these questions, the representation of silences is by far a more damning problem than the incorporation of multiple voices. In other words, although we have deployed multiple voices and theories to make sense of this conundrum, it may well be those voices that have not found their way even to the fringes of these "conversations" that may have the most to say.

CAN THE SUBALTERN SPEAK? THEORIZING
SILENCES IN THE GLOBAL DISCOURSE

For any identity to participate equally and meaningfully in a comity of identities, it has to ensure that its knowledge is accorded objective validity by all other parties at the very outset of the meeting. Without such a recognition, some identities are bound to be equal and more than equal, whereas others will be perceived as less than equal, for lack of an evenly realized universality. (Radhakrishnan, 1994, p. 321)

Existing as they do at the intersection of a variety of hostile and indifferent discourses, such as patriarchy, global capitalism, corporate interests, geopolitical contingencies, and academic fetishization of theories, many contemporary subjectivities are rendered unrepresentable within the confines of available conversations. Often, they end up being marginalized by the very discourses that set out as sympathetic to them. As Foucault and Deleuze glibly argue (Foucault, 1977a, p. 219), it is no longer possible or tenable for intellectuals to theorize about "ground realities," because those groups that need voice are now fully capable of speaking for themselves. In the context of our chapter, these scholars would argue that no intellectual has a right to represent the victims of feticide except the victims themselves, for they will find their voice in their own way. Such a perspective is vigorously challenged by many postcolonial theorists, notably Gayatri Spivak (1988), who notes that those who expect all subjectivities to have their own voices are obviously speaking from a specific perspective generated in late-capitalist Western societies, which may not be very relevant to the Third World. Intellectuals who affiliate themselves with marginalized subjectivities, Spivak argues, have a duty to represent their constituents, a duty that they can never renounce with a flourish.

At the center of this debate is, mostly implicitly, the problem of authorship (e.g., Foucault, 1977a). As we become authors (experts, professionals) within the institutions of our discipline, what we can say and how we say it define our possible realm of theory. Furthermore, this function of authorship guarantees for the discipline a discursive space and a normativity that allows for the constitution of an "outside of theory," of nonknowledge, of nonauthors. In that sense, theory constitutes the author and not the other way around. Said differently, theory constitutes our selves, our subjectivities, the subject positions we can take within our universe of professional discourse. We exist because our theory does.

The conditions of authorship and theory in the field are closely related to the problem of representation. In this case, we mean not only who can represent in the field (i.e., who does theory), but more important, what are the possible representations that constitute theory, what are the possible worlds that our theories configure, and whose are those possible worlds? The problem of representation resides within the allowable textuality with which we constitute knowledge in the field. As such, the practice of representation is one, among other micropractices, with which we become subjects of/in the field: who we are, who we can be.

Yet despite the tremendous problems associated with unreflective representation, the burden of representation is not one that a Third World scholar can disown. In the context of this argument, although we understand that our very presence in this discourse implicates us as being on a certain side of the power divide, we cannot afford not to articulate the problem of representation for those subjectivities that, ironically, have been left out of our own discourse.

And although discussions within postmodernism often point at the difficulties, if not impossibility, of escaping the conventions of representation within a field, others—particularly in the areas of postcolonial and globalization theorizing—offer a diversity of contingent subject positions with which to contest conventional representations.

For example, in the specific context of contemporary India, processes of coalition building, of linking issues of oppression, and of anchoring women's issues in the sociopolitical context of local issues have been an important strategy used by women activists throughout India. Activists seeking legislative protection against the practice of feticide have sought help from, and participated in, groups that have been formed to address diverse issues that affect dispossessed peoples. These coalitions have tackled issues such as the impact of the General Agreement on Trade and Tariffs on seed prices to farmers (*Frontline,* 1994), the effects of large dams on displaced villagers (Shiva, 1988), religious laws that deny women their democratic rights (Kumar, 1986), as well as the issue of sex determination tests and their feticidal consequences (Kulkarni, 1987). Indeed, the Indian government's edict banning sex determination tests has been the direct effect of intense lobbying on behalf of women's organizations at the governmental and bureaucratic level.

Such acts of organizing have been based on dynamic and shifting notions of identity and selfhood. In a sense, these women have used the entrenched notions of womanhood and birth as weapons in their attempt to mobilize power within the patriarchal setup. In the language of theory, one could argue that their subject position has been one of "strategic essentialism," a politics that, although acknowledging the power-encoded character of all social narratives, wishes to define a space for activism. This position, in Edward Said's (1990) view, suggests that avenues for activism need to be searched for in the arsenal of the repressive practices themselves. He argues for the political necessity "of taking a stand, of 'strategically essentializing' a position from the perspective of those who were and are victimized and continue to suffer in various ways from an unequal, capitalist, patriarchal and neocolonialist world order" (Krishna, 1993, p. 389). That is, although we all may be aware that social identities of any sort are historical fictions, it is often incumbent upon people to make use of those very social formations for articulating a stance against their own oppression.

Similar views have been articulated by Spivak (1988), who makes a point about a deliberate utilization of essentialism by various subjectivities when she notes that "I would read it as a *strategic* use of positivist essentialism in a scrupulously visible political interest" (p. 13). Ironically, the purpose of such "essentialism" is precisely to go beyond it, to render one's place and position unremarkable—silent as it were—into a world where differences are cause for neither celebration nor violence, but just are. Discursive figures such as Haraway's (1990) cyborgs, García-Canclini's (1990) and Nederveen Pieterse's (1994) hybrid cultures, and Moraga's (1983) theory in the flesh similarly promote the creation of other selves within theory. These and other experimental writings engage directly with the poetics and politics of representation (Clifford & Marcus, 1986) by expanding our "texts of knowledge," our theories, and, as such, help us craft other possible selves (Kondo, 1993) and other possible modes of existence as knowledgeable beings, for us and for others.

Still, is there any space between representation and the said for a theory of silence? The argument between representation and self-presentation in and of itself affords very little space for silence, but it may afford some space for a strategic "silence as said." Although our argument does not even come remotely close to affording a voice—that is, authorship—to silenced subjectivities, it has at least pointed toward the silence through our own fissured voices. The subjectivities themselves must find, and *do* find, their own way to ensure some representation. Their concerns and, indeed, their struggles are at the local level; and their interactions are often mediated by fluid coalitions, specific political alliances, and different modes of engagement. More important, their agency enacts and reenacts forms of knowledge and organizing that reside, and probably must continue to reside, outside of Western theorization (e.g., Alexander & Mohanty, 1997).

Thus, put bluntly, any theory/voice that seeks to gloss over these untheorizable spaces (of unfixable subjects and politics; of the "now you see it/now you don't" variety) of fundamental difference (with Western a priori notions of knowledge and the knowledgeable) is bound to remain trapped in its inability to produce a participative epistemology. Such is the challenge that any theory of global cooperation must withstand now, accepting that there are, indeed, limits to what they can address as global and to what they can expect as cooperation. Thus, the subaltern may or may not be able to speak, but is the West (knowledgeable enough to be) even capable of listening?

NOTE

1. Bennis used the term "men of knowledge" instead of "theorists."

13

FROM A DOMINANT VOICE TOWARD MULTIVOICED COOPERATION

Mediating Metaphors for Global Change

RENÉ BOUWEN

CHRIS STEYAERT

Dans n'importe quelle langue les hommes peuvent retrouver l'esprit, le souffle, le parfum, les traces du polylinguisme originel.[1]

Eco (1994)

More than a billion people live in inconsolable poverty and more than half a billion people go hungry every day. More than one hundred and twenty million people are formally unemployed. A large group of young people have no hope for societal integration through paid labor. More and more people, especially women, are increasingly confronted with vulnerability, isolation, marginalization, violence and uncertainty.

These data are not reported in a political pamphlet; they are part of the General Declaration approved by heads of state and prime ministers at the social summit in Copenhagen in March 1995. Remarkable achievements are also mentioned, such as economic growth in some countries, a general increase of life expectation, an increase in literacy, a decrease in child death, and more pluralism and democratization. But the formal engagement of country officials and the availability of financial means still have to be orchestrated and approved. There is no agreement expressed about the general influences driving the current situation. Economic globalization, escaping the control and steering capabilities of national and international authorities, is not directly linked to the existing problems. The General Declaration nevertheless formulates the principles and purposes of sustainable social development on a global scale in 10 engagements, signed by the leaders of a majority of governments.

Hence, there seems to be a growing general awareness of the inter-relatedness of the existing problems and challenges on a global scale. The increased interdependence of different actors on more and more domains of international social and economic life is being recognized, although the ideas about the direction to take within this situation differ a lot. In light of this growing awareness, organizational sciences also have to make a contribution to further the possibilities of understanding and intervention. Global issues have been formulated on a macro scale, and international relations and economic theories have been dealing with them for many years. In this chapter, we want to use insights from a micro and a meso level (e.g., interpersonal relationships, small groups and organizations) to shed some light on these global issues. In a research forum of the *Academy of Management Journal,* Smith, Carroll, and Ashford (1995) advocate a merger of levels of analysis and disciplines to deepen the understanding of processes of cooperation. To understand global issues, it is recommended that institutional, legal, and economic thinking be complemented by concepts about how interactions among parties are conceived on organizational and interpersonal levels. By doing this, organizational understanding is then moving toward less well-known territories. But we hope to suggest some ideas about how align-ment among parties and domain issues can be phrased and enacted. This seems particularly useful because there is always an organizational, direct, face-to-face moment emerging when parties start to deal with these global issues, be it in consultation and decision-making contexts or in implementation efforts in the field. These organizational moments probably can also be enlightened by making explicit how actors frame and phrase these issues and organize their talking and acting around them. Organizational theory from a social constructionist perspective has recently documented the process of dialogues among parties in contexts of change, innovation, and entrepreneurship (see Steyaert, 1995). We will emphasize language aspects that emerge in those organizational events by looking for metaphors that mediate organizing processes of global change.

First, we will try to capture the main challenges of globalization in relation to developmental, cultural, and ecological issues. These issues will be reformulated in organizational terms as a question of coupling and decoupling part-whole relationships. Second, dominant frames of aligning global issues will be explored and commented on; competition, by far the dominant frame of interaction, is often complemented by a language of cooperation, but the limits of competition will be sketched using the report of the Club of Lisbon. Third, alternative metaphors for interaction in a global context will be formulated and their potential for multivoiced cooperation explored. We will end with an attempt to formulate organizing principles and forms for understanding and enacting global change projects.

GLOBAL ORGANIZING VERSUS LOCAL DEVELOPMENT: CHALLENGES AND OPPORTUNITIES

Global Development on a Path Too Narrow

During the past decade, it became commonplace to talk about societal development in global terms. More and more domains of our society—economic as well as cultural, ecological, or political—are dealing with their core issues on a global scale. The development of technologies for communication and mobility contributed a lot to a more explicit formulation of societal issues in global terms, although these problems are not new.

The interrelationship of social groups, different cultures, and nations has been a pervasive issue as long as human history unfolds. The story of humankind is a history of how groups of different interests and power manage to live together or try to threaten each others' existence. The grand narratives and the important sagas of civilizations, from the Egyptians to the present, have stories to tell about the projects those people imagined to develop toward absolute hegemony or human brotherhood. One can trace a line from the Tower of Babel to the most recent meeting of the United Nations general assembly to picture the efforts of people to develop a global civil society. In the meantime, a wide variety of metaphors have been imagined or tested to "regulate" global relationships: from hegemony and slavery over colonization and worldwide power coalitions to the threat of a global nuclear disaster after another world war. So our collective memory is still full of images about histories of global relationships, most of them unequally satisfying to the different parties involved. This collective memory can teach us important lessons about viable, but most of the time about unviable, metaphors for a global community. Old habits have very deep roots, and old, dramatic models such as deadly competition or absolute hegemony are still pervasive in the strategic thinking of very powerful, so-called advanced institutions of our time.

Although these are certainly not new issues, the answers to be given are pressing for more urgency because the interdependencies became so pervasive that joint survival is directly at stake. Our capabilities to relate to each other using technological means have influenced the level of interdependencies in a dramatic way. There is a strange paradox in technological development. Aimed at creating more independence and mastery over the inconveniences of life, these technologies also extended human interdependencies toward the domains of global physical survival. Technologies reinforced the dominant thinking patterns and the main interaction patterns of our times. The conquest for the creation of wealth, which is the prevailing pattern for societal interaction, got a forceful fuel resource and is spreading worldwide.

Global development is very often a synonym for worldwide fierce economic competition. Management thinking and also organizational thinking, following the publications of the Academy of Management, are today still dominated by a win-lose strategy that is based on competition (Porter, 1985). Gaining competitive advantage is the ultimate success of the professional manager (Lawler, 1992; Pfeffer, 1994). The manager's ultimate task is to create the proper return on investment, there can be no doubt about this. Scientific thinking is documenting and advocating this approach as the only possible and meaningful approach. Since the crumbling of the Berlin Wall, there is now no thinkable alternative to the measurement of effectiveness than the application of the rules of high-level competition on a free market. Global competition is the name of the game and will deliver us the fruits of the only thinkable development, that is, worldwide economic progress through open competition. In management literature, global thinking is mainly documented as global market thinking. International management and even intercultural management are conceived mainly as easing the commercial transactions on a global scale, applying very consistently the rules of free-market exchange as they are developed in Western societies and negotiated as worldwide standards for human interactions. There are international organizations with other dominant logics, of course, but on the public international scene, the general rules are set by the commonly agreed-upon rules of institutions such as the World Bank, the International Monetary Fund, and the World Trade Organization. There is even a tendency among nongovernmental organizations (NGOs) to move toward a so-called no-nonsense development approach.

Projects that can lead to economic profitability are supported, whereas other projects have strong difficulties getting financial or technological support.

This is what we would like to call a global development launched on a path much too narrow. The dominant interaction metaphor of global open competition is only one metaphor to shape global exchanges. Having seen the dramatic inequalities that are the result of these interactions, we want to create some space here for additional thinking and imagining regarding other metaphors for global interrelationships.

Three Domains of Global Tensions and Opportunities

The globalization of societal problems, and mainly the global economic competition, puts severe constraints on the interrelationships among social groups of stakeholders. In general, one can distinguish three domains in which these globalization stresses are expressed: the North-South relationship between more developed and developing countries, ethnic issues within and between multicultural settings, and environmental issues from an ecological perspective. These domains are very much interrelated and can be considered as the economic, cultural, and ecological aspects of global developments. We want to develop an organizational perspective for a contribution to these issues. Therefore, it can be useful to look into these diverse situations to discover what the domains have in common organizationally. In each of these three domains, the organizational task concerns a part-whole relationship. Thinking in terms of a relational algorithm can help to conceptualize this (Weick, 1979).

In circles of NGOs working with problems related to developing countries, especially in our own country, Belgium, there is a feeling of discouragement after recent tragedies in some countries, mainly in Africa. After the openly exploitive and patriarchal relationship during colonialism, the humanitarian relationship of aid and support actions was introduced. In some places, the "no aid but trade" relationship was installed in an effort to neutralize or objectify the mutual interdependencies. These efforts also did not lead to the expected outcomes. We are now in a phase of rethinking the relationship, and perhaps an organizational-relational perspective can help find a new way to redefine the interdependencies.

Especially since the end of the cold war, there is also a growing ethnic awareness and rivalry. Multicultural settings in the big cosmopolitan cities are under enormous ethnic strains. In eastern Europe, the ethnic sensitivities seem to replace the social-economic sensitivities and play a key role in expressing self-value and social identity. Anthropologists speak about the "creation" of ethnicity (Roosens, 1989) to describe this new awareness of ethnicity. It is as if the grand theories of social class struggle are turned into old images, going back to old collective memories. The organizational-relational question is also important here. How can different parts relate to each other and be self-confident? Can organizational thinking contribute to this history-old issue, now that the interdependencies are also expressed in concrete organizational situations, where collaboration is needed for survival?

Ecological problems have been considered mainly as a domain to be covered by the physical and biological sciences. Pollution of water, air, and soil; the threat on several forms of life; and the disruption of ecological systems have been broadly and evidently illustrated. These scientific perspectives are certainly a core aspect of the problem definition. It is there that the symptoms are identified and that the "evidence" is documented. But is not the core issue the fragmentation in the gathering and application of knowledge, especially in the so-called objective scientific research and development? In isolated domains of physical and biological research, there has been an enormous expansion of detailed and fragmented knowledge that was often gathered with the expectation of direct, utilitarian use, even before the consequences of broader application could be tested. Here, the organizational dimension of the knowledge gathering and disseminating process comes into play. The organizing principle in research and application has been specificity and fragmentation. Here again, we see the part-whole relationship problem. From detailed analysis, knowledge could be constructed and then further applied, and the whole was assumed to be the sum of the details. Scientific domains are more and more specialized and fragmented, and the whole picture is lost out of sight. Organizational thinking can contribute to the understanding of the implicit and explicit organization of knowledge creation and knowledge dissemination processes. Beyond the specialization-cumulation metaphor, we are challenged to imagine other metaphors and forms of organizing research processes.

The Challenge to Rethink Part-Whole Organizing Relationships

When ecology is considered in a broad sense, then the cultural, social, and economic global issues can be thought of as perspectives of a global social ecosystem. The three domains that we described then become very much connected. This connectedness challenges our way of thinking and acting about part-whole relationships in these social ecosystems. In this chapter, we want to take up this challenge to develop organizational-relational theory and practice, which can help to overcome the fragmentation of our current thinking. Thinking is distinguishing and relating elements and parties involved. By the way we think, we create a relational network between the elements and the stakeholders involved in the process. Therefore, we consider it a vital question for the organizational sciences to reflect on the organizing patterns of our thinking activities in science and technology and the emerging relational-organizational forms and processes.

For the inspiration of such an organizational approach of global organizing, we want to draw on our experience with research in the domain of innovation and entrepreneurship in small enterprises and projects in larger organizations. We documented how innovation and entrepreneurship can be considered a dialogue among different action logics. It is the quality of the interaction process between the logics and parties involved that shapes the viability of new endeavors (Bouwen, Devisch, & Steyaert, 1992). Different patterns or forms of dialogue among the parties can be distinguished, and a confrontational learning approach can be characterized as the most promising dialogue form for creating viable new projects (Bouwen & Fry, 1991). Also, in the creation of new enterprises, the quality of interaction processes among the parties about the inputs from different action logics makes development of new ventures understandable (Bouwen & Steyaert, 1990). In particular, the dialogue processes, which allow for a simultaneous development of different voices, have been pointed out as crucial for understanding the perpetuation of the creative potential of high-tech firms (Steyaert, 1995).

Organizing for innovation can be considered from a social constructionist perspective as a meaning creation process (Bouwen et al., 1992). Meaning is constructed by building relationships around vital topics between the parties involved. Meaning making drives the organization-in-the-making. By unraveling the interaction and language processes, parties can get reflective insight in the dynamics of the construction. Later, we will document the importance of language in the process of meaning making. Meaning making in emerging organizational contexts is a play of working through dilemmas. Old and new, past and present, or present and future offer themselves as fields of tensions for making new meaning out of opposing or paradoxical forces. The organizing processes around global issues will be discussed for their relational qualities, the shaping of the language games, and the bridging of dilemmatic forces.

COMPETITION VERSUS COOPERATION AS
DOMINANT FRAMES OF ALIGNMENT

Competition as the Dominant Frame of Interaction

There seems to be an implicit agreement in the actual thinking about organizing that some form of competition is always necessary for effective and efficient performance. In the management literature, it is mainly since Porter (1985) launched the concept of competitive advantage that most introductions of articles and books start with referring to the contribution toward this competitive advantage in order to legitimize theories as well as proposals for practice. Even in the domain of human resource management, the reference to the contribution for enhancing competitive advantage is the rationale for programs of change, development, or improvement. Illustrations can be given from a variety of domains in social life, from the school system for elementary school children to later professional life, marked by stress and a career race. This chapter is not the place to document this position further; we just want to point out how widespread and pervasive the frame of competition is in leading the control of performance on all levels in our society. Pervasive competition in global problems creates local symptoms. Our way of organizing "here" has effects on our way of organizing "there," in other social and ethnic groups and in other spheres of activity. There is very little room to question the generally accepted theory of action, that pressure for performance can be steered only by competition. Nevertheless, there is emerging evidence that lasting improvements and sustainable development can be obtained only in environments where open testing and exchanging of ideas, free of direct threat, are possible.

The subject of the symposium "No Limits to Cooperation," which is a core idea in this book as well, is quite in contrast with the dominant way of organizing for high performance, which is advocated in the current management literature. "No limits to competition" seems to be a better descriptive phrase for actual thinking and practice. Often, the implicit competitive tone of large parts of the literature, communications in mass media, and even informal talk is not recognized. The war-and-conquest metaphor is very dominant and often not recognized by those using it (Lakoff & Johnson, 1980). Therefore, we want to address some underlying meanings in the use of concepts and metaphors to enhance the possibility of a more deliberate and documented choice. Then, it remains to be seen whether informed subjects find more energy in metaphors for appreciation and joint involvement than in metaphors for hegemony and depreciation of others.

Framing Cooperation at the Service of Competition

There seems to be no contradiction for many authors in combining cooperation and competition for the same purpose, namely, enhancing competition. "Collaborating to compete" is the general theory of action (Bleeke & Emst, 1993). It is also the overall tone of the research forum on cooperation in the *Academy of Management Journal* (Smith et al., 1995). The explicit recognition is that intra- and interorganizational cooperation is highly necessary and fundamental to management success in today's complex business world. Doing business is still widely covered by the war metaphor, and is this not a strange metaphor to promote cooperation? Management thinking seems to be caught in short-term and adversarial thinking. The win-lose paradigm is clearly dominant. But we will have to deal with the losing party, unless one can turn away from them in some way. But what, then, is the implication for the global interdependency? Our interconnectedness, through all communication and mobility technology, puts us straight away in direct contact with the losers. Even President Bush could not afford the final losses of his opponent in Baghdad during the Gulf War because of his growing concern about how to deal with the losing party.

How can we bind cooperation within a larger competitive frame? Theories about dominant power coalitions help to underscore this thinking (Kotter, 1979). But the dominant paradigm is still competition, even after social psychologists and industrial economists could document from game theory that, in the long term, it is cooperation that is lasting (Axelrod, 1984). There seems to be a governing dominant paradigm of competition that is still pervading the minds of managers and the writing of researchers. The concept of trust is nevertheless emerging as a researchable subject (Smith et al., 1995) and is treated as a variable in empirical research. Besides transaction cost considerations, firms seem to build on trust relationships (Gulati, 1995). Repeated contacts over a long period of time are characteristic for a trust relationship. It is difficult to consider trust as a variable that can be influenced from the outside. A positivist approach tries to identify controllable variables and needs strong evidence before a research conclusion can be turned into advice for practice. The special case for trust is that it is the outcome of a

continuously ongoing relationship that is essentially mutual and, by definition, not controllable from one perspective. A relational view is needed here
to conceptualize our thinking on trust relationships.

Limits to Competition (Club of Lisbon)

Also from within the field of macroeconomic analysis, voices are being
heard that put the dominant paradigm of competition in a new perspective.
Under the chairmanship of Riccardo Petrella, director of the technology
research programs of the European Union, a group of 17 distinguished
scholars, politicians, and businesspeople—called the Club of Lisbon to indicate the parallel with the efforts of the Club of Rome on ecological issues—
recently published their report *Limits to Competition* (Petrella, 1994). This
report is an in-depth analysis of the consequences of a generalized worldwide
competition. The Club of Lisbon states that global competition is no longer a
means but has become a goal in itself. This opens a perspective on a total and
global economic war with disastrous outcomes. They introduce the concept
of triadization to describe the process of integration through alliances and
extreme competition among the three dominant global actors: Europe, the
United States, and Japan, together with the new Southeast Asian dragons.
These three economic players will become more and more uncoupled from
the rest of the globe, and they can organize among themselves the distribution
of power and wealth. Petrella describes different scenarios for the future.
There can be fierce competition among the big three, followed by fragmentation and open war for survival. They can work toward a "pax triadica" among
the three key players and exclude the rest of the world. There is also a
possibility for regulated integration between the industrialized world and the
developing world. The Club of Lisbon sees the latter scenario as the most
desirable one, although they express a certain pessimism about it. To implement this scenario, they propose four global contracts: a contract about the
satisfaction of basic needs, a cultural contract, a democratic contract, and a
contract for the earth.

The Club of Lisbon's report challenges the myth of sacred competition
in the free market. The Club concludes that the world does not function
according to the assumptions of economists about a free market among equal
partners. This equality is never realized, and the existing interaction patterns
are the result of negotiated relationships based on the assets and power bases
of the different parties involved. Therefore, it is the players themselves who

determine how they shape the interrelationships. It is important to reflect on the language we use to do this negotiation task. The prevailing image has been and is still the free market idea and open competition. The core issue is that the play is not among equal partners but among partners who differ along very different lines of qualities and characteristics. A rational economic model in the language of some parties in the global play may not suffice to organize the global interaction and should be replaced by new metaphors that allow all, or as many players as possible, to join in the "play."

From a Dominant Voice to Multivoicedness

The dominant voice that is being heard in the exchanges based on the rules of competition is the voice of rational economic thought and positivistic, scientific research and development. The deductive, problem-solving mode of the exact sciences penetrated more and more the commonsense knowledge of larger groups of people in our Western society. The empirical language of facts and figures became more and more the shared language of large groups of people. They are educated in rational thinking and making judgments based on observable facts. The voice of rational technological thought and economic reasoning is heard in all domains of social life. Education, as well as free time and cultural activities, see the functioning of mass media and the growing influence of the technological base to regulate activities as planned and managed following the rational-economic mode. It is common sense and a sign of good management to always refer to the logical and economic bases for making and evaluating transactions. We want to explore further in this chapter whether the identification of the dominant versus the suppressed voices in social interaction can help us to understand better the global issues under consideration here.

We want to look into the characteristics of the dialogues going on in the different domains of global change. In developing countries, we can possibly identify how technological thinking is overpowering traditional and local voices. In ecological contexts, some voices probably have been excluded, and in intercultural contexts, even the natural languages of many groups of people are being excluded from the discussion. These different domains are equally characterized by the phenomenon of "single voicedness." To solve problems in, for example, developing countries, we can relate this issue to our way of thinking here. Global issues therefore have to be questioned here. *How are we framing issues here with a dominant voice in such a way that some other voices can no longer be heard?* This question can be reformulated in a more appreciative way: How can we frame global change so that all voices from different and unequal positions can be heard in an assembly with equivalent seats? How can we conceive a play in which the multiple voices can have a fully valid part in the dialogue instead of engaging once more in a classic performance through protagonists, antagonists, and chorus?

In the next section, we want to explore new and old possibilities for living together oriented in a multivoiced direction. Four metaphors will be explored for their potential for multivoicedness and how they add to the organization of global change. These metaphors are global change as "building the Tower of Babel," as "dialogical imagination," as a "polyphonic chorus," and as a "strangers' meeting."

METAPHORS FOR MULTIVOICED LIVING TOGETHER

Global Organizing: Building the Tower of Babel?

The story of the Tower of Babel from Genesis has a common interpretation in our collective mind as the first defeat of mankind to cope with a plurality of languages. Ever since the building of this divine construction ended in a Babylonian confusion of tongues, polylingualism was seen as problematic and to be prevented. In his book *La Recherche de la Langue Parfaite dans la Culture Européenne,* Umberto Eco (1994) retraces the search for a universal language throughout European literature (from Dante to d'Alembert, from the Kabbalah to artificial intelligence, from hieroglyphics to Esperanto) and tries to show the implications of this search for how Europe can cope today with its natural polyglot situation. In Eco's (re)search, the story of The Tower of Babel plays a prominent part. Historically, it is seen as the symbol of the *confusio linguarum,* of the transition of a universal language (as used by Adam) to a melting pot of languages. After Babel, the world was doomed to live with linguistic confusion and misunderstanding. Eco questions this interpretation of the Babel story: "Pourquoi interpréter la confusion comme un malheur?" (p. 24).[2] He tries to show that the solution to this confusion is not to find a universal language but to recognize an original polylingualism. The multiplication of languages is socially positive instead of destructive and conflictual. For finding an alternative evaluation, Eco (1994, p. 395) refers to another Biblical story that gives an alternative hope, namely, the apostles on Whitsuntide whose words could be understood by all cultures present. The question here is whether this was a case of one language understandable by everyone (glossolalie) or a case of simultaneous translation and multiple languages spoken by the apostles (polyglottism), as if the tongues of fire represented a mixture of languages. "Dans le second cas [polyglottism], il leur aurait été accordé la grâce de retrouver en Babel non pas le signe d'une défaite et une blessure à guérir à tout prix, mais la clé d'une nouvelle alliance et d'une nouvelle concorde" (Eco, 1994, p. 396).[3] Building the Tower of Babel is then an invitation to construe our world as a multiplicity of worlds. Development lies not in the reduction of languages; real, universal communication is a play of multiple languages that can interact through poly-formed organizing processes.

Because every language represents a world on itself, the care of our world can be approached through the care of languages. Because people agree on the preservation and protection of the ecology, a similar agreement is needed for languages (Ivanov, quoted by Eco, 1994, p. 382). "No language to waste"—that is the polyphonic cry that can ground every global development or cultural project. Solidarity from the perspective of languages means that every language, no matter how few people speak it, can be accepted as a possible world to nurture. However, the implications of a multilingual world community for language learning and translation are complex and require an interdisciplinary, grounded organizational answer (Steyaert & Janssens, 1997). Although this issue goes beyond the scope of this chapter, we want to focus on one aspect concerning translation and language learning. Steyaert and Janssens distinguish between two models of translation and language learning—instrumental and constructionist—that capture both interpretations of the Babel story. The first model, in which the source text is dominant, presumes a universal language that can guide correct translation from one language to another. Derrida (1987) brings us the link to Babel: "La traduc-tion, le désir de traduction n'est pas pensable sans cette correspondence avec une pensée de Dieu" (p. 217).[4] The second model, in which the target text is central, does not assume a metalanguage. Steyaert and Janssens suggest thinking of translation (and language learning) as a trialectical activity, where the transition between two languages requires a third language. This third language is a transition zone in which differences and specificities of each language can be explored and compared. One no longer follows a dualistic logic (true-false) but a principle of multivalence: The existence of multiple languages mirrors the validity of multiple truths, whereas translation can be a generative force to continue the development of a polyglot-based universal communication. Here, it becomes also clear that the myth of Babel mirrors our epistemological models. Characteristic of scientific and technological language is that only generalizable knowledge gets the status of validity. One assumes a process of accumulation of knowledge that is linear, logical, and unidirectional and that can be heaped on the mountain of science. This attempt for general and universally valid knowledge resembles the construction of a one-way world, as if the world could be seen as a village where everyone knows everyone else. From a social constructionist perspective, knowledge is generated through the interaction among all parties involved. Valid knowledge is not a priori useable but becomes useful in a concrete situation for different groups because it becomes locally reinvested or rediscovered.

In many ways, the search for a global change program can be compared to the search for a universal language and can be seen as an attempt to rebuild the Tower of Babel. At the same time, it is utopian and in danger of failure and becoming Babylonic, *Pure Babble.* Eco's second interpretation gives us the idea of avoiding this tower of babble and making the transition of a perfect babble of tongues toward a polyglot dialogue on "the plural of global." So, if the enterprise of the Tower of Babel is the start of our social, political, and scientific history, projects of global change, such as the Cleveland conference, should inscribe themselves in this reinterpretation. This means that global change is not approached in globalizing ways but as a construction of multiple worlds through local languages.[5]

This first metaphor on global change as a multivoiced initiative stresses in particular the interplay between national languages, whereas the next metaphor will go beyond this idea by emphasizing the interplay of social languages (of which national language is only one example). For this, we will turn now to the work of the late Mikhail Bakhtin, a Russian literary scholar who introduced the notion of multivoicedness. His vision of meaning and dialogue, initially used for analysis of literary texts (such as Dostoevsky and Rabelais), gets more and more attention in psychology (Gergen, 1994; Wertsch, 1991) and will be inscribed here in organizational theories of international communication and collaboration. From the first to the second metaphor implies also a transition from a semiotic to a literary form of text analysis.

Global Change: A Matter of Dialogical Imagination?

We want to look now to dialogue as a metaphor for global change. The idea is that development for global change does not require so much a transfer of knowledge from one part of the globe to another as it does the investment in different types of global dialogues that can create new knowledge contextualized in multiple sites. This requires investments in dialogues that can initiate localized creativity and imagination and foster new meanings and texts. The issue then becomes, In what ways can such dialogues be written? Although dialogue has received much attention in organizational theory in the context of communication and collaboration, we will turn to a literary model of dialogue as it is approached by Bakhtin. The construction of realities for Bakhtin is, in essence, dialogic, because every "utterance[6] is filled with dialogical overtones" (Bakhtin, 1986, p. 102; see also Wertsch, 1991, p. 54). It is through dialogue that space for new realities is created, as illustrated by one of his book titles, *The Dialogic Imagination*. New possibilities lie in the generative force of the dialogue, its quality, and its effects on the relationships among the different parties involved. Intercultural cooperation and understanding à la Bakhtin is essentially dialogic, with the creation and continuation of new realities as a result. The following quote can be illustrative for how understanding is linked to open dialogue:

> To understand another person's utterance means to orient oneself with respect to it, to find the proper place for it in the context. For each word of the utterance that we are in process of understanding, we, as it were, lay down a set of our own answering words. The greater their number and weight, the deeper and more substantial our understanding will be. Any true understanding is dialogic in nature. Understanding is to utterance as one line of a dialogue is to the next. (Wertsch, 1991, p. 54)[7]

We will now explore more in depth how Bakhtin approaches dialogue in relation to understanding meaning (creation).

Four principles can teach us how to engage in such a dialogue oriented to multivoiced meaning creation (Wertsch, 1991): (a) from literal meaning toward addressed meaning, (b) from isolated toward socioculturally situated meaning, (c) from a univocal toward a dialogic creation of text, and (d) from an authoritative toward an internally persuasive discourse. The first principle says that a priori meanings of words cannot guide us in conceiving a theory of meaning and understanding. It is not a word that is the unity of communication but the utterance, as it can be found in between other utterances, in the course of a dialogue or a text. Meaning comes during and not before the conversation.[8] Furthermore, an utterance gets a meaning because it is addressed, whereas a priori meanings suggest that there is no need for a reader and listener who answer by writing and talking back. Without an address, an utterance can never arrive. It is this principle of addressivity that makes every utterance imply at least two voices and places the dialogic dimension central in the creation of meaning.

There is no a priori meaning to be given to the word *global*: Every idea of global change will be filled with dialogic overtones that should be listened to and taken into account. In more general terms, the outlook and meaning of a specific project on global change should be seen as an addressed project in which listeners are talking back and creating their own meanings. As a consequence, several meanings of the project will emerge, and this is often explained as "a lack of understanding" and as "a disagreement." In Bakhtinian terms, this difference is a natural consequence of the double-voicedness of every utterance, and, importantly, it is this difference that creates continuity in the interaction between parties. For instance, at *Médicins sans Frontières* (MSF), the principle of "neutrality" is primordial for choosing partners and engaging in partnerships. However, there cannot be a single conception of neutrality; rather, this will change in the function of the addressees, be it an AIDS project for children in Thailand or a refugee camp in Somalia.

The second principle builds further on the first one and states that meanings are neither atomistic nor individually bound, but are socioculturally situated.[9] Bakhtin rejected the idea that isolated individuals create meaning. People cannot be cut off from their social context. Monologues are the expression of highly individualized inspiration. Every utterance refers to a rich and complex social background:

> For any individual consciousness living in it, language is not an abstract system of normative forms but rather a concrete heteroglot conception of the world. All words have the "taste" of a profession, a genre, a tendency, a party, a particular work, a particular person, a generation, an age group, the day and hour. Each word tastes of the context and contexts in which it has lived its socially charged life (Bakhtin, 1981, p. 293).

On the question of who is doing the talking, Bakhtin will not answer that it is the individual person, but with the person talking, other people, groups, parties, and backgrounds are taking part in the conversation.

The implication for our conceptions on global change is fundamental. The communication between people in multivalence groups is not so much an interindividual exchange, but every person is also a spokesperson through which other voices can be heard. Every conversation on global change is then an exchange between several social languages and cultural contexts. Becoming aware of the sociocultural world that we re-present in our suggestions on globalization then becomes an important task. Every utterance on what "global" means will refer to a certain local reality and will be socioculturally traced. Because there is no utterance that can have a global taste—after all, what would this mean?—the challenge is then to develop a multivoiced view on globality that tastes of the multiplicity of social communities. Such a multiplicity requires a different kind of view on dialogue and relations, which we will describe in Principles 3 and 4, respectively.

The third principle brings us to the core of the meaning of "dialogic" and how it is linked to creative interaction. Bakhtin distinguishes between a univocal and a dialogic function of text and talk. The first function concerns the transmission of information and ideas and gives communication an instrumental function. This univocal is well-known in organization theory and organizational behavior because it fits the sender/receiver model of communication. The assumption is that the sender, writer, or speaker can transmit his or her message intact so that the receiver can decode it correctly. The understanding of sender and receiver are equal. Communication is unidirectional here and involves one single voice. The dialogue is monologue. The dialogue function presumes a different dynamic in human communication and interaction. Communication is an active and dynamic process in which multiple voices are active simultaneously. Meaning is not created outside the interaction as something that can be packed up, sent, and later unpacked, and remain untouched during the transport. The aim of communication is not to conserve, but to create meanings. Receivers are active answerers, adding words and meanings, not out of the blue but in the stream of the speech communication, in between past and future utterance. As a consequence, a heterogeneity of meanings is constantly created. Neither function excludes the other. There is my message, information, view, proposal, which I can send as clearly as possible, but this brings new messages, as if other listeners can answer with their voices. We do not live only to inform each other but also to touch, reach, meet, influence, and awaken each other. Information processing does not count even half for true life, because it is always in tension with the creative replay of the listeners and with whatever new words and meanings come in through their consciousness and desire. The fourth principle considers the conditions in which other voices can come.

In our view, this dialogic function looks constructive for the discussion on global change. In this respect, global change can become a matter of "dialogic imagination." However, many times, we see a kind of sender-receiver model used in developmental projects, as if it is only a matter of transfer of (Western) knowledge, technology, aid, and so on. The dialogic function would suggest a meeting in which both parties explore each other, and themselves even more, in a transition zone in which new meanings, knowledge, and projects can be created. Developmental and cultural programs are never the development or cultural expression of one group but are the result of mutual development and performance.[10]

The fourth principle describes the quality of relations that can emerge in univocal or multivoiced texts. These relational differences try to explain why there are differences in how voices can "meet" each other. Who has the authority for starting this interplay among voices? Bakhtin discusses the difference between "authoritative" and "internally persuasive" discourse. Within authoritative discourse, the contact with other interlocutors, with other voices, gives no additional meaning creation. The meeting of voices is empty, without reply. There is no space to go further, "no play with its borders, no gradual and flexible transitions, no spontaneously creative stylizing variants on it" (Bakhtin, 1981, p. 343). Openness is characteristic for an internally persuasive discourse:

> The internally persuasive word is half-ours, and half-someone else's; it allows dialogic interanimation. . . . Its creativity and productiveness consist precisely in the fact that such a word awakens new and independent words, that it organizes masses of our words from within, and does not remain in an isolated and static condition. The semantic structure of an internally persuasive discourse is not finite, it is open; in each next contexts that dialogize it, this discourse is able to reveal ever new ways to mean. (Bakhtin, 1981, pp. 345-346)

Bakhtin gives us a vision on language that seems to be central in the construction of global realities. It helps us to see that understanding between the multiple parties on every global change project cannot start from an instrumental use of language, but that language is an important key for multivoiced interaction. Furthermore, these four principles of meaning creation can guide us in our conception of organizing processes for global change. New organizing forms can embody these principles: The rejection of literal meaning asks for organizational forms that are dynamic and changing and that can embody addressed meaning creation. The idea of socioculturally situatedness implies a contextualized organizing process that can favor the interaction between multiple social languages. The dialogic function invites us to conceive the organizing process as "multiperspectivistic," whereas the internally persuasive function of discourse stresses the relational qualities between the different parties. The challenge now becomes finding a metaphor that can help us to imagine organizing forms in a more concrete way.

Global Change: The Sound of Polyphony?

There are multiple metaphors that can give us a more concrete image of how multivoiced cooperation can be conceived. Many of these metaphors refer originally to a cultural and artistic world: literature (labyrinth, library, odyssey); theatre (improvisation, tragedy); music (polyphony, jazz improvisation, orchestra). We will turn here to a metaphor from music and explore its sound for multivoiced global change. Bakhtin (1984) himself refers to polyphony in his interpretation of Dostoevsky, whose novels he calls "a plurality of independent and unmerged voices and consciousnesses, a genuine polyphony of fully valid voices" (p. 6).

Polyphony is a metaphor from the oldest musical repertoires. In the 15th and 16th centuries, when the Flemish Primitives created a furor throughout Europe with their paintings, a musical composition form was developed at the same time that was initially performed in the Low Countries stimulated by the Bourgondic court, but it later became, via Italy and France, a medium for artistic production throughout all of Europe. This new composition technique was called polyphony, which literally means "multivoicedness." Two or more independent but organically related voice parts sound against one another. Traditional compositions consist of a melodic line and an accompaniment line. In a polyphonic partiture, we find multiple melodic lines, and every line could, in theory, be performed separately. But by performing all of these lines simultaneously, the result is a rich and complex musical totality. Next to the independent horizontal lines, vertical lines emerge that also form a totality. In this way, a network of horizontal and vertical lines is created in which every voice is meaningful on its own but, at the same time, gains meaning in relation to the other voices. Characteristic, especially to Flemish polyphony, is the equivalence of all parties. (There is no soloist part and chorus part.) The different voices are created simultaneously.

What, then, is the polyphonic sound of global change? Polyphony, as an image of totality—read, globality—and being a combination of horizontality and verticality, suggests an organizing process that sustains the development of multiple (horizontal) voices instead of a dominant voice that creates the rest of the world to its own likeness. Every voice has its own melody and rhythm. But the vertical dimension suggests that these voices are neither apart nor loosely coupled, as if local regions are isolated and uncoupled. The development of one region, culture, or ethnicity is only possible via the development of another region, culture, or ethnicity. Every voice needs the other voices for its own identity. These voices are not in competition with each other, but difference and contrast between voices is necessarily required and stimulated; otherwise, the play becomes univocal. Also, Bakhtin is aware of this kind of relational autonomy: "My voice can mean, but only with others: at times in chorus, but at the best of times in a dialogue" (quoted in Wertsch, 1991, p. 68). A polyphonic performance that starts from the autonomy of every voice is built up through the interaction process from within the group. Every voice is confident in the independence of the other voices so that each voice can resound with its full potential through and against the complex web of other, simultaneously created voices. In line with this principle, polyphonic music has been performed without a director but with a chorus of independent voices, where every voice is the owner of his or her own performance and where "a maestro di cappella" is indicating the tactus from within the choir.

Approaching global change from this polyphonic metaphor asks for the awareness of a so-called voice development, or what Bakhtin calls the creation of "the speaking personality, the speaking consciousness" (Holquist & Emerson, 1981, p. 434). The main aim of global change projects asks that every voice concentrate on and own its own part, and that each is able to find and create its voice through interaction with other voices. The musical metaphor of voice gives us an indication of how such an undertaking can be precious and equivocal. Typical for a voice is its directness and its need for presence. A voice wants and needs to be directly audible, again and again. But this also makes a voice vulnerable and dependent on the tone of the day or the night. It is never the same, because a voice is always in the process of finding out what one is inventing, singing out, expressing, or extinguishing. A voice contains the world in itself and expresses this world by blowing life to words. Development for voice development is creating space so that every party learns to reveal oneself for others and oneself. This asks for travel between the known and the strange that we will try to illustrate through a fourth metaphor, which looks at global change as a strangers' meeting.

Global Change: A Strangers' Meeting?

The metaphor of polyphony suggests a relational world of harmony in which all voices are balanced and equilibrated. Our fourth metaphor wants to counterbalance this idea. Voices are not only different and asymmetric, but they can be contrasting and conflicting. The dialogic function of Bakhtin creates a critical difference between the world of the talker, writer and the world of the listener, reader. Taking the idea of difference one step further brings us on the level of "the strange." The thesis we want to develop is that the strange can be an essential part for imagining how global organizing can be conceived.

Interestingly, the strange is seen as causing both cruelty and creativity, depending on how we learn to deal with strangers. The cruel side of strangeness can be learned from another biblical story, that of Cain and Abel. Even the most familiar relationship, brotherhood, has a strange side that can have fatal consequences. Because the first murder was a fratricide, the story is the first indication of a failure to deal with difference and strangeness, ending in a world of blood and murder and blowing up all bridges. Although we are inclined to approach brotherhood and familial relationships as a harmonious unity, in this story, the conflictual dimension is a main and essential part of this relationship. It sheds another light on the many fratricides of our time. With Cain and Abel, difference entered the world, differences in identity, way of life, religion, thinking, and more important, the task of learning to deal with this difference.

However, this learning task asks for a different view on the meaning of difference. Kristeva (1991) has suggested looking at difference in another way in her book *Strangers to Ourselves,* where difference can even become a source of creativity. Learning to see the strange in our (known) selves is the place where new, unknown, and potential elements can be found. Personal development will emerge more from unknown than known fields and from taking the known as unknown. Even the most familiar has a strange side, and paradoxically, there lies the potential for change and growth.

Concerning global change, we would like to look at it more as a meeting among strangers than among old friends. This creates two opportunities. First, dealing with the other as someone different and strange creates respect for this difference in such a way that it does not have to be bridged, and there is no need to become equals. Heterogeneity can be created only if we do not walk over the other. Second, the metaphor invites us to look for the strange in ourselves and to take this part as less self-evident. It becomes clear, then, that engaging in global change elsewhere requires local change and renewing on the homefront.

ORGANIZATIONAL PRINCIPLES FOR
GLOBAL ORGANIZING: ILLUSTRATIONS

We started this text from the general observation that there is a growing awareness of the global interdependencies in our present world on economic, sociocultural, and ecological issues. In this chapter, we want to make a contribution to this global awareness from a meso-level organizational perspective. The organizational perspective is focusing on how to couple and uncouple partners, functions, and domains in joint projects. The focus is on alignment and the search is for proper ways, given the specific conditions of global development projects. A very typical characteristic of these projects is that they usually bring together very unequal partners in certain aspects, such as rich and poor, highly skilled and unskilled, majority group and minority group, rural and urban, and so on. The existing literature is more about dealing with relationships among equal partners than about relationships between unequal partners. There is a lively debate nowadays about the appropriateness of cooperation versus competition to deal with intra- and interorganizational relationships. A lot of research is being done to define the conditions and contingencies for cooperation within a broader framework of global competition.

After this problem formulation, we moved to a language analysis on how we think and talk about interdependencies. It became clear how dominant voices from specific action logics shape our talking and acting. These dominant voices enclose the actors in their language and metaphors about interrelationships among parties, especially parties with unequal positions. Multivoicedness was proposed as a way out to set free the diversity of meanings and relationships among all parties involved. Does this analysis give us an outlook on new principles, and can the new generative metaphors presented above assist us in the task of dealing with diversity in these global domain issues?

As a form of conclusion, we want to point out some general principles that can enhance understanding and enacting the organizing of global projects and global institutions. Second, we want to be more specific and suggest via an illustration how the discussion of different proposals to address a change project can be arranged along a language of competition and multivoicedness.

Organizing Principles for Understanding and Enacting Global Change Projects

We want to propose the multivoicedness metaphor to address the organizing of global projects and institutions. This metaphor gives priority to four specific characteristics of such an organizing process.

- Multivoicedness means that it is an illusion to aim for one integrative language that encompasses all of the existing diversity. Absolute integration would mean the end of the original and creative inputs. The "strange" element can be recognized, and one can recognize the strangeness in oneself.
- The idea of general knowledge principles in one global language system has to be considered as an undesirable aim. It is local knowledge through sharing experiences that delivers useable knowledge. Knowledge is always knowledge *in context*.
- In this multivoicedness, no one is taking the dominant voice. The emerging pattern of interactions among the parties is aligning the voices.
- The relational quality of the dialogue among the parties contributes to shaping the emerging outcomes.

These principles can shape the interaction among the parties involved in global development projects. They shape the patterns of knowledge gathering and sharing, the content or substantial side of the organizing processes, and the patterns of relationships (i.e., how the social-relational structure is enacted). These principles can be applied on developing country issues (e.g., technology projects in Africa), cross-cultural issues (e.g., multiethnic art), and ecological issues (e.g., waste reduction). We will illustrate each domain shortly.

Large technological projects in developing countries in Africa have often been big failures; consider a large irrigation project in a rural area. Here, the relationship between the technical experts developing and implementing the project and the local farmers is very asymmetric. On each of the aforementioned principles, there is a fault line that has to be bridged. The language of the project stems from a dominant technological, economic, and instrumental paradigm. This voice is very dominant and experienced as an outside voice. Other voices can hardly been heard. The voice from cultural coherence, the voice of co-ownership, or the voice of aesthetics and meaning can seldom be heard. The relationship is framed as an expertise-dependency relationship. The knowledge that is transferred is experienced as distant, alien, and not connected to the local context, and certainly not to the local knowledge. Political relationships are often kept hidden and out of reach of local influence. The chances for common experiences among the parties involved, which provide new ground for a shared new metaphor that can shape the future relationship, are very low.

As an interesting experiment of cross-cultural multivoicedness, we want to mention the joint production of a musical by European and African actors, singers, and dancers. The title of the play was *Harlequin in Africa*. The script of the play itself was about an African group and a European group of theater players who tried to outperform each other's creations. The actual play was a mixture of dance, music, images, and pieces of scripts from both cultural groups. The performance was very successful, and the audience could easily identify with both groups of players. This is, perhaps, an example of an activity in which the dominant language and the dominant action logic are not defined mainly from one side, like we have in most technology transfer projects. Here, a broad variety of skills, emotions, and images come into play. Besides technical skill and performance, like the whole technical arrangement of the stage, also a variety of songs, dance, and text are involved. It is a broadband kind of contact, and the dialogue—the creative giving and taking from each voice—is really going both ways.

It is easy to give examples of the organizing principles discussed in the domain of ecological global change projects. Here, the distance or disconnection is between the users and the developers of products and services, and also between different groups of developers and producers who do not know each others' competencies or discoveries. The split is in the minds of the consumers, who cannot relate the different effects to each other. How difficult is it to realize that the use of certain products is having an effect on global warming? An aware consumer, who is acting consistently, would nevertheless have an enormous effect on the solution of this problem. The specialized organization of our research, production, and distribution makes it very difficult for the consumer to support informed-choice behavior. In this sense, these ecological problems are a direct consequence of our way of organizing productive activities. And these activities are a direct consequence of the way we organize knowledge through science and research. The split is also in the minds of the scientists and between the researchers and those who apply the findings of this research. The overall social relationship is on top of this, shaped mainly by profit-making and dominant economic exchange relationships. In crucial moments of the social interaction, important voices are left out and are not being heard in our way of organizing.

Our Western way of organizing is thus violating many of the organizing principles along the metaphor of multivoicedness. Important voices are excluded from the dialogue. Some voice or voices are always and for too long the dominant voice. There is even a strong unawareness of this process of exclusion of critical or competent voices in the ongoing debate about employment, ecology, and social development. Let it be repeated that our organizations here have to go through the same process of rethinking their organizing principles along a multivoiced metaphor. Our way of organizing, and first of all, our dominant way of organizing for competition, is the first lever to have an influence on the way of organizing in developing countries and in other cross-cultural settings.

Competition and Multivoicedness in the Discourse of a Global Development Project

Our way of organizing the process of knowing, as well as our way of organizing the knowledge-gathering process through scientific research in the narrow sense, shapes our writing and acting in global change projects. On a more concrete level, we can illustrate how specific interventions in the functioning of global change projects in the field follow a language of competition and/or multivoicedness. We will limit ourselves here to some illustrations in the strategy and functioning of NGOs in developing countries, based mainly on a brief field study in the Andes in Ecuador.

In their external and also their internal organizational strategies, NGOs express their mental models about development. We want to illustrate briefly how they talk in terms of aid, trade, expertise-transfer, and culture.

The discourse of *aid* was very popular in the past and still is in situations of urgency, although some aid organizations, such as MSF, also negotiate conditions of joint responsibilities. The external dependency effects are very evident here. Also, the internal relationships are characterized by a discourse of aid. Internal bureaucratization can also be a consequence. Internal and external politics (politicking) can even be a liability. During colonial times, this aid metaphor was underscored by the idea of conversion, as to a religion or culture. In some regions, this model is certainly still playing a role.

The no-aid-but-trade shift of strategy is expressed in a language of *doing trade*. This voice is, of course, very characteristic for all profit organizations that settle in developing countries. Within the rules of the market, they can contribute to the development. Inequality in terms of the relationship can make this approach detrimental for the weaker party, as could be observed so often. Local context is often not recognized, the relationship is not mutual, and the dominance of one party is even becoming more important at the end. Some NGOs are also on the way to adopting this no-nonsense development strategy. They intervene to support the local parties in imposing fair rules on the game by cooperative initiatives and other joint actions. Efforts to support small local businesses and shops also follow this line of thinking. Some NGOs act as savings-and-loan institutions under special conditions. These initiatives give the local people the chance to learn the rules and demands of a free market. It is helping them to join the dominant language for our Western world; in the short term, this may be a relief for some groups, but severe dependencies can also be the outcome.

There is a tendency for some NGOs to talk more and more in terms of *expertise-transfer.* One NGO that gives technical support in agriculture evaluates the projects they are supporting according to three criteria, in this order: economic rentability, organizational seriousness, and social relevance. This is a typical technological discourse toward sustainable development. One informant puts it this way: "What development workers need is strategic vision, management, and reflection, in this order." In this approach, the NGOs are acting as professional organizations and are responding to the organizing principles of professional bureaucracies.

In the Andes in Ecuador, the organizations of the Indian farmers are getting more and more involvement from large groups of people. They seem to talk in terms of *cultural development.* They base their interactions with the farmers on an ethnic-cultural base. The Indian culture is a strong subject for identification. In an interview with one of their representatives, Nina Pacari, who has a degree in law and is an important figurehead of the movement, she is pleading for an "integral development" concept. She calls upon the ancestral ties, the rights of land, the artisanal skills, the special knowledge of medicinal herbs, the convivial community forms, and so on as the multiple aspects of the society on which a development of broad scope has to be built. This idea of development goes far beyond economic development or transfer of technology. It is a global picture of a societal form in which all of the local voices are tuned in. The invitation she had toward the university as an institution was, "Help us to form our own university, an Indian university where the competence of the Indians and the local knowledge can be brought together and developed further." This is certainly a very different discourse that illustrates well the multivoiced principles we have been putting forward here: local knowledge, diversity, no dominant party, cultural-relational quality being more important than utilitarian use, and no absolute general knowledge.

Such ideas contrast very strongly with the concepts of large, also called integrated, development projects, conceived by national and international development organizations and NGOs. The basis is technical (an irrigation system), and it is organized on a provincial scale, with the involvement of about 30 different organizations and a large group of professional workers. The interfacing problems among the different organizations and with the local groups are enormous. Here we see one dominant technical voice that is constantly concerned about getting enough involvement from the locals. In the meantime, it is clear for all professionals that involvement is very crucial but also very difficult to obtain.

From a talk with a local anthropologist, Professor José Sanchez Varga from the University of Quito, we could learn some of the principles of organizing in traditional Indian communities: Conflict precedes consensus, integration on the local scale and fragmentation on the wider scale, and mechanisms of dissolution of power. This gives us a glimpse of the possible social resources that exist in this traditional society. Just from a conservation point of view, it would be important to preserve these cultures as expressions of the cultural variety, now that we become aware of the need for conservation of the biological variety. But conservation is possibly a discourse from a Western perspective, neglecting how this voice can influence and inspire more familiar voices.

These different discourses of organizing can also comprise some suggestions about possible roles for professionals. These roles will probably have the same mediating qualities. Knowledge transfer becomes local knowledge generation. Technical expertise becomes teaching and facilitating competence. Although it is an open question whether the role of an organizational or social facilitator has to be played in an explicit way, cultures that are very context-bounded and relational oriented do not reflect explicitly on those relational processes. They do it in ritual and ceremonial ways, and they celebrate community instead of using a reflective discourse. The relationship-building role of the organizational specialist perhaps has to be integrated in other roles, such as the participant role or the celebrating role. This needs to be studied further, but does it also then become a joint task for both cultures, here and there, to create at least a mutual understanding of what "study" means for both of us?

CONCLUSION

The main message of this chapter is that principles of organizing for global change need to have the following features: They should be relationally focused more than functionally focused, they should be multivoiced, they should be contextualized, and they should promote the development of local knowledge. When there is a strong, dominant mode of organizing that is functionally based, mainly along a technological or economic action logic, and oriented on general knowledge principles, projects of global organizing will suffer and not prosper. The transfer of general knowledge metaphor is seriously questioned, based on the principles of relational and contextual learning in organizations.

The concept of global development, meaning that there is going to be a general integration along one dominant economic action logic or metaphor, has to be reconsidered. The metaphor of global competition is not a viable concept. The same restrictions can be made on the domains of cross-cultural and ecological change.

In this chapter, we developed the metaphor of multivoicedness, or polyphony, in which all parties involved participate in their proper way, with their own voice and their own language. These voices can be unequal as well as equal in some respect. It is the common experiential basis from a Bakhtinian dialogue that creates new and alternative discourses. Creating new understandings and voices, and therefore new realities, is based on a transition from monologue toward dialogue:

> We must renounce our monologic habits so that we might come to feel at home in the new artistic sphere which Dostoevsky discovered, so that we might orient ourselves in that incomparably more complex *artistic model of the world* which he created. (Bakhtin, 1984, p. 272)

NOTES

1. "In every language, mankind can find the spirit, the breath, the perfume, the traces of an original polylinguism."
2. "Why should we interpret confusion as a misfortune?"
3. "In the second case, they would have received the grace to find in Babel not the sign of a defeat and a wound to be cured at any price, but the key of a new alliance and a new concord."
4. "Translation, the desire of translating, cannot be thought of without such a correspondence with a Divine thought."

5. A polyphonic reflex (and suggestion) would be to conceive forthcoming conferences on global change (and actually every international conference) as multilingual events. The monolinguist conception of many conferences (e.g., invitations only in English, papers and discussions in English without any facilities for translation and interpreting) puts a major limit on the multivoiced cooperation that such an initiative requires.

6. Bakhtin thought of utterance as the "real" unit of communication (Wertsch, 1991).

7. Wertsch cites from Voloshinov (1973, p. 102). The debate on the question of whether the texts of Bakhtin and Voloshinov are from one or more authors remains unresolved. We will refer here to the vision of Wertsch (1991, pp. 48-50), who discussed this issue extensively. We think one can best think of a kind of multiple authorship, by which Bakhtin has certainly made a contribution to the text with the name of Voloshinov, although it is not clear whether Bakhtin himself has actually written up (parts of) this text.

8. Remark the analogies with Wittgenstein's conception of meaning (see Krajewski, 1992; Wertsch, 1991).

9. This idea receives growing interest in psychology (see Bruner, 1990).

10. Examples in this orientation are given under Principle 4.

14

GLOBAL WOMEN LEADERS

A Dialogue With Future History

NANCY J. ADLER

As Vaclev Havel (1994), President of the Czech Republic, eloquently
states,

> There are good reasons for suggesting that the modern age has ended. Many
> things indicate that we are going through a transitional period, when it seems
> that something is on the way out and something else is painfully being born.
> It is as if something were crumbling, decaying and exhausting itself, while
> something else, still indistinct, were arising from the rubble. . . .
>   This state of affairs has its social and political consequences. The
> planetary civilization to which we all belong confronts us with global chal-
> lenges. We stand helpless before them because our civilization has essentially
> globalized only the surface of our lives. . . .
>   [Leaders] are rightly worried by the problems of finding the key to insure
> the survival of a civilization that is global and multicultural. . . . The central
> . . . task of the final years of this century, then, is the creation of a new model
> of co-existence among the various cultures, peoples, races and religious
> spheres within a single interconnected civilization. (p. A27)

Havel's appreciation of the transition that the world is now experiencing is
certainly important to each of us as human beings. "We are at a critical juncture

This chapter was adapted from an earlier managerial version by Nancy J. Adler that appeared in
International Management, 1(2), pp. 21-33.

in our history: Caught between the remnants of an industrial society with its paradoxes of progress and exploitation and the promise of a postmodern society with its emphasis on sustainability and transformation" (Bilimoria et al., 1995, pp. 71-72). The world situation challenges us to identify world leaders capable of the transnational vision, thought, and action needed to guide society into a 21st century worthy of being called human.

WHAT HAS CHANGED? ECONOMIC, POLITICAL, AND CULTURAL SPACES[1]

What has changed? Three major societal shifts outline the global challenges confronting 21st-century leaders. Historically, yet no longer true today, economic, political, and cultural spaces have always been highly overlapped. Traditionally, all three have been defined by the borders of the nation-state. Until recently, political leaders could therefore control all three domains simultaneously. Today, however, the three are no longer coincident (Kobrin, 1997; based on Kindleberger, 1975, p. 359).

Economic space has enlarged to become global. As is increasingly appreciated, economic competition transcends national borders; it encompasses the world. National borders no longer define, nor to an increasing extent even affect, the patterns and limits of economic activity.

Political space, by contrast, has remained defined by the borders of the nation-state. Because political space no longer encompasses economic space, national governments no longer control their own economies. Contrary to prior eras, political leaders are no longer capable of maintaining the economic well-being of their citizens. National leaders today can only attempt to create and maintain advantaged lifestyles for their citizens by educating and training them to attract the most interesting and well-paying jobs in the world, without regard to the nationality of the company doing the hiring (Reich, 1990, 1991). They can no longer legislate border controls to keep prosperity in and economic threat away.

Whereas economic space transcends the borders of the nation-state and political jurisdictions remain confined within national borders, the space defining cultural identity—answering the question, "Who am I?"—has shrunk to smaller, more homogeneously defined ethnic communities. Cultural space is thus increasingly synonymous with areas smaller than the nation-state. Whether it is Anglophone and Francophone Canadians, Czechs and Slovaks, or Malays and Chinese, people increasingly answer the question "Who am I?"

at a level both smaller than the nation-state and often not coincident with any particular country's national borders.

Thus, in observing major world trends, it is clear that economic space has expanded to become global, political space has remained nationally defined, and people's cultural identities have become more focused into areas generally smaller than a nation. Moreover, as the complexity, turbulence, and rates of change in the economic and political arenas increase, people worldwide appear to be retrenching into more narrowly defined cultural identities. It is therefore not surprising that Havel (1994) observed that "our civilization has essentially globalized only the surface of our lives [only our economic lives]. . . . [Leaders] are rightly worried . . . [about] the problem of finding the key to insure the survival of a civilization that is global [from an economic perspective] and multicultural [from the perspective of human identity]" (p. A27).

GLOBAL LEADERSHIP: WHO WILL
TAKE CARE OF THE WORLD?

In and of themselves, these trends do not appear problematic. They become problematic only because all of the major challenges to societal well-being today are transnational in scope, whereas the historic governance structures remain domestic. Beyond global economic competition, issues such as maintaining environmental quality, controlling population growth, and achieving peace and security are all transnational in their dynamics, impact, and potential for control. Even free speech, thanks to the Internet, has become transnational. The very nature and scope of each of these issues necessitates transnational thought, organizing, and action (Bilimoria et al., 1995). Yet "until recently in history, people have responded to global phenomena as if they were local" (Bilimoria et al., 1995, p. 72). Historically, people have failed to develop effective, transnational responses to global challenges that could predictably and positively alter the direction of global change (Bilimoria et al., 1995, p. 72).

Today's fundamental dilemma is that governments, which have had the historic mandate to provide for the welfare of their citizens, are encapsulated in increasingly obsolete domestic structures that often render them incapable of successfully addressing the very issues that most affect their citizens' social and economic well-being. By contrast, companies increasingly have the transnational structures and outlook necessary to address worldwide societal issues, but they lack the mandate to do so. This disjuncture raises the 21st century's fundamental leadership question: Who will take care of the world (Adler & Bird, 1988)? Economic leadership can no longer remain circumscribed within the narrow domain of a domestic economy nor the equally narrow domain of economics. Leaders, including business leaders, must move beyond their history of the past 500 years in which they considered "economics . . . [to be] the central issue" (Bilimoria et al., 1995, p. 74). If business is to accept the role seen for it "by its visionaries, a greater reflexivity and recall of the premises of business are crucial" (Bilimoria et al., 1995, p. 74). Leadership in the 21st century, whether economic, political, or cultural, must be inclusive in ways that were unheard of in the 20th or prior centuries. If individual countries are to remain capable of providing a high quality of life for their citizens, and if the community of nations is to remain capable of providing for the well-being of the world's population, leaders from all sectors need to begin thinking and managing very differently (see Drucker, 1992; Mitroff, 1987; Porter, 1990).

CHANGE: SHIFTING FROM THE 20TH TO THE 21ST CENTURY

Where are we going to find the kinds of leaders that we need for 21st-century society; leaders who differ so markedly from those of the past, leaders who can come "to grips with the dark side of a century of industrial 'progress'" (Bilimoria et al., 1995, p. 76; Harman & Hormann, 1990)? Clearly, we must look simultaneously at political, economic, and societal leadership. Equally clearly, we must look beyond the limited pool of traditional leaders—most of whom have been men—whose leadership styles fit better with the demands of the past century than with those of the century ahead.

What role might women play in 21st-century leadership? Women have always been scarce in elite leadership, both in politics and in business (Blondel, 1987; Genovese, 1993). Will the women who rise to the highest levels of leadership bring approaches that 21st-century society needs? Perhaps. Although it is too early to know for sure if studies of women in other roles will apply to women who are global leaders, most research suggests that women disproportionately bring some of the very cooperative, inclusive, participatory, and boundary-spanning approaches that society needs most in the 21st century (see Frenier, 1997; Gilligan, 1988; Helgesen, 1995; Noddings, 1984; Rosener, 1995).

We do know, however, that increasing the number of women leaders will contribute in one of two ways, both of which are positive for society. First, if women lead in ways similar to men, drawing on both women and men will expand the pool of potential leadership talent, thus ensuring, on average, a higher quality of leadership. Second, if women approach leadership in ways that differ from those of men, their styles will add new approaches, some of which appear to be a particularly good fit with society's needs or, at a minimum, to complement men's 20th-century leadership approaches (Adler, 1998).

Cambridge scholar and global management consultant Charles Hampden-Turner suggests that the competitive success of Western companies, and therefore Western societies, may, in fact, depend on their inclusion of values that are often labeled in the West as feminine and are more highly developed in Western women than in the majority of Western men. According to Hampden-Turner (1994),

> The ultra masculine corporate values system in such countries as the United States has been losing touch progressively with the wider world. It needs a change of values, desperately or it will continue to underperform, continue to lose touch with the values systems of people from the rest of the world, which ironically are much closer to the values in which American women are raised.
>
> Women . . . who are socialized to display values antithetical yet complementary to those of American men, have within their culture vitally important cures for Western economic decline.

The prescription is not for men to attempt to become like women or vice versa, nor for people from North America to act like Asians; that would be both stupid and impossible. Rather, it is for 21st-century organizations to include people from different backgrounds and to learn to use the inherent diversity to build stronger systems—what are referred to as culturally synergistic systems (Adler, 1997b). Twenty-first-century success will be achieved by those who know best how to use the complementarity of opposites (Hampden-Turner, 1994).

GLOBAL WOMEN LEADERS

What do we know about the women who hold the most senior global leadership positions? Who are the women who become political leaders—presidents

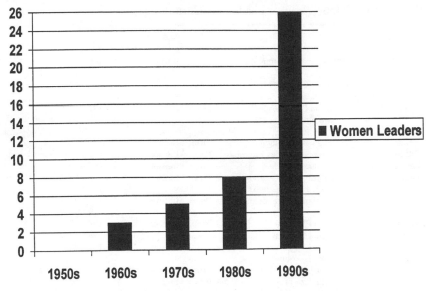

Figure 14.1 Global Women Leaders: Numbers Increasing

or prime ministers of their countries?[2] Who are the women who become global business leaders—presidents and CEOs of major global firms?

Women Political Leaders: Numbers Increasing

Although rarely recognized or reported in the media, one inescapable conclusion is that the number of global women political leaders is rapidly increasing, albeit from a negligible starting point. As shown in Figure 14.1, no women presidents or prime ministers came to office in the 1950s; three came to office in the 1960s, five in the 1970s, eight in the 1980s, and to date in the 1990s, 26 have already come to office. More than half of all women who have ever been political leaders have come into office since 1990: 26 of 42. At the current rate of increase, we would expect twice as many women to become president or prime minister in this decade as have ever served before. As shown in Table 14.1, countries as dissimilar as Bangladesh and Norway have elected women to lead them.

Global Women Business Leaders: Where Are They?

How many women CEOs and presidents of global companies are there? Do we see the same increase in the number of women business leaders as we

Table 14.1   Global Women Leaders: A Chronology

Country	Name	Office	Date
Sri Lanka	Sirimavo Bandaranaike	Prime Minister	1960-1965, 1970-1977, 1994-[a]
India	(Indira Gandhi)	Prime Minster	1966-1977, 1980-1984
Israel	(Golda Meir)	Prime Minister	1969-1975
Argentina	(Maria Estela [Isabel] Martínez de Perón)	President	1974-1976
Central African Republic	Elizabeth Domitien	Prime Minister	1975-1976
Portugal	Maria de Lourdes Pintasilgo	Prime Minister	1979
Great Britain	Margaret Thatcher	Prime Minister	1979-1990
Dominica	Mary Eugenia Charles	Prime Minister	1980-1995
Iceland	Vigdís Finnbógadottir	President	1980-1996
Norway	Gro Harlem Brundtland	Prime Minister	1981, 1986-1989, 1990-1996
Yugoslavia	Milka Planinc	Prime Minister	1982-1986
Malta	Agatha Barbara	President	1982-1987
Netherland-Antilles	Maria Liberia-Peters	Prime Minister	1984, 1989-1994
The Philippines	Corazon Aquino	President	1986-1992
Pakistan	Benazir Bhutto	Prime Minister	1988-1990, 1993-1996
Lithuania	Kazimiera-Danute Prunskiene	Prime Minister	1990-1991
Haiti	Ertha Pascal-Trouillot	President	1990-1991
Myanmar (Burma)	Aung San Suu Kyi	Opposition Leader[b]	1990-[b]
East Germany	Sabine Bergmann-Pohl	President of the Parliament	1990
Ireland	Mary Robinson	President	1990-[a]
Nicaragua	Violeta Barrios de Chamorro	President	1990-1996
Bangladesh	Khaleda Zia	Prime Minister	1991-1996
France	Edith Cresson	Prime Minister	1991-1992
Poland	Hanna Suchocka	Prime Minister	1992-1993
Canada	Kim Campbell	Prime Minister	1993
Burandi	Sylvia Kinigi	Prime Minister	1993-1994
Rwanda	(Agatha Uwilingiyimana)	Prime Minister	1993-1994
Turkey	Tansu Çiller	Prime Minister	1993-1996
Bulgaria	Reneta Indzhova	Interim Prime Minister	1993-1994
Sri Lanka	Chandrika Bandaranaike Kumaratunga	Executive President & former Prime Minister	1994-[a]
Haiti	Claudette Werleigh	Prime Minister	1995-1996
Switzerland	Ruth Dreifuss	State Councillor[c]	1995-[a]
Bangladesh	Hasina Wajed	Prime Minister	1996-[a]
Liberia	Ruth Perry	Chair, Ruling Council	1996-[a]
Ecuador	Rosalia Artega	President	1997
Bermuda	Pamela Gordon	Premiere	1997-1998
Bosnian Serb Rep.	Biljana Plavsic	President	1997-[a]
Ireland	Mary McAleese	Prime Minister	1997-[a]
New Zealand	Jenny Shipley	Prime Minister	1997-[a]
Guyana	Janet Jagan	Prime Minister, President	1997-[a]
Bermuda	Jennifer Smith	Premiere	1998-[a]

SOURCE. Adapted and updated from Adler (1996, p. 136).
NOTE. Those women whose names are in parentheses are no longer living.
a. Currently in office.
b. Party won 1990 election but prevented by military from taking office; Nobel Prize laureate.
c. Switzerland governed by Council of (7) Ministers, rather than a president or prime minister.

see in women political leaders? Although the pattern is not yet clear, initial surveys suggested that there are not very many global women business leaders. Think for a moment about the women CEOs of major global companies that you can name. Not many. Only in 1997, for example, did Britain gain its first woman chief executive of a *Financial Times* (FT-SE) 100 firm, Marjorie Scardino at Pearson Plc (Pogrebin, 1996).[3]

Are there really so few women chief executives of global companies, or could it be that we are looking in the wrong places? Have we primarily observed major corporations and concluded that there are very few women business leaders (see White & Hymowitz, 1997)? If so, our conclusion would be supported by fact. Most women in the 20th century did not attempt to climb the corporate ladder to the top of major corporations, and of those who did attempt the climb, few succeeded. For instance, according to the United Nations' 1995 report, *The World's Women,* there are no women running the world's largest corporations (as reported in Kelly, 1996, p. 21). Similarly, with almost 50% of the American workforce being women, Catalyst, a research and consulting organization, reports that only 2.4% of the chairs and CEOs of *Fortune* 500 companies are women (Wellington, 1996; as reported in Himelstein, 1996). Contrary to popular belief, however, women's scarcity in leading major corporations does not mean that they are absent as leaders of global companies. Unlike their male counterparts, most women chief executives have either created their own businesses or assumed the leadership of a family business. A disproportionate number of women have founded and are now leading entrepreneurial enterprises. According to the Small Business Administration, for example, women currently own one third of all American businesses (Kelly, 1996, p. 21). These women-owned businesses in the United States employ more people than the entire *Fortune* 500 list of America's largest companies combined (Aburdene & Naisbitt, 1992).[4]

In addition, for the first time in history, an increasing number of women are taking over the leadership of family businesses; succession is shifting from "first sons" to "first sons and first daughters" at an accelerating rate. This pattern is even echoed in royalty, where in December 1996, following the initial recommendation of Queen Elizabeth, Member of Parliament Jeffrey Archer introduced a motion that succession to the British throne go to the first child, rather than the first son. Sweden made succession to the throne gender neutral years ago.

Similar to narrowly searching primarily in corporations for women business leaders, have we also inadvertently misled ourselves by looking primarily in Western countries? Have we somehow implicitly assumed that economically advantaged countries offer more opportunities to women executives? They do not. If anything, economically advantaged societies act more conservatively than do some of their less economically privileged counterparts; perhaps because they believe that they have more to lose. As the list of women business leaders in Table 14.2 attests, the reality is that women from around the world are leading major companies. These global women business leaders come neither strictly from the West nor disproportionately from the West.

Focusing on the scarcity of women in senior corporate leadership rather than highlighting the increasing number of women chief executives of global entrepreneurial and family businesses appears to have caused scholars and executives alike to ask the wrong questions. Instead of considering the causes and potential impact of the increases, society has remained trapped in questioning why there are so few global women business leaders. Moreover, given the pervasive focus on scarcity, many executives and management scholars have misguidedly spent their time attempting to resolve what appeared to be the underlying dilemma:

"Do companies discriminate against women?"

or

"Are women just not effective as global leaders?"

rather than attempting to learn both how women succeed in acquiring global leadership positions and how effective they are once in such positions. Although the increasing number of women business leaders is still below the radar of most companies and almost all of the world's business press, a few forward-thinking companies—such as Avon, Motorola, and Nike—are not only planning for the scenario, they are taking advantage of it (see Adler, 1993-94).

GLOBAL WOMEN LEADERS: WHAT DO WE KNOW ABOUT THEM?

Beyond knowing that their numbers are increasing, what do we know about global women leaders that might help us plan for the 21st century? Three important patterns have emerged. First, diversity defines the dominant patterns. Second, women leaders' paths to power are unique. And third, women leaders leverage the fact that they are women.

Table 14.2 Global Women Business Leaders

How many of us recognize the names of the world's women business leaders? All of the women selected for inclusion on the following list lead companies with current revenues over US$1 billion, or for banks, with assets over US$1 billion:

Ernestina Herrera de Noble, Argentina, $1.2 billion: President and editorial director of Grupo Clarin, the largest-circulation Spanish newspaper in the world.

Francine Wachsstock, Belgium, $2.25 billion: President of the board of administrators, La Poste; Belgium's state-owned post office and largest employer.

Beatriz Larragoiti, Brazil, $2.9 billion: Vice president (and owner) of Brazil's largest insurance company, Sul America S.A.

Maureen Kempston Darkes, Canada, $18.3 billion: President and General Manager of General Motors of Canada.

Ellen R. Schneider-Lenne, Germany, $458 billion in assets: Former member of the board of managing directors, Deutsch Bank AG; deceased.

Nina Wang, Hong Kong, $1-2 billion in assets: Chairlady of Chinachem Group, property development.

Tarjani Vakil, India, $1.1 billion in assets: Chairperson and managing director, Export-Import Bank of India; highest ranking female banking official in Asia.

Margaret Heffernan, Ireland, $1.6 billion: Chairman, Dunnes Stores Holding Company; largest retailing company in Ireland.

Galia Maor, Israel, $35.6 billion in assets: CEO of Bank Leumi le-Israel.

Gloria Delores Knight, Jamaica, $1.86 billion in assets: Former president and managing director, The Jamaica Mutual Life Assurance Society; largest financial conglomerate in English-speaking Caribbean; deceased.

Sawako Noma, Japan, $2 billion: President of Kodansha Ltd.; largest publishing house in Japan.

Harumi Sakamoto, Japan, $13 billion: Senior managing director, The Seiyu, Ltd.; a supermarket and shopping centre operator expanding throughout Asia.

Khatijah Ahmad, Malaysia, $5 billion: Chairman and managing director, KAF Group of Companies; financial services group.

Merce Sala i Schnorkowski, Spain, $1.1 billion: CEO of Renfé; Spain's national railway system, currently helping to privatize Colombian and Bolivian rail and selling trains to Germany.

Antonia Ax:son Johnson, Sweden, $6 billion: Chair, The Axel Johnson Group; retailing and distribution, more than 200 companies.

Elisabeth Salina Amorini, Switzerland, $2.8 billion: Chairman of the board, managing director, and chairman of the group executive board, Société Générale de Surveillance Holding S.A.; the world's largest inspection and quality control organization, testing imports and exports in more than 140 countries.

Emilia Roxas, Taiwan, $5 billion: CEO, Asiaworld Internationale Groupe; multinational conglomerate.

Ellen Hancock, USA, $2.4 billion: Executive vice president and co-chief operating officer, National Semiconductor Corp.

(continued)

Table 14.2   Continued

The list grows to include many of the other countries of the world if companies are selected with revenues over a quarter million dollars, including such women business leaders as:

Donatella Zingone Dini, Costa Rica, $300 million: Zeta Group; fifth largest business in Central America, conglomerate.

Nawal Abdel Moneim El Tatawy, Egypt, $357 million in assets: Chair, Arab Investment Bank.

Colette Lewiner, France, $800 million: Chairman and CEO, SGN-Eurisys Group; world's largest nuclear fuels reprocessing company.

Jannie Tay, Singapore, $289 million: Managing director, The Hour Glass Limited; high end retailer of watches.

Aida Geffen, South Africa, $355 million: Chairman and managing director, Aida Holdings Ltd; residential commercial real estate firm.

Ann Gloag, United Kingdom, $520 million: Stagecoach Holdings Plc; Europe's largest bus company.

Linda Joy Wachner, United States, $1.1 billion (combined): Chairman of both The Warnaco Group ($789 million) and of Authentic Fitness Corporation ($266 million).

Liz Chitiga, Zimbabwe, $400 million: General manager and CEO, Minerals Marketing Corporation of Zimbabwe; in foreign currency terms, the biggest business in Zimbabwe.

SOURCE. Kelly (1996).

Diversity Defines the Dominant Patterns

The dominant pattern in the women leaders' backgrounds, paths to power, missions, records of achievement, and contexts in which they lead is diversity. No single "woman's style" of global leadership predominates.

Diverse Countries

Women leaders span the globe. The 42 women political leaders come from both the world's largest and smallest countries, the richest and poorest countries, the most socially and economically advantaged and disadvantaged countries, and from every geographical region. The largest cluster of women prime ministers is in South Asia, not in the advanced economies of Europe or North America.[5] The countries led by women represent six of the major world religions, with four women prime ministers having led predominantly Muslim countries.[6] As shown in Table 14.2, the women business leaders also come from all areas of the world (Kelly, 1996).

There is a myth that female-friendly countries produce more women leaders. However, facts refute the myth: Seemingly female-friendly countries (e.g., those that give equal rights to women) do not elect a disproportionate number of women presidents and prime ministers. Similarly, companies that select women for their most senior leadership positions are not those that implement the most female-friendly policies, such as day care centers and flextime (Wellington, 1996, as reported in Dobrzynski, 1996). For example, among the 61 *Fortune* 500 companies employing women as chairs, CEOs, board members, or one of the top five earners, only three are the same companies that *Working Woman* identified as the most favorable for women employees (Dobrzynski, 1996).

Although it should have been self-evident, we all seem to have missed the point. If we want to understand women's potential for global leadership, we cannot continue to confuse leaders with either managers or employees. Inadvertently, we appear to have assumed that the dynamics that apply to women in the lower ranks of organizations as they move into and up through management, often getting stopped at the so-called glass ceiling, also apply to women leaders. That is, we appear to have assumed that being a woman is so salient that, relative to being a woman, the difference between working as an entry-level employee and as a senior-level executive is irrelevant. From a dynamic perspective, we have inadvertently assumed that the influence of being a woman interacts neither with role nor with level in the organization. However, it now appears that our implicit assumption was wrong: The impact of being a woman is very different if one is a secretary, a manager, or a leader. For example, as much as eliminating sexual harassment has become an important consideration for companies wishing to improve the working environment for their female employees, no one (that I know of) ever suggested that Britain's former prime minister Margaret Thatcher skip a G7 meeting out of fear that she might be sexually harassed.[7] As shown in Figure 14.2, the role a woman holds in an organization and the impact of her being a woman interact: Although being a woman has often retarded the effectiveness and progress of women working at the lower levels of organizations, as will be discussed, being a woman appears to enhance women's leadership ability when working at the highest levels.

Diverse Backgrounds

In addition to coming from diverse countries, global women leaders also come from diverse personal backgrounds (see Adler, 1996). Some are rich and some poor. Some come from societally prominent families, whereas others come from families without substantial influence. Although most women

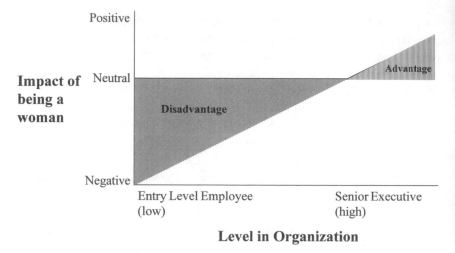

Figure 14.2 When Is Being a Woman an Advantage? The Relationship Between Role and Being a Woman

leaders are university educated, with many educated internationally, their academic backgrounds and professions reflect a diverse range of disciplines; from chemistry to demography, medicine to law, elementary education to political science, and history to engineering.

There is a widely held belief that most women leaders inherit power, with the implicit assumption being that they therefore have not gained power legitimately. The belief is false; most women leaders gain power on their own. Only one of the 42 women presidents and prime ministers, Argentina's Isabel Perón, inherited power. When Juan Perón died, after having appointed Isabel vice president, she automatically assumed the presidency. For nine other women presidents and prime ministers, membership in the "right family" was a necessary, but not a sufficient, condition for achieving power. In all but the case of Argentina's Isabel Perón, the women campaigned, often for more than a decade, before gaining their country's most senior leadership position. Among the political leaders, all 10 of the women from dynastic families come from Asia or Latin America, cultures in which family also dominates traditional male politics.[8]

Although no one as yet understands the dynamics surrounding the general public's appreciation, or lack thereof, of global women leaders, the current patterns raise some disquieting questions. Why does the pervasive, yet false, myth persist that women inherit power? Why is the importance of women political leaders seemingly discounted when they are thought to achieve power in ways that differ from those of prior leaders, all of whom, with only a few exceptions, have been men?[9] Is latent ethnocentrism, perhaps more so than any form of sexism, causing people from historically strong democracies (such as the United States) to imagine that women leaders achieve power in illegitimate ways as a way to discount both the reality and importance of their leadership? Given the changing demands of 21st-century society, one must question if society wants leaders, women or men, in the 21st century who gain power in exactly the same ways as the 20th century's predominantly male leadership.

Similar to the dynastic political leaders, women leading family businesses also tend to be discounted or rendered invisible as compared with the few women who lead global corporations. The appropriate question, of course, is not whether a particular woman chief executive does or does not have family connections, but rather, what she does with the business once having taken it over. Consider Italy's Wanda Ferragamo, for example, who certainly inherited the family business from her creative cobbler husband, Salvatore. However, it is Wanda who grew the business, expanded it internationally, and created one of the world's leading and most profitable fashion houses (de Gaspe Beaubien, 1994; Pearson, Hurstak, & Raiser, 1993). Similarly, Loida Nicolas-Lewis, originally from the Philippines, who took over TLC Beatrice International Holdings in 1994 following the sudden death of her African American husband, has made substantial and very profitable changes, including letting go of most of the prior executive team.[10]

Unique Paths to Power

Some strikingly unexpected patterns in the women leaders' paths to power differentiate them from most of their male contemporaries, and these very differences appear to fit well with the needs of 21st-century society. Most women leaders:

1. Are vision or mission driven
2. Transfer laterally into the most senior leadership positions
3. Develop and use broad-based popular support, rather than relying primarily on structural or party support
4. Leverage the fact that they are women

Each pattern will be discussed separately.

Vision or Mission Driven

First, most women political leaders are driven by a vision, mission, or cause. They are motivated by a compelling agenda that they want to achieve, not primarily by a desire for the office of president or prime minister, nor by a desire for power per se. Power and the presidency are means for achieving their mission, not the mission itself. As children, none of the women leaders dreamed or spoke about becoming her country's leader, as did so many prominent male political leaders, including the United States' Bill Clinton and Bob Dole, and Britain's Michael Hesseltine.[11] For example, Golda Meir's mission was to create the state of Israel and to ensure its survival as a Jewish state. Not only did she not dream of becoming prime minister, she rejected the position when it was initially offered to her. Likewise, Mary Robinson's compelling human rights agenda and desire to reconcile Ireland's civil war are what led her to seek the presidency, not a desire for the office per se.

Most of the dynastic leaders are similarly mission driven. They seek office to continue the legacy of their martyred father or husband, again not to gain office per se.[12] Perhaps the Philippines' Corazon Aquino and Nicaragua's Violeta Chamorro best exemplify this separation of mission and office. Both decided not to run for a second term, even when encouraged by colleagues to do so. Aquino explicitly explained that one of her goals was to leave a legacy of democracy to the Philippines, which meant, among other things, that she refused to run for a second term because she believed that Filipinos should have an opportunity to elect a new leader every 6 years (Col, 1993).

Are women business leaders similarly mission driven? The disproportionate number who choose to become entrepreneurs suggests that a substantial number are vision or mission driven. Picture, for instance, Anita Roddick, founder and CEO of The Body Shop, whose U.K.-based company has become world renowned for its societal commitments, including environmental campaigns, community-building hiring practices, and adherence to truth in packaging. Roddick (1991) describes her contemporary vision as "corporate idealism":

Leaders in the business world should aspire to be true planetary citizens. They have global responsibilities since their decisions affect not just the world of business but world problems of poverty, national security and the environment. Many, sad to say, duck these responsibilities, because their vision is material rather than moral. (p. 226)

Roddick's vision transcends traditional, narrowly defined economic goals; she is not motivated to be a traditional CEO, nor does she focus singularly on maximizing either profits or shareholder wealth. Whereas many observers have tried to explain that women become entrepreneurs because they cannot succeed in the corporate world, an alternative explanation suggests that they become entrepreneurs because they are vision or mission driven, and traditional corporations give them less latitude to express their vision. Similar to dynastic political leaders, women leading family businesses are also often mission driven, most frequently seeing themselves as carrying on the family legacy. Will we see mission-driven leadership among the women who are becoming leaders of global corporations? We do not know yet; the pattern of their global leadership style is, as yet, too new to be clear.

What are the implications of mission-driven leaders? Do leaders who are capable of significant global change efforts differ from traditional business and political leaders (Bilimoria et al., 1995, p. 82)? Yes; those capable of leading sustained global change are vision and mission driven. They are not driven simply by the acquisition of power, money, or a prestigious title. Whereas some male leaders are vision driven, it appears that a disproportionate number of women leaders are so driven. We certainly know that the 21st century needs leaders who will put society's well-being and that of their organization ahead of their personal career and financial success. We also know that, to date, no country with strongly individualistic values has an economy that has grown at a sustained rate of more than 2% per annum over the past decade, whereas every country that is growing at more than 4% per annum holds more communitarian values (Hampden-Turner, 1994). The 21st century can no longer tolerate or support the leadership of self-aggrandizement, nor can it support furthering of the interests of a small subset of the population (whether defined nationally, geographically, culturally, economically, or industrially) at the expense of the greater, now highly interrelated, whole—at the expense of the world's entire population and its physical, spiritual, and natural environment.

Lateral Transfer Into Leadership

Rather than following the traditional path up through the hierarchy of the organization, profession, or political party, most women leaders laterally transfer into high office.[13] For example, Gro Harlem Brundtland was a medical doctor; 6 years later, she became Norway's first woman prime minister.

Similarly, Tansu Çiller was an economics professor; 3 years later, she became Turkey's first woman prime minister. Likewise, most of the dynastic leaders, while either the daughter or wife of a prominent national leader—and therefore informally associated with the highest levels of leadership—did not hold any formal leadership position prior to becoming president or prime minister. Coming into leadership from outside, women frequently bring ideas, perspectives, and approaches that previously have not been a part of the mainstream.

A similar pattern of "outsiders" appears to be emerging among the women whom global corporations select as their chief executives. For example, Charlotte Beers became both Ogilvy Mather Worldwide's first woman chief executive as well as its first CEO brought in from outside of the firm (Sackley & Ibarra, 1995; Sellers, 1996). Marjorie Scardino, Pearson's first woman chief executive, is a double outsider. As the first American CEO brought in to lead this traditional British firm, she is a cultural outsider. In addition, because *The Economist,* where Scardino previously served as managing director, is only 50% owned by Pearson, she is an organizational outsider. The general public was so surprised by Pearson's selection of Scardino that Pearson's stock dropped initially on the announcement of her appointment (Pogrebin, 1996). Likewise, whereas Katherine Hudson stayed below the glass ceiling as the highest ranked woman—a corporate vice president and general manager of a major division—at Eastman Kodak, W. H. Brady brought her in from outside to become its first woman president and CEO (Schellbardt, 1993).

Will outsiders who laterally transfer into the highest level of leadership become a potential cost or benefit to society and to the organizations they lead? The 21st century needs integration across geographies, sectors of society, and professions; what Bilimoria et al. (1995) refer to as transborder integration. Society can no longer tolerate leaders with "chimney stack" careers that, in the past, have resulted in deep expertise in one area, organization, or country without any understanding of the context within which their particular organization or country operates, and therefore no skills at integrating across organizational and societal boundaries. Transferring across organizations, sectors of society, and areas of the world allows leaders to develop alternative perspectives and an understanding of context that is almost impossible to acquire within a single setting. Due to the historic pattern of promoting men and failing to promote women to the most senior leadership positions from within organizations—most often referred to as the glass ceiling—

women appear to have inadvertently become the prototypes of a career pattern that is needed more broadly among 21st-century leaders.[14]

Rather than lamenting the supposed scarcity of potential women leaders —or calculating one more time the number of years still needed for the "pipeline" to produce sufficient numbers of women candidates for leadership positions,[15] the question that organizations must ask themselves is, Do we look for potential leaders worldwide and from across all sectors rather than primarily from within our own country and company? Do we look for potential leaders with demonstrated skills at integrating across organizational boundaries and sectors of society? Do organizations fail to find potential global women leaders because they narrowly circumscribe the domain of their search? In looking for "insiders," do organizations focus on people, both women and men, who are least likely to have the breadth of experience and skills necessary to lead them successfully into the 21st century?

Broad-Based Support

Women leaders develop and use broad-based popular support rather than relying primarily on traditional party or structural support. This is particularly apparent among women political leaders, who often are not seriously considered as potential candidates by their country's main political parties. Consequently, they are forced to gain support directly from the people. Mary Robinson, for example, campaigned in more small communities in Ireland than any previous presidential candidate before either her party or the opposition would take her seriously. The opposition now admits that they did not seriously consider Robinson's candidacy until it was too late to stop her (Finlay, 1990). Not only did Robinson win, but she now enjoys a more than 90% approval rating (O'Neill, 1994). Similarly, Corazon Aquino held more than 1,000 rallies in 68 of the Philippines' 73 provinces, whereas incumbent Ferdinand Marcos held only 34 rallies in 22 provinces (Col, 1993, p. 25). Aquino, whose campaign and victory were labeled the People's Revolution, was elected as the Philippines' first woman president. Likewise, Benazir Bhutto campaigned in more communities in Pakistan than any politician before her. Her own party took her seriously only when more people showed up upon her return to Pakistan from exile than they, the opposition, or the international press had even expected (Weisman as cited in Anderson, 1993). Bhutto succeeded in becoming Pakistan's first woman and youngest ever prime minister. Following a similar pattern, Vigdis Finnbógadottir was originally elected president following Iceland's first countrywide women's strike—a strike intended to allow the people of Iceland to better appreciate women's contributions to society, business, community, and home.

Is there a parallel among women business leaders? Research on managers suggests that, on average, women use more inclusive approaches than do men. Based on a review of almost 400 studies, researchers found that women managers use more democratic and participative approaches than do their male counterparts (Eagly & Johnson, 1990, as cited in Vinnicombe & Colwill, 1995, p. 32). However, with no studies as yet focusing strictly on global women leaders, it is premature to suggest that the same pattern applies among women leaders as among women managers. As suggested previously in Figure 14.1, we must caution ourselves not to fall into the trap of overly inflating the salience of women leaders being women. To understand women leaders, we must observe women leaders; not simply assume that what is true for women in general —or for women managers in particular—is also true for women leaders.

How important is broad-based support for 21st-century organizations? As organizational structures flatten from hierarchies to globally dispersed networks, the importance of broad-based leadership becomes self-evident. Just as 21st-century political leaders need new agendas that better address the issues faced by the general populace, and not solely those of the people who previously held power, business leaders also increasingly need to understand and address the needs of a much broader constituency, both internally within their particular company and externally within complex networks of competitive and collaborative relationships with their clients, suppliers, competitors, and government agencies. As is already evident, the skills for such broad-based, inclusive, cooperative leadership are not those that were commonly used in 20th-century hierarchical organizations; which explains why some of the most successful companies of the past have faced failure and demise as they attempted to successfully make the transition to 21st-century dynamics (Hamel & Prahalad, 1993). For example, think of IBM's or Digital Equipment's recent history. Perhaps it is worth pondering the 21st-century maxim that "strong leaders create a weak people; strong people don't need strong leaders" (Steinem, 1994). Leadership within networks is not the same as the leadership of hierarchies. Hierarchies' historical "power over" is being replaced by the "power with" of 21st-century networks. Unfortunately, 20th-century society developed leaders' competitive skills to a much greater extent than their collaborative skills. In the 20th century, competition has so eclipsed cooperation that "by the end of the Second World War cooperation had largely disappeared from the vocabulary of social scientists" (Argyle, 1991, p. 12). Luckily, today, given the skills needed for 21st-century survival, let alone success, women appear to be bringing more cooperative approaches back to the forefront of leadership.

Leveraging the Fact That They Are Women

Rather than attempting to ignore it, hide it, or minimize it, women leaders leverage the fact that they are women. For leaders, difference is not necessarily a problem, but rather a potential advantage.

For the global women leaders, it is always salient that they are women. For example, the single most frequently asked question of Margaret Thatcher (1993), who was never accused of being a feminist, was, "What is it like being a woman prime minister?" (to which Thatcher generally responded that she could not answer because she had not tried the alternative). Women leaders worldwide are frequently compared to other women leaders. For example, the press refers to a number of the women leaders as the Margaret Thatcher of her country; including in such dissimilar countries as Colombia, Lithuania, Poland, Venezuela, and the United States.[16]

The question is not, Does it make a difference that she is a woman leader? Rather, the salient question is, When is it helpful that a woman leader is a woman, and when is it not? Overall, the primary advantages for women leaders are that being a woman:

1. Increases women leaders' visibility
2. Strengthens their relationship and closeness to people
3. Symbolizes progress, modernity, and change
4. Symbolizes unity

Increases visibility. Because women are new to the highest levels of leadership, they have the advantage of global visibility. For example, following the election of Mary Robinson as Ireland's first woman president,

> newspapers and magazines in virtually every country in the world carried the story. . . . [T]he rest of the world understood Ireland to have made a huge leap forward. . . . Mary Robinson had joined a very small number of women . . . who had been elected to their country's highest office. It was, quite properly, seen as historic. (Finlay, 1990, pp. 149-150)

Similarly, President François Mitterrand purposely created a worldwide media event by appointing the first woman, Edith Cresson, rather than another
man as France's prime minister. Likewise, in contrast to Benazir Bhutto's male
predecessor, who not only complained about receiving insufficient worldwide
press coverage while abroad but also fired the Pakistani embassy's public
relations officer when too few journalists showed up to cover his arrival in
London, Pakistan's former Prime Minister Benazir Bhutto always received
extensive media coverage no matter where in the world she traveled.

International businesswomen also receive more visibility than do their
male colleagues. Women expatriates as well as women on international business trips, for example, report being remembered more easily than their male
counterparts (Adler, 1994a). Compared with businessmen, global businesswomen gain access more easily to new clients, suppliers, and government
officials; receive more time when meeting with international contacts; and are
more frequently remembered (Adler, 1994a).

Strengthens relationships to people. Most of the women political leaders
use the powerful positive imagery surrounding women's family roles of
daughter, sister, mother, and grandmother to strengthen their relationship with
their constituents. For example, during her campaign, Turkey's former Prime
Minister Tansu Çiller "repeatedly insisted that she would be a 'mother' for the
youth, a 'sister' for the middle-aged and a 'daughter' for the elderly . . . [that
she would] embrace them all with motherly care" (Lazerges, 1993, p. 1).

Similarly, former Prime Minister Benazir Bhutto referred to herself as a
sister to the Pakistani people (Bhutto, 1989); Dominica's former Prime
Minister Eugenia Charles referred to herself as "mother of the people" (Opfell,
1993, p. 90); and Israel's Golda Meir "charmed the nation" with her grand-
motherly image (Opfell, 1993, p. 45). Using these familiar roles positively
and powerfully connects the women leaders directly to the people of their
respective countries without relying on the traditional mediating influence of
political party hierarchy. Moreover, using the familiar familial imagery of
daughter, sister, mother, and grandmother negates many of the undermining
sexual connotations often associated with women when the public, and
especially the media, implicitly and symbolically link them to such sexually
explicit roles as mistress and seductress. Whereas the influence of women
managers is frequently undercut by the sexual imagery surrounding the fact
that they are women, women leaders' influence appears to be enhanced by the
feminine imagery of being a close and cherished family member—a mother,
daughter, sister, or grandmother.[17] As we move from 20th-century dynamics

based on independence to 21st-century dynamics founded on interdependence, the symbolic importance of a leader's direct relationship and connectedness to the people he or she leads is heightened. As pointed out in a report by the World Commission of Environment and Development, "Positive, global change will only be feasible [in the coming century] with the creation of new organizational forms that are globally sophisticated in the dynamics of relationality" (as reported in Cooperrider & Bilimoria, 1993). Women leaders are bringing a new symbolism and a new reality to the dynamics of relationality.

Symbolizes change, modernity, and progress. Women's assumption of the highest levels of leadership brings with it the symbolic possibility of fundamental societal and organizational change. The combination of women being outsiders at senior leadership levels previously completely controlled by men and of beating the odds to become the first woman to lead her country or company produces powerful public imagery about the possibility of broad-based societal and organizational change. As "firsts," women by definition bring change.

If a woman can be chosen to be president, prime minister, or CEO when no other woman has ever held such an office and when few people thought that she would be selected, then other major changes become believably possible. In Mary Robinson's presidential acceptance speech, she captured the coupling of the unique event of a woman being elected president with the possibility of national change:

> I was elected by men and women of all parties and none, by many with great moral courage who stepped out from the faded flags of Civil War and voted for a new Ireland. And above all by the women of Ireland . . . who instead of rocking the cradle rocked the system, and who came out massively to make their mark on the ballot paper, and on a new Ireland. (RDS, Dublin, 9 November 1990, as reported in Finlay, 1990, p. 1)

People see Robinson "as a representative of a changing Ireland" (Opfell, 1993, p. 186). Similarly, commentators viewed Çiller's election as prime minister of Turkey as a sign and a confirmation of change: "It was the moment that signalled Turkish politics had changed forever" (Benn, 1995, p. A3). Because few women have played a major role in Turkish politics, Çiller's ascendancy was welcomed as a sign of Turkey's modernity (Lazerges, 1993, p. 1); as a sign of change. This was particularly important at the time of Çiller's election, as Turkey, a predominantly Muslim country, was trying to communicate its modernity to the Christian countries of Europe in its bid to gain acceptance into the European Union.

Do societies and organizations believe that the fundamental ways in which they operate can change? As we come to the close of the 20th century, what would make it possible to remarry idealism with contemporary reality? First and foremost, people would need to believe that change for the better is possible. The symbolic power of women assuming the highest levels of leadership is that change for the better becomes believably possible. Such symbolism is not insignificant for the 21st century.

Symbolizes unity. The fourth advantage that women leaders have is that they symbolize unity. For example, both Nicaragua's Chamorro and the Philippines' Aquino became symbols of national unity following their husband's murders. Chamorro even claimed "to have no ideology beyond national 'reconciliation'" (Benn, 1995). Of Chamorro's four adult children, two are prominent Sandinistas, whereas the other two equally prominently oppose the Sandinistas, not an unusual split in war-torn Nicaragua (Saint-Germain, 1993, p. 80). Chamorro's ability to bring all the members of her family together for Sunday dinner each week achieved near legendary status in Nicaragua (Saint-Germain, 1993, p. 80). As "the grieving matriarch who can still hold the family together" (Saint-Germain, 1993, p. 80), Chamorro gives symbolic hope to the nation that it, too, can find peace based on a unity that brings together all Nicaraguans. That a national symbol for a woman leader is family unity is neither surprising nor coincidental. Based on similar dynamics in the Philippines, Aquino, as widow of the slain opposition leader, was seen as the only person who could credibly unify the people of the Philippines following Benigno Aquino's death. Although Aquino was widely condemned in the press for naïveté when she invited members of both her own and the opposition party into her cabinet, her choice was a conscious decision to attempt to reunify the deeply divided country.

Given that women leaders symbolize unity, it is perhaps not surprising that a woman business leader, Rebecca Mark, chief executive of Enron Development Corporation, and not a male executive was the first person to successfully negotiate a major commercial transaction following the Middle East peace accords. Mark brought the Israelis and Jordanians together to build a natural gas power generation station.[18]

Focusing on unity inside the organization rather than between clients, Maureen Kempston Darkes, president and general manager of General Motors of Canada's $8 billion operations, surprised the world when she used a unifying strategy to attempt to settle General Motors's most recent major strike (Burrows, 1995). Rather than confining negotiations to the leadership of the union and of management, Darkes wrote a letter directly to her employees explaining the company's aspirations, dilemmas, and constraints. The strike was settled to both sides' satisfaction.

As we enter the 21st century and the interdependence in the world increases, the need for both symbolic and actual unity also increases. To achieve unity, leaders and the societies they lead must relearn the skills of cooperation and not continue to refine their ability to compete. "Research in almost every human science field since the late 1800s has indicated that cooperation is a superior form of relationship in nature and organizations, psychologically, physiologically, and economically" (Joba, Maynard, & Ray, 1993, p. 51, as cited in Bilimoria et al., 1995, p. 76). As suggested earlier, "the socialization of women . . . tends to reinforce cooperative modes" (Bilimoria et al., 1995, p. 76). Yet historically, world leaders have relegated cooperation to the status of a "neglected sibling of competition" (Bilimoria et al., 1995, p. 76). Today, the increasing number of women leaders is beginning to reintroduce cooperative, unifying modes into societal dynamics; they are beginning to welcome cooperation back into the family.

GLOBAL LEADERSHIP AND THE 21ST CENTURY

The confluence of 21st-century business and societal dynamics gives leaders a chance to create the type of world in which they, and we, would like to live. It demands, as Havel (1994) reflected, that leaders find "the key to insure the survival of . . . [our] civilization . . . a civilization that is global and multi-cultural" (p. A27). The increasing number of women business and political leaders brings with it a set of experiences and perspectives that differs from those of the 20th century's primarily male leadership cadre. The challenge is to use those differences to the benefit of organizations and society. As Octavio Paz (1985) expressed in his book *The Labyrinth of Solitude,* "What sets worlds in motion is the interplay of differences, their attractions and repulsions. Life is plurality, death is uniformity." The increasing interplay of women's and men's styles of leadership will define the contours and potential success of 21st-century society. The risk is in encapsulating leaders, both women and men, in approaches that appeared to work well in the 20th century but foretell disaster for the 21st century. Recognizing the growing number of women leaders is a first step in creating and understanding the types of leadership that will lead to success beyond the year 2000.

NOTES

1. Earlier versions of the following sections, including ideas on economic, political, and cultural spaces, were originally presented in Nancy J. Adler's John L. Manion Lecture in Ottawa on February 24, 1994, and subsequently published as Adler (1994b). They also appear in Adler (1995) and Adler and Boyacigiller (1995a, 1995b).

2. For a more in-depth discussion of global women political leaders, see Adler (1996).

3. The FT-SE 100 are the 100 largest firms on the London Stock Exchange, as listed by the *Financial Times* of London.

4. Similarly, according to the Bank of Montreal's Institute for Small Business (Michelle Fraser, as reported in Kirbyson, 1996), women-led businesses provide more jobs than the Canadian Business Top 100 companies combined.

5. The seven women leaders from South Asia are Khaleda Zia and Hasina Wajid in Bangladesh, Indira Gandhi in India, Benazir Bhutto in Pakistan, Sirimavo Bandaranaike and her daughter, Chandrika Bandaranaike Kumaratunga in Sri Lanka, and Aung San Suu Kyi in Myanmar (Burma).

6. The religions represented among the women leaders include Buddhism, Catholicism, Hinduism, Islam, Judaism, and various Protestant denominations. The women who have led Muslim countries include former Prime Minister Benazir Bhutto in Pakistan, the former and current prime ministers of Bangladesh, Khaleda Zia and Hasina Wajid, and the former prime minister of Turkey, Tansu Çiller.

7. The G7 is the Group of Seven most economically influential countries in the world, including Canada, Britain, France, Germany, Japan, and the United States.

8. Although most women leaders come to power without family connections, 10 were strongly advantaged by membership—either by birth or marriage—in highly prominent political families, including Violeta Chamorro in Nicaragua, both Khaleda Zia and Hasina Wajid in Bangladesh, Indira Ghandhi in India, Benazir Bhutto in Pakistan, Corazon Aquino in the Philippines, Sirimavo Bandaranaike and Chandrika Kumaratanga in Sri Lanka, and Aung San Suu Kyi in Myanmar (Burma).

9. For example, in Sri Lanka and Bangladesh, a woman followed another woman into office. In Sri Lanka, Sirimavo Bandaranaike was the world's first woman prime minister, gaining office in 1960. Her daughter, Chandrika Kumaratunga, was elected prime minister in 1994. When Kumaratunga was subsequently elected Executive President, she appointed her mother, Bandaranaike, to the position of prime minister. Bangladesh elected Hasina Wajid prime minister in 1996, following her successful campaign against Khaleda Zia, Bangladesh's first woman prime minister. Most other women presidents and prime ministers are the first to hold office in their respective countries.

10. For a discussion of Loida Nicolas-Lewis, see McCarroll (1996), Bulauitan (1995), Karlin (1995), and Munk (1995).

11. That the women did not imagine, let alone dream about, leading their country is not surprising. For all of the women political leaders except Sri Lanka's current executive president, Chandrika Kumaratunga, who followed her Prime Minister mother Sirimavo Bandaranaike into office, Bangladesh's Hasina Wajid, Ireland's Mary McAleese, and Bermuda's Jennifer Smith, there were no women predecessors and therefore no women role models.

12. Nine of the 10 dynastic leaders, all except India's Indira Gandhi, saw their husband, father, or both assassinated prior to assuming office themselves.

13. The two notable exceptions to the pattern of laterally transferring into office are Britain's Margaret Thatcher and Canada's Kim Campbell, both of whom had substantial political careers prior to becoming prime minister.

14. For an in-depth discussion of the ways in which highly successful women integrate a wide variety of experiences into their life and career paths, see Mary Catherine Bateson's *Composing a Life* (1989). For a discussion of the advantages of integrating such varied experiences, see Bateson's *Peripheral Vision* (1994).

15. *Business Week,* for example, predicted that it will be another 475 years before women reach equality as managers in the United States (K. Spillar, as quoted in Segal & Zeller, 1992).

16. For example, the press has referred to New Jersey's Governor Christine Heckman as the Margaret Thatcher of the United States, and to former Prime Minister Kazimiera-Danute Prunskiene as the Margaret Thatcher of Lithuania.

17. See Figure 14.2 for the interactive relationship between role and the influence of being a woman.

18. See Internet description: Amman. Joint Jordan-Israeli Energy Project promises a flying start to cooperation. Dataset from the Internet: Http://arabia.com/star/951228/bus1.html.

15

CORPORATIONS AS AGENTS
OF GLOBAL SUSTAINABILITY

Beyond Competitive Strategy

STUART L. HART

onsider that since the end of World War II, the human population has grown from about 2 billion to more than 5 billion (Keyfitz, 1989), the global economy has grown more than 15-fold (World Bank, 1992), consumption of fossil fuels has increased by a factor of 25 (Brown, Kane, & Roodman, 1994), and industrial production has increased by a factor of 40 (Schmidheiny, 1992). This would generally appear to be good news: The ability to provide for material and energy needs has far exceeded the rate of growth in human population, which means that people should be better off than they were 50 years ago despite the more than doubling in world population.

Unfortunately, the environmental and social impacts associated with this activity have also multiplied. For example, air and water pollution, toxic emissions, spills, and industrial accidents have created regional environmental and public health crises for thousands of communities around the world, especially in developing countries (Brown, Kane, & Roodman, 1994; Shrivastava, 1987). The composition of the atmosphere has been altered more in the past 100 years—through fossil fuel use, agricultural practices, and deforestation— than in the previous 18,000 (Graedel & Crutzen, 1989). Climate change,

This chapter draws heavily upon two previous publications by the author (Hart, 1995, 1997).

which might produce both rising ocean levels and further desertification, could threaten the very fabric of human civilization as we know it (Schneider, 1989). The world's 18 major fisheries have already reached or exceeded maximum sustained yield levels (Brown & Kane, 1994). If current consumption rates continue, all virgin tropical forests will be gone within 50 years, with a consequent loss of 50% or more of the world's species (Wilson, 1989). Reduced quality of life in the developed world, severe human health problems, and environmentally induced political upheaval in the developing world could all result (Homer-Dixon, Boutwell, & Rathjens, 1993; Kaplan, 1994).

In short, the scale and scope of human activity have accelerated over the past 40 years to the point where this activity is now having impacts on a global scale. Consider, for example, that it took more than 10,000 generations for the human population to reach 2 billion, but only a single lifetime to grow from 2 billion to more than 5 billion (Gore, 1992). During the next 40 years, the human population is expected to double again, to 10 billion, before leveling off sometime in the middle of the next century (Keyfitz, 1989). Even with world GNP currently at about $25 trillion, it may be necessary to increase economic activity 5- to 10-fold just to provide basic amenities to this population (MacNeill, 1989; Ruckelshaus, 1989). This level of economic production will probably not be ecologically or socially sustainable using existing technologies and strategies—a 10-fold increase in resource use and waste generation would almost certainly stress the Earth's natural systems beyond recovery (Commoner, 1992; Meadows, Meadows, & Randers, 1992; Schmidheiny, 1992).

It thus appears that few, if any, of our past economic and organizational practices can be continued for long into the future—they are simply not sustainable. Therefore, the next 40 years present an unprecedented challenge: To achieve global sustainability, we must alter fundamentally the nature of economic and human activity or risk irreversible damage to basic ecological and social systems.

THE ROLE OF CORPORATIONS
IN ADDRESSING GLOBAL CHANGE

The challenge of global sustainability can be conceptualized at several levels, each implying a different mechanism for appropriate intervention (Starik & Rands, 1995). Many, for example, believe that global-scale problems, such as those articulated above, require action at the global level through international agencies or other forms of world government (e.g. MacNeil, Winsemius, and Yakushiji, 1991; van Dieren, 1995; von Weizsacker, 1994). Others see the challenge as a composite of country- or community-level concerns, suggesting intervention at the national or local levels (e.g., Daly & Cobb, 1989; Greider, 1997; Korten, 1995; Schumacher, 1973). Still others frame the challenge as one requiring multilevel, interorganizational collaboration through partnerships, alliances, and networks (Cooperrider & Pasmore, 1991; Gray & Wood, 1991; Trist, 1983).

Although all three of the above perspectives are valid and important, this chapter takes a different point of view. I begin with the premise that sustainability can be ushered in only if *corporations* (firms, businesses, and companies), the main economic engines of the future, alter their behavior fundamentally (Fischer & Schot, 1993; Gladwin, 1992; Schmidheiny, 1992; Shrivastava & Hart, 1995). Incremental improvement by existing businesses and industries will not be enough: The scourges of the late 20th century—depleted fisheries, forests, and soils; choking urban pollution; poverty; and migration—appear to require fundamental restructuring of industries and infrastructures. Global industrial companies are the only transnational entities that actually produce things. As such, they are ideally positioned to introduce sustainable practices in economies around the world. In short, it would seem that corporations are the only organizations with the resources, technology, and global reach to facilitate sustainability.

Viewed in this light, the challenge of sustainable development presents a whole new class of needs and problems that is not recognized or served by existing industries and companies. Instead of looking to existing entities for the answers, I instead propose that the solution lies in the development of entirely new, more sustainable industries. New industries form when coalitions of companies and entrepreneurs combine their skills and knowledge in new ways to address unmet needs. Achieving sustainability thus implies the "creative destruction" of existing technologies and industries by emergent coalitions of firms and entrepreneurs with fundamentally different technical and social visions (Schumpeter, 1942).

I argue that existing corporations are in prime position to identify and drive the development of such new, sustainable industries. To capture these opportunities, however, corporations must fundamentally rethink their prevailing views about strategy, competition, and cooperation. Indeed, if existing corporations are to become agents of global sustainability in the coming decades, a fundamentally new conceptualization of strategy will be required. The existing competitive paradigm, in which a firm's success comes at the expense of other firms, the community, or the environment, will almost certainly not move us toward sustainability. Indeed, the purely competitive model of strategy has helped to create many of the problems articulated: In the quest for short-term profitability, firms have routinely externalized costs that harm not only the environment but also the firm itself in the long run.

To facilitate the transition to global sustainability, the traditional competitive model of strategy will have to give way to a new vision of collaborative strategy development. However, a purely cooperative mode, in which firms' behavior is based solely upon altruism and ethics, will also fail to facilitate the creation of a sustainable world. This chapter argues neither for pure competition (thesis) nor colloboration (antithesis). In the truest sense of the dialectic, global sustainability will be enhanced by corporations capable of *synthesis*—the simultaneous use of cooperative and competitive behaviors. In the end, the goal of the firm is still to do well for itself, but not necessarily at the expense of other firms (even competitors), and certainly not at the expense of society and the natural environment. In moving beyond competitive strategy, this chapter articulates a new model of success, one where corporations serve as agents of global sustainability through the creation of new industries that fulfill human needs in ways that do not lead to long-term social and environmental deterioration.

THE COMPETITIVE MODEL

The field of strategic management has long understood that business success depends upon the match between distinctive internal (organizational) capabilities and changing external (environmental) circumstances (Andrews, 1971; Chandler, 1962; Hofer & Schendel, 1978; Penrose, 1959). However, it has been only over the past decade that a bona fide theory, known as the resource-based view of the firm, has emerged articulating the relationships among firm resources, capabilities, and success (competitive advantage). Figure 15.1 provides a graphical summary of these relationships and some of the key authors associated with the core ideas.

Sustainable Competitive Advantage

The concept of competitive advantage has been treated extensively in the literature. Competitive advantage grows out of the value that a firm is able to create for its customers that exceeds the firm's cost of creating it, relative to competitors. Value is what customers are willing to pay, and superior value

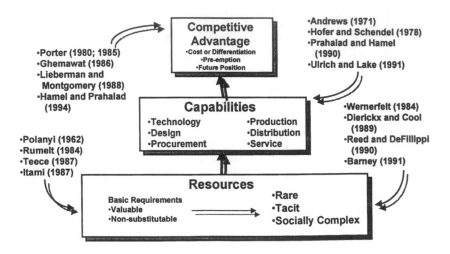

Figure 15.1 Resource-Based View

stems from offering lower prices than competitors for a given benefit, or providing unique benefits that more than offset a higher price. Thus, there are two basic sources of competitive advantage: cost leadership and differentiation (Porter, 1980, 1985). Cost leadership enables aggressive pricing and high sales volume, whereas differentiation creates brand loyalty and positive reputation, facilitating premium pricing.

Decisions concerning timing (e.g., moving early versus late) and commitment level (e.g., entering on a large scale versus more incrementally) are also crucial in securing competitive advantage (Ghemawat, 1986; Lieberman & Montgomery, 1988). By moving early, or on a large scale, it is sometimes possible to preempt competitors by setting new standards or gaining preferred access to critical raw materials, locations, production capacity, or customers. Preemptive commitments thus enable firms to gain a strong focus and dominate a particular niche, either through lower costs, differentiated products, or both (Porter, 1980). Finally, Hamel and Prahalad (1989, 1994) have emphasized the importance of "competing for the future" as a neglected dimension of competitive advantage. According to this view, the firm must be concerned not only with profitability in the present, and growth in the medium term, but also with its future position and source of competitive advantage. This requires explicit strategizing about how the firm will compete when its current strategy configuration is either copied or made obsolete.

The connection between a firm's capabilities and competitive advantage has also been well-established in the literature. Andrews (1971), and later, Hofer and Schendel (1978) and Snow and Hrebiniak (1980), noted the centrality of "distinctive competencies"—unique skills, resources, or capabilities —to competitive success. More recently, Prahalad and Hamel (1990) and Ulrich and Lake (1991) reemphasized the strategic importance of identifying, managing, and leveraging core competencies rather than focusing only on products and markets in business planning. The resource-based view takes this thinking one step further: It posits that competitive advantage can be sustained only if the capabilities creating the advantage are supported by resources not easily duplicated by competitors (Wernerfelt, 1984). In other words, firm resources must raise "barriers to imitation" (Rumelt, 1984). Thus, resources are the basic units of analysis and include physical and financial assets as well as employee skills and organizational (social) processes. Capabilities result from bundles of resources being brought to bear on particular value-added tasks (e.g., design for manufacturing, just-in-time production).

Although the terminology has varied (Peteraf, 1993), there appears to be general agreement in the strategic management literature about the characteristics of resources that contribute to sustained competitive advantage. At the most basic level, such resources must be valuable (i.e., rent-producing) and nonsubstitutable (Barney, 1991; Dierickx & Cool, 1989). In other words, for a resource to have enduring value, it must contribute to a capability with competitive significance that is not easily accomplished through alternative means. Next, strategically important resources must be rare and/or specific to a given firm (Barney, 1991; Reed & DeFillippi, 1990). That is, they must not be widely distributed within an industry and/or must be closely identified with a given organization, making them difficult to transfer or trade (e.g., a brand image or an exclusive supply arrangement). Although physical and financial resources may produce temporary advantage for a firm, they can often be readily acquired on factor markets by competitors or new entrants. Conversely, a unique path through history may enable a firm to obtain unusual and valuable resources that cannot be acquired easily by competitors (Barney, 1991).

Finally, and perhaps most important, such resources must be difficult to replicate because they are either tacit (causally ambiguous) or socially complex (Teece, 1987; Winter, 1987). Tacit resources are skill based and people intensive. Such resources are "invisible" assets based upon learning-by-doing that is accumulated through experience and refined by practice (Itami, 1987; Polanyi, 1962). Socially complex resources depend upon large numbers of people or teams engaged in coordinated action such that few individuals, if any, have sufficient breadth of knowledge to grasp the overall phenomenon (Barney, 1991; Reed & DeFillippi, 1990).

In sum, the goal of the competitive strategy model is to gain advantage over rivals through lower costs or differentiated products. Sustaining this advantage depends upon the cultivation of capabilities that cannot be quickly or easily acquired or imitated by competitors: To achieve this end, capabilities must be rare (firm-specific), tacit (causally ambiguous), or socially complex.

Collaboration to Ensure Legitimacy

Whereas the literature on competitive strategy focuses on competition among defined sets of players within industry sectors, other writers emphasize that a purely competitive approach may prove inadequate because issues of social acceptance and reputation are also extremely important to business success (Gray & Wood, 1991; Westley & Vredenburg, 1991). Institutional theorists, for example, have long recognized that to endure, competitive advantage must be created within a broader scope of social legitimacy (Bozeman, 1987; DiMaggio & Powell, 1983; Meyer & Rowan, 1977; Selznick, 1957).

Nowhere can this phenomenon be seen more vividly than in the chemical industry, where the creation of the Responsible Care program by the Chemical Manufacturers Association (CMA) helped rescue the industry from near oblivion. Following the Bhopal disaster in 1984 (in which 3,000 residents of Bhopal, India died as a result of a toxic chemical explosion at a Union Carbide plant), leading companies in the industry (e.g., Dow, DuPont, Monsanto) pressed for self-regulation to avert future chemical disasters that might threaten the continued survival of the industry. This culminated in 1988 in the adoption by the CMA of Responsible Care—a statement of environmental principles and codes of management practices that included provisions for community involvement. To give the program teeth, the principles and codes were made obligatory for CMA member companies, which comprised 90% of the chemical capacity in the United States; noncompliance was grounds for expulsion from CMA. Since 1988, Responsible Care has literally transformed the chemical industry's environmental behavior and helped to change the public perception of the industry from one of shameless polluter to more responsible actor.

As the Responsible Care example shows, when leading firms adopt "green" or socially responsible practices, they serve as models for other firms in the industry. Through industry-level collaborative processes, firms within a given sector (e.g., chemicals) come to resemble each other in terms of organizational structure and culture as well as environmental management and performance. Ultimately, pressure to mimic leading firms results in gradual improvement in the performance of the industry as a whole.

BEYOND COMPETITIVE STRATEGY

Although commendable and important, collaboration to ensure legitimacy serves only to incrementally improve the performance of existing industry participants. Sectoral collaboration is used to solidify the competitive positions of incumbents by rewriting the rules of the game in their favor. In this sense, collaboration among competitors serves to perpetuate the current industry structure. As a result, it fosters continuous improvement rather than reinvention or fundamental innovation.

But the more we learn about the challenges of global change and sustainability, the clearer it is that we are poised at the threshold of a historic discontinuity with the potential to transform many of the world's industries. Indeed, most existing energy- or material-intensive industries (e.g., oil, chemicals, mining, and transportation, to name but a few) are probably not sustainable in the long term. High levels of resource consumption, toxic contamination, or waste generation will ultimately limit the expansion of these industries, especially in the emerging markets of Asia, central and eastern Europe, Latin America, and Africa.

In the decades ahead, pressures for sustainable development will almost certainly open up opportunities for creative firms capable of envisioning and creating new, less impactful ways of fulfilling the needs of these massive and largely unserved populations. But although the opportunities are vast, few companies have the capacity or market power to unilaterally alter entire socio-technical systems. This suggests broader collaboration for system redesign —working with host governments, nongovernmental organizations (NGOs), the financial sector, and other companies to build entirely new, sustainable industrial systems.

Recently, a few writers in the field of strategic management have begun to recognize that fundamentally new technology and business creation requires intensive cooperation, sometimes with competitors, but more frequently with firms from beyond existing industry boundaries (e.g., customers,

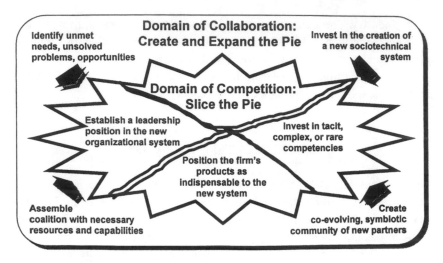

Figure 15.2 Creating New Sociotechnical Systems

complementors, regulators, and even stakeholders). They urge corporations to think in terms of building "coalitions" (Hamel & Prahalad, 1994), "co-opetition" (Brandenburger & Nalebuff, 1996), and "co-evolution" (e.g., Moore, 1996), rather than limiting their horizons to the traditional competitive model of defined industries and competitors.

The logic for this perspective is as follows: In a world of rapid techno-logical change and globalization of markets, traditional industry boundaries are easily crossed. As a consequence, successful companies increasingly may be those able to reinvent existing industries or create entirely new industries. As firms begin to think more in terms of solving customer problems rather than competing against a set of established players, the industry perspective becomes increasingly irrelevant. Strategy formulation in this context means thinking beyond the company and industry to find unmet needs, unsolved problems, and unexploited opportunities. Implementation then turns on put-ting together a coalition of players with the capabilities needed to create an emergent industrial system, because no single firm possesses all of the necessary resources (see "Domain of Collaboration," upper portion of Fig-ure 15.2).

For a given firm, strategizing thus begins by imagining how new coali-tions might evolve that better serve customers' and societies' needs, and finding ways to contribute to that development process. Sun Microsystems, for example, saw the emergence of the Internet as a social innovation of potentially vast proportions. Sun developed the Internet programming language called Java that greatly facilitated movement on the system. But rather than trying to sell Java in the near term as a product, Sun instead gave Java away to feed the Internet frenzy and reaffirm its image as a leader of the movement. Sun viewed Java as an investment in the creation of a new sociotechnical system that might one day become an important source of revenue as well as reputation for the firm (Brandenburger & Nalebuff, 1996).

Creating and expanding a new sociotechnical system also requires building coalitions with the necessary new resources and capabilities (see "Domain of Collaboration," lower portion of Figure 15.2). Often, this entails assembling a coevolving, symbiotic community of new partners that jointly creates the new system (Moore, 1996). As an example, Intel has led the way toward creation of coalitions that deliver functionalities based upon speed of information processing. Recognizing that its competitive success depends upon the emergence of software and services that take advantage of the speed of its chips, for example, Intel sought to create a new coalition of players to accelerate the development of advanced video applications, which require massive computing power for maximum effectiveness. Intel partnered with telecommunications companies to develop ProShare, a new videoconferencing system. Phone companies saw this development as in their own interest because they were already trying to sell the higher capacity ISDN phone lines necessary to drive the new system. Intel also partnered with Compaq to include ProShare on all of its new PCs. This arrangement helped differentiate Compaq's computers from others in an already crowded market for PCs. It also helped generate the necessary volume so that the ProShare program could be priced at a level attractive to a large base of potential users. Only by creating such a symbiotic community of partners was it possible to make this functionality available to the market.

However, it is no coincidence that Intel also assumed a critical role in the new system: Without its chips, the whole coalition collapses, whereas virtually any phone or computer company could complete the coalition. Thus, assuming a leadership stance in an emerging sociotechnical system is the best way to position the firm for competitive advantage once the contours of the new system have been defined (see "Domain of Competition," middle portion of Figure 15.2). A leadership position entails preemptive investments in competencies that are rare and difficult to imitate, and that are indispensable to the development of the new system. Given the indispensable nature of

Intel's products to this rapidly growing, emerging system, it should come as no surprise that over the past decade, the company has been among the most profitable in the world. Hardware companies and phone companies, although profitable, have not positioned themselves to capture the rent stream in the same fashion.

Cooperation would thus appear to be essential in creating and expanding the pie (new sociotechnical system), but competitive positioning determines which firms receive the largest slices of the pie (profits) once it is formed. Under this model, business success does not have to be a win-lose game. In fact, the most effective corporate strategies of the future may be those that solve problems and provide new functionalities by establishing thriving new communities of profitable, symbiotic partners.   /

CORPORATIONS AS AGENTS
OF GLOBAL SUSTAINABILITY

The challenge of sustainable development presents an opportunity over the next 10 years or so for a few companies—perhaps one or two in each industry—to drive the redefinition of their underlying sociotechnical systems toward sustainability. This will entail both aggressive development of new internal competencies and external coalition building (see Figure 15.3). Already, a few examples can be identified from selected industries:

■ *Chemical industry.* Must the industry be based upon the use of petroleum feedstocks and toxic materials (unsustainable), or is it possible to imagine an industry based upon biologically derived materials (potentially sustainable)? For example, Monsanto has committed to orienting its future strategy around biotechnology and sustainable development. By spinning off its bulk chemical businesses and investing heavily in biotechnology-based products that use dramatically fewer resources and create little to no waste, Monsanto has charted a course that will challenge the rest of the chemical industry over the next decade. Establishing an early position in the agricultural area has required extensive competency development in addition to new partnerships with farmers, seed companies, food manufactures, retailers, NGOs, and environmental groups. Monsanto aims to reinvent the world agricultural system, which it views as unsustainable in its present form because of high levels of dependency on agricultural chemicals and nonrenewable energy. Already, other companies have joined the push toward sustainable agriculture and "green" chemistry, including DuPont, Novartis, and Novo Nordisk. It is increasingly evident that

	Internal (Competitive)	External (Cooperative)
Pollution Prevention	Tacit e.g., TQEM	Transparency e.g., public disclosure
Product Stewardship	Socially Complex e.g., DfE	Stakeholder Integration e.g., external advisors
Clean Technology	Rare e.g., core competence	Technology Cooperation e.g., take-back systems
Sustainable Development	Path Dependent e.g., shared vision	Infrastructure Development e.g., new business systems

Figure 15.3 Corporations as Agents of Global Sustainability

the chemical industry is in the process of restructuring, with some companies remaining committed to petroleum- and chlorine-based chemical production while others focus on biological substitutes.

■ *Petroleum industry.* Must the industry be oriented around extracting and refining fossil fuels from the earth's crust (unsustainable), or is it possible to envision an industry that produces, refines, and distributes biofuels from the earth's surface (potentially sustainable)? British Petroleum and Sweden's OK Petroleum, for example, have recently come to the conclusion that their core competencies need not be tied to fossil fuels but to skills in refining and distributing renewable, liquid fuels. British Petroleum has announced its intention to transition to renewable sources of energy in the coming years. OK Petroleum has taken a leadership position by lobbying in favor of carbon taxes on fossil fuels and is aggressively pursuing alliances and joint ventures with the players necessary to create the new system. It appears that the restructuring of the oil industry is under way with global sustainability as the core driver.

■ *Metals industry.* Must the industry, with its vast technical knowledge for refining metals, be oriented around mining (unsustainable), or is it possible to envision an industry designed around recycling—mining the high-grade "ores" already circulating in the human economy? Today, for example, there is more copper above ground than below. Aluminum and steel are also extensively recovered, recycled, and reused. Efficient cycling of surface stocks may prove to be a better long-term proposition than the mining of fresh reserves. For example, Phillip Environmental, the rapidly growing, Ontario-based waste management firm, has emerged as an early leader in this capacity. Rather than emphasizing the treatment or disposal of waste materials (the dominant perspective in the waste management industry), Phillip has pioneered new technologies in material recovery and reuse, with thriving businesses in copper cable recycling and the recovery of foundry sands and scrap. Acquisition and joint venture have been the primary means by which Phillip has gained access to the new expertise. However, the strategy has also required the nurturing of numerous new relationships with suppliers and potential customers.

The Automobile Industry: Creative Destruction?

The automobile industry also presents tremendous opportunity when viewed through the lens of global sustainability. Over the past two decades, auto tailpipe emissions and fuel economy have improved incrementally through a combination of regulation, pollution prevention, and industry collaboration. Vehicle recycling has also been highly successful, especially in Europe, where product "take-back" requirements obligate manufacturers to take responsibility for their products at the end of their useful lives. Yet, at the same time, most environmental gains by the industry have been offset by volume increases (number of units sold) and growth in vehicle miles driven by individual drivers. Indeed, growth in emerging markets will generate huge additional car sales—and massive pollution—in the coming decades. Already the rush is on to stake out positions in China, India, and Latin America. More cars on the road spells continuing decline in air quality and increases in greenhouse gas emissions despite incremental improvements on a per-unit basis. It is difficult to imagine how the industry in its current form can be projected very far into the future.

Now step back and try to imagine a *sustainable* vision for the industry. What form could the opportunity take? Amory Lovins at the Rocky Mountain Institute has demonstrated the feasibility of building hypercars—vehicles that are fully recyclable, 20 times more energy efficient, 100 times cleaner, and cheaper than existing cars. These vehicles retain the safety and performance of conventional cars but achieve radical simplification through the use of lightweight, composite materials; fewer parts; virtual prototyping; regenerative braking; and very small, hybrid engines. Hypercars, which are more akin to computers on wheels than to cars with microchips, may render obsolete most of the competencies associated with today's auto manufacturing (e.g., metal stamping, tool and die making, and the internal combustion engine). Not surprisingly, investment in the concept has come not from the auto industry but from an emerging coalition of electronics, aerospace, and materials companies—firms that possess key technologies and skills needed to operationalize the hypercar concept.

Beyond Cars

Assume for a moment that clean technology, such as the hypercar or Mazda's soon-to-be-released hydrogen rotary engine, can be developed for a market such as China. Now try to envision a transportation infrastructure capable of accommodating so many cars. How long will it take before gridlock and traffic jams force the auto industry to a halt? Sustainability will require new transportation solutions for the needs of emerging economies with huge populations. Will the incumbents in the auto industry be prepared for this discontinuity in their business, or will they leave the field to coalitions of new ventures that are not encumbered by the competencies of the past? What might a new technological system look like that jointly solves the transportation and environmental problems of emerging economies? Who are the players with the knowledge and skills needed to speed the emergence of such a new system?

History suggests that major technological discontinuities occur when entrants from *outside* existing industries develop new capabilities (or combine existing ones) in ways that offer vastly superior functionality or dramatically lower cost (Cooper & Schendel, 1976; Foster, 1976). Suppliers of sailing ships, buggy whips, vacuum tubes, and propeller engines (to name but a few) were all displaced by new sociotechnical systems that emerged from outside of the existing industries. Initially crude and expensive, the new technology expands through successive rounds of experimentation, adaptation, and sub-market penetration. Incumbent firms either discount the significance of the emergent technology or fight back by seeking to improve the old technology. Most incumbents are usually not successful in building new capabilities needed to secure a competitive position in the emerging sociotechnical system. Ultimately, a new industry emerges with a different set of dominant competitors.

This pattern of technological discontinuity has occurred repeatedly over the course of the past century, with new industries emerging from the ashes of the old (Schumpeter, 1942). Industry incumbents that do not survive discontinuities do not see the new technology coming in time. Survivors generally evidence a higher degree of foresight and a propensity to invest and partner to acquire new competencies, rather than seeking only to shore up their current position. The challenge of global change may be signaling a series of approaching technological discontinuities of unprecedented proportions. The question is: Do today's existing corporations possess the foresight and agility to seize the opportunity before it is too late?

CONCLUSIONS AND RESEARCH QUESTIONS

As was noted at the outset, the challenge of global change and sustainability can be conceptualized at several levels, each implying a different point of intervention. For some, the problem appears to require action at the global level, through international agencies or other forms of world government. Others see the challenge as requiring national or community-level intervention. Still others frame the sustainability challenge as dictating multilevel, interorganizational collaboration.

In contrast, this chapter has taken the position that the world's industries and corporations are the best places to look for solutions. I argue that the corporate sector holds the key because it is the engine of most economic activity and development in the world. Indeed, it is asserted that corporations are the only organizations with the resources, technology, and global reach to affect global-scale problems directly. The arguments developed to support this basic premise can be stated in the form of several research propositions, which are summarized below.

1. *Successfully confronting the issues of global change and sustainability will require creation of fundamentally new sociotechnical systems, not incremental improvement within existing industries.* The traditional competitive model assumes that players in established industries battle each other for market share and industry leadership, with many costs externalized to society and the environment. In some cases, players within industry sectors may collaborate to reduce the negative impacts of their activities, thereby maintaining social legitimacy. But for corporations to become agents of global sustainability, entirely new sociotechnical systems need to be created that fulfill human needs with dramatically less social and environmental impact.

2. *Creating new sociotechnical systems will require a new model of strategic management, one that emphasizes coalition building across sectors with partners from outside the existing industry.* To respond to the sustainability challenge, a new conceptualization of strategic management is necessary— one that goes beyond the conventional model of competitive strategy. I argue that cooperation is essential to creating and expanding such new sociotechnical systems, but competitive positioning determines which firms receive the

largest slices of the profits once the new system is formed. In moving beyond competitive strategy, business does not have to be a win-lose game. In fact, the most effective strategies in the future may be those that solve social and environmental problems by establishing thriving new communities of profitable, symbiotic partners.

3. *Existing industry players can develop the foresight and agility to lead the transformation to sustainability.* Finally, I argue that the sheer magnitude of unmet needs and unsolved problems should serve as a magnet to attract self-organizing, coevolving coalitions of firms that are inventing new sociotechnical systems to address them. The question is whether or not the reinvention process will be led by current industry incumbents or by new players coming from outside of existing industry frameworks. Evidence suggests that some industrial corporations have acquired the skills and experience needed to lead the redefinition of industries through cooperation and coalition formation. Only time will tell whether or not the potential is realized.

REFERENCES

Aburdene, P., & Naisbitt, J. (1992). *Megatrends for women.* New York: Villard.

Ackoff, R. (1974). *Redesigning the future: A systems approach to societal problems.* New York: Wiley.

Adler, N. J. (1993-94). Asian women in management. *International Studies of Management and Organization, 23*(4), 3-17.

Adler, N. J. (1994a). Competitive frontiers: Women managing across borders. In N. J. Adler & D. N. Izraeli (Eds.), *Competitive frontiers: Women managers in a global economy* (pp. 22-40). Cambridge, MA: Basil Blackwell.

Adler, N. J. (1994b). Globalization, government, and competition. *Optimum, 25*(1), 27-34. (in English and French)

Adler, N. J. (1995). Competitive frontiers: Cross-cultural management in the 21st century. *International Journal of Intercultural Relations, 19,* 523-537.

Adler, N. J. (1996). Global women political leaders: An invisible history, an increasingly important future. *Leadership Quarterly, 7*(1), 133-161.

Adler, N. J. (1997a). Global leaders: A dialogue with future history. *International Management, 1*(2), 21-33.

Adler, N. J. (1997b). *International dimensions of organizational behavior* (3rd ed.). Cincinnati, OH: South-Western.

Adler, N. J. (1998). Societal leadership: The wisdom of peace. In S. Srivastva & D. L. Cooperrider (Eds.), *Executive wisdom and organizational change* (pp. 205-221). San Francisco: Jossey-Bass.

Adler, N. J., & Bird, F. (1988). International dimensions of executive integrity: Who is responsible for the world? In S. Srivastva (Ed.), *The functioning of executive integrity* (pp. 243-337). San Francisco: Jossey-Bass.

Adler, N. J., & Boyacigiller, N. (1995a). Global organizational behavior: Going beyond tradition. *Journal of International Management, 1*(1), 73-86.

Adler, N. J., & Boyacigiller, N. (1995b). Going beyond traditional HRM scholarship. In R. N. Kanungo & D. M. Saunders (Eds.), *New approaches to employee management. Vol. 3: Employee management issues in developing countries* (pp. 1-13). Greenwich, CT: JAI.

Afonso, C. A. (1990). NGO networking: The telematic way. *Development, 2,* 51-54.

Alderfer, C. A. (1976). Boundary relations and organizational diagnosis: A conceptual statement. In H. M. Meltzer & F. R. Wickert (Eds.), *Humanizing organizational behavior* (pp. 109-133). Springfield, IL: Charles C Thomas.

Alexander, M. J., & Mohanty, C. T. (1997). *Feminist genealogies, colonial legacies, democratic futures.* New York: Routledge.

Alvarez, K. (1994). *The twilight of the panther.* Sarasota, FL: Myakka River.

Alvarez, R., & Makhijani, A. (1988, August-September). Hidden legacy of the arms race: Radioactive waste. *Technology Review,* pp. 43-51.

Anderson, B. (1994). Exodus. *Critical Inquiry, 20,* 314-327.

Anderson, N. F. (1993). Benazir Bhutto and dynastic politics: Her father's daughter, her people's sister. In M. A. Genovese (Ed.), *Women as national leaders* (pp. 41-69). Newbury Park, CA: Sage.

Andrews, K. (1971). *The concept of strategy.* Homewood, IL: Irwin.

Annis, S. (1992). Evolving connectedness among environmental groups and grassroots organizations in protected areas of Central America. *World Development, 20,* 587-595.

Arena-DeRosa, J. (1990, Summer/Fall). Indigenous leaders host U.S. environmentalists in the Amazon. *Oxfam America News,* pp. 1-2.

Argyle, M. (1991). *Cooperation: The basis of sociability.* London: Routledge & Kegan Paul.

Argyris, C., & Schon, D. (1978). *Organizational learning: A theory of action perspective.* Reading, MA: Addison-Wesley.

Arora, D. (1996, February 17). The victimising discourse: Sex determination technologies and policy. *Economic and Political Weekly,* pp. 420-424.

Ashcroft, B., Griffiths, G., & Tiffin, H. (Eds.). (1995). *The post-colonial studies reader.* London: Routledge.

Astley, W. G., & Fombrun, C. (1983). Collection strategy: Social ecology of organizational environments. *Academy of Management Review, 8,* 576-587.

Axelrod, R. (1984). *The evolution of cooperation.* New York: Basic Books.

Bachrach, P., & Baratz, M. S. (1963). Decisions and nondecisions: An analytical framework. *American Political Science Review, 57,* 641-651.

Backer, T. E. (1991). *Drug abuse technology transfer.* Rockville, MD: U.S. Department of Health Services.

Bakhtin, M. M. (1981). *The dialogic imagination: Four essays.* Austin: University of Texas Press.

Bakhtin, M. M. (1984). *Problems of Dostoevsky's Poetics.* Manchester, UK: Manchester University Press.

Bakhtin, M. M. (1986). *Speech genres and other late essays* (C. Emerson & M. Holquist, Eds.). Austin: University of Texas Press.

Bahuguna, S. (1988). Chipko: The people's movement with a hope for the survival of humankind. *IFDA Dossier, 63,* 3-14.

Bajaj, J. K. (1988). Francis Bacon, the first philosopher of modern science: A non-Western view. In A. Nandy (Ed.), *Science, hegemony and violence* (pp. 24-67). New Delhi: Oxford University Press.

Baquedano, M. (1989). Socially appropriate technologies and their contribution to the design and implementation of social policies in Chile. In C. Downs, G. Solimano, C. Vergara, & L. Zuniga (Eds.), *Social policy from the grassroots: Nongovernmental organizations in Chile* (pp. 113-133). Boulder, CO: Westview.

Barker, D. (1980). Appropriate methodology: Using a traditional African board game in measuring farmers' attitudes and environmental images. In D. W. Brokensha, D. M. Warren, & O.

Werner (Eds.), *Indigenous knowledge systems and development* (pp. 301-306). Lanham, MD: University Press of America.

Barker, D., Oguntoyinbo, J., & Richards, P. (1977). *The utility of the Nigerian peasant farmer's knowledge in the monitoring of agricultural resources: A general report* (MARC Report No. 4). London: Chelsea College.

Barley, S. R. (1988). The social construction of a machine: Ritual, superstition, magical thinking and other pragmatic responses to running a CT scanner. In M. Lock & D. R. Gordon (Eds.), *Biomedicine examined* (pp. 497-539). Boston: Kluwer Academic Press.

Barnard, C. I. (1938). *The functions of the executive.* Cambridge, MA: Harvard University Press.

Barnes, B. (1983). On the conventional character of knowledge and cognition. In K. D. Knorr-Cetina & M. Mulkay (Eds.), *Science observed: Perspectives on the social study of science* (pp. 220-242). London: Sage.

Barnet, R. J., & Cavanagh, J. (1994). *Global dreams: Imperial corporations and the new world order.* New York: Simon & Schuster.

Barney, J. (1991). Firm resources and sustained competitive advantage. *Journal of Management, 17,* 99-120.

Barrett, D. (1995). *Reproducing persons as a global concern: The making of an institution.* Doctoral dissertation in progress, Stanford University.

Barrett, F. (1996). Creating appreciative learning cultures. *Organizational Dynamics, 4,* 36-44.

Barzetti, V., & Rovinski, Y. (1992). *Towards a Green Central America.* West Hartford, CT: Kumarian.

Bateson, M. C. (1989). *Composing a life.* New York: Atlantic Monthly Press.

Bateson, M. C. (1994). *Peripheral vision: Learning along the way.* New York: HarperCollins.

Bauman, Z. (1989). *Modernity and the Holocaust.* Cambridge, UK: Polity.

Bellah, R. H., Madsen, R., Sullivan, W. M., Swidler, A., & Tipton, S. M. (1991). *The good society.* New York: Vintage.

Benn, M. (1995, February). Women who rule the world. *Cosmopolitan.*

Bennis, W. (1963). A new role for behavioral sciences: Effecting organizational change. *Administrative Science Quarterly, 8,* 125-165.

Bergquist, W. (1993). *The postmodern organization.* San Francisco: Jossey-Bass.

Berkovitch, N. (1994). *From motherhood to citizenship: The world-wide incorporation of women.* Unpublished doctoral dissertation, Stanford University.

Berman, M. (1982). *All that is solid melts into air: The experience of modernity.* New York: Simon & Schuster.

Bezborua, R., & Banerjee, J. (1991). *Multi-agency collaboration for promoting a low-cost and sustainable rural energy source: The biogas case.* New Delhi: Ekatra.

Bhutto, B. (1989). *Daughter of destiny: An autobiography.* New York: Simon & Schuster.

Bilimoria, D., Cooperrider, D. L., Kaczmarski, K., Khalsa, G., Srivastva, S., & Upadhayaya, P. (1995). A call to organizational scholarship: The organizational dimensions of global change: No limits to cooperation. *Journal of Management Inquiry, 4,* 71-109.

Bingham, G. (1986). *Resolving environmental disputes: A decade of experience.* Washington, DC: Conservation Foundation.

Bleeke, J., & Ernst, D. (Eds.). (1993). *Collaborating to compete: Using strategic alliances and acquisitions in the global marketplace.* New York: John Wiley.

Blondel, J. (1987). *Political leadership: Towards a general analysis.* London: Sage.

Boje, D. M., Gephart, R. P., & Joseph, T. (Eds.). (in press). *Postmodern management and organization theory.* Thousand Oaks, CA: Sage.

Boli, J., & Thomas, G. M. (1995, February). *Organizing the world polity: INGOs since 1875.* Paper presented at the annual meeting of the International Studies Association, Chicago.

Boulding, E. (1988). *Building a global civic culture: Education for an interdependent world.* New York: Teachers College Press.

Boulding, E. (1990). Building a global civic culture. *Development, 2,* 39.

Bouwen, R., Devisch, J., & Steyaert, C. (1992). Innovation projects in organizations: Complementing the dominant logic by organizational learning. In D. Hosking & N. Anderson (Eds.), *Organizational change and innovation* (pp. 000-000). London: Routledge.

Bouwen, R., & Fry, R. (1991). Organizational innovation and beaming: Four paths of dialogue between the dominant logic and the new logic. *International Studies in Management and Organization, 21*(4), 37-51.

Bouwen, R., & Steyaert, C. (1990). Construing organizational texture in young entrepreneurial firms. *Journal of Management Studies, 27,* 637-649.

Bozeman, B. (1987). *All organizations are public.* San Francisco: Jossey-Bass.

Braimoh, D., & Sets'abi, A. M. (1994). *Improving the material conditions of rural communities in Lesotho through credit unions.* Nairobi: African Association for Literacy and Adult Education.

Brandenburger, A., & Nalebuff, B. (1996). *Co-opetition.* New York: Doubleday.

Bratton, M. (1992, January). *Civil society and political transition in Africa.* Civil Society in Africa Conference at Hebrew University of Jerusalem.

Bratton, M. (1994). Non-govemmental organizations in Africa: Can they influence public policy? In E. Sandberg (Ed.), *The changing politics of non-governmental organizations and African states* (pp. 33-58). Westport, CT: Praeger.

Brokensha, D. W., Warren, D. M., & Werner, O. (1980). *Indigenous knowledge systems and development.* Lanham, MD: University Press of America.

Brown, J. S., & Duguid, P. (1991). Organizational learning and communities-of-practice: Toward a unified view of working, learning, and innovation. *Organization Science, 2*(1), 40-57.

Brown, L. D. (1980). Planned change in underorganized systems. In T. G. Cummings (Ed.), *Systems theory for organization development* (pp. 181-193). New York: Wiley.

Brown, L. D. (1982). Interface analysis and the management of unequal conflict. In G. B. J. Bomers & R. B. Peterson (Eds.), *Conflict management and industrial relations* (pp. 60-78). Boston: Kluwer-Nijhoff.

Brown, L. D. (1991). Bridging organizations and sustainable development. *Human Relations, 44,* 807-831.

Brown, L. D. (1993). Development bridging organizations and strategic management for social change. In J. Dutton & D. Cooperrider (Eds.), *Advances in strategic management* (Vol. 9, pp. 381-405). Greenwich, CT: JAI.

Brown, L. D. (1998). Creating social capital: Nongovernmental development organizations and intersectoral problem-solving. In W. W. Powell & E. Clemens (Eds.), *Private action for the public good* (pp. 228-241). New Haven, CT: Yale University Press.

Brown, L. D., & Ashman, D. (1995). *Intersectoral problem solving, participation and social capital formation: African and Asian cases.* Working paper, Institute for Development Research, Boston.

Brown, L. D., & Detterman, L. B. (1987). Small interventions for large problems: Reshaping urban leadership networks. *Journal of Applied Behavioral Science, 23,* 151-168.

Brown, L. D., & Fox, J. (1996). *The struggle for accountability: The World Bank, NGO's and grassroots movements.* Unpublished manuscript, Institute for Development Research, Boston.

Brown, L., & Kane, H. (1994). *Full house.* New York: Norton.

Brown, L., Kane, H., & Roodman, D. (1994). *Vital signs.* New York: Norton.

Brown, L. D., & Korten, D. C. (1991). Working more effectively with nongovernmental organizations. In S. Paul & A. Israel (Eds.), *Nongovernmental organizations and the World Bank* (pp. 45-93). Washington, DC: World Bank.

Brown, L. D., & Tandon, R. (1993). *Multiparty collaboration for development in Asia.* New York: United Nations Development Programme.

Brown, R. (1981). *Social psychology.* New York: The Free Press.

Browning, L. D., Beyer, J. M., & Shetler, J. C. (1995). Building cooperation in a competitive industry: Sematech and the semiconductor industry. *Academy of Management Journal, 38,* 113-153.

Bruce, B., & Peyton, K. J. (1990). A new writing environment and an old culture: A situated evaluation of computer networking to teach writing. *Interactive Learning Environments, 1,* 171-191.

Brundtland Bulletin. (1991). Vol. 13. Geneva: Center for Our Common Future.

Brundtland Bulletin. (1993). Vol. 20. Geneva: Center for Our Common Future.

Brundtland Bulletin. (1994). Vol. 23. Geneva: Center for Our Common Future.

Bruner, J. (1990). *Acts of meaning.* Cambridge, MA: Harvard University Press.

Brysk, A. (1993). From above and below: Social movements, the international system, and human rights in Argentina. *Comparative Political Studies, 26,* 259-285.

Brysk, A., Pagnucco, R., & Smith, J. (1996). *Solidarity beyond the state: The dynamics of transnational social movements.* Syracuse, NY: Syracuse University Press.

Bulauitan, J. C. (1995, December 5). Loida Nicolas-Lewis. *Business World* [On-line]. Available: http://bizworld.globe.come.ph/oe121595/CorporateWorld/corpfeature.html;09/20/96.

Bunker, B. (1990). Appreciating diversity and modifying organizational cultures: Men and women at work. In S. Srivastva & D. L. Cooperrider (Eds.), *Appreciative management and leadership* (pp. 126-149). San Francisco: Jossey-Bass.

Burns, J. F. (1994, August 27). India fights abortion of female fetuses. *New York Times,* p. 5.

Burrows, M. (1995, Winter). Customer commitment: Global Focus: An interview with Maureen Kempston Darkes. *Canadian Business Review,*

Burton, L., & Timmerman, P. (1989). Human dimensions of global change: A review of responsibilities and opportunities. *International Social Science Journal, 121,* 297-313.

Burton, M., & Kirk, L. (1980). Ethnoclassification of body parts: A three-culture study (Massai, Kikuyu, U.S.A.). In D. W. Brokensha, D. M. Warren, & O. Werner (Eds.), *Indigenous knowledge systems and development* (pp. 271-300). Lanham, MD: University Press of America.

Cairncross, F. (1992). *Costing the earth.* Boston: Harvard Business School Press.

Carroll, J. E. (1986). Water resources management as an issue in environmental diplomacy. *Natural Resources Journal, 26,* 207-220.

CBSG (Conservation Breeding Specialist Group). (1993). *Futures search report.* Minneapolis, MN: Author.

Cernea, M. (1987). Farmer organizations and institution building. *Regional Development Dialogue, 8*(2), 1-24.

Chadha, P. (1991). *Employees' initiative in combatting industrial sickness: The case of Kamani tubes—India.* New Delhi: Centre for Workers Management.

Chambers, R. (1983). *Rural development: Putting the last first.* London: Longman.

Chandler, A. (1962). *Strategy and structure.* Cambridge: MIT Press.

Clark, H. (1985). Language use and language users. In G. Lindzey & E. Aronson (Eds.), *Handbook of social psychology* (pp. 185-209). New York: Random House.

Clayton, S. (1994). Appeals to justice in the environmental debate. *Journal of Social Issues, 50*(3), 13-27.

Clegg, S. R. (1990). *Modern organizations.* London: Sage.

Clement, C. (1993). SatelLife: Strategic health initiative. *Development, 3,* 60.

Clifford, J., & Marcus, G. E. (Eds.). (1986). *Writing culture.* Berkeley: University of California Press.

Club of Lisbon Report. (1994). *Limits to competition.* Brussels: Vubpress.

Cobb, C., Halstead, T., & Rowe, J. (1995, October). If the GDP is up, why is America down? *Atlantic Monthly,* pp. 59-78.

Col, J.-M. (1993). Managing softly in turbulent times: Corazon C. Aquino, president of the Philippines. In M. A. Genovese (Ed.), *Women as national leaders* (pp. 13-40). Newbury Park, CA: Sage.

Cole, R. E. (1989). *Strategies for learning.* Berkeley: University of California Press.

Coleman, J. S. (1990). *Foundations of social theory.* Cambridge, MA: Belknap.

Collins, H. M. (1983). An empirical relativist programme in the sociology of scientific knowledge. In K. D. Knorr-Cetina & M. Mulkay (Eds.), *Science observed: Perspectives on the social study of science* (pp. 162-181). London: Sage.

Combs, A. (Ed.). (1992). *Cooperation: Beyond the age of competition.* Philadelphia: Gordon and Breach.

Commoner, B. (1992). *Making peace with the planet.* New York: The New Press.

Compass. (1993). Vol. 57. Rome: Society for International Development.

Compton, J. L. (1980). Indigenous folk media in rural development in South and Southeast Asia. In D. W. Brokensha, D. M. Warren, & O. Werner (Eds.), *Indigenous knowledge systems and development* (pp. 307-320). Lanham, MD: University Press of America.

Cooper, A., & Schendel, D. (1976, February). Strategic responses to technological threats. *Business Horizons,* pp. 61-69.

Cooper, R., & Burrell, G. (1988). Modernism, postmodernism and organizational analysis: An introduction. *Organization Studies, 9,* 91-112.

Cooperrider, D. L. (1990). Positive imagery, positive action: The affirmative basis of organizing. In S. S. Srivastva & D. L. Cooperrider, *Appreciative management and leadership: The power of positive thought in organizing* (pp. 91-125). San Francisco: Jossey-Bass.

Cooperrider, D. L., & Bilimoria, D. (1993). The challenge of global change for strategic management: Opportunities for charting a new course. In P. Shrivastava, A. Huff, & J. Dutton (Eds.), *Advances in strategic management* (pp. 99-142). Greenwich, CT: JAI.

Cooperrider, D. L., & Pasmore, W. A. (1991). Global social change: A new agenda for social science? *Human Relations, 44,* 1037-1055.

Cooperrider, D. L., & Srivastva, S. (1987). Appreciative inquiry in organizational life. In W. A. Pasmore & R. W. Woodman (Eds.), *Research in organization development and change* (Vol. 1, pp. 129-169). Greenwich, CT: JAI.

Cordoba-Novion, C., & Sachs, C. (1987). *Urban self-reliance directory.* Nyon, Switzerland: International Foundation for Development Alternatives.

Cox, E. (1987). Networking among the rural women in the South Pacific. *Ideas and Action, 175,* 18-23.

Crook, S., Pakulski, J., & Waters, M. (1992). *Postmodernization.* London: Sage.

Crowfoot, J., & Wondolleck, J. (1988). *Environmental mediation.* Washington, DC: Island Press.

Crozier, M. (1964). *The bureaucratic phenomenon.* London: Tavistock.

Cruz, A. (1990). La incorporacion de las Nuevas Tecnologias de Informacion por las Organizaciones No Gubemamentales uruguayas. In F. Barreiro & A. Cruz, *Organizaciones No Gubernamentales de Uruguay: A nalisis y Reperiorio.* Montevideo, Uruguay: Institucion de Comunicacion y Desarrollo.

Dahrendorf, R. (1996). Economic opportunity, civil society, and political liberty. *Development and Chance, 27,* 229-249.

Daly, H., & Cobb, J. (1989). *For the common good.* Boston: Beacon Press.

Daniels, E. (1996). A future history of research on the human dimensions of global change. *Environment, 34,* 1-21.

Daudpota, Q. I. (1995). Information superhighway—Here we come! *The Way Ahead: Pakistan's Environment and Development Quarterly, 2*(2), 26-28.

DAWN Informs. (1989). Vol. 7/8, p. 6.

de Gaspe Beaubien, N., & de Gaspe Beaubien, P. (1994). *Wanda Ferragamo video program.* Montreal: Institute for Family Enterprise.

Denzin, N. K. (1989). *Interpretive interactionism.* Newbury Park, CA: Sage.

de Oliveira, M. D., & Tandon, R. (1994). *Citizens: Strengthening global civil society.* Washington, DC: CIVICUS.

Derrida, J. (1987). *Psyché: inventions de l'Autre.* Paris: Galilée.

DevCom Bulletin. (1987). Vol. 12.

Dierickx, I., & Cool, K. (1989). Asset stock accumulation and sustainability of competitive advantage. *Management Science, 35,* 1504-1511.

Dillin, J. (1994, April 22). U.S. probes crime's global reach. *The Christian Science Monitor,* pp. 1, 16.

DiMaggio, P., & Powell, W. (1983). The iron cage revisited: Institutional isomorphism and collective rationality in organizational fields. *American Sociological Review, 48,* 147-160.

Dimancescu, D., & Botkin, J. (1986). *The new alliance: America's R&D consortia.* Cambridge, MA: Ballinger.

Diong, I. C. (1994). *African regional NGOs: An overview of institutions.* Washington, DC: U.S. Forest Service, Office of International Forestry.

Dobrin, D. (1989). *Writing and technique.* Urbana, IL: National Council of Teachers of English.

Dobrzynski, J. H. (1996, November 6). Somber news for women on corporate ladder. *New York Times,* p. D1.

Doheny-Farina, S. (1992). *Rhetoric, innovation, technology.* Cambridge: MIT Press.

Dommen, A. J. (1975). The bamboo tube well: A note on an example of indigenous technology. *Economic Development and Cultural Change, 27*(2), 23-28.

Dougherty, D. (1992). Interpretive barriers to successful product innovation in large firms. *Organization Science, 3,* 179-202.

Drucker, P. F. (1992). *Managing for the future: The 1990s and beyond.* New York: Truman Tally Books/Dutton.

Duncan, R., & Weiss, A. (1979). Organizational learning: Implications for organization design. In L. L. Cummings & B. M. Staw (Eds.), *Research in organizational behavior* (Vol. 1, pp. 75-124). Greenwich, CT: JAI.

Durning, A. (1989). People power and development. *Foreign Policy, 2,* 66-82.

Dutton, J. (1993). The making of organizational opportunities: An interpretive pathway to organizational change. In B. Staw & L. L. Cummings (Eds.), *Research in organizational behavior,* Vol. 15, pp. 199-226. Greenwich, CT: JAI.

Eagly, A. H., & Johnson, B. T. (1990). Gender and leadership style: A meta-analysis. *Psychological Bulletin, 108,* 233-256.

Eberlee, J. (1995). Computer networks: A democratic tool for NGOs. *IDRC Reports, 23*(1), 16-17.

Eco, U. (1994). *La recherche de la langue parfaite dans la culture Européenne.* Paris: Editions du Seuil.

Economic and Political Weekly. (1992, May 30). pp. 1153-1155.

ElSheikh, E. O., & Wangoola, P. (1994). *IARA-HIKMA popular health programme for the urban poor in Greater Khartoum, Sudan.* Nairobi: African Association for Literacy and Adult Education.

Emery, M., & Purser, R. E. (1996). *The search conference: A powerful method for planned organizational change and community action.* San Francisco: Jossey-Bass.

Engardio, P. (1993, November 8). An ultrasound foothold in Asia. *Business Week,* pp. 68-69.

Engardio, P. (1994). Third World leapfrog. *Business Week* (Special Issue on the Information Revolution), pp. 47-49.

Epstein, J. (1994, December 8). Beaming the Americas into cyberspace: How Brazil activists tap the Internet. *The Christian Science Monitor,* pp. 1, 20.

Erikson, K. (1994). *A new species of trouble.* New York: Norton.

Etzioni, A. (1961). *Comparative analysis of complex organizations: On power, involvement, and their correlates.* New York: Free Press.

Etzioni, A. (1993). *The spirit of community: The reinvention of American society.* New York: Simon & Schuster.

Evans, P. (1996). Government action, social capital and development: Reviewing the evidence on synergy. *World Development, 24,* 1119-1132.

Evans, P. B., Jacobson, H., & Putnam, R. (1993). *Double-edged diplomacy: International bargaining and domestic politics.* Berkeley: University of California Press.

Eyoh, N. (1985/6). The Kumba workshop on theatre for integrated rural development. *Ideas and Action, 165,* 12-18.

FAO/FFHC. (1987). NGOs in Latin America: Their contribution to participatory democracy. *Development, 4,* 100-105.

Farrington, J., Bebbington A., with Wellard, K., & Lewis, D. J. (1993). *Reluctant partners? Non-governmental organizations, the state and sustainable agricultural development.* London and New York: Routledge.

Fenner, F., Henderson, D. A., Arita, I., Jezek, J., & Ladnyi, I. D. (1988). *Smallpox and its eradication.* Geneva: World Health Organization.

Finger, M., & Verlaan, P. (1995). Learning our way out: A conceptual framework for social-environmental learning. *World Development, 23,* 503-515.

Finlay, F. (1990). *Mary Robinson: A president with a purpose.* Dublin: O'Brien Press.

Fiol, M. C., & Lyles, M. (1985). Organizational learning. *Academy of Management Review, 10,* 803-813.

Fiorino, D. J. (1988, July/August). Regulatory negotiations as a policy process. *Public Administration Review,* pp. 20-28.

Fischer, K., & Schot, J. (Eds.). (1993). *Environmental strategies for industry.* Washington, DC: Island Press.

Fisher, J. (1993). *The road from Rio: Sustainable development and the nongovernmental movement in the Third World.* Westport, CT: Praeger.

Fisher, J. (1998). Nongovernmentals: NGOs and the political development of the Third World. West Hartford, CT: Kumarian.

Fleagle, R. G. (1994). *Global environmental change.* Westport, CT: Praeger.

Fleck, L. (1979). *Genesis and development of a scientific fact.* Chicago: University of Chicago Press. (Originally published in German in 1935)

Follett, M. P. (1940). How must business management develop in order to possess the essentials of a profession? In H. C. Metcalf & L. Urwick (Eds.), *Dynamic administration: The collected papers of Mary Parker Follett* (pp. 117-131). Evanston, NY: Harper & Row. (Originally published in 1925)

Foster, R. (1976). *Innovation: The attacker's advantage.* New York: Summit.

Foucault, M. (1977a). *Language, counter-memory, practice: Selected essays and interviews* (D. F. Bouchard, Ed.). Ithaca: Cornell University Press.

Foucault, M. (1977b). *Discipline and punish: The birth of the prison.* New York: Pantheon.

Foucault, M. (1978). *The history of sexuality, Volume 1: An introduction.* New York: Random House.

Foucault, M. (1988). *Politics, philosophy, culture: Interviews and other writings 1977-1984.* London: Routledge.

Frank, D. J. (1994). *Global environmentalism: International treaties and nation-state participation.* Unpublished doctoral dissertation, Stanford University.

Freedman, D. H. (1992). Is management still a science? *Harvard Business Review, 70*(6), 26-38.

Freire, P. (1973). *Education for critical consciousness* (M. Ramos, Trans.). New York: Seabury.

French, H. W. (1995, November 11). On the Internet, Africa is far behind. *New York Times,* p. A14.

Frenier, C. R. (1997). *Business and feminine principle: The untapped resource.* Boston: Butterworth-Heinemann.

Frisby, D. (1985). *Fragments of modernity.* London: Polity.

Frontline. (1994, May 29). Taking on GATT [On-line]. Available: www.the-hindu.com/fline/index.htm.

Fukuyama, F. (1995). *Trust.* New York: Free Press.

Ganley, G. D. (1992). *The exploding political power of personal media.* Norwood, NJ: Ablex.

García-Canclini, N. (1990). *Culturas híbridas: Estrategias para entrar y salir de las modernidad.* Grijalbo, México: Consejo Nacional para la Cultura y las Artes.

Garner, R., & Zald, M. N. (1985). The political economy of social movement sectors. In G. D. Suttles & M. N. Zald (Eds.), *The challenge of social control: Citizenship and institution building in modern society* (pp. 119-148). Norwood, NJ: Ablex.

Garrison, J. (1989). Computers link NGOs worldwide. *Grassroots Development, 2,* 48-49.

Genovese, M. A. (Ed.). (1993). *Women as national leaders.* Newbury Park, CA: Sage.

Gergen, K. J. (1991). *The saturated self.* New York: Basic Books.

Gergen, K. J. (1994). *Realities and relationships: Soundings in social construction.* Cambridge, MA: Harvard University Press.

Gergen, K. J., & Gergen, M. M. (1994). *Sandoz in the new century: An incorporative vision of communication for managerial effectiveness.* Basel: Sandoz Pharma.

Gergen, K. J., & Whitney, D. (1995). Technologies of representation in the global organization: Power and polyphony. In D. M. Boje, R. P. Gephart, & T. Joseph (Eds.), *Postmodern management and organization theory* (pp. 331-357). Thousand Oaks, CA: Sage.

Ghemawat, P. (1986). Sustainable advantage. *Harvard Business Review, 64*(5), 53-58.

Giddens, A. (1974). *Positivism and sociology.* London: Heinemann.

Giddens, A. (1994). *Beyond left and right.* Stanford, CA: Stanford University Press.

Gifford, C. A. (1993). TIPS: Developing a strong South-South bridge. *Development, 3,* 62.

Gilbert, D. T. (1991). How mental systems behave. *American Psychologist, 46,* 107-119.

Gilligan, C. (Ed.). (1988). *Mapping the moral domain: A contribution of women's thinking to psychological theory and education.* Cambridge, MA: Harvard University Press.

Ginsberg, F. D., & Rapp, R. (Eds.). (1995). *Conceiving the new world order: The global politics of reproduction.* Los Angeles: University of California Press.

Gladwin, T. (1992). The meaning of greening: A plea for organizational theory. In K. Fischer & J. Schot (Eds.), *Environmental strategies for industry* (pp. 37-62). Washington, DC: Island Press.

Golich, V. L., & Young, T. F. (1993). Resolution of the United States-Canadian conflict over acid rain controls. *Journal of Environment & Development, 2*(1), 63-110.

Gore, A. (1992). *Earth in the balance.* Boston: Houghton Mifflin.

Gore, A. (1993). *Earth in the balance: Ecology and the human spirit.* New York: Penguin.

Graedel, T., & Crutzen, P. (1989). The changing atmosphere. *Scientific American, 264*(9), 58-68.

Granovetter, M. (1973). The strength of weak ties. *American Journal of Sociology, 78,* 1360-1380.

Granovetter, M. (1982). The strength of weak ties: A network theory revisited. In P. V. Marsden & N. Lin (Eds.), *Social structure and network analysis* (pp. 105-130). Beverly Hills, CA: Sage.

Gray, B. (1989). *Collaborating: Finding common ground for multiparty problems.* San Francisco: Jossey-Bass.

Gray, B. (1996). Building collaborative alliances among business, government and stakeholders. In C. Huxham (Ed.), *In search of collaborative advantage* (pp. 57-79). London: Sage.

Gray, B. G., & Hay, T. M. (1986). Political limits to interorganizational consensus and change. *Journal of Applied Behavioral Science, 22,* 95-112.

Gray, B., & Wood, D. (1991). Collaborative alliances: Moving from practice to theory. *Journal of Applied Behavioral Science, 27,* 3-22.

Greider, W. (1997). *One world ready or not.* New York: Simon & Schuster.

Gricar, B., & Brown, L. D. (1981). Conflict, power and organization in a changing community. *Human Relations, 34,* 877-893.

Grimshaw, R. G. (1993). The Vetvier network. *Development, 3,* 64.

Gulati, R. (1995). Does familiarity breed trust? The implications of repeated ties for contractual choice in alliances. *Academy of Management Journal, 38,* 85-112.

Gupta, A. (1993). Honey Bee: An accountable global network of grassroots innovators and experimenters. *Development, 3,* 64-65.

Gurr, T. R. (1995, May). Communal conflicts and global security. *Current History, 94*(592), 212-217.

Haas, E. B. (1990). *When knowledge is power: Three models of change in international organizations.* Berkeley: University of California Press.

Haas, P. M. (1989). Do regimes matter? Epistemic communities and Mediterranean pollution control. *International Organization, 43,* 377-403.

Haas, P. M. (1992). Introduction: Epistemic communities and international policy coordination. *International Organization, 46,* 1-35.

Haas, P., Keohane, R., & Levy, M. (Eds.). (1993). *Institutions for the earth.* Cambridge: MIT Press.

Habermas, J. (1979). *Communication and the evolution of society.* Boston: Beacon Press.

Hadenius, A., & Uggla, F. (1996). Making civil society work: Promoting democratic development: What can states and donors do? *World Development, 24,* 1621-1639.

Hage, J., & Powers, C. H. (1992). *Post-industrial lives.* Newbury Park, CA: Sage.

Hall, B. L. (1993, October). *Global networks, global civil society? Lessons from international non-governmental organizations.* Paper prepared for the ARNOVA Conference, Toronto, Ontario.

Hall, P. D. (1989). Business giving and social investment in the U.S. In R. Magat (Ed.), *Philanthropic giving: Studies in variables and goals.* New York: Oxford University Press.

Hamel, G., & Prahalad, C. K. (1989). Strategic intent. *Harvard Business Review, 68*(3), 63-76.

Hamel, G., & Prahalad, C. K. (1993). Strategy as stretch and leverage. *Harvard Business Review, 73*(2), 75-84.

Hamel, G., & Prahalad, C. K. (1994). *Competing for the future.* Boston: Harvard Business School Press.

Hampden-Turner, C. M. (1994). The structure of entrapment: Dilemmas standing in the way of women managers and strategies to resolve them. In *The Deeper News.* Emeryville, CA: Global Business Network.

Haraway, D. (1990). A manifesto for cyborgs: Science, technology, and socialist feminism in the 1980s. In L. J. Nicholson (Ed.), *Feminism/postmodernism* (pp. 190-233). New York: Routledge.

Haraway, D. J. (1997). *Modest_witness@second_millenium.femaleman©_meets_oncomouse*™. New York: Routledge.

Hardin, G. (1968). Tragedy of the commons. *Science, 162,* 1243-1248.

Hardy, C., & Phillips, N. (1996). Strategies of engagement: Lessons from the critical examination of collaboration and conflict in an interorganizational domain. *Organizational Science, 9*(2), 217-230.

Harman, W., & Hormann, J. (1990). *Creative work: The constructive role of business in a transforming society.* Indianapolis, IN: Knowledge Systems.

Hart, S. L. (1995). A natural resource-based view of the firm. *Academy of Management Review, 20,* 986-1014.

Hart, S. L. (1997). Beyond greening: Strategies for a sustainable world. *Harvard Business Review, 75*(1), 66-76.

Hauzeair, R. F. (1984). FEPEC-Colombia. *ICVA News,* 118.

Havel, V. (1994, July 8). The new measure of man. *New York Times,* p. A27.

Hayek, F. A. (1945). Use of knowledge in society. *American Economic Review, 55*(1), 23-40.

Heimer, C. (1985). Allocating information costs in a negotiated information order: Interorganizational constraints on decision making in Norwegian oil insurance. *Administrative Science Quarterly, 30,* 395-417.

Helgesen, S. (1990). *The female advantage: Women's ways of leadership.* New York: Doubleday.

Helgesen, S. (1994). *The web of inclusion: A new architecture for building great organizations.* New York: Currency/Doubleday.

Helgesen, S. (1995). *The web of inclusion.* New York: Currency/Doubleday.

Himelstein, L. (1996, October 28). Shatterproof glass ceiling. *Business Week,* p. 55.

The Hindu. (1994, November 20). Section M, p. v.

Hofer, C., & Schendel, D. (1978). *Strategy formulation: Analytical concepts.* St. Paul, MN: West.

Hofstede, G. (1984). Motivation, leadership and organization: Do American theories apply abroad? In D. A. Kolb, I. M. Rubin, & J. M. McIntyre (Eds.), *Organizational psychology* (4th ed., pp. 309-334). Englewood Cliffs, NJ: Prentice Hall.

Holquist, M., & Emerson, C. (1981). Glossary. In M. M. Bakhtin, *The dialogic imagination.* Austin: University of Texas Press.

Holzner, B., & Marx, J. (1979). *Knowledge application: The knowledge system in society.* Boston: Allyn & Bacon.

Homer-Dixon, T., Boutwell, J., & Rathjens, G. (1993). Environmental change and violent conflict. *Scientific American, 268*(2), 38-45.

Horton, R. (1967). African traditional thought and Western science. *Africa, 37,* 155-187.

Houghton, I. (1994). *Promoting environmental protection through energy conservation in Kenya.* Nairobi: African Association for Literacy and Adult Education.

Howes, M. (1980). The uses of indigenous technical knowledge in development. In D. W. Brokensha, D. M. Warren, & O. Werner (Eds.), *Indigenous knowledge systems and development* (pp. 341-358). Lanham, MD: University Press of America.

Huber, G. P. (1991). Organizational learning: The contributing processes and the literatures. *Organizational Science, 2,* 88-115.

Hussain, A. (1991). *Collaborative efforts in rural immunization: The Bangladesh case.* Dhaka: Association of Development Agencies of Bangladesh.

IFDA Dossier. (1984). Vol. 42. The Asia-Pacific People's Environment Network. Nyon, Switzerland: International Foundation for Development Alternatives.

IFDA Dossier. (1987a). Vol. 61. ALOP—Trabajando por Latinoamerica (pp. 65-67). Nyon, Switzerland: International Foundation for Development Alternatives.

IFDA Dossier. (1987b). Vol. 59. ANEN—The African NGOs Environment Network (pp. 31-41). Nyon, Switzerland: International Foundation for Development Alternatives.

IFDA Dossier. (1987c). Vol. 69. ELCI elects Fazal as chairman (p. 81). Nyon, Switzerland: International Foundation for Development Alternatives.

IFDA Dossier. (1989). Vol. 74. South West Asian Ocean: A directory of activists (p. 88). Nyon, Switzerland: International Foundation for Development Alternatives.

IFDA Dossier. (1990a). Vol. 78. Asia: ARTA (p. 110). Nyon, Switzerland: International Foundation for Development Alternatives.

IFDA Dossier. (1990b). Vol. 77. Latin America: CLADES (pp. 99-103). Nyon, Switzerland: International Foundation for Development Alternatives.

IFDA Dossier. (1991). Vol. 80. Nyon, Switzerland: International Foundation for Development Alternatives.

Impact. (1992, Spring).

International Atomic Energy Agency. (1981). *The management of radioactive wastes.* Vienna: Author.

International Council of Scientific Unions. (1986). *The international geosphere-biosphere program: A study of global change.* Paris: Author.

International Tree Project Clearinghouse. (1987). *A directory: NGOs in the forest sector* (2nd Africa ed.). New York: United Nations, Non-Governmental Liaison Service.
IRED Bulletin. (1986). Vol. 21. IRED (Innovations et Reseaux pour le Developpement).
IRED Bulletin. (1988). Vol. 27. IRED (Innovations et Reseaux pour le Developpement).
Isen, A., Nygen, T., & Ashby, F. (1988). Influence of positive affect on subjective utility and gain and losses: It's just not worth the risk. *Journal of Personality and Social Psychology, 55,* 710-717.
Itami, H. (1987). *Mobilizing invisible assets.* Cambridge, MA: Harvard University Press.
IWRAW (International Women's Rights Action Watch). (1987). *The Women's Watch,* 1.
Jacobson, J. (1988). Planning the global family. In L. B. Brown & others (Eds.), *State of the world: A Worldwatch Institute report on progress toward sustainable society* (pp. 151-169). New York: Norton.
Joba, C., Maynard, H. B., Jr., & Ray, M. (1993). Competition, cooperation, and co-creation: Insights from the World Business Academy. In M. Ray & A. Rinzler (Eds.), *The new paradigm in business: Emerging strategies for leadership and organizational change* (pp. 50-56). New York: Tarcher/Perigee.
Johnson, P. C., & Cooperrider, D. L. (1991). Finding a path with heart: Global social change organizations and their challenge for the field of organizational development. *Research in Organizational Change and Development, 5,* 223-284.
Jones, W. T. (1969). *A history of Western philosophy: Kant to Wittgenstein and Sartre* (2nd ed.). New York: Harcourt, World & Brace.
Joseph, T., Tenkasi, R. V., & Cooperrider, D. L. (1994). Local-universal knowledge nexus in global organizing: An example from the eradication of smallpox. In A. Alkhafaji (Ed.), *Business research year book: Global business perspectives* (Vol. 1, pp. 710-714). Lanham, MD: University Press of America.
Kaczmarski, K. M. (1996). Evolution of the Mountain Forum: Global organizing for advocacy and support/A conversation with Dr. Jane Pratt, President and CEO of the Mountain Institute. *Global Social Innovations, 1*(1), 21-30.
Kaplan, R. (1994). The coming anarchy. *Atlantic Monthly, 273*(2), 44-76.
Karlin, B. (1995, July 20). Widow inherits food group and succeeds with a style of her own. *The Montreal Gazette,* p. D1.
Kaufman, S., & Duncan, G. T. (1990). Preparing the ground for mediation: Foothills revisited. *International Journal of Conflict Management, 1,* 191-212.
Keck, M., & Sikkink, K. (1994). *Transnational issue networks in international politics.* Unpublished manuscript, Yale University.
Kelly, C. (1996). 50 world-class executives. *Worldbusiness, 2*(2), 20-31.
Kennedy, P. (1993). *Preparing for the twenty first century.* New York: Random House.
Keyfitz, N. (1989). The growing human population. *Scientific American, 264*(9), 119-126.
Khandwalla, P. (1988). Strategic organizations in social development. In P. Khandwalla (Ed.), *Social development: A new role for the organizational sciences* (pp. 13-21). New Delhi: Sage.
Kindleberger, C. P. (1975). Size of firm and size of nation. In J. H. Dunning (Ed.), *Economic analysis and the multinational enterprise* (pp. 342-362). New York: Praeger.
Kirbyson, G. (1996). Small businesses a significant and growing force. *The Financial Post.* (Reprinted in *Women in Management, 7*[2], 6)
Kishwar, M. (1987). The continuing deficit of women in India and the impact of amniocentesis. In H. B. Holmes & B. B. Hoskins (Eds.), *Man-made women: How new reproductive technologies affect women* (pp. 89-101). Bloomington: Indiana University Press.
Kitschelt, H. P. (1986). Political opportunity structures and political protest: Anti-nuclear movements in four democracies. *British Journal of Political Science, 16,* 57-85.

Knight, C. G. (1980). Ethnoscience and the African farmer: Rationale and strategy (Tanzania). In D. W. Brokensha, D. M. Warren, & O. Werner (Eds.), *Indigenous knowledge systems and development* (pp. 205-232). Lanham, MD: University Press of America.

Kobrin, S. (1997). Transnational integration, national markets and nation-states. In B. Toyne & D. Nigh (Eds.), *International business: An emerging vision* (pp. 242-256). Columbia: University of South Carolina Press.

Kondo, D. (1993). *Crafting selves.* New York: Routledge.

Korten, D. (1995). *When corporations rule the world.* San Francisco: Berrett-Koehler.

Kotter, J. P. (1979). *Organizational dynamics.* Reading, MA: Addison-Wesley.

Kozmetsky, G. (1990). The coming economy. In F. Williams & D. V. Gibson (Eds.), *Technology transfer: A communication perspective* (pp. 21-40). Newbury Park, CA: Sage.

Krajewksi, B. (1992). *Traveling with Hermes: Hermeneutics and rhetoric.* Amherst: University of Massachusetts Press.

Krasner, S. D. (Ed.). (1983). *International regimes.* Ithaca, NY: Cornell University Press.

Krauss, R. M., & Fussell, S. R. (1991). Perspective-taking in communication: Representation of others' knowledge in reference. *Social Cognition, 9*(1), 2-24.

Krishna, S. (1993). The importance of being ironic: A postcolonial view of critical international theory. *Alternatives, 18,* 385-417.

Kristeva, J. (1991). *Strangers to ourselves.* New York: Harvester Wheatsheaf.

Kuhn, T. S. (1970). *The structure of scientific revolutions* (2nd ed.). Chicago: University of Chicago Press.

Kulkarni, S. (1987). Pre-natal sex determination tests and female feticide in Bombay City. *FRCH.*

Kumar, A. (1986). Muslim women's bill: The rising storm. *India Today* [On-line]. Available: www.india-today.com.

Kvale, S. (Ed.). (1992). *Psychology and postmodernism.* London: Sage.

Lakoff, G., & Johnson, M. (1980). *Metaphors we live by.* Chicago: University of Chicago Press.

Lavipour, F. G., & Sauvant, K. (Eds.). (1976). *Controlling multinational enterprises: Problems, strategies, counterstrategies.* Boulder, CO: Westview.

Lawler, E. L. (1992). *The ultimate advantage: Creating the high-involvement organization.* San Francisco: Jossey-Bass.

Lazerges, A. (1993, June 15). Tansu Çiller/Turkish "Mama." *Diario, 16,* 2.

Lévi-Strauss, C. (1966). *The savage mind.* Chicago: University of Chicago Press.

Levitt, K. (1970). *Silent surrender: The multinational corporation in Canada.* Toronto: Macmillan.

Lieberman, M., & Montgomery, D. (1988). First mover advantages. *Strategic Management Journal, 9*(special issue), 41-58.

Logsdon, J. (1991). Interests and interdependence in the formation of social problem-solving collaborations. *Journal of Applied Behavioral Science, 27,* 23-37.

Lopezllera Mendez, L. (1990). The struggle of the indigenous people and the new "reservations." *Fenix, 00,* 6-7. (Continuation of UNFAO's *Ideas and Action*)

Ludema, J. D. (1996). *Narrative inquiry: Collective storytelling as a source of hope, knowledge, and action in organizational life.* Unpublished doctoral dissertation, Case Western Reserve University, Cleveland, OH.

Lyotard, J. F. (1984). *The postmodern condition: A report on knowledge.* Minneapolis: University of Minnesota Press.

Machila, M. M. C. (1994). *Improving the material conditions of rural communities in the North Western Province of Zambia.* Nairobi: African Association for Literacy and Adult Education.

MacIntyre, A. (1984). *After virtue* (2nd ed.). South Bend, IN: University of Notre Dame Press.

Maclean, N. (1992). *Young men and fire.* Chicago: University of Chicago Press.

MacNeill, J. (1989). Strategies for sustainable economic development. *Scientific American, 264*(9), 155-165.

MacNeill, J., Winsemius, P., & Yakushiji, T. (1991). *Beyond interdependence.* New York: Oxford University Press.

March, J. G., & Simon, H. A. (1958). *Organizations.* New York: John Wiley.

Mather, L., & Yngvesson, B. (1980-81). Language, audience and the transformation of disputes. *Law and Society Review, 15,* 775-821.

Mathews, J. T. (1989). Redefining security. *Foreign Affairs, 68,* 162-167.

Mathews, J. T. (1991). *Preserving the global environment: The challenge of shared leadership.* New York: Norton.

Mayo, E. (1939). Foreword. In F. D. Roethlisberger & W. D. Dickson, *Management and the worker* (p. 5). Cambridge, MA: Harvard University Press.

Mazmanian, D., & Sabatier, P. (1983). *Implementation and public policy.* Glenview, IL: Scott, Foresman.

McAdam, D. (1982). *Political process and the development of Black insurgency, 1930-1970.* Chicago: University of Chicago Press.

McAdam, D., McCarthy, J. D., & Zald, M. N. (1996). *Comparative perspectives on social movements: Political opportunity, mobilizing structures, and framing processes.* New York: Cambridge University Press.

McAdam, D., & Rucht, D. (1993). The cross-national diffusion of movement ideas. *Annals of the American Academy of Political and Social Science, 528,* 56-74.

McCarroll, T. (1996, October 28). A woman's touch. *Time Magazine, 148*(20) (Internet back issue listing).

Mead, G. H. (1934). *Mind, self and society.* Chicago: University of Chicago Press.

Meadows, D., Meadows, D., & Randers, J. (1992). *Beyond the limits.* Post Mills, NY: Chelsea Green.

Meehan, P. (1980). Science, ethnoscience, and agricultural knowledge utilization. In D. W. Brokensha, D. M. Warren, & O. Werner (Eds.), *Indigenous knowledge systems and development* (pp. 383-392). Lanham, MD: University Press of America.

Mendlovitz, S. H., & Walker, R. B. (1987). *Towards a just world peace: Perspectives from social movements.* Boston: Butterworth.

Meyer, J. W. (1994). Rationalized environments. In W. R. Scott, J. W. Meyer, & Associates (Eds.), *Institutional environments and organizations: Structural complexity and individualism* (pp. 28-54). Thousand Oaks, CA: Sage.

Meyer, J., & Rowan, B. (1977). Institutionalized organizations: Formal structure as myth and ceremony. *American Journal of Sociology, 83,* 340-363.

Milbrath, L. (1989). *Envisioning a sustainable society: Learning our way out.* Albany: State University of New York Press.

Miles, M. B., & Huberman, A. M. (1994). *Qualitative data analysis* (2nd ed.). Thousand Oaks, CA: Sage.

Mitroff, I. (1987). *Business not as usual.* San Francisco: Jossey-Bass.

Mohanty, C. (1991). Under Western eyes: Feminist scholarship and colonial discourses. In C. T. Mohanty, A. Russo, & L. Torres (Eds.), *Third World women and the politics of feminism* (pp. 51-80). Bloomington: Indiana University Press.

Monday Developments. (1994). Vol. 12, No. 16.

Moore, G. (1980). New shoots from old roots. In D. W. Brokensha, D. M. Warren, & O. Werner (Eds.), *Indigenous knowledge systems and development* (pp. 393-398). Lanham, MD: University Press of America.

Moore, J. (1996). *The death of competition.* New York: HarperBusiness.

Moraga, C. (1983). *Loving in the war years: Lo que nunca pasó por sus labios.* Boston: South End Press.

Morgan, E. A., Power, G. D., & Weigel, V. B. (1993). Thinking strategically about development: A typology of action programs for global change. *World Development, 21,* 1913-1930.

Morgan, G. (1986). *Images of organization.* Newbury Park, CA: Sage.

Morgenthau, R. (n.d.). *International Liaison Committee for Food Corps Programs* (booklet). Waltham, MA: Brandeis University.

Morss, E. R. R., Hatch, J., Mickelwaite, D. R., & Sweet, C. F. (1976). *Strategies for small farmer development, Vol. 1.* Boulder, CO: Westview.

Mulkay, M. J. (1984). Knowledge and utility: Implications for the sociology of knowledge. In N. Stehr & V. Meja (Eds.), *Society and knowledge: Contemporary perspectives on the sociology of knowledge* (pp. 77-98). New Brunswick, NJ: Transaction Books.

Muller, R. (1993). *New genesis: Shaping a global spirituality.* Anacortes, WA: World Happiness and Cooperation.

Munk, N. (1995, November 20). The best man for the job is your wife. *Forbes,* pp. 148-154.

Nadelman, E. (1990). Global prohibition regimes: The evolution of norms in international society. *International Organization, 44,* 479-526.

Nagel, J. (1980). The conditions of ethnic separatism: The Kurds in Turkey, Iran, and Iraq. *Ethnicity, 7,* 279-290.

Nagel, J., & Whorton, B. (1992). Ethnic conflict and the world system: International competition in Iraq (1961-1991) and Angola (1974-1991). *Journal of Political and Military Sociology, 20,* 1-35.

Nederveen Pieterse, J. (1994). Globalization as hybridization. *International Sociology, 9,* 161-184.

Network '92. (1992). Geneva: Center for Our Common Future.

NGLS News. (1987). New York: United Nations, Non-Governmental Liaison Service.

NGO Management. (1986a). Vol. 1.

NGO Management. (1986b), Vol. 3

Noddings, N. (1984). *Caring: A feminine approach to ethics and moral education.* Berkeley: University of California Press.

Nyambura, G. (1994). *In search of development initiatives that make a difference.* Nairobi: African Association for Literacy and Adult Education.

Nyambura, G., Wangoola, P., Vera, E., Bodurtha, N., Lundgren, N., & Meyer, D. (1995). *Toward a new development paradigm: Findings from case study research of partnerships in Africa.* Nairobi: African Association for Literacy and Adult Education and Synergos Institute.

Nyoni, P. B. (1994). *Provision of expanded facilities for water and sanitation in Gwanda District, Zimbabwe.* Nairobi: African Association for Literacy and Adult Education.

Odurkene, J. N. (1994). *The revival of fishing villages in Nebbi District, Uganda.* Nairobi: African Association for Literacy and Adult Education.

Office of Science and Technology Policy. (1997). *Our changing planet: The FY 1997 research plan.* Washington, DC: Author.

Oliver, C. (1990). Determinants of interorganizational relationships: Integration and future directions. *Academy of Management Review, 15,* 241-265.

Oliver, P., & Marwell, G. (1988). The paradox of group size in collective action: A theory of the critical mass, II. *American Sociological Review, 53,* 1-8.

Oliver, P., Marwell, G., & Teixeira, R. (1985). A theory of the critical mass: Interdependence, group heterogeneity, and the production of collective action. *American Journal of Sociology, 91,* 522-556.

Olson, M. (1965). *The logic of collective action: Public goods and the theory of groups.* Cambridge, MA: Harvard University Press.

Olzak, S. (1992). *The dynamics of ethnic competition and conflict.* Stanford, CA: Stanford University Press.

O'Neill, J. (1994, July 21). Here's to you, Mrs. Robinson. *The Montreal Gazette,* p. B3.

Ong, A. (1987). *Spirits of resistance and capitalist discipline.* Albany: State University of New York Press.

Opfell, O. S. (1993). *Women prime ministers and presidents.* Jefferson, NC: McFarland.

Ormrod, R. K. (1974). *Adaptation in cultural ecosystems.* Unpublished doctoral dissertation, Pennsylvania State University, Pittsburgh.

Oxfam America News. (1989, Fall). Worldbeat, p. 3.

Padron, M. (1986). The Third World NGDO's Task Force: Origin, aims, evolution and present status. *IRED Forum, 18*, pp. 26-27.

Paige, J. (1975). *Agrarian revolution.* New York: Free Press.

Patel, S. J. (1992). In tribute to the golden age of the South's development. *World Development, 20*, 767-777.

Pearson, A., Hurstak, J. M., & Raiser, J. (1993). *Salvatore Ferragamo, spa case.* Harvard Business School case no. 9-392-023. Boston: Harvard Business School Press.

Penrose, E. (1959). *The theory of the growth of the firm.* New York: John Wiley.

Perlmutter, H. V., & Trist, E. (1986). Paradigms for societal transition. *Human Relations, 39*, 1-27.

Perrow, C. (1986). *Complex organizations: A critical essay* (3rd ed.). New York: Random House.

Peteraf, M. (1993). The cornerstones of competitive advantage: A resource-based view. *Strategic Management Journal, 14*, 179-191.

Peters, T. J., & Waterman, R. H., Jr. (1982). *In search of excellence.* New York: Harper & Row.

Petrella, R. (Chairman). (1994). *Grenzen aan de competitie* [Limits to competition]. Brussels: Vubpress.

Pettigrew, A. (1976, May). *The creation of organizational cultures.* Paper presented at the Joint EIASM-Dansk Management Center Research Seminar on Entrepreneurs and the Process of Institution Building, Copenhagen.

Pfeffer, J. (1994). *Competitive advantage through people.* Boston: Harvard Business School Press.

Piddington, K. W. (1989). Sovereignty and the environment: Part of the solution or part of the problem? *Environment, 31*, 18-20, 35-39.

Pogrebin, R. (1996, October 18). Pearson picks an American as executive. *New York Times*, p. D7.

Polanyi, M. (1962). *Personal knowledge: Towards a post-critical philosophy.* Chicago: University of Chicago Press.

Poole, M. S., & DeSanctis, G. (1994). Capturing the complexity in advanced technology use: Adaptive structuration theory. *Organization Science, 5*, 121-147.

Porter, G., & Brown, J. W. (1991). *Global environmental politics.* Boulder, CO: Westview.

Porter, M. (1980). *Competitive strategy.* New York: The Free Press.

Porter, M. (1985). *Competitive advantage.* New York: Free Press.

Porter, M. E. (1990). *The competitive advantage of nations.* New York: Free Press.

Postel, S. (1992). *Last oasis: Facing water scarcity.* New York: Norton.

Powell, W. W., Koput, K. W., & Smith-Doerr, L. (1996). Interorganizational collaboration and the locus of innovation: Networks of learning in biotechnology. *Administrative Science Quarterly, 41*, 116-145.

Prahalad, C. K., & Hamel, G. (1990). The core competence of the corporation. *Harvard Business Review, 68*(3), 79-91.

Prakash, G. (Ed.). (1995). *After colonialism: Imperial histories and postcolonial displacements.* Princeton, NJ: Princeton University Press.

Puliatti, E. (1990). Computer mediated communication—Systems and developing countries. *Development, 2*, 60-65.

Purdy, J., & Gray, B. (1994). Government agencies as mediators of public policy disputes. *International Journal of Conflict Management, 5*, 158-180.

Purnomo, A., & Pambagio, A. (1991). *Fostering local management of small irrigation systems.* Jakarta, Indonesia: Pelangi.

Putnam, R. D. (1993). *Making democracy work: Civic traditions in modern Italy.* Princeton, NJ: Princeton University Press.

Radhakrishnan, R. (1994). Postmodernism and the rest of the world. *Organization, 1*, 305-340.

Rahim, D. H. M. S. A. (1991). *Village technology centres for development of grassroots communities in Malaysia.* New Delhi: PRIA.

Rapp, R. (1991). Moral pioneers: Women, men and fetuses on a frontier of reproductive technology. In M. di Leonardo (Ed.), *Gender at the crossroads of knowledge: Feminist anthropology in the postmodern era* (pp. 383-395). Berkeley: University of California Press.

Rashid, A. (1991). *Self-financed, self-managed low-cost sanitation development in Orangi, Pakistan.* Karachi, Pakistan: Orangi Pilot Project Research and Training Institute.

Reddy, M. J. (1979). The conduit metaphor. In A. Ortony (Ed.), *Metaphor and thought* (pp. 232-272). Cambridge, UK: Cambridge University Press.

Reed, R., & DeFillippi, R. (1990). Causal ambiguity, barriers to imitation, and sustainable competitive advantage. *Academy of Management Review, 15,* 88-102.

Reich, R. (1990). Who is us? *Harvard Business Review, 68*(1), 53-64.

Reich, R. (1991). Who is them? *Harvard Business Review, 69*(2), 77-88.

Richards, P. (1975). Alternative strategies for the African environment: For community oriented agricultural development. *African environment special report, No. 1: Problems and perspectives.* London: International African Institute.

Ridgeway, G. L. (1938). *Merchants of peace: The history of the International Chamber of Commerce.* Boston: Little, Brown.

Ring, P., & Van de Ven, A. (1994). Developmental processes of cooperative interorganizational relationships. *Academy of Management Review, 19,* 90-118.

Roddick, A. (1991). *Body and soul: Profits with principles.* New York: Random House.

Rogers, E. M. (1983). *Diffusion of innovations.* New York: Free Press.

Rogers, E. M., & Kincaid, D. L. (1981). *Communication networks: A new paradigm for research.* New York: Free Press.

Rondinelli, D. (1983). *Development projects as policy experiments.* New York: Methuen.

Roosens, E. (1989). *Creating ethnicity.* London: Sage.

Rosaldo, M. (1980). The use and abuse of anthropology: Reflections on feminism and cross-cultural understanding. *Signs, 53,* 389-417.

Rosas-Ingnacio, M. A. D. (1991). *Collaborative effort in development: The case of the Tondo Foreshoreland/Dagat-Dagatan development project.* New Delhi: PRIA.

Rosenau, J. N. (1990). *Turbulence in world politics: A theory of change and continuity.* Princeton, NJ: Princeton University Press.

Rosener, J. B. (1995). *America's competitive secret: Utilizing women as a management strategy.* New York: Oxford University Press.

Ross, L., Green, D., & House, P. (1974). The false consensus phenomenon: An attributional bias in self-perception and social perception process. *Journal of Experimental Social Psychology, 13,* 279-301.

Rothermel, R. C. (1993). *Mann Gulch fire: A race that couldn't be run.* USDA, Forest Service, General Tech. Report INT-299.

Rucht, D. (1996). *Mobilizing for "distant issues": German solidarity groups in non-domestic issues areas.* Working Paper, University of Michigan, Advanced Studies Center, International Institute.

Rucht, D. (1997). Environmental policy for the European Community: Problems of mobilizing influence in Brussels. In J. Smith, C. Chatfield, & R. Pagnucco (Eds.), *Transnational social movements: Solidarity beyond the state.* Syracuse, NY: Syracuse University Press.

Ruckelshaus, W. (1989). Toward a sustainable world. *Scientific American, 264*(9), 166-175.

Rumelt, R. (1984). Toward a strategic theory of the firm. In R. Lamb (Ed.), *Competitive strategic management* (pp. 556-570). Englewood Cliffs, NJ: Prentice Hall.

Sabur, M. A. (1986). The AFCOD experience. *IFDA Dossier, 55,* pp. 67-70.

Sackley, N., & Ibarra, H. (1995). *Charlotte Beers at Ogilvy & Mather Worldwide.* Harvard Business School case no. 9-495-031.

Said, E. (1990). Narrative, geography and interpretation. *New Left Review, 180,* 81-107.

Saint-Germain, M. A. (1993). Women in power in Nicaragua: Myth and reality. In M. A. Genovese (Ed.), *Women as national leaders* (pp. 70-102). Newbury Park, CA: Sage.

Salancik, G. R. (1977). Commitment and the control of organizational behavior and belief. In B. M. Staw & G. R. Salancik (Eds.), *New directions in organizational behavior* (pp. 1-54). Chicago: St. Clair.

Sawadogo, A. (1990). The state counter-attacks: Clearly defined priorities for Burkina Faso. *Voices from Africa, 2,* 59-64.

Schearer, S. B. (1993). *Building development projects in partnership with communities and NGOs: An action agenda for policymakers.* New York: UNDP.

Schell, J. (1987). Introduction. In A. Michnik, *Letters from prison* (pp. xvii-xlii). Berkeley: University of California Press.

Schellbardt, T. D. (1993, December 7). Kodak's top female executive resigns to be president, CEO at W.H. Brady. *Wall Street Journal,* p. B3.

Schmidheiny, S. (1992). *Changing course.* Cambridge: MIT Press.

Schneider, B. (1988). *The barefoot revolution.* Paris: Report to the Club of Rome.

Schneider, S. (1989). The changing climate. *Scientific American, 264*(9), 70-79.

Schumacher, E. F. (1973). *Small is beautiful.* New York: Harper & Row.

Schumpeter, J. (1942). *Capitalism, socialism, and democracy.* New York: Harper & Row.

Schutz, A. (1964). *Studies in social theory.* The Hague: Martinus Nijhoff.

Scott, P. T., & Trolldalen, J. M. (1993, Winter). International environmental conflict resolution: Moving beyond Rio. *NIDR Forum,* pp. 44-51.

Sebenius, J. K. (1992). Challenging conventional explanations of international cooperation: Negotiation analysis and the case of epistemic communities. *International Organization, 46,* 3-32.

Segal, A. T., & Zeller, W. (1992, June 8). Corporate women: Progress? Sure. But the playing field is still far from level. *Business Week,* p. 76.

Sellers, P. (1996, August 5). Women, sex, and power. *Fortune,* pp. 42-57.

Selznick, P. (1957). *Leadership in administration.* New York: Harper & Row.

Senge, P. (1990). *The fifth discipline: The art and practice of the learning organization.* New York: Doubleday/Currency.

Shaftoe, D. (1993). *Responding to changing times: Environmental mediation in Canada.* Waterloo, Ontario: The Network: Interaction for Conflict Resolution.

Shiva, V. (1988). *Staying alive: Women, ecology and development.* London: Zed.

Shiva, V. (1992). *Women reconnect technology, ecology and development.* Berkeley: University of California Press.

Shrivastava, P. (1983). A typology of organizational learning systems. *Journal of Management Studies, 20,* 9-21.

Shrivastava, P. (1987). *Bhopal: Anatomy of a crisis.* Cambridge, MA: Ballinger.

Shrivastava, P. (1996). *Greening business: Profiting the corporation and the environment.* Cincinnati, OH: Thomson.

Shrivastava, P., & Hart, S. (1995). Creating sustainable corporations. *Business Strategy and the Environment, 4,* 154-165.

Sikkink, K. (1993). Human rights, principled issue-networks, and sovereignty in Latin America. *International Organization, 47,* 411-441.

Smart, T. (1993, November 8). GE's brave new world. *Business Week,* pp. 62-71.

Smith, A. D. (1991). *National identity.* Reno: University of Nevada Press.

Smith, J. (1994). *The transnational social movement sector, 1983-1993.* Unpublished manuscript, Kroc Institute for International Peace Studies, Notre Dame, IN.

Smith, J., Pagnucco, R., & Romeril, W. (1994). Transnational social movement organizations in the global political arena. *Voluntas, 5*(3), 121-154.

Smith, K. G., Carroll, S. J., & Ashford, S. J. (1995). Intra- and interorganizational cooperation: Toward a research agenda. *Academy of Management Journal, 38,* 7-23.

Snow, C., & Hrebiniak, L. (1980). Strategy, distinctive competence, and organizational performance. *Administrative Science Quarterly, 25,* 317-335.

Snow, D. A., & Benford, R. D. (1992). Master frames and cycles of protest. In A. D. Morris & C. M. Mueller (Eds.), *Frontiers in social movement theory* (pp. 133-155). New Haven, CT: Yale University Press.

Soros, M. (1986). *Beyond sovereignty: The challenge of global policy.* Columbia: University of South Carolina Press.

Spector, B. I., Sjostedt, G., & Zartman, I. W. (1994). The dynamics of regime-building negotiations. In B. I. Spector, G. Sjostedt, & I. W. Zartman (Eds.), *Negotiating international regimes* (pp. 3-8). London: Graham & Trotman/Martinus Nijhoff.

Spivak, G. (1988). Can the subaltern speak? In C. Nelson & L. Grossberg (Eds.), *Marxism and the interpretation of culture* (pp. 308-341). Chicago: University of Illinois Press.

Srivastva, S., & Associates. (1983). *The executive mind.* San Francisco: Jossey-Bass.

Srivastva, S., & Cooperrider, D. L. (1990). *Appreciative management and leadership: The power of positive thought in organizing.* San Francisco: Jossey-Bass.

Stack, J. F., Jr. (1981). Ethnic groups as emerging transnational actors. In J. F. Stack, Jr. (Ed.), *Ethnic identities in a transnational world* (pp. 17-45). Westport, CT: Greenwood.

Starik, M., & Rands, G. (1995). Weaving an integrated web: Multilevel and multisystem perspectives of ecologically sustainable organizations. *Academy of Management Review, 20,* 908-935.

Starke, L. (1990). *Signs of hope: Working towards our common future.* Oxford, UK: Oxford University Press.

Steedman, M. J., & Johnson-Laird, P. N. (1980). The productions of sentences, utterances and speech acts: Have computers anything to say? In B. Butterworth (Ed.), *Language productions: Speech and talk* (pp. 58-96). London: Academic Press.

Stefflere, V. J. (1972). Some applications of multidimensional scaling to social science problems. In A. K. Romney & S. C. Weller (Eds.), *Multidimensional scaling theory and applications in the behavioral sciences* (pp. 211-243). New York: Seminar Press.

Steinem, G. (1994). *Moving beyond words.* New York: Simon & Schuster.

Sterling, C. (1994). *Thieves' world: The threat of the new global network of organized crime.* New York: Simon & Schuster.

Stern, R. N., & Barley, S. R. (1996). Organizations and social systems: Organization theory's neglected mandate. *Administrative Science Quarterly, 41,* 146-162.

Stern, P., Young, O., & Druckman, D. (1992). *Global environmental change: Understanding the human dimensions.* Washington, DC: National Academy Press.

Steyaert, C. (1995). *Perpetuating entrepreneurship through dialogue: A social constructionist approach.* Unpublished doctoral dissertation, Catholic University, Leuven, Belgium.

Steyaert, C., & Janssens, M. (1997). Reconsidering translation and language in an international business context: Beyond an instrumental approach. *Target: International Journal of Translation Studies, 9,* 131-154.

Stone, P. B. (1992). *The state of the world's mountains: A global report.* London: Zed.

Sudan Council of Voluntary Agencies. (1988, January). Conference on the role of indigenous NGOs in African recovery and development, Khartoum, Sudan.

Susskind, L. E. (1994). What will it take to ensure effective global environmental management? A reassessment of regime-building accomplishments. In B. I. Spector, G. Sjostedt, & I. W. Zartman (Eds.), *Negotiating international regimes* (pp. 221-232). London: Graham & Trotman/Martinus Nijhoff.

Susskind, L. E., & Cruikshank, J. (1987). *Breaking the impasse.* New York: Basic Books.

Swanson, R. (1980). Development interventions and self-realization among the Gourma (Upper Volta). In D. W. Brokensha, D. M. Warren, & O. Werner (Eds.), *Indigenous knowledge systems and development* (pp. 67-92). Lanham, MD: University Press of America.

Swieringa, J., & Wierdsma, A. (1994). *Creating learning organizations.* Reading, MA: Addison-Wesley.

Synergos Institute. (1993). *Working together to overcome poverty: Report of activities.* New York: Author.

Szakonyi, R. (1990). 101 tips for managing R&D more effectively. *Research and Technology Management, 33*(4), 31-36.

Tandon, R. (1993). *Holding together.* New York: UNDP.

Tarrow, S. (1995a). The Europeanization of conflict: Reflections from a social movement perspective. *West European Politics, 18*, 223-251.

Tarrow, S. (1995b). *Power in movement: Social movements, collective action and politics.* New York: Cambridge University Press.

Tavis, L. A. (Ed.). (1982). *Multinational managers and poverty in the Third World.* South Bend, IN: University of Notre Dame Press.

Taylor, F. W. (1911). *The principles of scientific management.* New York: Norton.

Teece, D. (1987). Profiting from technological innovation: Implications for integration, collaboration, licensing, and public policy. In D. Teece (Ed.), *The competitive challenge* (pp. 185-220). Cambridge, MA: Ballinger.

Tendlar, J. (1989). *Whatever happened to poverty alleviation?* New York: Ford Foundation.

Tenkasi, R. V., & Mohrman, S. A. (1995). Technology transfer as collaborative learning. In T. Backer, S. L. David, & G. Soucy (Eds.), *The behavioral science knowledge base on technology transfer* (pp. 147-168). Rockville, MD: U.S. Department of Health Services.

Thachankary, T. J., Tenkasi, R. V., & Cooperrider, D. L. (1996). *Processes of global organizing: Learnings from the eradication of smallpox.* Unpublished paper, Case Western Reserve University, Cleveland, OH.

Thatcher, M. (1993). *The Downing Street years.* New York: HarperCollins.

Theunis, S. (1992). *Non-governmental development organizations of developing countries: And the South smiles. . . .* Boston: Martinus Nijhoff.

Thoele, M. (1995). *Fire line: The summer battles of the West.* Golden, CO: Fulcrum.

Thomas, K., Swaton, E., Fishbein, M., & Otway, H. J. (1980). Nuclear energy: The accuracy of policy makers' perceptions of public beliefs. *Behavioral Science, 25*, 332-344.

Thoolen, H. (1990). Information and training in an expanding human rights movement. *Development, 2*, 86-90.

Tilly, C. (1978). *From mobilization to revolution.* Reading, MA: Addison-Wesley.

Towle, J., & Potter, B. G. (1989). *Organizational profiles of who is doing what in support of programs for sustainable development and environmental management in the Eastern Caribbean: A guide to donor assistance agencies.* St. Thomas, U.S. Virgin Islands: Island Resources Foundation.

Trist, E. (1983). Referent organizations and the development of inter-organizational domains. *Human Relations, 36*, 269-284.

Trist, E. (1986). Quality of working life and community development: Some reflections on the Jamestown experience. *Journal of Applied Behavioral Science, 22*, 223-238.

Trolldalen, J. M. (1992). *International environmental conflict resolution: The role of the United Nations.* Washington, DC: World Foundation for Environment and Development.

Tudge, C. (1991). *The last animals in the zoo.* London: Hutcheson.

Tugendhat, C. (1972). *The multinationals.* New York: Random House.

Turner, B. L., Clark, W. C., Kates, R. W., Richards, J. F., & Mathews, J. T. (Eds.). (1991). *The earth as transformed by human action.* New York: Cambridge University Press.

Ullman, R. (1983). Redefining security. *International Security, 8*, 129-153.

Ulrich, D., & Lake, D. (1991). *Organizational capability*. New York: John Wiley.

UNDP. (1992). *Human development report, 1992*. New York: Oxford University Press.

Union of International Associations. (1993). *Relationships between international non-governmental organizations and the United Nations system. Geneva: United Nations.*

Union of International Associations. (Ed.). (1997). *Encyclopedia of world problems and human potential*. New York: Springer-Verlag.

United Nations Development Program. (1993). *Human development report*. New York: Author.

United Nations Environment Program (UNEP). 1989. *Environmental perspectives to the year 2000 and beyond*. Narobi: Author.

Uphoff, N. (1992). *Learning from Gal Oya: Possibilities for participatory development and post-Newtonian social science*. Ithaca, NY: Cornell University Press.

Uvin, P., & Miller, D. (1995). *Scaling up: Thinking through the issues*. Unpublished manuscript, Brown University, Providence, RI.

Van Den Berg, J. H. (1974). *Divided existence and complex society*. Pittsburgh, PA: Duquesne University Press.

van der Veer, P. (1995). *Nation and migration: The politics of space in the South Asian diaspora*. Philadelphia: University of Pennsylvania Press.

van Dieren, W. (1995). *Taking nature into account*. New York: Springer-Verlag.

Van Liere, K. D., & Dunlap, R. (1980). The social bases of environmental concern: A review of hypotheses, explanations and empirical evidence. *Public Opinion Quarterly, 44*, 181-197.

Vernon, R. (1977). *Storm over the multinationals: The real issues*. Cambridge, MA: Harvard University Press.

Vickers, G. S. (1968). *Value systems and social processes*. New York: Basic Books.

Vinnicombe, S., & Colwill, N. L. (1995). *The essence of women in management*. London: Prentice Hall.

Voloshinov, V. N. (1973). *Marxism and the philosophy of language*. New York: Seminar.

von Moltke, K., & DeLong, P. J. (1990). Negotiating in the global arena: Debt-for-nature swaps. *Resolve, 22*(1), 3-10.

von Weizsacker, E. (1994). *Earth politics*. London: Zed.

Waddock, S. (1993). Lessons from the National Alliance of Business compact project: Business and public education reform. *Human Relations, 46*, 777-802.

Wade, J. S., Tucker, J. C., & Hamann, R. G. (1994, April). Comparative analysis of the Florida Everglades and the South American Pantanal. *Proceedings of the Interamerican Dialogue on Water Management, Miami, Florida: South Florida Water Management District*, pp. 31-70.

Waldrop, M. M. (1992). *Complexity*. New York: Simon & Schuster.

Waterman, R. H., Jr. (1990). *Adhocracy: The power to change*. Memphis, TN: Whittle Direct Books.

Weick, K. E. (1979). *The social psychology of organizing*. Reading, MA: Addison-Wesley.

Weick, K. E. (1990). Cognitive processes in organizations. In L. L. Cummings & B. M. Staw (Eds.), *Information and cognition in organizations* (pp. 185-210). Greenwich, CT: JAI Press.

Weick, K. E. (1993). The collapse of sensemaking in organizations: The Mann Gulch disaster. *Administrative Science Quarterly, 38*, 628-652.

Weick, K. E. (1995). *Sensemaking in organizations*. Thousand Oaks, CA: Sage.

Weisbord, M. (1987). *Productive workplaces*. San Francisco: Jossey-Bass.

Weisman, S. R. (1986, April 11). A daughter returns to Pakistan to cry for victory. *New York Times*, p. 2.

Wellington, S. W. (1996). *Women in corporate leadership: Progress and prospects*. New York: Catalyst.

Wernerfelt, B. (1984). A resource based view of the firm. *Strategic Management Journal, 5,* 171-180.

Wertsch, J. (1991). *Voices of the mind.* London: Harvester Wheatsheaf.

Westley, F., Gray, B., & Brown, L. D. (1996, August). *Domain analysis, organizing factors, and social capital formation in interorganizational collaboration.* Paper presented at the Academy of Management Meeting, Cincinnati, Ohio.

Westley, F., & Vredenburg, H. (1991). Strategic bridging: The collaboration between environmentalists and business in the making of green products. *Journal of Applied Behavioral Science, 27,* 65-90.

White, J., & Hymowitz, C. (1997, February 10). Broken glass: Watershed generation of women executives is rising to the top. *Wall Street Journal,* pp. A1, A6.

Willetts, P. (1982). *Pressure groups in the global system: The transnational relations of issue-orientated non-governmental organizations.* New York: St. Martin's.

Williams, F., & Gibson, D. V. (1990). *Technology transfer: A communication perspective.* Newbury Park, CA: Sage.

Williamson, O. E. (1975). *Markets and hierarchies.* New York: Free Press.

Wilmot, T. B. (1996). Inquiry and innovation in the private voluntary sector. *Global Social Innovations, 1,* 5-13.

Wilson, E. (1984). *Biophylia.* Cambridge, MA: Harvard University Press.

Wilson, E. (1989). Threats to biodiversity. *Scientific American, 264*(9), 108-116.

Winter, S. (1987). Knowledge and competence as strategic assets. In D. Teece (Ed.), *The competitive challenge* (pp. 159-184). Cambridge, MA: Ballinger.

Wittner, L. S. (1988). The transnational movement against nuclear weapons, 1945-1986: A preliminary survey. In C. Chatfield & P. Van den Dungen (Eds.), *Peace movements and political cultures* (pp. 265-294). Knoxville: University of Tennessee Press.

Wood, D. (1992, June). *"Dams or democracy?"—Stakeholders and issues in the Hungarian-Czechoslovakian hydroelectric controversy.* Paper presented at the International Association of Business and Society Meeting, Leuven, Belgium.

Wood, D. (1995, October 30). US foreign policy is a private interest. *The Plain Dealer,* p. 9-B.

Wood, D., & Gray, B. (1991). Toward a comprehensive theory of collaboration. *Journal of Applied Behavioral Science, 27,* 139-162.

World Bank. (1992). *Development and the environment.* New York: Oxford University Press.

World Bank. (1994). *The World Bank and participation.* Washington, DC: Author.

World Commission on Environment and Development. (1987). *Our common future.* Oxford, UK: Oxford University Press.

Wright, P. F., Kim-Farley, R. J., de Quadronos, C. A., Robertson, S. E., Scott, R. M., Ward, N. A., & Henderson, R. H. (1991). Strategies for the global eradication of poliomyelitis by the year 2000. *New England Journal of Medicine, 325,* 1774-1779.

Yin, R. K. (1984). *Case study research.* Beverly Hills, CA: Sage.

Young, O. R. (1989). *International cooperation: Building regimes for natural resources and the environment.* Ithaca, NY: Cornell University Press.

Young, O. R. (1991). Political leadership and regime formation: On the development of institutions in international society. *International Organization, 45,* 281-308.

Young, O. R. (1994). *International governance: Protecting the environment in a stateless society.* Ithaca, NY: Cornell University Press.

Zacchea, N. (1992). Technology transfer: From financial to performance auditing. *Managerial Auditing, 7*(1), 17-23.

INDEX

REDESCA. *See* Regional Network of NGOs
for Sustainable Development in Central
America
Regimes. *See* Global issue regimes
Regional Committee of Emergency and
Solidarity (CRED), 220
Regional Coordination Program for Popular
Education in Costa Rica (ALFORJA),
220
Regional Coordinator of Socioeconomic
Studies (CRIES), 220
Regional Network of Environmental Experts
(ZERO), 215-216, 223
Regional Network of NGOs for Sustainable
Development in Central America
(REDESCA), 218, 220
Relational process, 264-266
Reseau Africain pour le Developpement
Integre, 222
Resource mobilization theory, 177
Retrospect, effect on sensemaking, 44, 54
Richards, P., 128
Rio Earth Summit. *See* United Nations
Conference on Environment and
Development
Robinson, Mary, 334, 337, 339, 341
Roddick, Anita, 334-335
Rumsey, Walter, 48

SADCC. *See* Southern African Development
Coordination Committee
SADCC Food Security Network, 223
Salient cues, effect on sensemaking, 44, 54
Sallee, Robert, 48
SAN. *See* Southern Africa Energy Network
Sanchez Varga, José, 317
Sandoz Pharma, 267-269
SatelLife, 231-232
SATIS. *See* Appropriate Technology
International Information Services
Save the Children Federation, 214
Scardino, Marjorie, 327, 336
Schell, J., 49-51
Science:
critiques of, 274
differences between Western and ethno-,
124, 127-128
positivism, 301
SDC. *See* Switzerland, Agency for
Development and Cooperation

SDNP. *See* Sustainable Development
Network Pakistan
Seal, Ulysses, 94-95, 99, 103-104, 110
Search conferencing, 134-135
Sensemaking, 39-40, 76
definition, 41-42
distinction from decision making, 42
effect of organizational designs, 43, 46,
48-49, 52-54
Mann Gulch firefighters example, 47-49,
55-56
properties, 42-46
Worker's Defense Committee example,
49-54, 56
Settlements Information Network Africa
(SINA), 225
Silences, representation of, 287-289, 290
SINA. *See* Settlements Information Network
Africa
SINENFAL. *See* Information Exchange
Service for Non-Formal Education
and Women for Latin America
Six S Association, 227
Slave trade, 181, 182
Smallpox, eradication of, 10-11, 125-126, 134
SMOs. *See* Social movement organizations
Social capital, 142
as factor in successful cooperation,
149-152, 163, 165
creation of, 163, 167
Social constructionism:
approaches to knowledge, 27-28
meaning creation process, 297
reflexive deliberation, 29
relativistic view of ethics, 264
Social context, effect on sensemaking, 43,
53-54
Social learning:
as factor in cooperation, 156-160, 164-166
processes, 143, 156
Social legitimacy, of businesses, 352-353
Social movement organizations (SMOs), 171
creation of, 179-180
globalization of, 171-176, 183-184
state-supported, 180-181
transnational, 216-217
See also Global social change
organizations; Nongovernmental
organizations
Social movements:
impact of, 181-182

ABOUT THE EDITORS

David L. Cooperrider is Associate Professor of Organizational Behavior and Chair of the Social Innovations in Global Management (SIGMA) Program at the Weatherhead School of Management, Case Western Reserve University. He is a former chair of the National Academy of Management's Division of Organizational Development and Change. From 1994 to 1997, he served as Principal Investigator of a $3.5 million grant from USAID working with international organizations dealing with global issues of human health, environment, peace, and development. As part of this grant (renewed for 1997-2000), he and his colleagues have organizational learning projects in 57 organizations in more than 100 countries. Most of these efforts are inspired by the "appreciative inquiry" methodology for which he is known.

Professor Cooperrider has published in journals such as *Human Relations, Administrative Science Quarterly, Journal of Applied Behavioral Science,* and *Contemporary Psychology,* and he has participated in research series, including *Advances in Strategic Management, Research in Organization Development and Change,* and *Inquiries in Social Construction.* He is editor of a new Sage book series, **Human Dimensions of Global Change.** He has served as researcher-consultant to a wide variety of organizations, including BP America, GTE, Touche Ross Canada, World Vision, Nature Conservancy, Cleveland Clinic, Imagine Chicago, TechnoServe, Omni Hotels, and the Mountain Forum.

Jane E. Dutton is the William Russell Kelly Professor of Business Administration at the University of Michigan Business School. She taught at New York University for 6 years before joining the Michigan faculty. Her research focuses on invisible relational work in organizations—what it is and why it matters. She is searching for ways to write and ways to theorize that put the relational side of organizational life center stage. Right now, she is doing all of her work on the construction of care for place and is studying people who do cleaning in all kinds of contexts. Her research articles have appeared in *Administrative Science Quarterly, Academy of Management Review,* and *Academy of Management Journal,* as well as a variety of other journals. She serves on the editorial boards of *Administrative Science Quarterly* and *Organization Science.* She is co-director of the Interdisciplinary Committee of Organization Studies (ICOS) at the University of Michigan.

ABOUT THE CONTRIBUTORS

Nancy J. Adler is Professor of Organizational Behavior and Cross-Cultural Management at the Faculty of Management, McGill University in Montreal, Canada. She conducts research and consults on strategic international human resource management, global women leaders, international negotiating, culturally synergistic problem solving, and global organization development. She has authored numerous articles, produced the film *A Portable Life*, and published the books *International Dimensions of Organizational Behavior* (3rd ed., 1997), *Women in Management Worldwide* (1988), and *Competitive Frontiers: Women Managers in a Global Economy* (1994). She has consulted for private corporations and government organizations on projects in Europe, North and South America, the Middle East, and Asia. She is a recipient of the American Society for Training and Development's International Leadership Award, the Society for Intercultural Education, Training, and Research's Outstanding Senior Interculturalist Award, the YWCA's Femme de Mérite (Woman of Distinction) Award, and the Sage Award for scholarly contributions to management.

John D. Aram is Professor of Management Policy at the Weatherhead School of Management at Case Western Reserve University. He received his doctorate in management from the Sloan School at MIT in 1968. His current interests focus on the social and organizational impacts of global capitalism and on institutional structures capable of combining ideals of liberalism and community. At the Weatherhead School, he is faculty director of the Executive Doctorate in Management Program, which is an interdisciplinary program of doctoral studies available for advanced professionals working full-time.

Darcy Ashman teaches courses in organizational behavior at the School for International Training (SIT) in Brattleboro, Vermont and the Global Partnership for Non-Governmental Organization (NGO) Studies, Education and Training in Dhaka, Bangladesh. She is SIT's Chairperson of the Global Partnership, a joint venture between SIT and two distinguished NGOs in Bangladesh and Zimbabwe offering graduate and undergraduate degree programs in grassroots development and NGO leadership and management. She also serves as a Research Associate of the Institute for Development Research (IDR) in Boston. Her research interests are in the areas of interorganizational relations; organizational development of NGOs; and women's organizations, management, and leadership. She is completing her doctoral dissertation on the roles of NGO networks in the democratization of Bangladesh at Boston University.

René Bouwen is Professor in Organizational Psychology and Group Dynamics at the Catholic University of Leuven in Belgium. He has been involved as a visiting professor in projects in Asia, Latin America, the United States, and several European countries. His research and publications focus on three main topics: innovation, entrepreneurship, and change processes in organization; conflict and conflict management; and the development and effectiveness of groups. A common thread in his work is a social constructionist and multivoiced approach of dynamic and emergent multiparty social contexts. He is involved with change projects in business and social profit organizations, especially through the advanced professionla training of process consultants.

L. David Brown is President of the Institute for Development Research and Professor of Organizational Behavior at the Boston University School of Management. His research and consulting focus on interventions to strengthen civil society organizations and institutions that promote democratic governance and sustainable development. He works with nongovernmental support organizations in Asia and Africa as well as international organizations and coalitions concerned with these issues. He is an author of several books and more than 50 articles in professional journals and books. He is currently coediting *The Struggle for Accountability: The World Bank, NGOs, and Social*

Movements, which reports results of a multicountry study of efforts to reform World Bank policies and projects.

Marta B. Calás is Associate Professor of Organization Studies and International Management at the School of Management of the University of Massachusetts–Amherst. She was born in Cuba and has lived and worked in various countries. She holds an MBA from the University of California at Berkeley and a PhD in organization studies and cultural anthropology from the University of Massachusetts–Amherst.

Julie Fisher is a Program Officer at the Kettering Foundation in Dayton, Ohio, with responsibilities related to its International Civil Society Consortium for Public Deliberation. Until recently, she was a Scholar in Residence at the Program on Nonprofit Organizations at Yale University and one of several professors teaching a course on global population issues at Yale. She is the author of *The Road From Rio: Sustainable Development and the Nongovernmental Movement in the Third World* (1993) and *Nongovernments: NGOs and the Political Development of the Third World* (1998), as well as a number of articles. As an independent consultant on international development, her clients have included Save the Children, Technoserve, Lutheran World Relief, the International Council for Educational Development, UNICEF, Interaction, and CARE.

Kenneth J. Gergen is Mustin Professor of Psychology at Swarthmore College in Pennsylvania. He is a major contributor to theory and research in social construction, and his writings treat a wide range of topics, including postmodernism, organizational process, education, technology, and the self. He is an Associate Editor of *The American Psychologist* and *Theory and Psychology,* as well as a co-founder of The Taos Institute. Among his most important works are *Toward Transformation in Social Knowledge, The Saturated Self,* and *Realities and Relationships.*

Barbara Gray is Professor of Organizational Behavior and Director of the Center for Research in Conflict and Negotiation at The Pennsylvania State University. She has been studying organizational and international conflict and negotiation processes for more than 20 years. She has published two books, *Collaborating: Finding Common Ground for Multiparty Problems* and *International Joint Ventures: Economic and Organizational Perspectives* as well as numerous journal articles. Her publications have appeared in *Administrative Science Quarterly, Academy of Management Journal, Academy of Management Review, Journal of Applied Behavioral Science, Human Relations,* and *Journal of Management Inquiry,* among others. She is also a trained mediator and has served as a consultant to numerous public and private sector organizations.

Stuart L. Hart is Associate Professor of Strategic Management at the Kenan-Flagler Business School, University of North Carolina at Chapel Hill. Previously, he taught corporate strategy at the University of Michigan Business School and was Director of the Corporate Environmental Management Program (CEMP), a joint initiative between the Business School and the School of Natural Resources and Environment. His research interests center on effective strategic and organizational change. He is particularly interested in the implications of environmentalism and sustainable development for corporate strategy and the management of technology and innovation. He serves on the editorial board of the *Strategic Management Journal* and has published more than 40 papers and authored or edited four books. He has also served as consultant or management educator to a number of private and public organizations.

Kathryn M. Kaczmarski is a doctoral candidate in organizational behavior at Case Western Reserve University. Her research focuses on the forms of leadership involved with global social change initiatives. Having left a career in corporate human resources to pursue her doctorate, she has consulted in both the private and public sectors, most recently with international development and nongovernmental organizations. One of her current projects is the United Religions Initiative, a global movement to create a United Nations-like organization of the world's religions. She has coauthored an article, "Leadership for a Global Spiritual Movement" and authored numerous other articles on leadership appearing in *Global Social Innovations,* a publication of the Global Excellence in Management Initiative of the Weatherhead School of Management, Case Western Reserve University.

Raza A. Mir is Assistant Professor in Management/Marketing at Monmouth University. He grew up in India and has been witness to the exponential expansion of international capital there, particularly over the past 15 years. His research interests are based on those experiences; for his dissertation, he is studying the processes of "knowledge transfer" in multinational corporations, and the political and power-laden dimensions that undergird them.

Susan Albers Mohrman is senior research scientist at the Center for Effective Organizations in the Marshall School of Business at the University of Southern California. Her research and consulting activities have been in the areas of organizational design and large-scale organizational transformation. Recently, she has been a principal investigator in a study of 10 major corporations undergoing fundamental change in their business model. She is a coauthor of *Self-Designing Organizations: Learning How to Create High Performance* (1989) and *Designing Team-Based Organizations* (1995).

Linda Smircich is Professor of Organization Studies at the School of Management of the University of Massachusetts–Amherst. In her collaborative scholarly work with Marta Calás, she applies perspectives from cultural studies and postmodern, feminist, and postcolonial theorizing to question current understandings of organizational topics such as leadership, business ethics, and globalization. She is coeditor of the Americas (with Calás) of the new journal *Organization: The Interdisciplinary Journal of Organization, Theory, and Society.* Her articles and book chapters have appeared in several national and international publications.

Chris Steyaert is Associate Professor of Human Resource Management at the Institute of Organization and Industrial Sociology, Copenhagen Business School, Denmark. In 1996, he received his PhD in Psychology from Katholieke Universiteit Leuven. He has published in international journals and books in the area of entrepreneurship and organizational innovation. His current research topics include organizing creativity, language and translation, forms of performing/writing research, and intercultural communication in society.

Ramkrishnan V. Tenkasi is Associate Professor at the Graduate School of Business and Health Administration, Benedictine University. His research examines the impact of cognitive, affective, and communicative processes in organizational knowledge and learning, and their mediation by organizational design choices. A special interest is the role of information technology in facilitating knowledge creation and learning processes in organizations. He is the author of articles and book chapters that have appeared in publications such as *Organization Science, Journal of Engineering and Technology Management, Journal of Organizational Change Management, Journal of Applied Behavioral Sciences, Employee Relations, Research in Organizational Development and Change,* and *ACM Proceedings in Computer Supported Cooperative Work.*

Karl E. Weick is the Rensis Likert Collegiate Professor of Organizational Behavior and Psychology at the University of Michigan and is also the former editor of *Administrative Science Quarterly,* the leading research journal in the field of organizational studies. In 1990, he received the highest honor awarded by the Academy of Management, the Irwin Award for Distinguished Lifetime Scholarly Achievement. He studies such topics as how people make sense of confusing events, the social psychology of improvisation, high reliability systems, the effects of stress on thinking and imagination, indeterminacy in social systems, social commitment, small wins as the embodiment of wisdom, and linkages between theory and practice. His writing about these topics has been collected in four books, one of which—the coauthored *Managerial Behavior, Performance and Effectiveness*—won the 1972 Book of the Year Award from the American College of Hospital Administration.

Frances Westley is Associate Professor in the strategy and organizations area, Faculty of Management, McGill University. She teaches, does research, and consults in the area of strategies for sustainable development. Her particular interest is in organizational design and process and its effects on environmental sustainability.

Mayer N. Zald is Professor of Sociology, Social Work, and Business Administration at The University of Michigan. He has published widely on complex organizations, social welfare, and social movements. In 1990, he edited (with Robert L. Kahn) a volume of essays titled *Organizations and Nations: New Perspectives on Conflict and Cooperation.* In 1996 (with Doug McAdam and John McCarthy), he edited a collection of essays, *Comparative Perspectives on Social Movements: Political Opportunities, Mobilizing Structures and Cultural Framings.* Aside from essays on social movements, he is currently engaged in a reformulation of social science as science and humanities. Several recent publications reflect this theme. He has been a fellow at the Center for Advanced Studies in the Behavioral Sciences (1986-1987, 1994) and was Distinguished Scholar of the Organization and Management Theory Division of the Academy of Management (1989).